THE
IRISH CATHOLIC
EXPERIENCE

A HISTORICAL SURVEY

PATRICK J. CORISH

GILL AND MACMILLAN
Dublin

Published in Ireland by
Gill and Macmillan Ltd
Goldenbridge
Dublin 8
with associated companies in
Auckland, Dallas, Delhi, Hong Kong,
Johannesburg, Lagos, London, Manzini,
Melbourne, Nairobi, New York, Singapore,
Tokyo, Washington
© Patrick J. Corish 1985
Reprinted 1986
Hardback 0 7171 1236 5
Paperback 0 7171 1486 4

British Library Cataloguing in Publication Data
Corish, Patrick J.
The Irish Catholic Experience: a historical survey.
1. Catholics — Ireland — History
1. Title
282'.415   BX1503
ISBN 0-7171-1236-5
Print origination in Ireland by Keywrite.
Printed and bound in Great Britain by
Biddles Ltd, Guildford and King's Lynn.

THE IRISH CATHOLIC EXPERIENCE

A Historical Survey

Contents

Introduction

This, I know, is an impossible book. If there is any justification for it, I can only plead that the thought has been in my mind for quite a long time. It probably first came into focus in 1961, when we celebrated the mission of St Patrick in ways that today would certainly be called 'triumphalistic'. In that year I proposed to a group of scholars that we make our contribution by producing *A History of Irish Catholicism*. With a certain inevitability, I found myself unanimously appointed editor.

It was the beginning of more problems than I had anticipated, as I tried to marshal a team of contributors to deliver the work they had undertaken. In the end I was only partly successful, and the project suffered further because, in order to be published at all, it had to be published as a series of separate fascicles, the order of publication being determined by the very practical, but not primarily scholarly, criterion of order of availability. In consequence, each contribution had to stand very much on its own, because there was never that overall view that might have helped to weld the individual contributions into a whole.

It must have been sometime during these years, as I watched the pile of correspondence grow almost as fast as the pile of printer's copy, that the thought first invaded my mind that it might have been a more realistic proposition if I had tackled the whole thing myself. As with many an attractive idea, it looked attractive until I faced up to doing something about it. The fascicles of *A History of Irish Catholicism* appeared between 1967 and 1972. By the time the decision had to be taken regretfully that no further fascicles would be published it had become clear that things were beginning to happen to 'Irish Catholicism' that nobody had anticipated only a decade before. The reasons for the change passed under the general name of 'Vatican II', but this was a great simplification of a complex cultural challenge to what now began to appear as an unexpectedly fragile inheritance. A society that had been in many ways static was thrown open to what were quite literally winds of change. At times they seemed gales of change.

Historians enjoy no privilege of insulation from the world they live in. Successive generations rewrite history because each generation asks its own questions of the past. The historian may claim that it is not for him to assess contemporary developments, for they are not yet history, but he cannot ignore the questions these developments pose to his interpretation of what is indubitably history.

Over these same years the new approaches to religious history which had for some time been established in continental Europe, and which had played their own part in the great religious questioning, began to make their way into Ireland, with a time-lag of a generation or more, as is so often the case. John Bossy's book, *The English Catholic Community, 1570-1850* (London 1975), might perhaps be singled out among those showing the Irish Catholic historian ways he might think of going. His fresh approach to Irish questions in 'The Counter-Reformation and the People of Catholic Ireland' (*Historical Studies*, viii (Dublin 1971), 155-69) provided a certain stimulus for my own *The Catholic Community in the Seventeenth and Eighteenth Centuries* (Helicon History of Ireland, Dublin 1981). From there I was led to the present attempt by the suggestions of a publisher who had been very long-suffering with *A History of Irish Catholicism*.

This book can make no pretence to being other than preliminary and tentative. The sources for Irish Catholic history are fragmentary and scattered. I know them better at some points than at others: there are places where I have obviously relied heavily on other people's work, but even here I would like to think that I have asked my own questions. There are crucial areas as yet only marginally explored, for example the traditional prayers in Irish and the rich heritage of folklore. The work seemed worth while, however, especially at a time which seems to be calling for a cold assessment of the Irish Catholic inheritance, its weaknesses as well as its strengths. This assessment must in the end be theological, but in the first instance it must be historical. The first step is to try to find out what happened.

Here one can only regret the curious dichotomy in Ireland between the professional study of theology and the study of the humanities in the general university world, for in this task of exploring a heritage theology and the humanities need one another. Theology must take from the humanities some philosophical structure, a certain sense of language, and a certain sense of history. In return the humanities may expect to receive a certain sense of involvement, a realisation that a bell tolls through all human experience, and that it tolls for me. This may have weakened for the humanities because they have been overawed by the methods of the scientists, though with these same scientists there are indications of a kind of stumbling on a God who is not 'the God of the gaps' but much more like the God at the centre. What relevance the scientists may feel the churches and their theologies have to this God is an intriguing question. At times one may fear that the points of contact will not be great. In retrospect it does seem strange that Catholic theology did not enter the National University after 1908, stranger still that it did not do so after 1921, in a political jurisdiction over 90 per cent Catholic, and strangest of all that nothing has happened in the twenty questioning years since the Second Vatican Council.

These twenty years I have rigorously excluded, for they are not yet material for the historian. In these years the theological framework of Irish Catholic life has changed dramatically, but it is still hard to see anything distinctively Irish about it. The country of origin may have changed, but it still looks imported.

In a book like this annotation and bibliography present insoluble problems. I can only hope that my compromises are not too uneasy. Detailed annotation is impossible, so there will always be an arbitrary element in choosing what to annotate. As to bibliography, I have confined it to mentioning a few things at the head of the notes to each chapter, in the hope that they will lead the reader seeking further information to a more extensive literature.

I have used the bibliographical abbreviations set out in *Irish Historical Studies*, supplement I (January 1968).

Patrick J. Corish
Maynooth
November 1984

1

Saints,
Kings and Vikings

According to what has from a very early date been the established tradition, Ireland was substantially converted to Christianity in the lifetime of one great missionary figure, St Patrick the Briton, and as the result of his personal mission. All this took place about the middle of the fifth century. While firm historical evidence is not easily come by at this distant time, there is enough that is reasonably firm to suggest that the true story must be a little more complex.

In the first place, the Irish secular power structures were so complex and fragmented that it is hard to accept that one missionary figure, no matter how gifted and dedicated, could have conducted an effective mission over the whole country. This argument is strengthened by the consideration that at the time of Patrick's mission these power structures were in an exceptional state of flux even by Irish standards. The rise of two powerful new dynasties was central to this political instability — the Uí Néill in the north and the Eóganacht in Munster. While anything like a firm chronology is beyond recovery, it does seem highly likely that during St Patrick's mission in the north of Ireland, or at the very latest shortly after it, the lands which had been at the centre of his missionary activity were overrun by the Uí Néill. At the same time the Uí Néill also intruded on the northern part of what had been the territory of the Laigin. The date of the rise of the Eóganacht in Munster is similarly uncertain, but it may be associated, at least in north Munster, with Óengus mac Nad Froích (his annalistic obit, for what it is worth, is given as 490/92). Of the southern ecclesiastical 'founding fathers', Declan of Ardmore and Ciarán of Saighir may well be contemporaries of Óengus, while the figure who rose to be the chief patron of Munster, Ailbe of Emly, may belong to the next generation (the annals record his death at various dates between 527 and 542).

In all this there is one date which seems to be firm beyond all doubt, because it comes from a contemporary written source, the *Chronicon* of Prosper of Aquitaine. Here under the year 431 Prosper has the entry 'Palladius, ordained by Pope Celestine, is sent to the Irish believing in Christ as their first bishop.' Prosper ties this information about Palladius into a quite credible background of papal interest at this time in the affairs of the northern islands. But then Palladius, to all intents and purposes, disappears. By the seventh century his mission is firmly subordinated to that of Patrick, and it is stated to have been rather brief and unsuccessful, ending according to one version in martyrdom, and according to another in his leaving the country disappointed and discouraged. The fragments of topographical information that cling to his name locate his mission in Leinster.

There are, however, suggestive indications that this may not be alto-gether true. The key figures here are three bishops, Secundinus, Auxilius and Iserninus, whose death-dates, for what they are worth, are recorded in the annals. Even more suggestive are the churches with which they were later associated. Secundinus (d. 447/8) is associated with Dunshaughlin in present-day Co. Meath, Laigin territory under attack by the Uí Néill during his lifetime. Auxilius (d. 459/60) is associated with Killashee near Naas in north Leinster, and Iserninus (d. 465/8) with Aghade near Tullow in the south. All three places are closely associated with royal sites.

Developed tradition associated these three figures with Patrick in a subordinate capacity, even providing an entry in the annals under the year 439: 'Secundinus, Auxilius and Iserninus are sent to help Patrick; nevertheless not they but Patrick alone held the apostleship.' The very form of this entry suggests a later construct: if they were in fact subord-inate to Patrick, contemporaries would not have felt it necessary to emphasise it so explicitly. The fact is that these three figures are closely associated with Leinster royal sites. That they worked in the middle of the fifth century is as certain as anything can be in that uncertain age. The state of Irish politics at the time makes it impossible to believe that they worked in close association with Patrick. It is a reasonable hypothesis that their mission in Leinster derived from that of Palladius; and Palladius, it will be recalled, was sent 'to the Irish believing in Christ'. Though the Leinster and Patrick missions took place at the same time, Patrick was teaching the faith for the first time to pagans, whereas the Leinster missionaries were in some sense consolidating a position.

On this hypothesis, we may well have contemporary evidence for what might be called the first and second stages of the conversion of the Irish. The evidence for the first stage comes, of course, from Patrick himself. No one has ever seriously called into question the authenticity of his two letters, written towards the end of his life, the *Confession* and the *Letter to the Soldiers of Coroticus*. The evidence for the second stage is in the document known as the 'First Synod of Patrick', which has traditionally carried the heading 'Here begins the synod of the bishops, namely, Patrick, Auxilius and Iserninus.' It is very hard to associate the Patrick of his own writings with the canons of this synod, whether one considers their content or the quality of their Latin. It is not hard to see circum-stances in which his name came to be added later. There are no real problems in associating the canons with Auxilius and Iserninus. This would place them sometime in the 450s, after the death of Secundinus. The Christian situation they reflect is 'second-generation missionary', and this, it is reasonable to assume, was the position in Leinster in the middle of the fifth century.

Set in this context, a satisfactory picture of the progress of evangelisation emerges from these three documents. His missionary technique is one thing that does emerge with reasonable clarity from Patrick's highly personal and often frustratingly uncertain prose. Allowance must be made for the fact that this missionary technique was regarded as quite unorthodox, and drew on him criticism from the leaders of the British church, all the more pointed because Patrick was so successful. Above all, he appears as his own man. He does not share authority. He is the bishop, and there is no mention of other bishops. His mission is highly personal and highly successful. He preached to the limits of human habitation and baptised great numbers of people. Everywhere he ordained clerics to baptise and preach. He was quite fearless. He continually faced plots and dangers, and at least once was taken captive and in danger of his life. However, he was sensible in his bravery, paying money — the word 'bribe' would be a total anachronism — to kings and brehons and to the company of young nobles who went about with him. He communicated his bravery to others, to the slave-women who became Christians despite terror and threats, and to the young men and women of higher rank who decided to become monks and nuns despite reproach and even persecution from their parents. He makes it clear that there are many such people, but nowhere does he speak of any community structures for them. While this does not necessarily mean that such structures did not exist, it does imply that this aspect of the religious life was not of primary importance for Patrick.

We are in a different world in the so-called 'First Synod of Patrick'. This is partly because we are here dealing with a people among whom Christianity is longer established, though the situation is still missionary and paganism still powerful and even dominant. But in addition, the people who drew up these canons have a stamp of mind very different to Patrick's. They are organising 'the Irish believing in Christ'. There are several bishops, each with his own diocese, his area of authority, which must be respected by other bishops. They have authority over the activities of the clergy of their dioceses. All the grades of clergy are in existence, and the clergy of all grades, up to and including priests, are envisaged as married. A cleric may be of any rank in society, even a slave, but his clerical ordination does not alter his servile state, as it was to do after Christianity had become more fully integrated into society. As with Patrick, there are monks and virgins, but here they are explicitly subject to religious superiors. There are problems about Christian marriage, as indeed there were to be for a long time to come. Superstitions linger on, and they too were to have a long life. A number of regulations try to ensure that Christians settle even secular disputes among themselves instead of approaching the civil authorities, who are clearly still pagan and applying pagan standards of justice.

By the middle of the sixth century Christianity had become the dominant religion all over Ireland. Paganism still lingered — it has been said of the high king Diarmait mac Cerbaill (544-564/5) that it is quite impossible to decide if he were pagan or Christian, or perhaps a bit of both. What little is known of early Irish paganism strongly suggests that it was unlikely to put up a forceful resistance to the preaching of Christianity. Inevitably, ways from the pagan past lingered on, even with people who had generations of Christianity behind them. One reason for this undoubtedly was that as the Christian mission gained momentum the conversion of a leader usually brought the conversion of all his people as well. Another was the fact that the Christian missionaries practised a system of 'adaptation' such as Pope Gregory the Great was later to recommend explicitly in the mission to the Anglo-Saxons — pagan practices and festivals were not abolished, but worked into the new creed.

The Christian church was organised as it was in every other place, around diocesan bishops and their clergy. Up to about 550 the great majority of ecclesiastics whose deaths were recorded in the annals were bishops. By about this date the 'new druids' had been allocated their niche in the social structures — the bishop being equated with the king, and the clergy being accepted as another element in the *aes dána*, the men of learning. The pagan sages retained their place in this class, according to legend because of the intervention of Colum Cille at the convention of Druim Cett in 575. One function they had to yield to the Christian clergy was the role of intermediaries with the other world. In the second half of the sixth century the two cultures reached an accommodation which in certain matters remained uneasy.

By this date too a great change had come over the ecclesiastical structures of Irish Christianity. Leadership was rapidly passing from the diocesan bishops to the abbots of great monasteries, who were coming to preside over a number of far-flung monastic communities that formed a *paruchia* (this is the normal Latin word at the time for diocese; it survives in the Modern Irish *fairche*). As time went on, the offices of bishop and abbot become divided. Colum Cille, the most famous of the monastic founders, was not himself a bishop.

How and why this development took place is far from certain. The influence of British Christianity can hardly be discounted, for while the evidence is late and unsatisfactory, it does seem to represent a deep and real tradition. In Britain the invasions of the pagan Angles, Saxons and Jutes in the fifth century had driven the native Christians into the mountainous north and west. In this great movement of peoples the existing diocesan organisation had broken up. It was replaced by great monasteries and famous abbots, such as Iltud, Gildas, David and Cadoc, represented in the later evidence as the masters of the Irish monastic founders. That the Christians in Ireland should turn to great abbots as their leaders was a natural thing, for reasons both religious and secular. An inheritance from paganism still permeated the lives of Christians, and it was natural to believe that the full Christian life was possible only for those with monastic vows. The sixth-century Penitential of Vinnian lays down an extremely severe code of morality for Christians, especially of sexual morality. It makes no concessions to a society accustomed to divorce, remarriage and concubinage, and in the end grudgingly concedes that lay Christians who observe its standards may expect the 'thirtyfold reward', that is, just about save their souls; while the Old Irish Treatise on Commutations, probably of the eighth century, has the wintry remark that there is hardly a single layman or laywoman who has not some part in manslaughter.[1]

Because of the nature of Irish society, the new religion needed its heroes, and it got them in the great monastic founders. It would be a mistake to regard this development simply as the watering down of Christianity by superstition. In fact this array of new heroes, and of new holy places — this was particularly important with a people so much influenced by places and their associations, the *dindsenchas* — was a significant novelty that was very effective in leading people from paganism to Christianity.

The development of the monastic *paruchiae* fitted into the structures of Irish civil society. Land belonged to the extended family group, the *derbfine*. When part of this was alienated by agreement to form the endowment of a monastery it remained an interest of the family group but was freed from secular obligations. This made a monastic foundation particularly attractive to branches of ruling families that were losing out in the dynastic struggles, and as secular overlordship tended to become concentrated in fewer hands the monastic *paruchiae* were built up.

The overall development was not quite as tidy as this. It is scarcely an accident that Colum Cille came from the highest ranks of the aristocracy, though monasteries with founders of humbler origin could become power centres in their own right and develop extensive *paruchiae*. The names of the great founders show that not all were of noble blood — Ciarán of Clonmacnois was *mac in tsaír*, son of the carpenter. What is certain is that the new heroes multiplied. After the year 600 the great majority of those regarded as worthy of commemoration in the annals were not bishops but abbots.

They ruled over numbers of monastic communities, each possessing lands with lay tenants, for whom they provided spiritual ministrations. Indeed, the civil law tracts regarded these lay tenants of monastic lands as in some sense ecclesiastics — the word they use for them is *manaigh*, monks. But great as were the possessions of the monastic *paruchiae*, most of the country had lay overlords. Here the spiritual ministration must have been provided by that common feature of early medieval western Europe, the 'proprietary church', that is, the church provided for the people by the lay overlord. The 'First Synod of Patrick' had tried to exclude this development, insisting that all churches be under the control of the bishop, but in Ireland as in Europe the very structures of society encouraged its growth. The history of these proprietary churches is very difficult to recover, for the surviving sources chronicle the affairs of an aristocracy, whether ecclesiatical or lay. Even when the penitential literature deals with the laity. it must be presumed that the primary concern is with the monastic tenants, the *manaigh*. The very location of what must have been great numbers of tiny churches scattered over the countryside must be sifted from placenames and genealogies, and the work of sifting has scarcely begun.[2]

The pattern of Christian living centres in community, first the primary community of the family, and then the more ecclesial community of aggregations of families, this in its turn centring on the Sunday Eucharist, a Christian practice traceable back to the New Testament itself. In the beginning, when Christians were few, each community gathered round its bishop. As numbers increased, and especially as the rural areas came to be evangelised, there came to be many Sunday communities, each gathered round a priest who represented the bishop. Gradually the terminology sorted itself out in the western church: the bishop's area was his diocese, while the priest's community was his parish.

In early medieval Europe this structure was everywhere substantially modified by the growth of 'proprietary' churches. If we regard the churches in the great monastic aggregations as 'proprietary', and this is where they fit in the general structures of the church at the time, Ireland must be regarded as representing a very far-reaching development of the 'proprietary' church. Inevitably, this affected the position and authority of the bishop.

Despite the conservatism of its structures, Irish society in the early centuries was not static, but continually evolving, so that some division into periods is necessary. One turning-point may be placed about the year 800, which saw the emergence of a notable reform movement, that of the *Céli Dé* or Culdees, and the beginning of the Norse incursions. A second comes about the year 1100, with the extension to Ireland of the papally inspired reform of the eleventh century. The whole context of this reform was changed by the arrival of the Normans in 1169.

Within each period it will be necessary to consider, or at least try to consider, the impact of Christianity on different groups of people. Here again a threefold division suggests itself. In the first place come the religious properly so called. Numerically they were always a small minority, but the monastic institute was such a powerful social force that in important respects they must have set the tone of society as a whole. Next came their dependent laity, the *manaigh* of the civil law tracts. And finally there are those outside the great monastic aggregations, 'the little churches of the laymen' as they are described in one of the documents emanating from the Culdee reform.

To begin with, a general word on church structures — how did these basic elements, the diocesan episcopate and the parish clergy, fare in the unusual circumstances of Ireland? It seems most likely that the original pattern had been that there was a bishop in every *tuath* or petty kingdom, and as many of the *tuatha* were small this in itself meant that, even at the beginning, many bishops could not have been very powerful figures. The episcopal office survived, however, if only because there had to be bishops to perform the ecclesiastical functions proper to their order. A large monastic community could regard maintaining a bishop as part of its functions. Originally bishop and abbot may have been the same person — this may well have been the case with such shadowy figures of the early days as Mel, Macarten or Asicus. This pattern was not known outside Ireland: an example is Martin of Braga in north-western Spain, who died in 580. But in Ireland as time went on the two offices of bishop and abbot were divided.

Though the abbot was head of the monastery, the bishop remained an important figure. In the civil law tracts, which are preoccupied with questions of status, he stands at the top of the ecclesiastical ranks, equal in dignity to the king. The ecclesiastical sources show that the bishop of the *tuath* is still in evidence as a figure of authority at the end of the eighth century. An eighth-century tract that passes under the name of the Rule of Patrick (*Riagail Pátraic*) describes his office and functions:

> Every *tuath* should have a chief-bishop (*prim-epscop*) to ordain its clergy, to consecrate its churches, to give direction to its chiefs and nobles, and to sanctify and bless their children after baptism. For the *tuatha* and territory which have no bishops to perform these functions see the law of their faith and belief perish.

It has frequently been said that in the Irish 'monastic' church the abbot exercised the 'power of jurisdiction', while the bishop exercised only the 'power of orders'. No such sharp distinction could have existed in the early Irish mind, if only because it was first elaborated by the scholastic theologians of the twelfth and thirteenth centuries. The earlier theology of holy orders, which has enjoyed something of a revival in recent times, saw the bishop as having the fullness of sacramental order, and his priests as participating in the priesthood of their bishop. Within this framework of thought it is hard to see the pre-eminence of the episcopate being obscured, no matter how much the direction of affairs — what later centuries were to call the power of jurisdiction — had passed to the abbot.

Behind the bishop, at least in the ideal scheme of things, stood the synod and the metropolitan. Neither institution flourished in Ireland. It is true that when fresh contacts were opened up with Rome and the continent in the seventh century an attempt was made to give them life by a party known at the time as *Romani* or Romanisers, but the native social structures of the great monastic *paruchiae* proved too strong. However, the effective rise of the church of Armagh, and with it the acceptance of Patrick as the national apostle, may well have drawn some of its strength from an association with the *Romani*: Armagh appears to have been the first northern church to join the Romanising party. Armagh's claims are set out in the *Liber Angeli*, which existed there before the end of the seventh century.[3] These claims are extensive. Armagh claims direct authority over the north-east. It also claims, as the heir of Patrick, the right to a tax from all 'free churches' and all 'monasteries of cenobites'. Indeed, it claims that 'every free church, every city of episcopal rank, and every place which is called *domnach*', that is, every church not absorbed into the monastic *paruchiae*, is subject to Armagh, and claims further that even the monastic *paruchiae* originated in a usurpation of the universal authority of Patrick. Finally, it is claimed that Armagh is the court of appeal from all the churches of Ireland, and that appeal may be carried further, to Rome, only when the sages of Armagh are baffled.

Claims and acceptance of claims are two different things. Nevertheless, Armagh gradually extended its claim. However, it did this in the context of Irish social structures rather than of Roman canon law, by promulgating the 'Law of Patrick' ever more widely, though there are clear indications that attempts to impose it on Munster were long resisted and came to be accepted only at the end of the tenth century as part of a political agreement. There is no evidence that it was accepted in Leinster.

The debates in the seventh century brought the see of Rome back into the picture. Here later clarifications of the concept of 'jurisdiction', exacerbated by disputes arising from the sixteenth-century Reformation, have tended to obscure the real question — how did the early Irish church see its relationship with Rome? Rome was a unique centre in the west, adding to the prestige of the old imperial capital the fact that it was the west's one patriarchal see. The peoples from outside the empire, the Goths for example, saw the acceptance of Christianity as an important step in their Romanisation. The texts in which Patrick himself is made to appeal to the authority of Rome are of questionable value, but his own writings show clearly that he identified being Roman with being Christian. In so far as the Irish are pagan, his mission is to 'live among barbarians, a stranger and exile for the love of God', but he can identify himself with those of them who 'have received one and the same baptism, and have one and the same God for a father': 'we are Irish'.[4]

These phrases come from Patrick's *Letter to the Soldiers of Coroticus*. Coroticus, a British war-lord, had raided Ireland. Among his victims were some of Patrick's newly baptised Christians. Some had been killed, others carried into captivity. The swell of Patrick's indignation mounts not merely against Coroticus, but against all in Britain who have denigrated his mission to the 'barbarians': 'For them it is a disgrace that we are Irish.' This certainly provides a context into which may be fitted the third of the 'sayings of Patrick' preserved by Tirechán at the end of the seventh century: 'church of the Irish, nay of the Romans'. The authenticity of the saying itself is subject to scholarly dispute, but there can be little doubt that it reflects the mind of Patrick. For a fifth-century Briton, to become a Christian was to be admitted into the world of Rome.

For more than a hundred years after Patrick's death there is no evidence from Ireland about its relationship with the Roman see, but there is from the Christians of Britain, who, as has been seen, almost certainly played an important part in the development of Irish monasticism. These hard-pressed British Christians counted it an honour to be 'Romans', in contrast with the pagan invaders who had despoiled them of their best lands. What reopened direct Roman contacts with the insular churches after more than a century of isolation was the Roman mission to these still largely pagan peoples in 597.

The first contacts had their problems. The British Christians found it hard to accept their one-time pagan foes as brothers in Christ. In addition, the long-isolated insular churches had developed their own special practices. The one that caused most debate arose from the fact that by now their method of computing the date of Easter differed from the Roman one. It was a practical problem, for the date of Easter determined the whole cycle of the church's liturgical worship, and it was made more intractable by prickly insular pride.

The dispute led to an Irish embassy to Rome, probably in 631. For this we have a primary witness, a letter from Cummian, probably Abbot of Durrow, to Ségéne, Abbot of Iona. Cummian is precise and explicit. When the Irish failed to agree among themselves they decided on the embassy, in accordance with a synodal decree that major causes should be referred to the chief of cities. His remark that God granted them a good journey, in that some of them got to Rome and after three years some returned, is sufficient indication that in that age consulting Rome was not a thing to be undertaken lightly. At Rome the envoys came to realise that the Irish were out of step with the rest of the world. When they came back with this news the Irish who had sent them immediately adopted the Roman practice, and after some hurt pride it became universal.

It is important not to see Roman authority in the context of later refinements of the idea of jurisdiction. For Cummian, the Irish went to Rome 'as children to their mother'. The authority of a church rested on the quality of its witness to the faith. This in turn rested on the witness of its saints and martyrs, past as well as present, the dead even more than the living, if only because there were so many more of them. This witness of the dead is made tangible by the fact that they rest in the church's cemetery. The Irish word for cemetery, *reilig*, denotes it as the place where rest the earthly remains of the saints, their *reliquiae*. But Old Irish had another word for cemetery which Modern Irish has lost. The word is *ruam*. It occurs in several senses, three of them ecclesiastical: the city of Rome itself; a great monastic settlement that may justly be compared to Rome; and a cemetery, usually the cemetery of such a monastery. It is in these senses that the Prologue to the *Félire* of Óengus, composed about the year 800, speaks, for example, of 'thronged Glendaloch, the *ruam* of the western world'. Rome was the chief witness to the faith, the incomparable city of saints and martyrs. The highest compliment that could be paid to another church was to compare its witness to that of Rome.

The great Columban can be fitted convincingly into this framework. He has acquired a reputation, not indeed undeserved, for chiding popes sharply, Yet his letters to the popes are a mixture of asperity and humility: he sees it as desperately important that the pope be right. Perhaps his real mind emerges in his incidental remarks. There is one that recurs in each of the three letters he wrote to a pope, twice, perhaps significantly, in his closing salutation. In his letter to Pope Boniface IV he had accused the pope of heresy, a subtle Greek heresy that Columban clearly did not know much about, but its repercussions were disturbing his mission to the Lombards in northern Italy. The Irish, he claims, have never been in heresy, 'followers of Peter and Paul, bound to the see of Rome'. And he concludes: 'For the rest, holy father and brethren, pray for me, a most wretched sinner, and for my fellow-pilgrims beside the holy places and the ashes of the saints, and especially beside Peter and Paul.' Popes may be questioned, but the witness of Rome lies in Peter and Paul and in the ashes of its saints.[5]

Turning from popes to priests, the evidence for their role and function, scanty as it is, is convincing. Just as the original pattern was that of a bishop in his diocese, so it was of the priest in his parish. Here in particular the evidence of the earliest penitential, that of Vinnian in the sixth century, appears conclusive. It even positively excludes monks from the parish ministry. Later evidence, from the end of the eighth century, shows that the pattern of the priest attached to the parish community still survives: the *clericus plebis*, the *clérech tuaithe*, the *fer-gráid do mhin-eclaisib tuaithe* — a phrase one is tempted to translate as 'the country curate' — who provides

the rites of baptism and communion (that is, the sacrament) and intercessory prayer for the living and the dead, and Mass every Sunday and every chief high day and every chief festival.[6]

On the estates of the monasteries it would be natural to expect that monastic priests provide for the lay *manaigh*. Even here, however, priests were often in short supply. At this time, in Ireland as elsewhere, only a minority of monks were priests. But there must have been many small proprietary churches, and even small monasteries, that had the services of a priest only intermittently. The non-monastic clergy, institutionally weak, do not seem to have survived the Norse disruptions. Thereafter the references are to monastic priests only, but then the sources are of monastic provenance.

Because the monastic institute became dominant in the early Irish church, the monastic ideal set the general cultural pattern of Christianity. Most of the great monastic founders and lawgivers are known to us only through lives written quite some time after they had died, and written with the primary purpose of emphasising the power of the saint in order to support and extend the claims of the churches which owed obedience to his *comarba* or successor. In this development much if not all of the authentic Christian witness of the founding father is heavily obscured. There are exceptions, two in particular. Columban is known to us in his own writings, and Colum Cille does come through the serene and luminous pages of his biographer, Adomnán, as a living, saintly human individual, though even Adomnán to some extent transmutes him into something of a superhuman figure of heroic saga. There is also some valuable information from the Venerable Bede (d. 735) concerning the Irish monastic church as he came into contact with it, for Bede did have a genuine historical sense which is without parallel for his time.

It was in the world of the great monastic jurisdictions that the Christian and native traditions were fused, helped by the close association that developed between the great monasteries and the ruling aristocracies. In this process the *file* or poet had to surrender any claims to mediation with the other world: this became the province of the Christian church. Indeed, what historical reality may lie behind the story of Colum Cille's intervention at Druim Cett in 575 suggests that the office of *file* may have been in some danger because of the confident advance of Christianity. The danger was averted, however, and the outcome was a Christian church that in some respects accommodated itself to the paganism that had hitherto permeated society. In this it was far from unique in early medieval Europe.

The confidence of Christianity may be seen in its literature in Latin, ranging over biblical commentaries, theology, canon law, music and hymnody, grammatical texts, and the first ventures into hagiography. The monastic *scriptoria* were also important centres in the emergence of the annals, and in the commitment to writing of secular literature such as the sagas and the civil law tracts. From all this amalgam there emerged a culture decidedly Christian but also distinctively Irish. As Kathleen Hughes summed it up:

> A consciousness of the supernatural must have pervaded early Irish society. The storytellers move from reality to magic as if they do not recognise any boundary. There are visitors from the *síd*, a man may enter a fairy dwelling, or have a fairy lover. The poet was also a 'seer', so that vision and prophecy were his proper medium. In historical sagas and saints' lives the writer seems sometimes unable to distinguish fact and fiction, in the religious literature he is close to the powers of the spiritual unseen. This is the tradition in which he lived. The Irish audience did not ask, as we do, 'Is this story true?' meaning 'Is it literal fact?' They wanted to be amused. They wanted their heroes to behave well. And sometimes they wanted to share an experience of beauty, which might mean entering into a world of enchantment.[7]

The same confident blending of ancient pagan concepts, foreign borrowings and Christian themes appears strikingly in early Irish Christian art. This art was abstract by choice. When occasionally the artist deviated into realism he showed that he could master this technique as well. A striking example is the portrayal of cats with birds on the Cross of Muiredach at Monasterboice. One can only surmise what prompted the artist to depict them, speculating that the cat may be the monastery's Pangur Bán, and that the domesticity of the theme prompted the unusual break into realism. The universe the Irish artist likes to inhabit is not so much a country of the mind as of the limitless imagination. His work is 'the plastic equivalent of that country of all wonders which haunts the mind of the Irish poets'.[8] Heaven is the land of the living, the goal of the voyage not only of Brendan but of Bran.

The creative imagination might wander, but the daily life of the monk was girt round with austerity. In its first flowering it nourished a wonderful dedication in poverty and charity, as may be seen, for example, in the writings of Columban or in Bede's account of Aidan of Lindisfarne. It appears too in Adomnán's Life of Colum Cille, notably in the spare and moving final chapter where he describes the saint's death:

> And when he came to that verse of the thirty-third psalm where it is written, 'But they that seek the Lord shall not want for anything that is good' he said: 'Here at the end of the page I must stop. Let Baithene write what follows.' . . . So, he gave his last commands to the brothers: 'I commend to you, my children, these last words, that you keep among you unfeigned love with peace.'[9]

And a real Christianity and a real humanism keep breaking through in the later lives of the saints, written to boost the authority of a church by glorifying the power of its founder. There is the saying attributed to Ciarán of Clonmacnois, 'the golden rule is enough for the Christian life without any further reading', or Ita's summary of 'the things which please God — true faith with a pure heart, a simple life with religious observance, and generosity with love', or the plaint of the monks of the austere Colmán Elo, that will strike a chord in everyone trying to be a Christian: 'We are afflicted with labour and many tribulations, and we know not what are the rewards of the world to come.'[10]

This church must certainly have sustained its world; equally certainly, the world dragged down its church. The controversies of the seventh century had been concerned with more than the introduction of Roman usages on certain points of discipline. It is clear from surviving synodal legislation, notably the so-called 'Second Synod of Patrick' and the collection of canons known as the 'Hibernensis', that the 'Roman' party sought a radical restructuring of the church in Ireland. These sources emphasise themes always dear to ecclesiastical reformers: an episcopal church with its clergy free of lay control, and church appointments free of simony. In these matters the reformers were not successful. The power centres of the church in Ireland continued to be the great monasteries, each trying to extend its power and influence by the wider promulgation of the *cáin* or 'law' of its founder. The word itself suggests that the right to tribute was an essential part of the *cána*, but their contents indicate wider concerns. As the commentary to the *Félire* of Óengus summed it up:

> These are the four *cána* of Ireland: Patrick's law, not to kill the clergy, and Adomnán's law, not to kill women; Daire's law, not to kill cattle; and the law of Sunday, not to transgress thereon.[11]

It was in the nature of things that these churches, in effect ecclesiastical territorial states, should become heavily secularised. They became part of the framework of power. Battles between monasteries are recorded from the middle of the eighth century, and it seems fairly certain, notwithstanding the ambiguity of the word *manach*, that monks properly so called took part in these battles. Nevertheless, the great monasteries were the indispensable framework of the Christian church in Ireland. The 'Roman' reformers had not changed this framework, and the next reformers, the Culdees, set out to work within it.

At this stage there may be an uneasy feeling that St Patrick has fallen out of the story. It is right that the feeling should be uneasy. It may be that his acceptance as national patron is to some extent due to later historical developments, and it may be too that some of those who helped to make him the national patron saw the mission of the Christian church in terms that would have horrified Patrick himself. Nevertheless, it is not just Patrick's real stature, but a certain quality in that stature, that made it very fitting he should be the national patron. It should be borne in mind too that from the seventh century onwards his authority was sought not only by the power-seekers but by the reformers, both those who tried to impose a 'Roman' framework on the Irish church and those who decided to work within the native one.

We know the real Patrick only through his own short writings, the *Confession* and the *Letter to the Soldiers of Coroticus*. The number of people who might be expected to mention Patrick and who do not is quite striking. Columban is silent, so is Jonas the biographer of Columban, Cogitosus the biographer of Brigid, Adomnán, and even that Anglo-Saxon monk with a real sense of history, the Venerable Bede. Neither can other documents allegedly closely connected with Patrick be regarded as authentic. The documents in Irish, the 'Breastplate' and the Hymn of Fiacc of Sletty, can be ruled out on linguistic grounds. On internal evidence the Latin hymn attributed to Secundinus can hardly have been composed in Patrick's lifetime; and though it may well be the earliest external testimony about him, its eulogies are so generalised that it tells us little about Patrick the man. His earliest biographers, Tirechán and Muirchú, wrote at the end of the seventh century. They draw on Patrick's writings, but their additional material is aimed at exalting Patrick (and in consequence Armagh) as a focus of power and authority. The hymns of Fiacc and Secundinus also echo Patrick's writings. The ninth-century Book of Armagh shows that the *Confession* was preserved and treasured there, even if with discreet editing to play down any seeming human weaknesses in Patrick.

At first sight Patrick's writings do not seem to be promising material. This is not only because they are short. He himself admits to his poor command of Latin. He had no intention of giving a coherent account of his life. His writing is clumsy with frequent anacoloutha that sometimes tail into meaninglessness or at best uncertainty. Yet a powerful personality comes through clearly, more clearly than most figures from his age. It is not stretching things to compare him in this respect with Augustine of Hippo. He is a man of great courage, a missionary, a bishop. He is no academic theologian: the 'rule of faith' which he gives in the fourth chapter of the *Confession* concentrates on the essentials and echoes the Apostles' Creed more clearly than the theological controversies of his day. It may well be that his one book was the Scriptures, but these he had fully assimilated into an intense religious experience based on a life of personal prayer. His God is above all the person who has loving care for the helpless, and a certain feeling that he needed such protection never left Patrick himself.[12]

One gets a real sense that Patrick and his Irish converts inhabited the same country of the mind. 'We the Irish' was a phrase which must have had real meaning for Patrick in his old age. Not altogether the same country of the mind, perhaps. Whoever penned the 'Breastplate of St

Patrick' probably took heathenism more seriously than he did:

> I summon today all those powers between me and these evils...
> against incantations of false prophets,
> against black laws of heathenry...
> against craft of idolatry,
> against spells of women and smiths and wizards...

but what follows rings true:

> Christ to protect me today...
> Christ with me, Christ before me, Christ behind me,
> Christ in me, Christ beneath me, Christ above me,
> Christ on my right, Christ on my left,
> Christ where I lie, Christ where I sit, Christ where I arise,
> Christ in the heart of every man who thinks of me,
> Christ in the mouth of every man who speaks of me,
> Christ in every eye that sees me,
> Christ in every ear that hears me...[13]

Every Christian society inevitably makes its compromises with the stark demands of the gospels, where two points in particular may be singled out as central to the demands of charity: what counts above all is the interior disposition, not the external act; and the interior disposition of love of one's neighbour must extend not only to friends but also to enemies. These are searching demands for human beings in any walk of life, and they were particularly searching for the warlike aristocratic kin-societies of early medieval Europe. The Christian evangelists had to set out to change society slowly. Pope Gregory the Great (590-604) was to set out the rules in connection with the mission to Anglo-Saxon England: pre-Christian religious customs, where they cannot be abolished, are to be given a Christian form and meaning: 'for no one can doubt the impossibility of changing everything at once in rude and untrained minds, just as a person who sets out to scale the heights must do so step by step and not by leaps and bounds'.[14] The Irish missionaries had already followed this practice. They had followed it with great confidence, and with the inevitable consequence that a heritage from paganism passed over to Christian Ireland, and one may suspect that neither they nor Gregory really suspected how long this paganism would take to die.

The principal sources for the story of the Christianising of Ireland are the penitentials and the synodal legislation. Neither is altogether satisfactory. Synodal decrees tend to depict things as the legislators would wish them to be rather than as they actually are. At first sight the penitentials might seem more promising material, but they too need to be used with caution. They were drawn up in the first instance for the spiritual guidance of monks. In many cases they do deal explicitly with the laity, but these laity are those to whom the monastic discipline of penance came to be extended, and it may well be that these are in the main the lay *manaigh*, that is, the tenants of the monastic estates. At first sight the penitentials as we have them appear to be a boring compilation of a list of penances appropriate for every thinkable sin, but it may be that we have not begun to ask the right historical questions of the penitentials (we have indeed asked them few really historical questions). Recent work elsewhere[15] suggests that a useful framework for approaching all these gradations of sin implied in the gradations of penances is to relate them, not to the degree the sin in question offends God, but to the degree in which it disturbs the public peace (this would afford a credible explanation of what might otherwise be seen as an unhealthy pre-occupation with sex, for most societies have strongly believed that un-restrained sex is a great disturber of the public peace).

Such an analysis of the penitentials might add considerable detail to what we now perceive as the general shape of society at the time Christianity came to dominate it in the second half of the sixth century. As far as the clergy were concerned, Christian dominance must have been a great social leveller, allowing persons of lowly origin an opportunity of rising in the ranks by being accepted as *aes dána*. There would have been no such change in the social position of the Christian laity. We see their society, even the experts are agreed, in an uncertain half-light, but we can see the layman as existing in a web of kinship and clientship. There is a sense in which this is true of all societies at all times, but in ancient Ireland kinship and clientship were the very legal framework of society. A person's claims, obligations and loyalties were bound up with his kin-group, his *derbfine* or 'certain kin', those descended from a common great-grandfather. The vertical social links were provided by clientship. What the client had to offer was an important economic factor in sustaining the position of the lord, while he could expect in return for his contribution some protection against arbitrary violence.

This system had some resemblances to the emerging feudal societies of Europe, but there were differences. In particular, the legally free man was a more important element in Ireland. Irish society had its equivalent of the feudal villein, and it had its slaves, but its basic unit was the person with enough possessions to be able to seek clientship of a lord.

It was in this society that the Irish became Christian, and in it they continued to be linked to the *derbfine* and to the lord. This had an immediate impact on the basic society of the family and on the institution of marriage. Here there were conflicts between civil law and church law. For one thing, the church forbade marriages between kindred to an extent genuinely difficult to observe in Irish society. Further, the civil law recognised marriage unions that were neither permanent nor mono-gamous. The church had always found it difficult to impose Christ's uncompromising teaching on marriage, to have it accepted that a marriage between Christians was of its nature a lifelong sacred bond. Everywhere in early medieval Europe the civil law regarded marriage as a contract terminable in certain circumstances, and in Ireland as elsewhere Christians entered marriages which they were prepared to terminate should circumstances demand it. Both lords and clients needed sons from their marriages. If there were none, both could remarry, and the lord might have several wives and concubines; the fact that sons by slave-girls could not inherit made them in some respects more valuable, for such sons had no temptation to be disloyal to their father. The early Penitential of Vinnian[16] insists on a strictly Christian view of marriage, but there may be indications in later sources that it was not to be expected that all Christians were living in Christian marraige. There may even be a suggestion that it was only among the *manaigh* or tenants of the monasteries that all the laity 'served the church in lawful marriage'. Indeed, the civil jurists felt confident enough to point out to ecclesiastical critics that in the Old Testament 'the chosen people of God lived in plurality of unions'.[17]

The number of priests to minister to these communities was always inadequate. This can be seen from such things as the relaxation of the earlier discipline that did not allow priests to resume their ministry after grave sin; the fact, as noted in the *Riagail Pátraic*, that one priest may have the charge of three or four churches; or the suggestions of the eighth-century reformers that boys 'given to the church' for education should be pressed to receive orders[18] (these would have been the sons of *manaigh*, the free clients of the church, not villeins, as they would have frequently been in feudal Europe). While the ascetic tradition rejected clerical marriage, it would appear that members of the clergy were in fact married. The civil law recognised not merely married priests but also married bishops, and the priest of the lay proprietary church in particular would have found it hard to live the life that was his lot without the support and help of a wife.

The dependent economic status of the clergy lessened episcopal control. Attempts by ecclesiastical reformers to introduce a system of tithes were resisted. The *fer gráid do mhin-eclaisib tuaithe* moved in the circle of his kin and his lord rather than of his bishop, while the priest of the lay *manaigh* was economically dependent on the monastery. For education all priests depended on the monastic schools, and the level of clerical education must have been decidedly higher in Ireland than in continental Europe. Indeed, Ireland must have had an unusually high number of literate laity, for the monastic schools opened their doors to laymen as well as to monks and priests, thereby setting up close links between the church and secular society, links epitomised by Cú Cuimne 'the wise', for example, who, after a monastic education and a life as a layman, later returned to the monastery. The Annals of Ulster, recording his death in 747, add a little poem, that reads, in Professor Kelleher's sprightly translation:

> Cú Cuimne in youth
> read his way through half the truth.
> He let the other half lie
> while he gave women a try.
>
> Well for him when in old age
> he became a holy sage.
> He gave women the laugh.
> He read the other half.[19]

Learning in the monastic schools was, as it had been for Patrick, first and foremost the Scriptures. Knowledge of scriptural themes was assimilated not only from the sacred text itself or from written commentaries, but also, to an extent hard to grasp in an age of printing, from Christian art. Much of that art has perished. Only a fraction remains even of the high crosses carved in durable stone. The Cross of the Scriptures still stands at Clonmacnois, but nothing remains in Clonenagh of the many crosses which once stood where Óengus the Culdee first read his psalms. Less durable things were even more vulnerable, like the wall-paintings of the great church at Kildare described by Cogitosus in the seventh century. But everywhere about him the student in the monastic school would see depicted the history of salvation.

The duties of priest and bishop are listed in a number of places, notably in the reform tracts that pass under the name of the 'Rule of Patrick' and the 'Rule of the *Céli Dé*' — preaching the gospel, baptism, Mass, the recitation of the canonical hours, prayers for the living and the dead, the last rites for the dying. It is stressed that the baptism of infants is the right and obligation of the priest of the community, the *clericus plebis*. Some problems regarding the administration of baptism in Ireland surfaced during the seventh-century controversies. The precise nature of these problems is obscure, but it is agreed that they concerned points of ritual only and not the substantial validity of the sacrament. Indeed, the threat to the ecclesial significance of Irish baptism may well have arisen from another quarter, its natural significance to the kin-group, and this was to have a long history. Baptism involved godparents. In the eyes of the church, their function was to watch over the spiritual development of the newly baptised. In the eyes of the kin-group, they served to bind new-born children into it; and this, coupled with the custom of fosterage, must have threatened to obscure the sacramental significance of baptism.

Penance does not figure prominently in the lists of clerical duties. Yet, as is well known, in this matter Irish Christianity took a significant step forward in extending frequent private penance to the laity. The penitentials themselves are quite explicit in reserving the formal reconciliation of a penitent sinner to a priest or bishop, but they are more concerned with what we call satisfaction than with what we call absolution. Indeed, what they extend to the laity is essentially the frequent spiritual counselling that marked the monastic life, and it is reasonable to assume that for layman as well as monk the director or *anamchara* was himself a monk. From this it would appear to follow that penance was rarely available to the faithful in the lay proprietary churches, but in the present state of our knowledge this can be no more than a hypothesis. What is clearer, however, is that many reformers set themselves against the long penances imposed and introduced the idea of commuting them into shorter and sharper ones. This was because numbers of people would appear to have been assigned to a kind of perpetual penance. Indeed, a single penance might extend over several years, and, in the eyes of the reformers, anything that excluded Christians from communion at least at Easter was bad pastoral practice.

The Sunday Eucharist is always listed as a priestly and episcopal function: 'What else signifies it that the Lamb is taken *in one house*, but that Christ is believed and communicated under one roof of faith?'[20] The Sunday ritual in the great monastic centres was an elaborate affair. At Armagh, for instance, according to the *Liber Angeli*,

> Christians are seen to live together in religion from the time when the faith first came until the present day; to which aforesaid city three orders indeed adhere, virgins and penitents and those serving the church in lawful marriage. And it is permitted to these three orders to hear the word of preaching in the church of the north quarter on Sundays always. In the southern basilica bishops and priests and authorities of the church and other religious offer well-pleasing phrases.[21]

Cogitosus is even more detailed on seventh-century Kildare. Here, in the great new church,

> The interior contains three large oratories, divided from one another by walls of timber, but all under one roof. One wall, covered with linen curtains and decorated with paintings, traverses the eastern part of the church from one side to the other. There are doors in it at either end. The one door gives access to the sanctuary and the altar, where the bishop, with his school of clerics, and those who are called to the celebration of the holy mysteries, offers the divine sacrifice to the Lord. By the other door of the dividing wall, the abbess enters with her virgins and with pious widows in order to participate in the supper of Jesus Christ, which is his flesh and blood. The remainder of the building is

divided lengthwise into two equal parts by another wall, which runs from the western side to the transverse wall. The church has many windows. Priests and lay persons of the male sex enter by an ornamented door to the right hand side; matrons and virgins enter by another door on the left hand side. In this way the one basilica is sufficient for a huge crowd, separated by walls according to state, grade and sex, but united in spirit, to pray to Almighty God.[22]

The 'state and grade' of the priests who assist with the laymen is particularly interesting. They are not monks, for they are distinguished from the 'school of clerics' (*regularis schola*) who stand with the bishop. It may be that they are priests of some of Kildare's outlying congregations, come with their people to assist at the liturgy in the mother church. Such an attendance of priests must have contrasted with the lot of the churches in lay patronage, many of which, as already suggested, may well have had the services of a priest only intermittently.

The Christian leaven worked slowly. The example of Columban shows that Christian preachers were not afraid to correct the mighty, but with these especially pagan influences must have lingered on. The most unambiguous pagan elements may have disappeared from the ritual inauguration mating of king and *tuath*, but the ceremony persisted: it was too important for the good fortune of the people. Everybody needed luck, and most of all a people needed a lucky king. The King of Leinster, for example, had five 'lucky things'. One was to preside over the *oenach* of Carman, and the holding of this assembly every third year was believed to bring plenty and peace to his kingdom. The new sacred places of the saints could not altogether supplant the old sacred places: an entry in the Annals of Ulster for 784 suggests an attempt to marry the two traditions — 'the arrival of the relics of the son of Erc at the city of Tailtiu' (St Erc of nearby Slane had died early in the sixth century).

Above all, superstition clung to the great mystery of death, and was to cling to it for long centuries to come, despite all attempts to Christianise it, by viaticum, by Mass, prayer, fasting and almsdeeds for the good of the soul departed. Even reforming churchmen felt a kind of pagan dread:

> Even one in orders who brings the sacrament to a sick man is obliged to go out of the house at once thereafter, that the sick man die not in his presence; for if he be present in the house at the death, it would not be allowable for him to perform the sacrifice until a bishop consecrate him.[23]

And when the sick man died the *caoin* was raised, despite the penances prescribed by confessors for this unchristian activity. Unchristian or not, it had a long life ahead of it.[24]

The great monasteries were at the heart of this Christian leavening. Inevitably, they became associated with the now established major dynasties, and in consequence became centres of secular power. The development by which the head of the monastery became a married layman, though still with the title of abbot, was too logical to be altogether shocking. Monastic armies fought with kings and against kings; they fought one another. The basis of their growing power was an amalgam of paganism and Christianity. An ever-widening circle sought clientship from them, for they could offer protection against the greatest risk of all, the perils of judgment day. What they offered was the protection of their saintly founder, and the Lives composed to glorify him show how paganism had diluted Christianity, for in them the saint appears as a figure of power, strong to bless, no doubt, but especially strong to curse. This development can be seen clearly in the successive Lives of Patrick: the holy, humble Christian of his own writings becomes a kind of arch-druid, marching around the country threatening people if they do not accept his authority and pay him tribute.

So these great monasteries, while they were the essential support of the Christian mission, developed their own threat to its inner meaning. But they did become the new sacred places, and their glories are evoked in the Prologue to the *Félire* of Óengus, written about 800:

> The little places that were occupied by twos and threes,
> they are *ruama* with multitudes, hundreds and thousands.
> Tara's mighty burgh perished with the death of her princes:
> great Armagh with its numberless sages lives on.
> Rath Croghan has vanished with Ailill child of triumph:
> fair beyond kingdoms is the majesty of the city of Clonmacnois.
> The proud burgh of Allen has perished with its boastful throng:
> great is triumphant Brigit, fair is her crowded *ruam*.
> The burgh of Emhain has faded away save that its stones remain:
> thronged Glendaloch is the *ruam* of the western world.

The payment of clientship dues was well rewarded by being permitted to await the day of judgment beside the ashes of the saints.

In the second half of the eighth century there were many reform movements in the western church. The reform leaders in Ireland called themselves the *Céli Dé*, or, in what is now an acceptable anglicisation, the Culdees.[25] The words may be a translation of the long-established Latin phrase, *servus Dei*, 'servant of God', or they may have a more native background, stressing that the reformer is a client or *céle* of God and not of any abbot or monastery. Despite annalistic references to a *céle Dé* who came from across the sea, the Culdee movement as it developed is totally native in its inspiration. It generated a considerable literature, associated in particular with the two chief centres of the reform, 'the two eyes of Ireland', the monasteries of Tallaght and Finglas. From this literature it would appear that this new reform derives in a real sense from the seventh-century reformers who had called themselves the *Romani*, but whereas these latter had sought reform in a context of Roman legal structures the Culdees sought reform within the native tradition. Though they could be critical of the laxity and secularisation of the 'old monasteries', they did not propose to replace them. What they proposed was a reform of monasticism.

The movement produced many monastic rules, some explicitly in the name of the Culdees, others attributed to great figures of an earlier age, such as Colum Cille or Ailbe. It is not easy to sum up the ideals of the reformers, for the texts are diffuse and difficult. Essentially they called for a renewal of the ancient ascetic tradition, with special emphasis on study and the anchoretic or hermit life. The devotional literature of the Culdees is very distinctively Irish, with its imaginative freshness and its constant repetition of phrases expressing trust and abandonment, as in the 'Broom of Devotion' or the 'Alphabet of Piety':

> O holy Jesu, O gentle friend, O morning Star, O midday Sun adorned . . . O Son of the Merciful Father without mother in heaven, O Son of the true Virgin maid Mary without father on earth, O true and loving brother . . .

Above all, this spirituality expressed itself in highly personal religious poetry. By any measure, religious or literary, this poetry is a very splendid thing, and it continued to express the aspirations of what is confessedly a religious elite through the iron centuries that lay ahead.

The central weakness of this reform movement will be clear from what has been said. It lacked structure. The rules composed by contemporary continental reformers like Chrodegang of Metz or Benedict of Aniane set out a structure for life, but the Irish rules pointed to an ideal for it. So the development of the Culdee movement was not uniform. In some monasteries, such as Tallaght and Finglas, all the monks were *céli Dé*. In others, Roscrea for example, they formed a separate community closely associated with the old monastery. In others they lived the life of anchorites within it. A ninth-century hermit poem begins: 'All alone in my little cell, without a single human being along with me: such a pilgrimage would be dear to my heart before going to meet death', but it ends, more realistically: 'Let the place which shelters me amid monastic enclosures be a hermit's cell, with me alone therein.'[26] The renewed ascetic tradition needed the protection of the structural strength of the great monasteries if it was to survive.

The Culdees were interested in more than monasteries and hermits: they were also concerned about the weaknesses in the general pastoral mission. Here too their reform efforts must have been exercised mainly through the monasteries and their schools. Above all, they sought more priests and better-educated priests:

> It is right to show reverence to ordained priests, and to fulfil their behests, just as if they were God's angels among men, seeing that it is through them the kingdom of heaven is to be won, by means of baptism and communion and intercession, and by the sacrifice of the body and blood of Christ, and by preaching of the gospel, and by building up the church of God, and by unity of law and rule; and this is what is pleasing to God on earth.[27]

They were also concerned with the observance of Sunday as a day of rest. Here church practice had vacillated between a strict sabbatarianism and treating Sunday as a day of work like other days. Again, there are suggestions of continental influence, for the matter was causing some concern at this time. Under the year 887 the annals note: 'An epistle came with the pilgrim to Ireland, with the *Cáin Domnaig* and other good instructions.' The *Cáin Domnaig* or 'Law of Sunday' survives as a brehon law tract, providing for secular enforcement of Sunday observance. Its effect must have been limited, especially because of the disruptions caused by the Norsemen.

Their first raid came in 795, and thereafter no coastal settlement was safe. A generation later they began to strike inland, and before the middle of the ninth century they had established permanent bases. The development of such bases at least gave the Irish something to attack, and by the end of the century the threat seemed contained, with evidence of intermarriage and the beginnings of absorption. It erupted again early in the ninth century, as the Norse were contained abroad, in England by Alfred and in Normandy by the Frankish kings. But despite the new onslaught, the pattern of absorption and assimilation continued, and the permanent Norse settlements developed into trading towns with the introduction of that great lubricant of commerce, coinage, first Anglo-Saxon pennies and then coins from their own mints.

They were certainly a powerful new force on the Irish scene, but the brief summary just given indicates that some modification may be necessary to the traditional depiction of the Norse as ruthless pagan raiders who savaged Irish Christianity. This is certainly the picture given by the Irish sources. These, however, concentrate on what was undoubtedly the ruthless side of the Norse raids. Because the annals are of monastic provenance, they naturally concentrate on the sufferings of the monasteries, but the monasteries were raided not because they were Christian but because they were wealthy. The later, 'saga'-type literature, like *Cathréim Cellacháin Caisil* or *Cogadh Gaedhel re Gallaibh*, is designed to glorify the Irish kings who fought the Norse, and naturally tends to portray the Norse as almost invincible. But before the Norse came there were lay abbots in Ireland, and rich and secularised monasteries. These developments grew during the Norse period, but not necessarily because of the Norse raids. What did happen in this period was a striking centralisation of power in both church and state. Again, this was not altogether new. In Irish society the weaker had always tended to go under, but it may not be altogether wrong to see the process accelerating under the new pressures.[28]

The striking development in secular policies is the rise of the Dál Cais in Munster after the death of the Eóganacht king Cellachán in 954. Brian Bóruma, King of Munster, divided Ireland with Maelsechnaill of the Uí Néill, and five years later he won recognition as high king. The limitations on his authority appear clearly in the line-up at the battle of Clontarf in 1014, especially the thorny independence of Leinster. But the concept of 'high king', slowly developing as the great dynasties consolidated, had taken another step forward. In particular, the Norse kingdoms have been further integrated into Irish society. They relate to other power centres, and the relationship is frequently one of subordination.

The same process of centralisation went on in the ecclesiastical establishment. Poverty was no protection against the Norse. In 824, according to the Annals of Inisfallen, 'Sceilg was plundered by the heathens, and Etgal was carried off into captivity, and he died of hunger on their hands.' It must have been harsh treatment indeed to bring to such a death a man who had lived on that bare poor rock. But even wealthier places were not safe if their political strength was inadequate. Bangor was raided in 823, and, according to the same annals, 'The shrine of Comgall was broken by them, and its learned men and its bishops were put to the sword.' Bangor's situation was very exposed, but the weakness of the Dál nAraide, its political support, may have been a more important factor in its rapid decline and, apparently, extinction. Bernard's account of the complete collapse of Christian life in the area before the monastery of Bangor was restored by Malachy in 1125 is hardly an exaggeration.

Even the greatest were not immune. Iona was dreadfully exposed, so much so that as early as 804 the decision was taken to set up a new head-quarters at Kells in Ireland. That this move involved some subordination to Armagh is still testified to by the inscription on the high cross at Kells: 'The cross of Patrick and Colum Cille'. Iona continued to be a venerated spot, but its ecclesiastical power continued to decline.

By contrast, the monastic centres that had solid political underpinning increased their power, even though they were very frequently raided because of their wealth. Kildare in its open plain was very vulnerable and suffered a great deal. More refugees from Kildare may be sensed in Carolingian Europe than from any other monastery, but they surface because of their literary remains, which in itself testifies to the continuity of the monastic schools at Kildare, and the great monastery survived and grew because of its position as the chief church of Leinster. Clonmacnois, traditionally associated with the Connacht dynasties, transferred its allegiance to the rising power of the Clann Cholmáin of Meath at the end of the ninth century. The Clann Cholmáin king, Flann Sinna, built a new church at Clonmacnois, and the great Cross of the Scriptures, as its inscription still testifies (though now faintly), was erected by Abbot Colmán in honour of King Flann.

The greatest beneficiary of this process of consolidation was Armagh. That Armagh was Patrick's principal church is as certain as anything can be in the fifth century. Yet Patrick's personal mission, though highly successful, was localised, and he may well have ended his days amid the political defeat of the people he had Christianised. Nevertheless, by the middle of the seventh century Armagh appears to have enjoyed some position of pre-eminence in the northern half of Ireland, and by the end of the century it is extending its claims to the whole island in the name of Patrick.[29] For both the *Romani* and the Culdees, Patrick was in some sense a 'national' figure, and by about 700 it is clear that Armagh is associated with the dominant northern power of the Uí Néill. Thereafter the 'Law of Patrick' is widely and regularly promulgated by capable ecclesiastical jurists who worked effectively within the native traditions. Inevitably, Armagh's wealth left it open to secularisation and drew the Norse raiders on it, but this did not check its growing power. Indeed, its prestige may at times have helped it even against the pagans. The *Three Fragments of Annals* record under the year 851 a fight in Dublin between the Norse and the newly arrived Danes. The Danes decided to invoke the help of 'Patrick, archbishop and head of the saints of Ireland', whose church had suffered so much from the Norse. After their victory they filled a great trench with gold and silver 'for Patrick', and doubtless sent it to Armagh.

When the Munster kings set their thoughts on the high kingship of Ireland they knew they had to reach agreement with Armagh. This is clear as early as Fedelmid mac Crimthainn, who died in 847. Agreement was finally reached between Armagh and the new Munster dynasty of the Dál Cais in 973, and thereafter the 'Law of Patrick' was accepted in Munster. When Brian Bóruma visited Armagh on his triumphant circuit of Ireland in 1005 he had his *anamchara* or confessor write in the Book of Armagh:

> St Patrick, when going to heaven, decreed that the entire fruit of his labour, as well of baptism and of causes as of alms, should be rendered to the apostolic city which in the Irish tongue is called Arddmacha. Thus have I found in the records of the Irish. This I have written, namely Calvus Perennis, in the presence of Brian, emperor of the Irish: and what I have written he has determined on behalf of all the Kings of Cashel.

The context of this entry seems clear. In 962 Otto the Great had entered

Rome, restored the Holy Roman Empire, and set out to use its strength to rescue the papacy from its degradation. The Irish parallel may not be exact in all respects, but here too there was essentially the same vision of relationships between the heads of civil and ecclesiastical authority. After Brian's death at Clontarf his body was carried to Armagh for burial.

These, then, were the great centres whose power was the necessary protection of the structures of Christian life, however much their government may have become secularised. Here and only here could learning flourish. The schools of Armagh continued to rework the Patrick legend. A Latin quatrain preserved on the fly-leaves attached to a scriptural commentary of Bede, the 'Laon fragment', mourns the death of Cathasach, 'the wise and learned master, the dutiful, virtuous youth, the decorous superior'. Under the year 897 the Annals of Ulster record his death, '*tanase* abbot of Armagh, a pious young man'. Promotion in the ecclesiastical hierarchy did not necessarily exclude either learning or virtue. Two ninth-century continental manuscripts, the St Paul Codex from Carinthia and the St Gall Priscian, were written by Irishmen, quite possibly refugees from Kildare. Their marginalia and glosses are particularly interesting. The St Paul Codex contains the well-known and charming poem on the scholar's cat, Pangur Bán, while the St Gall Priscian has the beautiful quatrains idealising the work of the scribe:

> A wall of woodland overlooks me, a blackbird's song sings to me, praise that I shall not hide. Over my lined book the chant of birds sings to me. A clear-voiced cuckoo sings to me in a green cloak of bush-tops, a lovely utterance. The Lord be good to me on judgment day! Well do I write beneath the woodland trees.[30]

At the same time the marginalia show somewhat unregenerate human nature still struggling for expression: 'A blessing on the soul of Fergus. Amen. I am very cold' . . . 'Nightfall and time for supper' . . . 'Love lasts as long as property lasts, Maellacán.'

It may have been cold in the *scriptorium*, but there were books, and protection, and even supper, and the mind could stray to that 'hermitage of the heart' so dear to the Culdees. In the world outside conditions were harsher, as the great ecclesiastics got more drawn into the ways of an iron world. Fedelmid mac Crimthainn, King of Munster, abbot and possibly bishop, died in 847. His life was a succession of wars, against lay and clerical dynasts. Yet the Annals of Ulster salute him at his death as 'best of the Irish, scribe and anchorite'. Cormac mac Cuileannáin, likewise King of Munster, scholar, bishop and celibate, died in battle in 908, a battle he would have wished to have avoided but which was forced on him by dynastic politics. All that was Christian in Ireland recognised him as a saint and martyr, and it may well be said that the cause of his martyrdom was the limitations of Irish Christianity in his day. The assimilation and

Christianisation of the Norse must have also helped to coarsen the Christian life. The old gods returned, Norse gods this time, as in the case of Helgi, whose mother and grandmother would have been Irish and Christian, but who is said to have been 'very confused in matters of faith. He put his trust in Christ and named his homestead after him, but during stormy weather, in the stress and strain of battle, and generally when things were critical, his prayers were directed to Thor.' The churches of the Irish homesteads, the proprietary churches, disappear from our sight, no doubt absorbed into the growing concentrations of power. With them disappear their priests, who even in better times had always been too few in numbers to conduct a fully effective mission. To say that they drop out of the record is not to say that they ceased to exist, but one can reasonably suspect that they became even fewer as times got harder for smaller people. For good or ill, the pastoral mission now depended almost exclusively on the services of the great monasteries.

The period after Clontarf is usually referred to as that of 'kings with opposition', but what was new was not the opposition but the fact that the claim to high kingship was now more far-reaching than before. The opposition led to unending warfare, with churches being regularly burnt as part of it. True, there was a certain superstitious respect for ecclesiastical sanctuary, but the right of sanctuary tended to be effective only when it was backed by force. In the great churches all offices had now become hereditary, including the office of priest, though hereditary office in the Irish sense did not always or necessarily imply a succession from father to son. While the surviving sources strongly suggest that there were not many priests, it must be remembered that these sources are interested only in the affairs of an aristocracy. Towards the end of the century, when the great Norman Archbishops of Canterbury, Lanfranc and Anselm, interested themselves in the affairs of the Irish church, their concern is not so much that the sacraments are not administered in Ireland but that they are administered irregularly (marriage is a predictable exception: to Lanfranc Irish marriage, governed by brehon law, is not marriage but fornication).

The chronicling of the ecclesiastical aristocracy allows us to see some aspects of their acitvities. One is care for the poor, as with Cummascach ua hErodáin at Armagh, 'head of a thousand poor', or Conn *na mBocht* at Clonmacnois, a married man who was also 'head of the *céli Dé* and anchorite'. Another reasonably well-documented activity is the related theme of pilgrimage and hermitage. The unique charters of Kells allow us to see the organisation of a *disert* or hermitage for those who had re-nounced the world and left their kindred, something which appears to have been not uncommon for people coming to the end of their days who may have felt they had much to do penance for.

Irish ecclesiastical learning remained very insular: the traces of the new learning now stirring on the continent are faint indeed. One indication that the great stream of Irish learning may at this time be coming into its maturity or even into its autumn appears with the gathering of the learning of the past into the great 'books of lore', those slightly later compilations from the twelfth century, such as the Book of the Dun Cow, Rawlinson B 502 and the Book of Leinster. Some literature of more general piety has survived from this period: reworking of the legends of the saints, voyage and vision literature. Pagan and Christian themes intermingle like the interlacings of the artist of the Book of Kells. Yet the most authentic Christian vision can suddenly break from a seemingly unpromising morass. The Notes to the *Félire* of Óengus date from about this time. Kenney has described them as 'at times neither trustworthy nor edifying, a vast and heterogeneous mass of myth, legend, folklore, and the debris of history and literature'. But there are islands of authenticity in the bog:

> Once upon a time Moling was at prayers in his church and he saw a lad coming towards him, a goodly lad arrayed in purple raiment.
> 'Who art thou?' says Moling.
> 'I am Christ, son of God,' says he.
> 'I know not that,' says Moling. 'When Christ would come to have speech with the Culdees, 'twas not in purple raiment or in kingly guise that he would come, but after the fashion of hapless men, as a leper or a man diseased.'[31]

That great figure from the first age of monasticism, Colum Cille of Iona, came to occupy the centre of this lore. In his own day he was reputed to have protected the poets of Ireland, and from the eleventh to the thirteenth centuries many nameless poets produced a literature they attributed to him. This poetry gathers up the highest aspirations of the monastic church: the love of solitude, asceticism, and scholarship, and the acceptance of exile as the 'white martyrdom', the greatest sacrifice man can make for Christ. Colum Cille was the great and archetypal exile, who for love of Christ abandoned 'the three best-beloved places', Tír Luígdech his birthplace, Durrow with its 'cuckoos calling from the woodland on the brink of summer' (the hermit poetry is full of woods and birdsong), and lastly Derry, 'noble angel-haunted city . . . calm and bright, full of white angels from one end to the other'.[32]

The old Irish church was distinctively itself. Soon it was to be opened up to a wider world. In far-off Rome the papacy was stirring. The popes had freed themselves from domination by the local nobility with the support of the German emperors. Now in the persons of popes like Leo IX (1049-54), Alexander II (1061-73) and Gregory VII (1073-85) they set out to discard imperial support and lead the reform of the church from their own resources. In the eleventh century Ireland was drawn into closer contact with Rome. Pilgrims increased in number as the journey became safer. At the end of the century there was an Irish monastery in Rome — the Annals of Inisfallen record the death of its abbot, Eógan, in 1095, and a manuscript in the Vatican library has two lists of its monks from about the same date. There are five names on one list and four in the other.

This papal reform centred on a clergy independent of lay control, organised in diocese and parish. The first stirrings of this came to Ireland as the Christian Norse towns organised their churches. Dublin got its first bishop about 1030. It is almost certain he was consecrated in Canterbury, and it should be recalled that the King of England at the time was a Dane, Canute. Waterford got its first bishop in 1096. He too was consecrated in Canterbury. The archbishop now was a Norman, Anselm, who like his predecessor Lanfranc wished to reform the Irish church (the Normans had set themselves up as patrons of the papal reform). However, by this date there was an organised reform party in Ireland. They wanted a reform under the leadership of Rome, not of Canterbury. They had just established this reform at a series of synods in the twelfth century when the Normans arrived in Ireland.

2

Normans,
but no King

The twelfth-century world that the Irish were now brought into full contact with was pulsing with life and development at every level. Ecclesiastical reform was coming under the firm guidance of the papacy. The central feature of this reform seemed to provide exactly what was most lacking in the Irish experience, namely a firm structure supported by law within which the round of Christian duties could be set. The popes of this period set their reform efforts within a legal framework, from Gregory VII (1073-85) through Alexander III (1159-81) to Innocent III (1198-1216).

However, the successful application of this great concept to the daily lives of Christians demanded stable institutions at a local level, the diocese and the parish. For these to function effectively, civil peace was needed, and civil peace was increasingly summed up in the person of the monarch. The popes had need of 'the holy kings'. Charlemagne's great achievement had faltered, but his Holy Roman Empire was restored in 962 in the person of Otto the Great. The authority of his line was, however, confined to the German lands, but by the reign of Louis VI (1108-37) France began to develop as a centralised state.

Such centralised states were made possible by feudalism. The central strength of the feudal system lay in the fact that it extended the links of kinship on which previous societies had been based. This it did by balancing the right to exploit land and the labour of those who worked the land by the obligation of military service. This was embodied in the pledge of homage, whereby the person receiving the right bound himself to fulfil the duty. In this way a warlike aristocracy was brought under central royal control.

The most extraordinary single achievement in this age of rapid development was that of the Normans. In 885 they had sailed up the Seine as freebooters to besiege Paris. In 911 they had been enfeoffed by the French king with the land that came to be called Normandy. In one century thereafter they had adopted the feudal system within the framework of the rapidly developing structures of French law. They did this for purely pragmatic reasons, seeing in the system of law the firm structure of a state. They did not make the mistake of confusing law with morality: moral considerations never prevented a Norman from seizing any chance that might offer. In consequence, this gifted and now disciplined people began to expand rapidly. In 1066 they conquered England. In 1042 a scion of the obscure house of Hauteville became Count of Apulia, and in 1130 his descendant Roger was King of Sicily. Bohemond of Taranto went on the first crusade and in 1099 became Prince of Antioch. Kingdoms were there for the taking. In August 1167 the first few Norman knights had arrived in Ireland, by a kind of political accident; but although, like the Hautevilles in the south, and initially with less difficulty, they established themselves in the country, it was only in a qualified sense that they brought the overall legal system that was their strong foundation.

As well as kings to establish the rule of law, the popes needed saints to inspire the religious revival, and they got them. Many of them founded religious orders, which came to play a much greater part in the church's life. The first half of the twelfth century is often called 'the age of St Bernard', so complete was the dominance of the great Cistercian abbot (1090-1153). Bernard is essentially a feudal aristocrat: for him the Christian life is the knight-service to God. But already in his own lifetime Bernard was becoming a figure of the past, as society and the individuals who made up society became more complex, especially under the impact of the growth of towns and increased contact with non-Christian peoples. Among other things, this had brought about a theological development that was deeply suspect to Bernard. For him theology had been the Scriptures and the Fathers. Now there was a new desire to produce a systematic overall view of the truths of faith by rational reflection. It flourished in the new institution of the university. At the beginning of the thirteenth century a new concept of the religious life appeared with the friars, bound by vows but dedicated to the active apostolate. It was natural that they should concentrate their mission in the towns, and equally natural that they should enter the universities in force.

So that old Irish church, so distinctively itself, was to be opened up to a multiplicity of new influences. It needed a programme like the papal one: it needed the saints, and it needed the kings. It got the programme and the saints, but what it did not get in sufficient measure were the kings.

The foreign contacts were built up through the eleventh century, contacts with Rome and contacts with Canterbury, since 1070 ruled by the great Norman archbishops Lanfranc (1070-89) and Anselm (1093-1109). In Ireland a native reform party established itself. It was centred on Munster, where the Dál Cais dynasty provided a measure of stability. Toirrdelbach ua Briain (1063-86) had been approached by Pope Gregory VII and Archbishop Lanfranc, both of them detailing the abuses in the Irish church and urging that a reform synod be called. The principal abuses detailed were: the anomalous position of the Irish episcopate (in Ireland bishops were consecrated to exercise what the new theology was to define as a 'power of orders', not to exercise authority, 'the power of jurisdiction', over a diocesan community); the prevalence of simony (the conferring of ecclesiastical office for temporal considerations, a prime target of the reformers, and inevitably widespread in Ireland both because of the anomalous position of the bishop and the hereditary nature of ecclesiastical succession); and widespread abuses in connection with marriage and sexual morals generally.

The synod assembled in Cashel in 1101. King Muirchertach Ua Briain (1086-1119) had handed over this historic royal fortress to the church, not without some political interests, for the royalty that Cashel represented had been the Eóganacht dynasty displaced by the Dál Cais. It was presided over by Máel Muire Ua Dunáin, 'chief legate, chief bishop and chief senior of the island of Ireland, with authority from the pope himself',[1] that is, as papal legate, the first of a line that was to continue until after the Norman invasion. The decrees of the synod have survived in a terse form which is not always clear. What is clear, however, is that they made a beginning in tackling the abuses. The legislation on marriage would not have satisfied the foreign reformers, but it probably represents a situation where the Irish reformers realised that change would have to come gradually. Neither did they tackle the anomalies concerning bishops and dioceses, but they did lay down that within the Irish system there should be only one person in authority in each church and that he should not be a layman.

It was on this issue that the north of the country was brought into the reform movement. By now it was universally accepted that Patrick's church of Armagh ranked first in honour among the Irish churches. However, its very prestige, and the wealth which went with it, had made it a particularly bad example of secularisation: for over a century it had been held in hereditary succession by one family. But Armagh too had its reform party, and when a member of the ruling family, Cellach (latinised Celsus), succeeded in 1105 he decided to head the reform by receiving priestly ordination at once and episcopal consecration in Munster in the following year. The way was now open for a reform synod representing the whole of Ireland. It met at Rathbreasail in the midlands in 1111, and was presided over by Gilbert, the Bishop of Limerick, as papal legate.

The main achievement of Rathbreasail was to tackle the problem left untouched at Cashel, namely the drawing of a clear distinction between the world of the monastery and the world of the diocese by establishing a diocesan episcopate. There were to be two metropolitan sees, Armagh and Cashel. Each was to have twelve suffragans, Armagh in Ulster, Meath and Connacht, and Cashel in Munster and Leinster. Inevitably, the dioceses would have to coincide with civil territorial divisions if they were to be viable units. Indications of the problems facing the reformers are to be found in the proviso that Leinster and Connacht might change the scheme proposed at the synod provided there were no more than five dioceses in each province, and in the fact that Cashel was left with only eleven suffragans, a pointed emphasis on the omission of Dublin with its tradition of bishops consecrated in Canterbury. Nevertheless, a study of the episcopal obits in the annals over the next forty years indicates that this shaky scheme did in fact establish itself. The greatest single obstacle was overcome sometime in the 1120s, when at the urging of Cellach Dublin took its place among the Irish dioceses.

The great archbishop died in 1129. On his death-bed he named as his successor Máel Máedóc Ua Morgair, better known as St Malachy (1095-1148). Malachy's father had been a teacher in the schools of Armagh. He was ordained priest in 1119 and appointed Bishop of Down and Connor about 1124. St Bernard has given an account of what he found there, and making all allowance for the great Cistercian's rhetoric, it is a chilling possibility that he may not be too far from the truth, especially when it is remembered that the spiritual centre of the district, the abbey of Bangor, had suffered very severely at the hands of the Norse. He met beasts, not men, said Bernard, shameless in their morals, wild in their rites, impious in their faith, unclean in their lives. They did not enter on lawful marriage; they made no confessions; and the few priests who existed had lost heart and 'lived idle lives among the laity'.

There were a few years of fruitful reform, but then Malachy and his monks at the restored monastery of Bangor were driven into exile because of local hostilities; they fled to the furthest recesses of Munster, where the continuing vitality of the reform is witnessed to this day by the romanesque beauty of Cormac's chapel on the Rock of Cashel, which was then being built (it was consecrated in 1134). It is small wonder that Malachy reacted to Cellach's death-bed legacy by declaring that he would not return north until he had some assurance of being received as Archbishop of Armagh. Predictably, the family of Cellach had intruded one of their members, who could count on support from the traditionalists and the unsophisticated. Malachy faced a stiff struggle after he had been persuaded to return. It ended in 1136 in a compromise which he found acceptable. He resigned the archbishopric, but the hereditary succession was broken by the appointment to Armagh of Gelasius, the Abbot of Derry (this in itself being an indication that this great Columban monastery had joined the reform party).

Malachy returned to the diocese of Down, now separated from Connor, but he remained in a very real sense the leader of the reform movement. That is why it was he who set out for Rome in 1140 to tidy up the achievements of the reformers and in particular to ask the pope to grant the *pallia*, the symbols of metropolitan jurisdiction, to the two Irish archbishops. On his way he stayed at Clairvaux, where he and Bernard immediately developed a great respect for one another. This was to lead to the first Irish Cistercian foundation at Mellifont in 1142. Fourteen more Cistercian houses had been founded by the date of the Norman invasion.[2]

Malachy's name is also associated with the Augustinian canons regular. In many respects these had a greater impact on the reform of the Irish church: there were over sixty houses in existence by 1170. Most of them were in the north of Ireland, and here most, under Malachy's inspiration, followed the rule of the house at Arrouaise in northern France, which he had visited in 1140. The question of the canons regular is complex, as they were not a unitary organisation like the Cistercians. For long centuries there had been attempts to get the clergy attached to the larger churches, especially the cathedrals, to live under a rule, the *vita canonica*. There were differences of opinion as to whether this rule should include personal poverty. Those who favoured personal poverty moved out and founded their own separate communities. In order to define their way of life more exactly they came to adopt what was known as the Rule of St Augustine. A new division appeared among these 'Augustinian canons regular': should their life be monastic or should they engage in the care of souls? Some congregations went in one direction, others in the other. The rule of the canons of Arrouaise, so favoured by Malachy, inclined towards the strict monastic observance, but this appears to have been modified in Ireland even in houses that called themselves Arroasian. Though much of the detail is beyond recovery, it seems quite certain that most of the old Irish monastic centres adopted the Augustinian rule of Arrouaise as part of their reform, but continued some measure of pastoral care. And, as in Europe, convents of women following the Augustinian rule developed, frequently in close association with the houses of men. The vast majority of the relatively small number of women religious in medieval Ireland were Augustinian canonesses, and a considerable proportion of the convents would describe themselves as Arroasian.

When Malachy arrived in Rome the pope confirmed the arrangements which had been made at Rathbreasail. He appointed Malachy papal legate in Ireland, but said he would not grant the *pallia* until a request for them came from an Irish synod. Why the pope laid down this condition can only be conjectured. It is true that Archbishop Theobald of Canterbury and other bishops from England had been in Rome shortly before Malachy; and that Canterbury still retained its interest in Ireland is indicated by the fact that he consecrated a Bishop of Limerick in 1140. It is also true, however, that if Malachy wished to urge caution on the pope he was not without evidence to back his opinion. The fact is that Ireland had been in political and military turmoil since Toirrdelbach Ua Conchobair had begun his bid for the high kingship in 1114, and there was no sign of improvement (though if it was Theobald who urged his consideration on the pope, it must have been in full consciousness of the fact that at this time England was in no better state of civil peace). But the disturbed conditions in Ireland may well explain why Malachy failed to assemble his synod until 1148. Once again, unwilling and ailing, he set out for Rome to request the *pallia*, but he died at Clairvaux on 2 November. Bernard in effect canonised him by singing the final prayer of the requiem from the Mass of a confessor-bishop. Formal papal confirmation of his sainthood was given in 1190.

Bernard himself died five years after Malachy, and the Cistercian pope, Eugene III, died in the same year. The great figures of an older age were passing away. Their last achievement in Ireland was at the Synod of Kells in 1152. This time the papal legate was a Roman cardinal, John Paparo. On his journey to Ireland his passage through England was obstructed by King Stephen, as indeed Malachy's passage had been obstructed in 1148. He did succeed in arriving, however, and presided over the Synod of Kells. The still continuing abuses were again legislated against, notably those concerning marriage practices, but the synod's great achievement was the establishment of a diocesan system that with minor changes has lasted to the present day.

It seems to have come as a surprise that Paparo brought with him four *pallia*, not two. The proposal for the establishment of a new metropolitan see in the west at Tuam must be explained as a recognition of the rising power of the O'Connors, and must also indicate that the Roman authorities were keeping themselves informed on the situation in Ireland. The elevation of Dublin to metropolitan status confirmed its dissociation from Canterbury and absorption into the Irish system. In all, thirty-two suffragan sees were recognised, nine in Armagh, six in Tuam, twelve in Cashel, and five in Dublin. The increase in number over Rathbreasail indicates that more centres than was ideally desirable could not be denied the status of an episcopal see; while the notable difference between the two synods in what places must be deemed the seat of a bishopric reflects the political instability of the forty years between them.

While the diocesan system did prove substantially permanent, it was still in important respects only a declaration of intent. In particular, the bishops still had to establish a system of parishes. The cumulative synodal legislation against abuses was also in important respects only a declaration of intent — simony, hereditary succession, regular adminis-tration of the sacraments, abuses connected with sex and marriage. Yet the old ways were giving way to the new. The extraordinary efflorescence of the monastic scribal tradition in those great compilations of lore in the Irish language, both secular lore and lives of the saints, may well be under-stood as an indication that it had now reached its end. Whether the com-pilers were conscious or not that they were at the end of a tradition can hardly be established, but it is a fact that after the twelfth century the scribal tradition passed from the monks to lay learned families.

Two persons may be singled out to show the vitality of the new ways.

One is Laurence O'Toole (1128-80), Abbot of Glendalough in 1156 and Archbishop of Dublin in 1161, the first prelate of that see to be consecrated by an Irish prelate, namely the Archbishop of Armagh. His first care was to provide a worthy clergy for his diocese; his cathedral clergy became Arroasian canons, and he himself lived by the rule and spent his days in preaching and charity. The second is a temporal ruler, Donnchad Ua Cerbaill, King of Oirgialla (Louth). A eulogy of his work was copied into a sixteenth-century antiphonary of Armagh:

> A prayer for Donnchad Ua Cerbaill, supreme King of Oirgialla, by whom was made the book of Cnoc na nApstal at Louth and the chief books of the order of the year, and the chief books of the Mass. It is this illustrious king who founded the entire monastery, both stone and wood, and gave to it territory and land for the prosperity of his soul in honour of Paul and Peter. By him the church was reformed throughout the land of Oirgialla, and a regular bishopric was made and the church was placed under the rule of a bishop. In his time tithes were received and marriage was assented to and churches were founded and temples and belfries were made, and monasteries of monks and canons were rebuilt and hermitages were made. These are especially the works that he did for his prosperity and rule in the land of Oirgialla; namely the monastery of monks on the banks of the Boyne [Mellifont], stone and wood, implements and books and territory and land, in which there are one hundred monks and three hundred conventuals, and the monastery of canons at Termon Feichin and the monastery of nuns and the great church of Termon Feichin and the church of Lepad Feichin and the church of ... [3]

The fact is that since the stresses of the Norse invasion Ireland had moved closer to the concept of unitary kingship without finally achieving it. Powerful dynasties had been consolidated by the absorption of smaller lordships, and this had inevitably done away with the strict law of kinship succession. There were even the beginnings of what must be described as 'feudalism'.[4] But no one dynasty was able to emerge as supreme, and a number of them were determined to keep trying. In 1155 the pope gave Ireland a king. In view of the future developments of Irish history, it was ironical that the king was the King of England and the pope the only Englishman ever to have occupied the chair of Peter. It is only to be expected that the event should have passed into the national legend as English aggression.

Henry II had been accepted as King of England on 19 December 1154, and in his long reign of thirty-five years undid the anarchy of the nineteen years of Stephen. In contrast to Ireland, the English anarchy had been only an interlude: Henry could build again on the work of his Norman and even Saxon predecessors. It is only in a qualified sense that he can be described

as English. He was King of England, but was lord of even greater territories in France. These he saw as the centre of his dominions, and there
he spent most of his time.

The Englishman Nicholas Breakspeare, who became pope on 4
December 1154, fifteen days before Henry became king, was by now
international rather than English. He had left England in his youth,
became a wandering scholar, and then a cardinal at Rome. From 1152 to
1154 he had been papal legate in Scandinavia, doing a job very like what
John Paparo was doing in Ireland at the same time. True, his election as
pope had caused national pride in England, and a delegation of three
bishops had gone to Rome to congratulate him. With them was John of
Salisbury, secretary to Archbishop Theobald of Canterbury. It was on this
occasion that the pope granted Ireland as a lordship to Henry and confirmed his grant with the bull *Laudabiliter*. The purpose of the grant, as
the pope explained, was that Henry should further the interests of the
church in Ireland. The indications are that Henry himself had very little to
do with this development. It was brought about by ecclesiastics. It is difficult to dismiss the thought that the now thwarted ambitions of
Canterbury had something to do with it, though it did not result in the restoration of Canterbury's authority in Ireland. It must also be remembered
that there was now a Roman cardinal in Rome, John Paparo, who could
report on Irish problems from first-hand experience.

Henry himself would have been no Norman if he had never entertained
the thought of adding Ireland to his dominions, but the fact that he did
not arrive until 1171 indicates it was not his first priority. His first
priority when he did come was to curb his own barons. His second was to
placate a pope outraged by the murder of Archbishop Thomas Becket by
dutifully taking up the papal mandate of 1155. One can see the point of
John Watt's remark that 'a reform movement that could produce spiritual
leaders of such calibre [Malachy and Laurence] deserved better of the
papacy than it was to get',[5] while bearing in mind that the problems of the
Irish reform movement did not arise from the quality of its spiritual
leaders but from the political instability of the country. The pope decided
that Henry's lordship was the best solution. The Irish bishops agreed,
partly because their reform had been very consciously dependent on papal
authority, but also in the possibly bitter realisation that Henry's lordship
held out the only hope of the necessary civil peace. Unfortunately it did
not result in bringing the peace of a unitary feudal lordship in Ireland.

It will be convenient to speak of 'Irish' and 'Normans' during the later
twelfth and thirteenth centuries, though the 'Normans' belonged to an
international culture that was basically French. In the early fourteenth
century the Normans suffered a series of misfortunes that permanently
altered the balance of power in the country. Very quickly after the
invasion they established themselves over the greater part of it. It was not

just the Irish ecclesiastics who accepted Henry: the Irish lay leaders at this stage had no inhibitions about admitting this new element into the Irish power game, though from the beginning there should have been enough to disquiet them, notably Henry's grant of Meath to Hugh de Lacy in 1172. And even apart from formal royal grants, the land-hungry Normans proved uncontrollable. Laurence O'Toole was the Irish leader in an attempt to control their expansion. The Treaty of Windsor (1175) recognised Rory O'Connor as both King of Connacht and overlord under the crown of the other Irish kings. The treaty did not stop Norman expansion. Laurence's own brother was killed by the Normans in 1178. He himself died on 14 November 1180, at Eu in Normandy, on his way to appeal to Henry II, who was then, as so often, in his French dominions.

A line drawn on a map can give a misleading impression of reality. Everywhere there were Gaelic enclaves. The border, the 'march', was never far away, psychologically or physically, and the march meant warfare. In this respect, however, Ireland was not so different from much of Europe. Even in England the 'land of peace' had its marches, in the north and in Wales.

What made a 'land of peace' was control by the king through his courts of common law, to which all free men had access. What may well have been the greatest single factor in leaving the conquest incomplete was the denial of this right to Irishmen except by individual privilege (in Wales, where Norman penetration had taken place at an earlier date when the framework of common law was much less developed, it had been easier to envisage each lordship developing its own 'mixed' law). The consequences of this denial of English law to the Irish was far-reaching. The surviving Irish lords had no title to their territories that could stand up in the king's court. The many Irish in Norman lordships lacked that right so basic that it was almost the definition of a free man, namely the right to appear in person before the king's courts, and not to have to content himself to sue or be sued in them through his lord. The only exceptions, for clergy as well as laity, were by grant of personal privilege or when a bishop litigated on behalf of his church. Many of the Irish in the Norman lordships were, of course, not personally free. The Normans had no wish to drive out those who worked the land, and the Irish lower classes remained as villeins or *biataigh*.

The Normans set out to exploit the land by more intensive agriculture, with increased emphasis on tillage. This demanded a greater population than the Irish could supply, so favourable terms were offered to attract immigrants from England, and they came in what appear to have been large numbers. The density of settlement varied, from areas like Fingal in Dublin or Forth in Wexford, where it seems to have been almost total, to the Ulster lordship and perhaps much of Connacht, where the Norman lordship represented little more than the imposition of a military aristocracy. The Normans also developed towns, and here too there were Irish, but only among the poor. There is only one Irish name among the 224 members of the Dublin guild merchant of 1226,[6] and at an early date the Irish were formally excluded from guild membership.

The bishops and diocesan clergy — but not the religious orders — seem to have been the most successful in adapting themselves to this difficult situation, but even they must have lost hope after the failure of the attempt led by Archbishop David Mac Cerbaill of Cashel in 1280 to have English law extended to all. It may well be that the sharp legal division meant rather less in day-to-day experience, but for the Irish there was always a sense of insecurity and humiliation. With the Normans, the situation nurtured a sense of racial superiority. A poem on the death of Piers de Bermingham in 1308 praises him at length for his continuing hostility to the Irish and for the numbers of them he has killed.[7] Irish resentment can be clearly seen in the remonstrance addressed to Pope John XXII by the Irish princes in 1317 justifying their support of Edward Bruce:

> For not only their laymen and secular clergy but some also of their regular clergy dogmatically assert the heresy that it is no more sin to kill an Irishman than a dog or any other brute.... All of them, indifferently, secular and regular, assert with obstinacy that it is lawful for them to take away from us by force of arms whatever they can of our lands and possessions of every kind, making no conscientious scruple about it even when they are at the point of death.[8]

By the middle of the thirteenth century about a third of the Irish episcopate was Norman, a proportion rather less than might have been expected, for Norman ecclesiastics were as predatory as Norman laity. The situation varied from see to see. Dublin was at one extreme, very consciously Norman since the provision of John Cumin in 1181 on the death of Laurence O'Toole began a long line of archbishops actually born in England. In 1191 Cumin set up a new cathedral chapter, that of St Patrick's, richly endowed and heavily staffed with clerics in the king's service. At the other extreme were certain dioceses dominated by the Irish, in Ulster and Connacht, where the old principle of kin-succession yielded only slowly. But over the thirteenth century as a whole the bishops were freely elected by the cathedral chapters, frequently from among their number, and in consequence were well acquainted with local needs. The king had a natural interest in the election of a bishop, for a bishop was a great landed magnate. The agreement with the papacy embodied in Magna Carta was extended to Ireland in 1216. In practice, the king was content if licence to elect and confirmation for the person elected was sought, and if the new bishop posed no political risk. Crown influence was regularly used, but not always on behalf of Normans, and it was not always successful. It was unusual for the papacy to attempt to nominate a candidate: it was content to act as arbiter in disputes.

The system of common law held out many attractions for the bishops. Even in Ireland every bishop could litigate in the king's courts in the affairs of his church. Common law and canon law also moved, as it were, in the same orbit: at the worst, they could dispute within an agreed system. Common law also recognised the competence of church courts over clerics charged with felony, over public sinners, and over matrimonial and testamentary matters, though it jealously guarded its jurisdiction over real property. Brehon law, on the other hand, while giving ecclesiastics the same juridical authority as any other lord in their own lands, gave them no authority outside them, and retained many elements the church could not accept. So there was widespread co-operation between bishops and the king's officers, but it had very real limits. Even at the height of royal authority the king's influence was very minimal in the dioceses of Derry, Raphoe, Kilmore, Clogher and Dromore. No convocation of clergy developed in Ireland, and the disputes over precedence between the Archbishops of Armagh and Dublin severely limited the activites of the former outside his province, even after the see had fallen to the Normans in 1303.

The typical medieval bishop survives as an administrative figure, through his synodal legislation and in the records of his church courts. What little survives from thirteenth-century Ireland makes it difficult to see any bishop even in his administrative role, especially as it has to be remembered that much synodal legislation was borrowed because it had been found good elsewhere, and it is hard to estimate its exact relevance to local conditions. The thirteenth-century bishops come even less into focus as religious leaders, and inevitably the Irish bishops are even less clearly focused than the Normans.

It has already been noted that from the twelfth century new religious orders had played an important role in the church. The Cistercians had come in strength before the invasion, and so had the canons regular, especially in the northern half of the country. The Normans were great founders of abbeys.[9] A people of practical piety who were prepared to pay so that others could do what they knew they themselves were doing not at all or badly, they regarded a monastic foundation as a solid insurance policy against the day of judgment. So they added new Cistercian abbeys and houses of canons, especially in the southern half of the country. They introduced the military orders, the Hospitallers and the Templars, who seem to have colonised their lands very thoroughly and in general acted as a kind of police force. A particularly interesting development was the introduction of the Brothers of the Cross, sixteen houses in all, who, in contrast with the Knights Hospitallers, did make the provision of hospital services their primary concern. There were Irish houses from 1180, but the first English house came only in 1244, and the order was never strong there. It is by no means impossible that they came to Ireland directly from Italy, especially in view of the fact that the Italian south was a Norman land.

A real new development came with the friars, who arrived at a quite early date, the Dominicans in 1224 and the Franciscans about 1230. In addition to practising corporate as well as individual poverty, the friars placed preaching and pastoral care at the very centre of their lives. They came to Ireland through England, they founded their houses in the Norman lands, and, as everywhere, they concentrated on the towns. However, like the other religious orders, it was normal that there should be Normans and Irish in the same house. By the time the friars arrived this had already led to strife in the monastic orders.

The older Irish monastic traditions had shown some power of revival under the impulse of the twelfth-century reform, but the revival was short-lived and the new imports carried the day. The Irish found these in many respects strange and uncongenial. About 1216, for example, four canons from the newly founded Premonstratensian house at Tuam turned up in Prémontré, asking, apparently, to be told what it was all about. They had to be provided not merely with books containing the observances of the order but even with the religious habit — they did come clad in habits, but they were 'age-worn and thin in texture'.[10] However, the most serious problems arose with the Cistercians. They came to a head in the 'conspiracy of Mellifont' at almost the same date as the Tuam canons turned up in Prémontré. They were resolved, in so far as they could be resolved, by a firmly conducted investigation by the Norman-English Cistercian abbot, Stephen of Lexington, in 1228. He was clearly shocked by what he found, and while it would be an anachronism to interpret his decisions in a 'racist' sense, he did clearly lay down that the Irish were to be Cistercians precisely as the French were, and that their control over their local affairs was to be limited until they had shown themselves capable of this. Though local control was restored later in the century, the tensions continued and did much to reduce the contribution of the Cistercians to the church in Ireland.

The friars enjoyed what in retrospect must seem an abnormal peace for over fifty years. A register has survived for the Dominican house in Athenry, founded in 1241 by Meiler de Bermingham. It shows that the house received patronage and benefactions from both Irish and Norman. For the friars it was even more important than for the monks to have Irishmen in the Norman houses because of the need to preach in Irish in the 'land of peace'. Here, as in religious houses in general, the government was prepared to approve positively an Irish presence, provided the Irish did not become superiors. By about 1285 it is clear that the Irish friars were coming under suspicion as a kind of Trojan horse, not altogether without reason, it would seem. Disputes at the meeting of the Franciscan chapter in Cork in 1291 led to at least sixteen friars being killed.

The parish clergy were of even more basic importance than the friars. In 1172 the Synod of Cashel had ordered the payment of tithe, because the establishment of tithing was the necessary foundation for a parish system. This system came about rapidly as the Normans divided their lordships into manors. A manor implied a church, a parish and a priest, and soon much of Ireland was covered with what have endured under the name of 'civil parishes'. Because they were so closely linked with the manorial system, many of them had drawbacks as ecclesiastical units, being either too big, too small, or even too scattered. The next problem was to provide a priest in the parish, and here all the problems common to the medieval church presented themselves. Pluralism was not of great importance, though it did exist: the Irish parish benefice was normally too poor to attract the pluralist. Impropriation was a more serious problem, that is, the grant to a religious house of the right to parish tithes. Such grants became a normal part of the endowments of monasteries. In return the monastery had the right and the duty to appoint a vicar to serve the parish. Conscientious bishops tried to establish 'perpetual vicarages', with a third of the tithe guaranteed to the vicar, but in rural parishes the parish priest might often have as little as three marks a year, the wage of an agricultural labourer. If he was Irish, he might be even worse off, whether he worked among the Normans or ministered to the Irish *biataigh* as a separate community, as seems to have been often the case. The rural parish priest, Norman as well as Irish, had no high social standing.

The development of a parish system in the independent Irish lordships was inevitably more uncertain and is much harder to chart. It seems to have proved hard to put together enough wealth to support priests and even bishops, especially as they remained subject to exactions from lay rulers. The wealth of the old monastic centres remained with the families who had established their right to them. These were the coarbs and erenaghs. These were not priests or monks, but laymen. They were expected, even if sometimes at a low level, to represent the learned tradition: they might be poets or historians or keep a school of law or medicine. The remnants of a more ecclesiastical tradition may be seen in the fact that they sometimes kept houses of hospitality. Some might be laicised clerics, but were not obliged to proceed to major orders and were allowed to marry. Their obligations varied, but normally included the duty of paying certain taxes to the bishop and of sharing with the priest the upkeep of the church. This system was widespread, and in some instances the coarb or erenagh lands may never have been monastic property.[11] In addition, some of the ancient proprietary churches may have survived — at least that is a possible explanation of the use of such terms as *plebania* or *rectoria plebis*. New monastic houses would have impropriated to them the right to parish tithes, but these were relatively few in the Irish lordships. All in all, the parish system in the Irish lordships would appear to have had a slow untidy growth, and there may have been places it just did not reach. The population was thinner than in the manorial lands, with in consequence more large parishes where there might be many chapels but with irregular services in most of them. Finally, beginning with the pontificate of John XXII (1316-34), the papacy began to grant dispensations to priests' sons to proceed to ordination, and the hereditary system of succession returned.

It is worth while to attempt even an impressionistic picture of art and architecture, even though the architecture is mostly in ruins and only pitiful fragments of the art survive, because the bulk of the population must have had their religion impressed on them in the first instance by such tangible things. Little sculpture from the thirteenth century has survived the iconoclasm of the Reformation, though there is some, notably some wooden statues of the Blessed Virgin, for example those from Waterford, Kilcorban, Athlone and Clonfert. It was the Cistercians who first brought the new experience of Gothic to Ireland, but it was the Normans who developed it. Irish thirteenth-century Gothic is simple, reflecting the fact that Ireland was a relatively poor country, but it was graceful too. The churches still in use have generally been heavily modified over the centuries, like Christ Church and St Patrick's in Dublin. St Canice's in Kilkenny is much more faithful to its thirteenth-century beginnings. The most impressive single building is possibly the Cistercian church at Graiguenamanagh, Co. Kilkenny, now sensitively restored as a parish church. The thirteenth century can be felt too in the Dominican Black Abbey in Kilkenny. Of the parish churches still in use, it can be sensed best in the nave of St Audoen's in Dublin, and in the ruins in places such as New Ross, Gowran and Thomastown. The wealth generated by the Normans from the rich lands is very apparent in places like Trim, where the achievements of feudal lord, church and borough stand so close to one another. And yet the very Norman character of places like Trim stirs memories of older things, like the stone heads in the tympanum of the west doorway at Clonfert, or, earlier still, the cats and birds of the Cross of Muiredach at Monasterboice, and prompt reflections on what might have sprung from a real fusion of Irish and Norman culture.

When one turns from these tangible remains to literary sources in search of a religious consciousness one gets a sense of things eluding the grasp, not just because so much has perished but because of a real inability of all medieval literature not only in Ireland to observe and record critically concrete detail about persons. There is a wealth of detailed documentation from the Normans, but it is about legal and administrative affairs. If it is almost impossible to bring a thirteenth-century bishop into focus as a religious person, it is even harder to bring to focus a priest or a layman.

Religion seems to have sat easily on a conservative and orthodox population. There is no mention of heresy in the thirteenth century, and very little afterwards. The church at the centre of the manor was a homely, multipurpose building, with little of the character of a sacred place set apart that it was to acquire later. A well-known snatch of song proclaimed:

> I am of Ireland
> And of the holy land of Ireland.
> Good sir, pray I thee
> For of *saint charité*
> Come and dance with me in Ireland,

suggesting a touch of the idyllic that a church with its emphasis on tithe and administration may not have always inspired. Yet any obvious signs of resentment or dissent came from a few goliardic sources, like the Irish 'Vision of Mac Conglinne' in the twelfth century or the satirical poems in B.L. MS Harley 913.[12] Authors of such highly disrespectful satire were quite possibly clerics who had taken the tonsure because they were unwilling to dig and not ashamed to beg, or even as a useful insurance against the hangman. A prudent prelate confronted with them could certainly have thought of his jail, but they were, of course, quite untypical.

The rural priest was probably poorly educated. There were poorly educated rural priests in all countries, but Ireland fared worst than most because it had no university, where by now clerical education was concentrated. Some Irish clerics made their way to Oxford, but these were unlikely to serve in a parish worth three marks a year. The comparatively few Irishmen who won fame as theologians in the middle ages did so abroad. The towns were certainly more sophisticated: there was a great gap between the manorial priest and the canon of St Patrick's in Dublin, but, as has been seen, the canon was likely to be a king's clerk, building his career in the royal administration. But on a humbler level the town still had advantages. There was a religious aspect to the activities of the guilds. They maintained chantry priests in their own special chapel, where all were expected to attend on the patron's day. Above all, however, the towns were able to call on regular ministrations from the friars, at the heart of whose vocation was preaching. Little survives even in the way of names — Geoffrey of Waterford, John of Kilkenny, Malachy of Limerick — and even less in the way of actual texts, but it is enough to show that in Ireland the friars drew on the common stock of moralising and homiletic material they used all over Christendom. The drawback in this kind of material lies precisely in the fact that it is common stock, and it is hard to form any concrete idea of how exactly it was used.

Fortunately there is a single surviving document that adds this personal element. The B.L. MS Harley 913 contains a number of religious poems. One is certainly by a 'Friar Michael of Kildare', for he names himself in it, four more almost certainly, and yet another quite probably. They are sermons in verse on the common topics of the time: the fifteen signs of the day of judgment, the salvation history of the fall and the redemption, the ten commandments, the seven deadly sins, on Jesus the only hope of mankind, the shortness of life, the vanity of riches, the need for penance and active charity to the poor, the fact that in the end the passion of Christ will be both our judgment and our salvation.[13] The themes are stereotyped, the verse is not great poetry, but it is direct and arresting. Friar Michael was a good preacher, and one can almost see him in the pulpit:

> Me to speak, and you to lere,
> That it be worship, Lord, to thee,
> Me to teach, and you to hear,
> That helpful to our souls it be.

At the core of his preaching is

> Sweet Jesus, hend and free,
> That was istrawght on roode tree;

one can almost see him pointing dramatically to the crucifix above the pulpit:

> They nailed him in hands and feet,
> As ye may all isee;
> For the apple that Adam ate,
> Death he tholed upon the tree.

And one can see him drawing the moral lesson, in reference to a habit that many generations of preachers after him tried to break in Ireland:

> When ye swear great oaths
> On rood thou puttest him again.

There is a curious timelessness about him; he might almost be giving a mission sermon in the Ireland of not so many years ago, in the atmosphere of what was then called 'traditional Irish Catholicism'.

The friars travelled the countryside also, but the very pattern of distribution of their houses must have meant a smaller presence in the Irish lordships (in the thirteenth century the Franciscans had no house northwest of a line between Claregalway and Carrickfergus). We have no idea of the quality of instruction in a rural parish, but it must often have been meagre enough. The scribal tradition in Irish had passed to the laity and expressed itself especially in the highly stylised bardic poetry. There is fairly widespread agreement that in general these poems, composed by a professional class for personal reward, are not particularly marked by freshness and spontaneity: an authority as weighty as David Greene has said that sometimes 'they can be very bad indeed'.[14] The religious poetry shares the same characteristics; possibly the religious poems were recited to the chieftains like the secular poetry, to show off professional skill. They certainly drew on the *exempla* of the friars' preaching and the general stock of medieval apocrypha. They added to it themes more properly Irish; a delight in nature they inherited from the earlier and more spontaneous poets, in which some, for example Robin Flower, have seen a growing Franciscan influence, and the practice of using terms from the aristocratic Irish world to explain the Christian truths — Christ's redemption is a war waged on our behalf, his payment for us of the *eiric* or blood-price to his Father; our own life is the hardship of the hosting, the moral struggle is the tribute we pay to God. And when the poet comes to judgment he will expect heaven as the price of his poems.

Irish and Norman shared the same general heritage of superstition, devotion to relics, pilgrimages to shrines both in Ireland and abroad. Many of the great shrines of Ireland disappeared in the Reformation, like that of the Bachall Íosa in Christ Church, Dublin, or of Our Lady of Trim, but some that were to survive were already known: Croagh Patrick, for example, or St Patrick's Purgatory at Lough Derg, Co. Donegal, which had a European reputation from the twelfth century, when it was celebrated in a work of devotion so popular that it came to be called the Golden Legend. The annals, those chronicles of an aristocracy, are curiously silent about the pilgrimage — they mention it only in 1397, in passing, because a Catalan nobleman on pilgrimage called on Niall Mór Ó Néill on his way, and in 1497, when a papal order, which seems to have been quite ineffective, ordered the famous 'cave' to be sealed up because of the abuses connected with it. Yet from an early date this pilgrimage centre maintained an ecclesiastical establishment large enough to indicate great numbers of pilgrims, the great bulk of whom must have been Irish. The greatest religious poet of the century, Donnchad Mór Ó Dálaigh, who died in 1241, made his pilgrimage there, to no profit indeed, he lamented, because for all his mortifications he had not obtained true repentance:

> Truagh mo thuras ar Loch Dearg.

The fact that he went to seek repentance through mortification indicates that he saw the reward of the Christian life as more than something due to him by God for having composed court poetry in his praise.

It was not only in Ireland that signs of trouble began to appear early in the fourteenth century. They were widespread in western Christendom, and the papacy, which had been so central to the building up of the medieval achievement, was now at the centre of its problems. To a great degree by accident, the popes found themselves at Avignon in 1305, and they were to remain there until 1378. The consequences were in many ways disastrous. With control of the papal states in Italy lost, other sources of finance had to be found. The reforming papacy had always insisted on its ultimate control over all offices in the church, but hitherto this control had been exercised sparingly. Now the popes reserved more and more appointments to themselves, quite simply in order to tax the incoming office-holder. The system fed on itself — more reservations needed a greater bureaucracy, which in turn demanded more money to pay it, and more money could be got only by further reservations. By the pontificate of John XXII (1316-34) the system was already irresponsible.

In 1378 the papacy dragged itself back to what was left of Rome. The Great Schism began that same year and lasted until 1417. Now there were two popes (and later three), each demanding expensive support, and between them inevitably provoking questionings of the nature of the papal office. That office had been weakened when in 1417 there was once again a single agreed pope. A generation later the popes became patrons of the Renaissance, first its art, then its politics and statecraft. By the end of the fifteenth century there were popes who were petty Renaissance princes and little more. The appointment to every church office worth taxing had been reserved to the papacy. The care of souls was the last consideration in making an appointment. A system that had been irresponsible at the beginning of the fourteenth century had become quite shameless by the end of the fifteenth.

Everywhere the quality of Christian life suffered because the wealth which had been set aside to provide the care of souls was now largely diverted to clerical careerists at all levels from the papacy downwards. The church in Ireland shared these international problems, and compounded them by problems peculiar to itself. The political peace of the country had always been precarious. Now things worsened as the balance between the two nations changed. The Irish grew stronger, and the other nation weaker. Hitherto the term 'Norman' has been used as a convenient shorthand to describe it, but the term 'Anglo-Irish' becomes more suitable as their basic culture changed from French to English (and, indeed, in important respects to Irish) in the early fourteenth century. Overall, the 'land of peace' contracted; but it is even more important now than it had been a hundred years before not to visualise the situation in terms of lines drawn on a map. Even in the thirteenth century there had been great potential for instability: in the 1240s no less than four great lordships were in serious trouble because of failure or deficiency of heirs. The de Lacy lordship of Meath and the great Marshal inheritance in Leinster were divided between several coheiresses, and the lords of these lands were now absentees.

What has traditionally been regarded the real turning-point was the Bruce invasion, from 26 May 1315, when Edward Bruce landed at Larne, to his death at the battle of Faughart on 14 October 1318; and there is no doubt that the events of these years did bring important and lasting changes. The Irish supported Bruce; with insignificant exceptions the Normans did not. When it was all over the two nations looked at one another with even more suspicion, dislike, and even active hatred. The three and a half years of war had caused very great physical damage over most of the country. Churches and church resources suffered heavily. And in Ireland as in Europe the harvest failed, and there was famine in three successive years, 1315, 1316 and 1317.

The emergence of the great earldoms that were to be such a lasting feature of Irish history is to be seen partly as a reward for services and partly as a realisation by the central government that some devolution was now necessary. John de Bermingham, the victor at Faughart, was created Earl of Louth in 1319, but the title became extinct when he was murdered in 1329. Already an earldom of Kildare had been created in 1316, Ormond was to follow in 1328, and Desmond in 1329. It became clear that the realities of power were to rest with these local magnates when the de Burgo Earl of Ulster died without male heirs in 1333 and the Norman presence in Ulster shrank to a coastal strip. Another de Burgo branch held sway over much of Connacht, though their earldom of Clanricard did not come until 1543. Much of Carlow and Wexford, already weakened by division and absenteeism consequent on the division of the Marshal lordship, fell to the resurgent MacMurrough Kavanaghs.

The Black Death came first in 1348, and returned several times. It appears certain that the towns and more densely populated countryside of the Anglo-Irish suffered most. Here almost half of the population may have died. Before long what was left of the working class began to return to England in considerable numbers; and even though more land was given over to pasture at the expense of tillage, the reduced workforce in most rural areas in Anglo-Ireland must by now have been heavily Irish.

The well-known 'Statutes of Kilkenny' of 1366 can be seen in these circumstances to have been a purely defensive measure. Yet it was not for another eighty years that the word 'Pale' was first used. Even in 1366 the concept of a 'land of peace' from which the Irish can be excluded and within which they can and must be anglicised seems to have been rather a scheme devised in England rather than a solution emerging from the realities of life in Ireland. The ecclesiastical legislation of the provincial synod convoked by Archbishop Thomas Minot may be closer to these realities, namely that effective power was in the hands of the great magnates, Irish and Anglo-Irish, and that they all had a great measure of independence from the central government. The Irish kings may have submitted to Richard II at the end of the century, but his hopes of turning them into loyally dependent subjects were quite unreal. Power lay with the lordships. Even when in the second half of the fifteenth century people had come to accept 'the Pale' as a small and fairly clearly delimited area, they also recognised that what viability its borders enjoyed derived to a great extent from the attitude of the neighbouring magnates.

The phrase 'more Irish than the Irish themselves' has passed into the national legend. It has given rise to much silly romantic froth, and perhaps the simplest thing to say about it is that on balance it is more untrue than true. Though they might adopt many Irish ways and usages, very few Anglo-Irish became totally assimilated. Even the most 'Irish' of them still regarded the real Irish as basically inferior. If a son married an Irish-woman, he was a younger son, and in Ireland as in Wales the children fol-lowed the father's 'blood'. So there are various regions and power groups of different degrees of acculturation, but no Anglo-Irish lord was ever totally Irish, much less 'more Irish than the Irish'. 'Gearóid Iarla', the third Earl of Desmond (*c.* 1335-1398), stood where three cultures met, French, Irish and English. He wrote poetry in Irish, and he pioneered the use of Irish poetry to express the French traditions of 'courtly love'. Yet he served in the king's government, and even headed it as Justiciar (1367-9). When towards the end of his life he wished to send his son to the O'Brien King of Thomond for fosterage he first sought government permission. Even in the later fifteenth century it would be wrong to visualise the king's government in Dublin as effective only 'within the Pale'. There was hardly any lord who did not have some relationship with Dublin, even if it was tenuous and intermittent. And just as the Anglo-Irish were in some respects getting like the Irish, so too the Irish were in some respects getting like the Anglo-Irish. They were learning to make war like them, with castles, body-armour and mercenary soldiers. Irish lords found much in the common law to bolster their position as rulers. And if the whole situation added up to almost continuous war, that war was mostly in the Irish tradition, small-scale and sporadic. But it did continue to a degree the rest of the world was coming to regard as intolerable. As a would-be reformer wrote in 1515, there was

> no land in this world of so long continual war within himself, nor of so great shedding of Christian blood, nor of so great robbing, spoiling, preying and burning, nor of so great wrongful extortion continually as Ireland.[15]

This lengthy summary has been necessary to give some idea of the com-plexity of the patterns of culture in which Christianity existed in Ireland in the fourteenth and fifteenth centuries. It is all the more necessary to keep these complexities in mind because the nature of the source material allows little more than an impressionistic survey of the Christian religion 'among the English' and 'among the Irish', these latter including many who must be described as 'Irish' in a cultural and therefore religious sense, though politically they were 'Anglo-Irish'. The area which is both politically and culturally Anglo-Irish was contracting to the towns and the 'Pale' stretching from the Dublin mountains to Dundalk, and inland about twenty miles. Even within these narrow bounds the Anglo-Irish were a small elite, because so many of the English working class had returned to England. 'The Pale' was a state of mind of a small rural and urban aristocracy.

They had been shaken by the Bruce invasion, but the blow was by no means mortal. The Black Death was far more serious. It is possible to form a very good impression of Anglo-Ireland in the first half of the fourteenth century by reading through the annals written by John Clyn, a Franciscan friar of Kilkenny: the entries for this period may be assumed to describe events of his own lifetime. He makes it clear that the Anglo-Irish community felt a real sense of betrayal when the Irish supported Edward Bruce. One senses the 'march' drawing closer in the catalogue of murders and maimings that form the bulk of his entries. Then there was the burning for heresy of Petronella of Meath at Kilkenny in 1324, 'a thing before her unheard of in Ireland'. In 1332 the tower and a great part of the nave of the cathedral of St Canice collapsed, and though there was some restoration in 1343, it was a patched-up affair, possibly indicating that resources were more straitened than a century before. On the other hand, the friars were extending their churches, and the market cross was erected in 1335. Then the plague came, in August 1348. Clyn describes it graphically. It struck first in Drogheda and Dublin. The mortality was heavy. In Drogheda twenty-five Franciscans died, in Dublin twenty-two. It arrived in Kilkenny in the spring of 1349. Eight Dominicans died in one day, 6 March. As he watched the havoc and the panic Clyn wondered if any 'of the race of Adam' could survive. He assumed that he himself would die, and as his entries came to an abrupt end it may be very reasonably inferred that he did.

The first half of the fourteenth century also saw the only recorded cases of doctrinal heresy in Ireland, and this may be as good a place as any to say a word about them. In so far as they were genuinely doctrinal heresy, they must be set in the context of ideas let loose by the Englishman John Wiclif (1330-84), but there are strong political overtones to the three recorded burnings. The case of Petronella of Meath in Kilkenny in 1324 does not figure prominently in local accounts, and the details of the alleged heresy emerge clearly only in a letter of Pope Benedict XII ten years later. It is a reasonable surmise that the real tensions at Kilkenny arose from strife between some local magnates and the English bishop, Richard Ledred. It is hard to dissociate the burning of Adam Duff O'Toole at Hoggen Green in Dublin on 11 April 1328 from the tensions that followed the Bruce invasion. Similarly, the burning of two MacNamaras in Clare in 1355 is associated with the recapture of Bunratty castle from the Irish. No burnings are recorded afterwards. It seems reasonable to conclude that Irish medieval Christianity, whatever its faults — and they were many — was not greatly addicted to doctrinal heresy.

The state of religion among the Anglo-Irish in the first half of this century is, by Irish standards, unusually well documented. There are four synods for the province of Dublin, and the work of Archbishop FitzRalph of Armagh (1346-60) can be followed from his sermon-diary.[16] It is clear that there were continuing problems with the diocesan clergy. They were still on the whole poorly educated, largely because of the failure of Archbishop Bicknor's attempt to found a university in Dublin in 1320. There were complaints of moral laxities of various kinds, complaints too of tensions with the friars, who claimed to be better educated, and probably were. These tensions centred on the administration of the sacraments. The diocesan clergy were the main offenders in the problem of the celebration of clandestine marriages without publication of banns (such marriages were at this time valid, but their clandestine nature could pose many problems, especially if the partners wanted to get out of them). The friars were particularly blamed for abuse of the sacrament of penance. Since the fourth Lateran Council in 1215 every Christian was obliged to confess at least once a year to his parish priest. The complaint against the friars was that they attracted penitents by offering easier terms, being prepared to absolve, without insisting on reparation, even those excommunicated for murder. There are already complaints that the pedlars of indulgences are threatening to bypass sacramental penance altogether by claiming authority to absolve from the guilt of sin, *a culpa et poena*. It might be surmised that deficiences in confessional practice had an important role in maintaining racial tensions, especially in so far as they condoned homicide. Archbishop FitzRalph certainly believed this to be true. He himself struggled against what he called this 'inveterate hatred' with at best limited success. He had no high opinion of the merchant communities of Dundalk and Drogheda, where any chastening effect of the Black Death seems to have been short-lived. He accused them of usury, fraud, and oppression of the poor. They sinned against charity by refusing to take Irish apprentices, and what they claimed to be the religious activities of their guilds were marred by superstition and ostentatious feasting on the day of their patron. The Dublin provincial synods afford glimpses of increasing disorder in the countryside. It is clear that the churches were used to store goods to protect them from plunder. This led to a further loss of the sense of the church as a place of worship, and sometimes to a violation of sanctuary not just in the case of people's goods but in the case of people themselves.

The strange lack of episcopal registers means that little is known of day-to-day detail for the later middle ages. Next to nothing is known, for example, of what must have been the distinguished episcopate of Archbishop Richard Talbot of Dublin (1417-49). What can be said with certainty is that things got worse. Even less suitable candidates had to be accepted as priests, their numbers thinned by the Black Death, and the growth of papal provisions made bad worse. Education was always a problem. Our information is meagre, and too much should not be made of the fact that the catalogue of complaints about individuals which make up so much of the papal letters seldom mention insufficiency of learning. It is true that Irish clerics continued to go to Oxford in particular in large numbers, but at the best these were a minority. What little we know of the few chantry foundations does not suggest that education was one of their principal concerns, and the monasteries were in increasingly bad shape to make any contribution.

No new monastic house was founded after the Black Death, and the existing houses became more and more secularised, their wealth increasingly used to make provision for younger sons of more than dubious monastic vocation. In 1498 the Cistercian Abbot of Mellifont reported to the general chapter that only in Mellifont and Dublin was the rule kept or even the habit worn. He asked to be dispensed from visitation of the Irish houses, because he judged it not only useless but dangerous. The worst feature of this monastic decay was the fact that in so many parishes the monasteries controlled the tithes, and in consequence the appointment of the parish priest. By contrast, the orders of friars reformed themselves in the fifteenth century, but this reform began in the north and west and spread to the Pale only much later.

So we have to content ourselves with impressions. For the city of Waterford, chance has preserved a set of documents dealing with Dean John Collyn in connection with his foundation of the chantry of St Saviour in the city.[17] A native of Kilkenny, he became dean in 1441, resigned the office in 1480, and died in 1484. He appears in the records as a very good man of business. In the course of his life he accumulated a large number of books. The precise number is not stated, and very few are named, apart from the liturgical service-books. He also wrote a book himself, *De Sacramentis et de Arte Moriendi*. Some of these books came to him as the fruit of his business as banker-cum-pawnbroker. A number were pledged by the Cistercian abbey of Graiguenamanagh, now controlled by the Kavanaghs, for example a Bible in two volumes, pledged for half a mark, prompting the thought that the monks may have preferred money to Bible-reading. The fact that they also pledged two gilt chalices for six pounds of silver might prompt further interesting reflections, and the most interesting of all might be prompted by the pledge of the crosier of the Archbishops of Cashel for fourteen gold marks.

So it is not surprising that when Dean Collyn decided in 1468 to found a chantry he was able to drum up a good list of benefactors, enough to build a chantry chapel in the cathedral to support two priests to offer Masses, the divine office, and prayers for the founder and his relatives and benefactors. Ten years later he founded a hospice for the maintenance of twelve old people, who were to offer their prayers likewise, and specifically to rise to pray three times during the night, at eight, at midnight, and 'at the first stroke of matins', on pain of having to provide their own rations on the following day.

Dublin is the best-documented centre, though even here the evidence is fragmentary. It is still the most consciously 'English' place in Ireland, even though its inhabitants are less 'English' and more 'Anglo-Irish' at the end of the fifteenth century than they were two hundred years before. In all, twelve liturgical books have survived from medieval Dublin.[18] At a time when popular catechesis scarcely existed the liturgy was an important means of instruction, in particular the additions made to the liturgy to satisfy popular piety. Two Dublin manuscripts of the fourteenth century afford glimpses of these additions. The most telling must have been the office of the Sepulchre on Easter morning. It had been composed by St Ethelwold in tenth-century Anglo-Saxon England and may very well have come to Dublin quite early. In the darkened church 'three persons each with covered heads, wearing surplices and silk capes and each carrying a box as if for ointments, represent the three Marys seeking Jesus'. They approach the sepulchre, sadly declaring their mission to anoint his body, to be confronted with the apparition of an angel demanding: 'Whom seek ye in the tomb, O friends of Christ?' and announcing that he is risen and that the tomb is empty. 'In the meantime two persons, representing the apostles John and Peter, come barefoot to the choir entrance, dressed in albs without embroidery, and carrying tunics', and the liturgy returns in the joyful dialogue of the sequence of Easter, surely losing little of its impact by being in Latin, especially when accompanied by that miracle of religious music, Gregorian chant.

The office of the Sepulchre is the root of European drama. The next developments were the miracle and morality plays. Here there are two fifteenth-century manuscripts with Dublin associations: *The Pride of Life* from the first half of the century, and *The Play of the Sacrament* from the second half.[19] There is no direct evidence that they were actually performed in Dublin, but it may be taken as certain that they were. Indeed, as early as 1366 there is evidence from the synod of Archbishop Thomas Minot that such plays were detaching themselves from the liturgy and probably from the clergy, for he complains of 'theatrical shows' (*ludi teatrales*) as well as dances and fighting taking place in churches and cemeteries, especially on feast days, an indication perhaps that already not all the theatrical themes were religious.

This tradition of religious drama was also nurtured by the guilds.[20] There was a religious aspect to all guilds, and some had been founded for an exclusively religious purpose. The Guild of St Anne in Dublin, founded in 1430, maintained six priests and two clerks for religious services in its chapel in the south aisle of St Audoen's, to offer Mass for its members, especially on the patron day, to preside at their funerals, and to pray for the living and the dead. The Guild of St George, founded about 1425, staged a religious pageant on St George's Day. By 1466 it is clear that many of the guilds were presenting pageants on Corpus Christi (the Council of Vienne in 1311 had urged that this feast be celebrated with solemnities and processions). There are details of the pageants presented by each guild in 1498. Not all the themes are Christian: 'the vintners acted Bacchus and his story, the carpenters that of Joseph and Mary'. No texts of these pageants have survived, so that it is impossible to be certain if they were plays in the true sense of the word or simply some kind of tableaux. The brief descriptions certainly do not exclude the possibility that they were real plays: we know that in Kilkenny the book of mystery plays was recopied in 1637 because it had become worn out from use.

Another feature of fifteenth century Europe, particularly associated with the towns, was the growth of lay piety, manifesting itself in lay religious associations and the multiplication of books of piety. There is no direct contemporary evidence for this in the towns of Ireland, but the evidence may well have been lost because the town merchant classes suffered very severely in the calamities of the seventeenth century. We have two lists of the books of the Earls of Kildare. One, which may be taken as representing the library of Garret Mór FitzGerald (d. 1513), does contain quite a number of religious books, but they are almost all in Irish. The second indicates the additions made during the life of his son, Garret Óg (d. 1534). It shows the impact of the Renaissance and, even more, of the controversies stirred up by the Reformation. It is a reasonable assumption that there were wealthy merchants in places like Dublin, Drogheda or Waterford who would have regarded the earls' library at Maynooth as a little old-fashioned and provincial, but no trace of their own libraries remains.

That there continued to be contacts between the churches among the Irish and the Anglo-Irish appears clearly in the surviving records of the Archbishops of Armagh, beginning with Archbishop FitzRalph (1346-60). All these prelates were English or Anglo-Irish. Half their diocese and most of their province was Irish territory, yet they did exercise authority there, helped no doubt by the fact that the Irish continued to have a great reverence for the coarb of Patrick, even though he might be a cultural stranger living on his Louth manors of Dromiskin or Termonfeckin. The archbishops regularly visited the city of Armagh, to carry out visitation of the dean and chapter and of the Augustinian priory. A record has survived of a visitation of the then vacant see of Derry by Archbishop Colton in 1397. The coarb of Patrick, an Englishman born, was given his due honour as he moved in what to him must have been a very unfamiliar world of coarbs and erenaghs. The archbishops even managed to reach a working agreement with the civil powers, represented principally by the O'Neill kings; and while there were inevitably problems, they were no worse than those faced by ecclesiastics in the lands of the common law.

It was no mean achievement to have devised a system that worked, for there were real differences between the two cultures. Among the Irish, as elsewhere, clerical standards declined. This was partly because of the ravages of the Black Death — later visitations in the fourteenth century seem to have struck the Irish districts severely — but a much more important factor was the increase in papal provisions, and most important of all the increased facility in getting papal dispensations for the ordination of sons of priests. The hereditary system, almost successfully challenged in the thirteenth century, returned in force. The Irish clergy became great 'Rome-runners', much more than the Anglo-Irish. Why this should have been so is in some ways a mystery, if, in contrast to the Anglo-Irish, to whom every benefice was fair game,[21] an Irish cleric could hope to get possession of a benefice only if it was accepted as belonging to his kin-group, and it cost time, money and trouble to get a provision in Rome. But the evidence of the papal letters is incontrovertible: they applied to Rome in great numbers, and Roman corruption spilled over into Ireland. There is need of many local studies before it becomes clear what precisely prompted them to apply.[22]

Despite its increasing deviation from the general norms of canon law, the church among the Irish was not devoid of certain innate strengths. The clergy retained the social position of a learned class, the *aes dána*. As such they mingled on equal terms with the poets, the brehons, the lay erenaghs, these latter frequently the keepers of the small hospices or houses of hospitality that speckled even remote districts and still kept some tradition of Christian service. Christianity fitted this society with the comfort of an old shoe. But the price paid was heavy. There are clerical figures who remain quite unbelievable as Christians even after making every effort of the historical understanding and even of the historical imagination. There is, for example, Matthew Ryan, Cistercian Abbot of Holy Cross at the end of the fifteenth century, growing rich by trading in wine, and often, it seems, his own best customer. Thady Dowling, chancellor of the diocese of Leighlin, notes under the year 1522 that Maurice Doran, the Bishop of Leighlin, a good and learned man, was killed after an episcopate of only twenty months by his archdeacon, Maurice Kavanagh, because the bishop had rebuked him for his crimes and tried to get him to mend his ways. This Maurice was the son of the Cistercian Abbot of Graiguenamanagh, just possibly the same abbot who had raised some money by pawning the abbey's books and chalices with Dean Collyn of Waterford. Dowling notes that Kavanagh was hanged, drawn and quartered by Garret Óg FitzGerald in 1525, 'at the head of Glan Reynald by Leighlin', obviously as a public example.

Other clerical figures yield a little at least to the historical imagination. In 1476 Cormac Magauran was appointed Bishop of Kilmore by papal provision. He had been prior of the Augustinian canons of Drumlane, Co. Cavan, and had succeeded his father both as prior and bishop. In 1480 Thomas MacBrady got a papal provision to the same see. He lived until 1511, and Cormac until the following year. For at least part of this time both were recognised as bishops, no doubt because each was so powerfully supported by his kin-group that he could not be dislodged. At synods of 1492 and 1495 each signs as Bishop of Kilmore, a strange spiritual bigamy disquieting not only to the canonist but to the theologian. Yet MacBrady, who seems to have won sole recognition in the end, is saluted in his obit in the Annals of the Four Masters as 'a luminous lamp that enlightened the laity and clergy by instruction and preaching'.

Bishop MacBrady's daughter Siobhán married Thomas, son of Cathal Óg MacManus Maguire, chief compiler of the Annals of Ulster. Cathal Óg, who died in 1498, had held many ecclesiastical offices. He was Dean of Lough Erne, canon choral of both Armagh and Clogher, and parson of Inishkeen. He had over a dozen children, some of them certainly born after he had acquired these offices. These same annals salute him at his death, not only for his learning and hospitality, but as a gem of purity and a dove of chastity.

The figure of a cleric from a very different culture may help the historical imagination. Archdeacon Grantly of Barchester was in some respects a good man, in some respects even a Christian man. The lives of the poor in his rectory of Plumstead would have been much harder without his ministrations, and one can suspect that they would have been even harder without the ministrations of Mrs Grantly. And if Cathal Óg MacManus Maguire was a faithful husband to his wife and family, we can begin to see why the Annals of Ulster should praise him for his chastity.

In the twelfth century popes and Archbishops of Canterbury had denounced marriage abuses in Ireland. The Irish reformers who tackled the problems were quite conscious that they faced a heavy task. To a great extent they failed. Irish chiefs and nobles continued to take wives and discard wives as allowed by the brehon law but very definitely forbidden by canon law in the name of Christian marriage. Poorer people could hardly afford matrimony on this scale, but in a closely-knit kin-society many of their marriages must have been invalid in the eyes of the church because they were within the forbidden degrees of kindred. Yet it would be an error to see in this situation something unique to Ireland. In Europe too the canon-law marriage faced problems of acceptance, and the registers of the Archbishops of Armagh, for example, show that numbers of Irish people were concerned that their marriages should be in accordance with canon law.

Decay in the monastic institution was even more advanced among the Irish than among the Anglo-Irish. In contrast, the Irish friars did reform themselves in the fifteenth century, and this 'Observant' reform must have been by far the single most powerful factor in lifting up the Christian mission. A simple enumeration of the geographical location of new foundations in the fifteenth century will be enough to show the pattern, for they were nearly all Observant. There were forty in the ecclesiastical province of Tuam, twenty-eight in Armagh, eighteen in Cashel, and only four in Dublin. The older houses adopted the reform, but here again the movement, by and large, was from north and west to south and east. The appearance of the Franciscan Third Order Regular is particularly interesting. Over forty houses were founded. There was nothing like it in England and little in Europe, and it does seem to have been an especially Irish manifestation of the lay piety so widespread at the time. It did not survive the Reformation, and little is known about it in detail. But it is known that it concerned itself especially with education, and this may well have had a real effect in raising the standards of the diocesan clergy, while the Observant friars as a body must have fitted very well into the structures of Irish society, where the territorial parish always faced difficulties and, as already noted, may never have established itself in certain areas.

The Irish lords had the resources and the willingness to endow the new friaries. To some extent their motives may have been less than purely Christian. A man conscious of defects in his own life may have thought it a good investment to pay the friars to do for him what he knew he was not doing. Again, he might find the friary useful as a place of retirement if secular politics went disastrously against him. But above all, the founder might expect the privilege of being buried in the friary cemetery, so that when the last trump sounded he might grasp a friar's hand and claim clientship. He might also expect to be received into the order on his death-bed and be buried in the habit — a certain insurance, for were not the theologians agreed that religious profession was a second baptism that blotted out all sin?

But the Observant movement was a genuine religious reformation. A list of the books owned by the Observant Franciscans of Youghal has survived. Youghal had always disputed with Cork for the honour of having been the first Franciscan friary in Ireland. It had became Observant unusually early for a town friary, in 1460, but by then the Desmond lands where it was situated were remote from Dublin. In 1491, when the list of its books was first drawn up, it had a mixed community of Irish and Anglo-Irish, with an Irish guardian. The community's books would not support deep studies in speculative theology, but the collection was well designed to serve the needs of a body of men who were taking seriously their duties in the pulpit and the confessional. They were keeping in touch with European developments in these fields, and at least one of their books was not manuscript, but printed.[23]

The culture of Ireland did not take easily to the printing-press long after the year 1500, but its enduring scribal tradition has left evidence, lacking for Anglo-Ireland, on what was being read in the fifteenth century. Bardic poetry continued, shut up, it seems, within its own narrow canons of perfection. This influences the religious poetry too, even when the poet is a friar, like Pilib Bocht Ó hUiginn, who died in 1487 and was called in the Annals of Ulster 'the best and greatest religious poet in these latter times'. Religious poetry in Irish might perhaps have best broken out of its constrictions through the traditions of the love-poetry, though it is remarkable that no Irish poet seems to have experimented with a foreign metre. Yet there are individual poems which suggest tantalisingly what might have been — a certain Franciscan spirit, as Robin Flower liked to think,[24] or, even more tantalisingly, a distant stirring of Christian humanism?

Original religious prose had died by the fifteenth century, but in its place there were many translations of standard works of popular medieval piety, again with a strong Franciscan influence. The texts have survived because they were copied and recopied, and in some cases we know the names of the translators. It is not so easy to be sure who actually read these works, but outside the Pale and the towns what religious literature both Anglo-Irish and Irish possessed would have been in the Irish language, as is shown by the library of Garret Mór FitzGerald. And even if the nobility themselves were not great readers, they may have been prepared to listen to their friars as well as to their bards.

It was in some ways an archaic world, in some ways a closed world, but not altogether closed and not altogether archaic. Thady Dowling in his annals gives a detailed picture of an individual who summed up in himself a great deal of it:

Nicholas Maguire, Bishop of Leighlin, called in the vulgar tongue McSyr Moris, was born in Tulmoginan in Idrone in Leinster, the son of a priest. Thady Dowling commends him for hospitality and the number of cows that he grassed without loss (so well was he beloved) upon the woods and mountains; but Thomas Brown his chaplain who also wrote his life reporteth that he studied in Oxford, although it was but two years and three months, yet he profited so much in logic, philosophy, the seven liberal sciences and divinity that in his later days he seemed to excel; he was made prebendary of Killard, when he preached and delivered great learning with no less reverence, being in favour with the king and nobility of Leinster, who together with the dean and chapter elected him Bishop of Leighlin. . . . This Nicholas had obtained of the Bishop of Rome letters of provision and was consecrated bishop being but thirty years of age; to the great loss of the church he died in the year 1512, having began many learned works; and death preventing his purpose he could not finish any saving one chronicle summarily by him collected.[25]

So, despite the administrative shambles, there were good bishops, who could and did preach, like Thomas MacBrady of Kilmore, or Nicholas Maguire of Leighlin, 'McSyr Moris', the son of priest Maurice. It is when we move down to the parish level that the questions come much more easily than the answers. What happened on Sundays? What was the function of the priest? Formal catechesis in the modern sense is to a great extent a development of the Reformation controversies: in this matter the medieval church as a whole had been quite negligent. Reforming bishops had urged that the work be done, but for the most part it was not. In 1281 Archbishop John Pecham of Canterbury, a Franciscan, had composed a catechetical tract that came to be widely used in England.[26] It was a simple exposition of the Apostles' Creed, the commandments, the two great precepts of love of God and of one's neighbour, the seven corporal works of mercy, the seven capital sins and the seven virtues. In the diocese of Armagh every parish priest was obliged to have a copy and to use it to instruct his people four times a year. It is probable that it was more widely used throughout Ireland, but how effectively it was used in any part of the country we simply do not know. For the Irish districts, it may be that a more useful approach might be to study the catechetical methods of the Observant friars, but here too there is a great dearth of detailed information.

One is forced back on speculation based on later evidence. It is quite possible that some of the folk-prayers in Irish antedate the Reformation, and they have impressive theological sinew. An Irish prayer, the 'Lament of the Three Marys', must surely derive from the office of the Sepulchre, adapted to a simpler society that could not provide half a dozen figures clad in albs to act out the drama of Easter morning. In Anglo-Irish Wexford a quite distinctive tradition of carol-singing at Christmas has persisted down to the present day. A bishop at the end of the seventeenth century listed among his library 'two old script carol books', and it is more than possible that they antedated the Reformation. At about the same time a priest from the same area noted that in the barony of Forth 'there are very many crosses in public roads, and crucifixes, in private houses and churches . . . builded of stone, timber or metal, representing the dolorous passion of our Saviour Jesus Christ, which, wherever found, were totally defaced, broken or burned by Cromwellian soldiers'. Many of these may have been pre-Reformation (surviving examples in Co. Meath date from about 1470).[27]

For Mass on Sundays there was need of a church. Very few churches were built in the fifty years after the Black Death, that is, the second half of the fourteenth century. In the following hundred years there was a great deal of church-building, especially in Munster and Connacht. The most striking group of new buildings were those erected by the Observant friars. Everywhere, however, even in the Pale, there are clear indications that Ireland was becoming more isolated from developments in England and on the continent. By and large, Irish builders are using the old techniques and not using them so well as they did before. The churches are heavy and massive. The Cistercian abbey of Holy Cross, Co. Tipperary, for example, was very extensively renovated in the third quarter of the fifteenth century. It is hard to believe that this massive pile is contemporary with the development of the Perpendicular style in England. One obvious reason for the massiveness was that such buildings might frequently have to serve as fortified refuges. The Benedictine house at Fore, Co. Westmeath, situated in what had become decidedly border land in the fifteenth century, looks much more like a fortress than a monastery.

The meticulous restoration of Holy Cross does not conceal the massiveness of the building. How much more light and graceful the early Cistercian buildings were in the thirteenth century appears quite strikingly from restoration work of similar quality at Graiguenamanagh. It naturally takes an effort of the imagination to realise that the many buildings that now stand in stark ruin, all the starker because of the removal of the softening but destroying ivy, looked much less stark when they were in use. Just after the middle of the fifteenth century the Plunketts built a new church on their manor at Dunsany. In his will, dated 1461, Sir Christopher Plunkett endowed this church richly, with arras, scarlet hangings, crosiers and chalices of silver and gold, made by a local goldsmith at Trim, a wealth of service-books, vestments of cloth-of-gold and satin, and a chaplet of pearls for the statue of the Virgin. The interior walls of churches would also frequently be painted with scenes designed to bring home religious truths to the congregation. All that remains of this, or remained long enough to be described and copied, is no more than pitiful fragments. The technique is not fresco. The paintings are simple coloured-in line-drawings, very difficult to date. In the Cistercian abbey of Knockmoy, Co. Galway, there are the remains of a painting based on the popular morality narrative 'The Three Living Kings and the Three Dead Kings' and also of St Sebastian. The little cell of Knockmoy on remote Clare Island has quite elaborate decoration. Most of the subjects are not obviously religious, but it is quite possible they are an elaborate allegorisation based on the medieval bestiaries. Similarly, the scene showing hunters and a stag in Holy Cross, Co. Tipperary, may also be part of an allegory, and not a depiction of a purely secular scene, as is sometimes assumed. But it is from these scraps that we have to try to form an idea of what religious thoughts the church paintings of late medieval Ireland set out to convey.

The churches would also have been adorned with statues. Here again, much even of what is known from literary sources to have existed has perished at the hands of the iconoclasts. The stone sculpture has naturally proved more durable, and there was much more of it in the fifteenth century, especially on tombs. Even at its best it lacks inspiration. It is crude and stiff, and shows no signs of a developing artistic technique. The wooden statuary has inevitably suffered more severely.[28] Examples from ports like Waterford show signs of continuing influence from abroad, but as one moves up country figures like the Kilcorban St Catherine indicate what is basically a folk-art cut off from the mainstream. There are a few surviving carved figures to indicate that the great native tradition had not dried up, especially if they are to be dated in the later medieval centuries, as seems accepted. The two most striking are those of St Molaise on Inishmurray and St Maelruan at Crossabeg, Co. Wexford. These are striking indeed. Their expressions recall the vision that shines through, say, the stone heads of the portal of Clonfert cathedral. It owes little to the mainstream of European art, and it has no need to. One can look at the face of Maelruan and have a deeper perception of what it meant to be a Culdee. The preservation of Maelruan's cult in an area so thickly settled by the Normans is quite remarkable, but his 'pattern day' was observed there well into the nineteenth century. The preservation of such a statue in such an area is even more remarkable, especially if its date is comparatively late; and its creation is more remarkable still.

These tangible things, in all their ruin, have an important role in fleshing out our ideas of late medieval Christianity in Ireland. It seems to me that it is fundamentally misleading to say that in medieval Ireland Christianity never expanded outside a purely religious sphere of life and had no impact on the general social system (in regard to marriage, the example specifically given, I have already indicated reasons to believe that the Irish practice did not differ quite so starkly from that of medieval Europe).[29] What is true — and in this respect Ireland was not unique in the later fifteenth century — is that the failure of leadership in the church, spiritual, theological and administrative, above all in the papacy, gave a particularly good opportunity to a primitive but enduring human temptation, to regard the good and the holy as existing in two quite separate compartments of human experience.

Ireland was not helped by what appears to have been a great and on the whole increasing isolation. The evidence to substantiate the view of Edmund Curtis that 'in literature as in all else, the native race was taking on the impress of a new, a Renaissance Europe'[30] is indeed thin and uncertain. As might be expected, there are some indications that the towns in particular were more open to outside influences, even to the first stirrings of humanism, but in cultural and religious matters the evidence is sparse and indirect. On the whole, the Irish system is closed. It is a subtle interaction of several cultural influences, which may be given concrete expression in the legal systems, the church law, the common law, and the brehon law. Where Ireland suffered especially was in the lack of civil peace. It had been a problem for its Christian church in the twelfth century, and it was still a problem at the end of the fifteenth. Churches were already falling into disrepair and even into total ruin in the 'land of so long continual war within himself'. It is one of the many ironies of Irish history that when Ireland entered the modern world at the beginning of the seventeenth century, and a king's writ ran unchallenged through the whole island, the bulk of the Irish people had set up a new problem for themselves by not accepting that king's religion.

3

King
or Pope?

Like every other country in Europe, but more disastrously than most, Ireland entered the modern world through the gate of the sixteenth century. Henry VII had recognised the limitations on his control in Ireland in the agreement to share power which he made with Garret Mór FitzGerald, Earl of Kildare and Lord Deputy, at Salisbury in August 1496, and even this shared power was effective only in a small part of the island. At the century's end Hugh O'Neill, the last of the independent Irish lords, surrendered to the English Lord Deputy at Mellifont in March 1603. Hereafter there was to be no legal limitation on the royal power in any part of the island. Even those ancient islands of independence, the corporate boroughs, were shortly to find that independence circumscribed by new charters bringing them much more directly under royal control.

Poynings' parliament in 1494 had enacted, fairly realistically, that ditches should be made about the English Pale (c. 34), but it was more as a declaration of intent that it had enacted 'that no peace or war be made with any man without licence of the governor' (c. 32). It had taken the whole century to put this declaration of intent into practice, but now in 1603 there was only one army, the king's army. There was only one civil jurisdiction, the king's, exercised through the king's officials. There was only one legal ecclesiastical jurisdiction, the king's church, in law the church of Ireland. It was already clear that the church of Ireland in law was only to a limited extent the church of Ireland in fact. Perversely, most of the king's Irish subjects had given their allegiance to a church which was not the church of their civil ruler.

In an attempt to comprehend this unique development several cautions are necessary. It is essential to see the religious conflicts of the sixteenth century as part of a wider pattern of cultural change, not peculiar to Ireland, but occurring also in England and in Europe generally. Everywhere, in one measure or another, national monarchies were trying to control hitherto unruly nobilities and independent burghers; and everywhere, in one measure or another, this change was resisted.

Well before controversies arose among Christians these monarchs had been trying to get greater control over the church in their kingdoms. The great religious divide that opened up after Martin Luther's protest in 1517 offered kings both prospects and problems: on the one hand, the expectation of greater control over a church which had renounced the pope, but on the other hand, a fear of greater civil disorder in so far as imposing a new religion threatened long-established social patterns.

To a very great extent it was fortuitous that the English monarchy found itself imposing a Protestant religion as part of its political programme in the sixteenth century. It is true that there were real roots to English Protestantism, in the persistent Lollard tradition, in the criticisms of the clergy being voiced by better-educated laymen, and in the small groups of clerics in the universities, more particularly Cambridge, who were coming under the influence of Luther. These forces were much weaker in Ireland. Of Lollardy there are no real traces, despite its getting the attention of an act of Poynings' parliament (c. 29). Recent scholarship has emphasised the element of humanism, and its frequent concomitant, some measure of anticlericalism, in the towns and the Pale. Any evidence for an impact of the new religious controversies shaking Europe after 1517 is thin indeed, but what there is — the catalogues of the library of the Earls of Kildare — suggests an interest in works refuting the new ideas rather than in the ideas themselves.[1]

In any case, whatever pressures for change existed had little connection with what happened in the 1530s. For reasons ranging from the statesmanlike to the unworthy, King Henry VIII had to be free of his marriage to Catherine of Aragon. For an equally wide range of reasons, Pope Clement VII refused to grant his request. Henry's reply was to abolish papal authority in England. The formidable monarch was otherwise conservative in religious matters, and after the fall and execution of Thomas Cromwell in 1540 those who favoured the new ideas of Martin Luther discreetly held their peace in the face of the orthodoxy of the aptly named King's Book of 1543. When Protestantism established itself within the Church of England in the reigns of Edward VI and Elizabeth I, it derived from Calvin rather than Luther. This English Calvinsim was tempered by factors not easily paralleled elsewhere. They arose from the essentially political wish to enable the great majority of Englishmen to accept the national church, the *ecclesia Anglicana*. This national church preserved many of the structures of the papal days, and its creeds were framed to be inclusive rather than exclusive. Through a judicious mixture of sword and word, pressure and preaching, the national church established itself in the ancient pattern of bishopric and parish, with dissent no greater than what was politically acceptable.[2]

There was more than 'reasons of state' to recommend the new religion. By any standards, the old religion needed reform and revitalisation. Calvinism did offer a new discovery of God in Christ through the Scriptures, with its vernacular Bible, its trained pastors, its systematic instruction, its modern devotions, well fitted for those in any way touched by the Renaissance belief in personal development through education. Calvinism also could be perceived by its adversaries, not altogether without reason, as threatening a general wreckage of the old order, a ruthless destruction of the 'idolatry' of the old religion, carried out by wealthy minorities who had seized the machinery of government. And the 'old religion' had its virtues as well as its faults. Calvinism, with its doctrine of predestination and election, and its emphasis on education and on the printed word, was an elitist creed. The destruction of the old religion and its replacement by Calvinism would be for many a real loss in religious terms, for while the old creed set its sights low it was so woven into the fabric of society that for many people it achieved what it set out to do. However, the days of such a religion seemed over once the papal church had reformed itself. The Counter-Reformation priest was as revolutionary in his demands as was the Protestant pastor. Both demanded systematic instruction and regular devotions as foundations for the Christian moral life. Both these revolutionary figures were to find the old religion surprisingly resilient.

The new Anglican religion developed its identity pragmatically. The monarch replaced the pope, and a new form of worship was introduced. Both these steps were taken by 'the king in parliament'. It was only after they had been introduced that the church drew up its theological formulae of belief.

No penalties had been attached to the act of the Irish parliament of 1536 declaring Henry VIII supreme head of the church. However, two further acts supplied the deficiency. To defend the authority of the Bishop of Rome was punishable with the penalties of *praemunire*, aptly summarised as 'everything short of death', while the Act of Slander made it high treason, punishable by death, to call the king a heretic, a schismatic or a usurper. These acts were repealed in the reign of Mary and were not re-enacted under Elizabeth. They were replaced by the Act of Supremacy (1560), declaring the queen to be supreme governor in things spiritual as well as temporal. An oath to this effect had to be taken by a wide range of people — all ecclesiastical persons, officers under the crown, mayors of corporate towns, members of a university, heirs minor on suing out livery. For non-compliance there was one sensible and logical penalty — lifelong incapacity for the office in question. The penalties for active defiance of the new law were loss of property for a first offence (a year's imprison-ment if the property were worth less than £20); the penalties of *praemunire* for a second offence; and the dread penalty of treason for a third.

'The king in parliament' also decided how public worship should be carried out. Here too penalties were laid down for those who did not observe the law and for those who actively defied it. These penalties increased in severity in successive Acts of Uniformity, passed in England in 1549 and 1552 (Edward VI) and 1559 (Elizabeth). No parliament was held in Ireland in the reign of Edward VI, and as the king was a minor much uncertainty attached to attempts made to impose this legislation in Ireland. It may be taken that there was some measure of success in imposing the first act, but none with the second. The Elizabethan act of 1559 was passed in an Irish parliament in 1560 and was therefore unquestionably in force. It imposed, with some modifications, the Book of Common Prayer of the act of 1552. This, beyond all possibility of doubt or equivocation, fundamentally changed the form of public worship. The act also laid down penalties for those who would not comply and for the defiant. The penalties of the 1549 act had been more lenient than what came after, and those of 1552 never applied in Ireland, so it will be sufficient to summarise the penalties laid down by the act of 1560.

The penalties for defiant clergy had been laid down in 1549: for a first offence, six months in prison and loss of a year's revenue; for a second, twelve months in prison and loss of benefice; and for a third, the penalties of *praemunire*. Those for defiant laity had been substantially set out in 1552. After 1560 they were: for a first offence, a fine of 100 marks or six months' imprisonment in default; for a second, 400 marks or twelve months' imprisonment; and for a third, the penalties of *praemunire*. For laity who would not comply, but absented themselves from church services, there had been ecclesiastical censures in the act of 1552; under Elizabeth these were supplemented by a fine of twelve pence for each absence. The fine was to be levied by the churchwarden, and offenders could be presented in either the civil or ecclesiastical courts.

The articles of belief were sanctioned by the monarch and convocation of clergy in England in 1553 and 1563. The corresponding formulary for Ireland was the Twelve Articles, issued in 1566 by authority of Lord Deputy Sidney and the bishops.[3]

Though no further ecclesiastical legislation was passed in the two other parliaments to be held in Elizabeth's reign, the new religion was sufficiently defined, in both doctrine and legal status, to set out on its way to become the religion of the country. By the end of the reign it had become precisely that in England, by a judicious mixture of 'sword' and 'word'. By the same date its failure in Ireland was becoming evident. Some of the reasons for that failure lay in deficiencies in both 'sword' and 'word'.

The primary task of the Tudor government in Ireland was to establish its authority in secular affairs. Here as in other matters the Irish parliament played a negligible role. It remained a small body, in no sense representative; it met only six times between 1536 and 1603. The government was forced to rely on prerogative authority, expressing itself in proclamation and martial law, and ultimately on physical force of arms.

By the end of Elizabeth's reign Ireland had been militarily conquered.

The imposition of religious change had to take second place. Indeed, an influential view, which became the dominant one, argued that it necessarily took second place: 'civility' imposed by conquest was a necessary preliminary to preaching the gospel. But military conquest was expensive, and the Tudors did not like spending money, especially in Ireland. In consequence, there were long periods of hesitant religious toleration, punctuated by forceful action. No really consistent attempt was made to enforce the Reformation statutes until the mid-1570s. By this date discontent with the new regime was ready to boil over in many places — in Munster, even in the Pale (or at least in its more peripheral areas, with Viscount Baltinglass or with the Nugents of Delvin), and later, of course, in Ulster. In all cases the more obvious discontent was with a political programme that threatened traditional local liberties, but the new religion would have appeared very definitely as an element in that programme. By this date Counter-Reformation Catholicism was active enough to make its challenge for the allegiance of a population to whom the queen's religion was a social and political threat, but in other respects quite unknown because it had scarcely been preached to them.[4]

This is a very important point. The success of Counter-Reformation Catholicism was made immeasurably easier by the failure of the mission of the state church. The word 'failure' is strong, but accurate. It will be sufficient for the present purpose to trace this failure through the long reign of Elizabeth. Before this we can scarcely speak of a 'state church', for its character changed from reign to reign, and even to some extent within reigns. The years from 1558 to 1603, however, were a lengthy spell during which in England the church by law established became the church of the nation in fact. This it markedly failed to do in Ireland.

One obvious and underlying reason was its administrative weakness. In all matters, not merely those of the church, the Irish administration was slow to benefit from the reforms being introduced in England. There the ecclesiastical Court of High Commission, with various subsidiary and local bodies, played an important role in the 'sword' of religious change. Such a court was set up in Dublin in October 1564, but in so far as its working has been studied it appears as spasmodic and ineffective. As for the 'word' of religious change, Ireland was not well equipped with clergy who could preach when the Reformation came upon it, and the situation deteriorated fairly quickly. The principal reason was the plundering of the resources of the church. The church in Ireland had been fairly wealthy, as wealth went in Ireland, but this wealth had been badly distributed, and the parochial benefices were poor. As has been seen, many of them were impropriate to monasteries, and their revenues were lost in the monastic confiscation. Revenues that had never been monastic tended to stick to greedy fingers at this time of general confiscation. In all this the queen's government was the worst offender. And even when the revenues survived it was frequently said that it was necessary to put three, four or even more of them together to provide a minimum support for a minister. On top of this was the problem of finding ministers who could preach. Beyond question, many beneficed clergy, bishops as well as priests, were prepared to go along with the state church if they found themselves in a position where they had to make a choice. Their motives were seldom so simple as an unashamed desire to keep their livings. They themselves were so poorly instructed that the choice as it presented itself must often have been quite blurred; and despite their apparent change of allegiance, their commitment, if one may use so strong a word, still tended to be to the old religion. ' The ragged clergy are stubborn and ignorantly blind,' wrote Bishop Hugh Brady of Meath; even in Dublin itself, 'from bishop to petty canon, none but disguised dissemblers, they say themselves they be old bottles and cannot away with this new wine';[5] or, as the wrathful Bishop Bale complained of the new service in Waterford — loyal Waterford — it was 'altogether used like a popish Mass, with the old popish toys of Antichrist, in bowings and beckings, kneelings and knockings'.[6] Hopes for a new generation of clergy were doomed by the failure to provide a university in Dublin until 1592. By this time the opportunity had passed.

Complaints that the supply of ministers able to preach is totally inadequate recur year after year during this long reign. In 1561 the newly appointed Bishop Craik of Kildare lamented that he had 'not a preacher to assist me in setting forth of God's word, saving one Mr Lofthowse; my own chaplain is but lately come over to me'.[7] Fifteen years later Lord Deputy Sidney was asking the queen in growing desperation that a search for ministers be made in the English universities (though he admitted that they could probably find their church in ruins, that it was quite uncertain if they would be paid, and that in many cases they would need to know Irish). Failing the English universities, he wrote, search should be made in Scotland.[8] At that time Scotland was so short of ministers that lay readers were being appointed even to officiate at baptisms and marriages; and the queen might have preferred papists to some at least of the Scottish ministers. In any case, Sidney got no reply. In 1584 the prebendaries of St Patrick's lamented: 'There is an infinite number of impropriate churches in Ireland.... There is not in any one impropriation a preacher. There is scant a minister to be found among them but rather a company of Irish rogues and Romish priests.' The reason, they said, is that the tithe farmer seeks 'a priest who will serve his care cheapest'.[9] In so far as the church by law established was becoming established, it was beginning to look remarkably like what had been there before.

One can only speculate on what would have been the effect on the state church in Armagh had the archbishopric gone, as for political reasons it might have gone, to Dean Terence O'Donnelly, foster-brother of Shane

O'Neill. We are a little better informed, though not nearly as well informed as we would like to be, on Hugh Brady, the queen's Bishop of Meath from 1563 to 1584. Brady was a native of Dunboyne in the heart of the Pale. He was a graduate of Oxford, and it is beyond doubt that he had been fired by religious reform in its Protestant guise, and that he sincerely set out to preach his religious convictions, not without some hope when he began. 'A great number of the simple people,' he noted, 'and especially where I was born, are greedy hearers, and such I hope will be unfeignedly won.'[10] He did have his troubles with new arrivals from England — in their eyes he was a 'wog' — but his diocese, much of it peaceful and by Irish standards wealthy, should have offered possibilities to a sincere reformer like Brady. Yet by 1576 Sidney had to report that even Meath was in bad shape: the odds against the reform were too great. Of 224 parish churches, 105 were impropriate, all of them leased out to tithe farmers, and each served by 'a very simple or sorry curate', most of whom were 'Irish rogues' living 'upon the bare altarages'. There were 52 incumbents appointed by the bishop, where things were better but not good, and 52 appointed by lay patrons, with things still better but nevertheless overall not good.[11]

At some remove from Hugh Brady was Miler Magrath, queen's bishop since 1567 and Archbishop of Cashel from 1571 to 1622, fifty years which certainly ruined the prospects of the state church in Tipperary. In a sense he was unfortunate to have been born a century too late. A hundred years earlier he might have passed comfortably enough, though even then this man from Ulster would scarcely have been comfortable in the metropolitan see of the south. His primary preoccupation was to ward off the hostility of the local gentry and clergy. This he did by tactics more appropriate to a *taoiseach* or war-lord than to a reforming archbishop. From quite an early date Counter-Reformation agents were active in Cashel — 'the great traitor Dr Craghe', the Catholic Bishop of Cork and Cloyne, was sheltered by Lord Dunboyne. There was little by way of Prayer Book service, and much massing, not just by Counter-Reformation missionaries, but also, it would appear, by beneficed clergy, the archbishop's own wife, Anny, being denounced by his enemies as 'the massmonger', and his own religious sympathies probably inclining in that direction as well.[12] That he was not removed from office is a fairly striking testimony to the weakness of the established church.

In 1610 Sir John Davies described the state church as Lord Deputy Chichester had found it in Cavan in the previous year. The problem of impropriation was everywhere — the worst offenders had been the abbey of Fore, now farmed by Lord Delvin, and the abbey of Kells, farmed by Gerard Fleming. The vicarages were so poorly endowed that ten of them would scarcely support a minister. The churches were mostly in ruin: those of them described as 'in reparation' were rudely thatched. As for the incumbents,

Both parsons and vicars did appear to be such poor, ragged, ignorant creatures ... as we could not esteem any of them worthy of the meanest of those livings.... The bishop, Robert Draper ... hath two dioceses ... but there is no divine service or sermon to be heard within either. ... He is diligent in visiting his barbarous clergy to make benefit out of their insufficiency.[13]

And the laity? In the eyes of observers like Sir Henry Sidney,

Surely there was never people lived in more misery than they do, nor as it should seem of worse minds, for matrimony among them is no more regarded in effect than conjunction between unreasonable beasts; perjury, robbery and murder counted allowable; finally, I cannot find that they make any conscience of sin, and doubtless I doubt whether they christen their children or no; for neither find I place where it should be done, nor any person able to instruct them in the rules of a Christian; or, if they were taught, I see no grace in them to follow it; and when they die I cannot see they make any account of the world to come.[14]

Plus ça change...? There is more to it than that. We clearly have here a people already learning the art of concealment. This reinforced Sidney's conviction that they were not 'civilised'. It may have been true even in 1567 that their culture was degenerating under new strains. It was certainly true by the end of the century. To balance the picture we might look at a visitation report on Armagh *inter Hibernos* from 1546 that has chanced to survive.[15] The archbishop's visitators were Gaelic clerics, and they clearly met a great deal of frankness, even if they were not always told the truth. The manuscript is heavily damaged, and they did not record the same information everywhere, so that neat percentages are difficult. There is information of some kind on sixteen parishes and their incumbents. The church buildings are satisfactory in 50 per cent of cases, the church furnishings in 75 per cent, and the church services in about 66 per cent. In the matter of concubinage, we have definite information on eighteen priests. Four keep concubines, ten do not, four say they do not but some of their parishioners say otherwise. Under the phrase 'orat et celebrat' ('he recites the office and says Mass') there is explicit information on eight priests only. Seven do, one does not. The picture of religious observance would not have satisfied John Calvin or Ignatius Loyola. Two Jesuits, a Frenchman and a Spaniard, had visited Ulster in 1542 and had not been impressed by what they saw. No doubt they would have had reservations even about Dean Edmund MacCawell, whose obit is recorded in the surviving Antiphonary of Armagh. He died on 28 January 1549, having chanted the full office on the day of his death, though suffering intolerable pain. Before his death he had given the poor all that was due them under the church's law; and, while chastising his own body, he had discharged the duty of hospitality towards all.[16] This is far from Sidney's 'unreasonable beasts' or from the 'barbarous clergy' of Cavan as they filed in front of their new masters. And it takes us on to the real question, and therefore the difficult question: what was the quality of the religious observance of these people, and how was it taken up into Counter-Reformation Catholicism?

The sources are sparse, even by Irish standards. At other times it is usually possible to put together a reasonably documented account of clerical activities. The Counter-Reformation clergy, or those who were to develop into Counter-Reformation clergy, have left no consecutive account of their activities. Government documentation portrays them as either unco-operative or, later, as hostile. The available papal documentation comes mostly from the last thirty years of the century, and is nearly all of a political character. The *Calendar of Papal Letters* is just reaching the beginning of the century, at a pace that prompts thoughts about 'world enough and time', all the more so as the real religious business of the papacy will almost certainly be found increasingly concentrated in the series in the Vatican archives known as the 'Lateran briefs'. It is high time these were calendared or at least listed.

It was becoming clearer that what was to be effectively the 'Church of Ireland' was drawn from the 'New English', those who arrived in Ireland after the Reformation. True, there were some others who ended up in it, like the family of Primate Ussher, and there were New English who for one reason or another ended up in Counter-Reformation Catholicism. Both categories were exceptional, however. The great bulk of those who had been in Ireland before the Reformation went to make up the great bulk of the Irish Counter-Reformation Catholic church.

Ireland in the later middle ages had been a divided country, and its divisions had been complex. Two different traditions had lived together in it, the Gaelic and the Anglo-Norman. Inevitably, they had influenced one another, so that there were many shadings of Gaelicisation between the Pale and the towns on the one hand and the Gaelic lordships on the other. Under the stresses of the sixteenth century the pattern sorted itself out into: the New English, as described above; the 'Old English', now extended from the towns and the Pale to take in all, or almost all, of Anglo-Norman ethnic origin; and the Old Irish. Despite greatly differing experiences in the crisis of the sixteenth and seventeenth centuries, these last two groups gave their religious allegiance to Counter-Reformation Catholicism.

For each of them the religious choice was only an element in a wider cultural crisis, which was so different in each case that they must be taken separately. It will be convenient to begin with the world of Gaelic Ireland, where the crisis presented itself in the starkest terms.

The church in Gaelic Ireland had many weaknesses, but it had one great strength: its accepted and respected place in society, which would undoubtedly have been harsher had it not been there. It is true that the clergy endangered the respect due to them as a branch of the *aes dána* by misconduct of various kinds. They murdered: an example has already been given, the murder of the Bishop of Leighlin by his archdeacon. They made war: at the battle of Knockdoe in 1504 O'Neill protested at the presence of ecclesiastics in the camp;[17] while a report on the diocese of Ardagh in 1517 describes the cathedral as being in ruins, the cathedral city reduced to three or four wooden houses, all this mainly because of the warlike life of the late bishop, William O'Ferrall (1480-1516), before his consecration Cistercian Abbot of Granard.[18] Inevitably, many of them had little learning, and many did not honour the obligations of celibacy. As everywhere in Europe, the clergy were over-ripe for reformation.

Inevitably, among the people there was an appallingly low level of religious instruction, scandalous to Protestant and Catholic reformer alike. Writing on 26 October 1571, Edmund Tanner, professed Jesuit, soon to be Catholic Bishop of Cork and Cloyne, declared that while few Irish accepted the state church, a pious Catholic could scarcely be found, and the clergy were the worst of all. Few could repeat the Lord's Prayer, the creed and the commandments, and fewer understood them. Many had never heard a sermon. The sacraments were rarely administered and more rarely understood. Many who lived their lives in grossest sin had no consciousness of guilt because they did not know what sin was.[19] Naturally, to balance this sense of outrage we should compare like with like. There was, for instance, the old man from Cartmel in Lancashire, who, when asked about Jesus Christ, remarked: 'I think I heard of that man you spake of once in a play at Kendal, called Corpus Christi play, where there was a man on a tree and blood ran down.'[20] Ignorance of the very rudiments was not confined to Ireland.

The main difficulty in analysing Gaelic Ireland in the sixteenth century is a problem of sources: that society seems to have been very slow to analyse itself and what was happening to it. There are times when it appears that there was very much the same level of incomprehension in the first 'surrender and regrant' agreements of the 1540s, when the nature of the threat must have been quite obscure, and in the mass defections of Hugh O'Neill's *uirríthe* after Kinsale, when it should, one feels, have been crystal clear. Recent attempts to analyse the people who should have been most articulate, the poets, have led only to disagreement.[21] It does seem most likely that, with one or two exceptions, the horizon of the poets was limited to their local patron and their own place in society, and that they perceived a threat only when it was directed against one or other of these aspects of things.

The clergy, normally the principal historical witness to how things are going for the church, are even less articulate than the poets, and this leaves us little alternative to the witness of outsiders, with all its drawbacks. There can be little doubt that the least satisfactory of these witnesses are the English or New English of the reign of Elizabeth. However it be explained, they had developed a propaganda in connection with a war of conquest, which made it necessary to portray the Irish natives as uncivilised by either of the accepted criteria of civilisation, namely by having a high level of secular culture or by being Christian. If conquest were to be justified, the Irish must be shown to have neither, to be 'a people who did not have the law'. There was ample justification in the Old Testament not merely for divine permission to God's elect, but even for a positive divine command, to deal very roughly with such people.

The articulate Anglo-Irish are more promising, if what they say is used carefully and critically, not so much perhaps the rather priggish humanists of the first half of the century, like Sir Thomas Cusack, who could see the problem as primarily how English civilisation might be mediated to Gaelic Ireland through Anglo-Ireland,[22] but rather the grittier reflections of the next generation, when Anglo-Ireland itself faced its crisis of identity. Some of these men are Protestants, like Rowland White of Down; others are moving from Protestantism to Catholicism, like Richard Stanihurst of Dublin; others again are totally committed to Counter-Reformation Catholicism, like the Jesuits Edmund Tanner of Cork and David Wolfe of Limerick. Useful reflections come from a few others, the English Jesuit Nicholas Sanders, and a Spaniard or two.

While opposite poles of the religious reform can sometimes come close to agreement — compare the 'barbarians untamed and ferocious' of David Wolfe the Jesuit with the 'not Christian civil or human creatures' of Andrew Trollope the Calvinist[23] — all observers not totally hostile are agreed that the Irish are in some sense religious. They are often puzzled as to what this may mean — Cuellar the Spaniard, for example, genuinely finds it hard to understand the religion of the 'savages', even though they 'call themselves Christians' and 'Mass is said among them and regulated according to the orders of the Church of Rome'. He does, however, recognise Bishop Redmund O'Gallagher of Derry who helped him as quite simply 'a very good Christian'.[24] What does seem to be the central problem for outside observers is not so much the lack of religious rites 'according to the orders of the Church of Rome' but the lack of any real link between religious observance and moral goodness. I think we can dismiss the view put forward by English observers, that children were not baptised. The overwhelming likelihood — which is indeed supported by positive evidence, Spenser for example — is that they were baptised, but not in the established church, a practice made all the more plausible if one considers the importance of the element of natural kinship associated in the Irish mind with what the church preached as a sacrament of personal regeneration. As for marriage, all observers were agreed that old usages in regard to marriage and sexual habits generally changed only very slowly. Stanihurst could not accept that keening at funerals was compatible with a Christian attitude to death — and he would appear to have been right. And everywhere there was the appalling ignorance of even the rudiments of the faith, among the clergy as well as the laity, the increasingly intermittent sacramental life as outside pressures on society increased, the gross superstitions, and, shadowing everything, the yawning gap between a sense of religion and a sense of moral goodness. How could one explain the reasoning of the mind that prayed for success in a robbery or even in a murder, and gave thanks for that success afterwards? All these ambiguities clearly underlie the reverence shown for holy places — respect for sanctuary is often mentioned — and for holy people, priests and most especially friars. The regard for friars is noted by everyone, friends and enemies: John Derricke, for example, is obsessed by them, in those jog-along stanzas that express a loathing of the whole Irish scene:

> Thus friers are the cause
> The fountaine and the spring
> Of hurleburles in this land
> Of eche unhappy thing.[25]

There is widespread agreement, however, that if the Irish are great sinners, they are also quick to repent, and that the repentance is often sincere: as Stanihurst put it:

> The lewder sort, both clerks and laymen, are sensual and over-loose in living: the same, being virtuously bred up or reformed, are such mirrors of holiness and austerity that other nations retain but a shadow of devotion in comparison of them.[26]

What might be the other side of the coin comes in a comment from the puritanically-minded Sir Henry Wallop, grimly mindful no doubt of the doctrine of election:

> The great affection they commonly bear to the popish religion ...agreeth with their humour, that having committed murder, incest, thefts, with other execrable offences, by hearing a Mass, confessing themselves to a priest, or obtaining the pope's pardon, they persuade themselves they are forgiven. And hearing Mass on Sunday or holyday they think that all the week after they may do what heinous offence soever, and it is dispensed withal.[27]

Yet Edmund Tanner may have put his finger on a point of some importance when he said that swift repentance could come with one word of admonition or reproof from a good man. This, it may be argued, had always been an essential element in the Irish religious experience. In the days before the Reformation and the wars of conquest, reverence had been extended to the friars not only because they were holy and therefore powerful, but because they were good, and this surely is the distinction between personal and interior religion and some kind of shamanism.

The pattern revealed so far is what has been well called 'conservative survivalism'. If anything, we would expect religious values to coarsen as the society they lived in faced radical changes, imposed at best by peaceful means, more frequently by ruthless warfare. What sustained the values was a combination of traditional strengths, especially the friars and most especially the Franciscans, with a stiffening of the new Counter-Reformation vitality. Unfortunately neither of them is particularly well studied or even documented.

The friars were important: 'the false and crafty bloodsuckers, the Observants, as they will be called most holiest, so that there remains more virtue in one of their coats and knotted girdles than ever was in Christ and his passion', as a wrathful reformer wrote in 1538.[8] There was some reason for his wrath, if one is to accept the chatty reminiscences of the convent of Donegal written by Donagh Mooney, one of the last friars to be received there, and the first superior of St Anthony's, Louvain. He records in particular Father Bernard, who died in 1549, having won national fame as a miracle-worker. He recalls with special pride the fact that for diseases of animals water blessed by Father Bernard kept people from going for 'curing prayers' to 'wise women' and magicians.[29] This is uncomfortably close to 'if you can't beat them, join them'. As the screw tightened, however, the quality of the friars seems to have stiffened. Something of the scale of their activity may be seen in a report from Galway in 1572.[30] Up to twenty friars had gathered in the city, from as far away as Ulster. An Ulster friar had preached in the friary (which was still standing), and had preached rebellion. Several aldermen had been present, including Denis Kirwan, mayor in the previous year, and the godly had been very much afraid. As Munster went up in the flames of James FitzMaurice's war the friars played a prominent role. Two Franciscans in particular who were put to death seem to have taken special pains to ensure that their role was seen as a religious and not a political one: Daniel Nelan, who had refused to leave off his habit like the others did, though this made his capture and execution inevitable, and Thady O'Daly, friar of Askeaton, who when captured and condemned to death asked to be hanged in his habit.[31] At about the same time two lists preserved in Rome mention the activities of another Munster friar, Eugene O'Donohue, the Irish provincial, who travelled the whole country preaching despite the fact that he knew no English.[32] Then there was Thady Sullivan, friar of Kilcrea, who died on 17 December 1597. He had studied in Spain and was a doctor of divinity. He too travelled the whole country preaching, in the towns, in the houses of nobles, but, according to Mooney, especially in the wilder areas, where there was room for much preaching on fundamentals.[33] The friars too, especially the Franciscans, were numerous among the bishops appointed in Ireland during the century. Their activities were normally not restricted to their dioceses, and they link the church in Ireland to the wider concerns of the continent, where young Irishmen, and others not so young, some still pursuing the old game of Rome-running and some fired with a broader vision, were gathering at Rome, Louvain and elsewhere. Stray tantalising hints may be gathered from the 1560s,[34] but we still have to await the systematic exploration of the papal archives; and, by a cruel misfortune, the matriculation registers of Louvain from 1569 to 1616 disappeared during the era of the French Revolution.[35]

This is the world in which James FitzMaurice, with papal backing, launched the crusade to dethrone the heretic Elizabeth that was to leave the whole Desmond inheritance devastated and ripe for plantation. FitzMaurice had impressed David Wolfe, the Limerick Jesuit who had been appointed papal nuncio in Ireland in 1560. Writing in 1574, he spoke of him as 'a good Catholic and a brave captain. He was minded to enter some religious order, or to quit Ireland to live in some Catholic country, but by the advice of the good prelates and Catholic religious he stayed where he was for the good of the country.'[36] The old and the new were meeting in James FitzMaurice in the 1570s, just as they were meeting in all of Gaelic and Gaelicised Ireland. They clashed as they met, and we are still far from understanding the clash fully. When the name of James FitzMaurice first came up he appeared as the kind of person most would agree Irish society was well rid of, the swordsman and idle retainer *par excellence*. His future did not look bright as his master, the Earl of Desmond, faced the problem of making his terms with the crown, for swordsmen could have no place in a reconstructed lordship. To survive, FitzMaurice had to start a war. This he did in 1569. He rationalised it into a 'holy war', arguing that the most obvious indication of how the English were threatening the whole of society was their suppression of the monasteries and the whole complicated system of services, obligations and hospitality under which they operated. The threatened church was a microcosm of the threatened society.[37] FitzMaurice certainly grew out of his fixation on the past, especially when he went abroad after his surrender in 1575, and particularly perhaps when in the Rome of Gregory XIII he grew into the Counter-Reformation. When he returned as the Catholic crusader in 1579 with a pitifully small force a massive revolt broke out despite his own death in a petty skirmish a month after he had landed. But those in arms were almost all what FitzMaurice had been in 1569, swordsmen whose way of life was threatened, and not what FitzMaurice had become ten years later, the leader of a crusade against heresy. By this date it might be safely said that Gaelic and Gaelicised

Ireland would not become Protestant. It was not yet altogether clear in what sense it would be Catholic.

The conquered Desmond lands were planted, and the structures of the state church were consolidated. There were newcomers, laymen like Sir William Herbert or ecclesiastics like Bishop William Lyon of Cork and Ross (1583-1617), who gave their energies to spreading their religion.[38] Essentially, however, this religion was to be imposed as part of the conquest: eloquent praise of the bishop's mission of preaching must be balanced against the fact that he did not know any Irish. In 1588 it was reported that great numbers were attending services of the established church, but within a decade they were gone. It appears certain they attended what they called 'the devil's service' only under compulsion,[39] and according to one local witness,[40] not a dispassionate one it is true, they dared to show their contempt by disrupting the service. Another far from dispassionate witness, but passionate on the other side, summed it up in one vivid incident.[41] It was a Saturday afternoon in Kilmallock in October 1600. James FitzGerald, son of Earl Gerald, who had been killed in 1583, had just been restored to the title of Earl of Desmond and sent home to Munster in the hope of stabilising the situation there. Huge crowds had converged in Kilmallock to welcome him (this surely gives the lie to the much-repeated contention that 'the plain people' were only waiting to be delivered from the oppression of their chiefs). Next morning the young earl, just thirty, emerged to make his way to service in the Protestant church. The same crowds appealed to him not to go, but he went. When he came out they reviled him and spat on him.

So conquered Munster has made up its mind by 1600. At the other end of the country James Archer, Jesuit from Kilkenny, wrote to his general in Rome, on 10 August 1598, from O'Neill's camp, 'in haste'. It was a tense time, for O'Neill was deploying his forces for the great victory of the Yellow Ford in a few days' time, but the Jesuit was thinking of spiritual victories.[42] He has, he says, heard two thousand confessions; instructed the ignorant; got a nobleman to put away his concubine and take back his wife. Extraordinary crowds came to Mass and confession. In the north — here speaks the Palesman — they are barbarians, but they are free to profess their religion and they show great respect for religious. In the south many are afraid to give them public support, but even these help in every way they can. The reform of the clergy is essential and will be difficult, for they are ignorant and undisciplined. He himself in a short time has induced ten of them to put away their concubines and abjure heresy (far away in the south Bishop Lyon was lamenting that his ministers were forsaking their benefices to become massing-priests, many by persuasion of the seminary priests).

The religious practices of Gaelic Ireland up to late in the reign of Elizabeth — we have, of course, to depend very largely on outside observers — are only beginning to be affected by the ways of the Counter-Reformation. Much of the Counter-Reformation ways was mediated through the Anglo-Irish, who now demand our attention. They are a better-documented group, more vocal in themselves, and discussed in more detail by the administration. The crisis of identity they faced was more subtle, and it will always probably remain something of a mystery why they did not accept some reasonable form of Anglicanism when the pressure came on them in the reign of Elizabeth — and there can be little doubt a very reasonable Anglicanism would have satisfied the queen.

They were a social group who did not fit easily into the patterns of romantic nationalism. In consequence, they have been little written about, even by professional historians. The general image of them that survived is of a people without any real culture, sheltering behind the defences of the Pale, a colonial outpost incapable of any real initiatives. Recent studies have done something to put features on their facelessness, but we are still at an early stage in understanding them. In particular, there has been no real attempt to correlate the sparse information we have about the situation in Ireland with the increasingly well-documented story of what was happening in towns elsewhere, for this society in Ireland was essentially town-centred. Even where it spread furthest outside the town walls, in the Pale, the overall area was small, magnate families were closely linked with one another, and Dublin and Drogheda were not far away. Ideas circulated easily and freely; as well, and probably more important than the ideas in circulation, there was the fact that these towns still had a very large measure of self-government. Even in Dublin the city fathers were by no means at the beck and call of the Castle.

What ideas were in circulation? Something that might be called humanist, certainly, though this may have been more explicit in political thought than in religious concern. Something more akin to the *devotio moderna* may be closer to the mark — a genuine concern for religious values; inclined to place its trust in the autonomous lay spirituality that had proliferated so much in the fifteenth century, and certainly without any great hope that a genuine religious reform could be led by the clergy, clergy like Bishop Thomas Dillon of Kildare, 'a simple Irish priest, a vagabond, without learning, manners or good quality, not worthy to be a holy water clerk'.[43] They were realistic in appreciating that the malaise of the church was part of the general malaise, and that without 'the special grace of God' of a reformed church 'this land may never be reformed'.[44] They were sceptical of the capacity of the prelates to reform the church, but may not have been without hope that the secular authority might reform both church and prelates.

Though conscious they were not 'English' as the English were, they were loyal to England with a loyalty that went deeper than mere self-interest, though they did expect England to bail them out without giving very much by way of positive return. They had welcomed the fate of the Earls of Kildare, for, as seen from Dublin or Drogheda, Maynooth had looked very Irish. They had welcomed an English Lord Deputy, assuming that their own merits would be duly rewarded by an invitation to serve on his council. True, they were not altogether without fears, for at least in the early stages of the rebellion of Silken Thomas some of them had been forced into compromising positions. When they gathered in parliament on 1 May 1536 the fears were certainly real, but so were the hopes that they might have a part to play in the reform of both church and land.

These necessarily general considerations are far from explaining the fact that the bulk of the antipapal legislation which had been so cautiously and lengthily put through parliament in England was passed by the Irish parliament in one month, May 1536, with no opposition except from the representatives of the lower clergy in the House of Commons. The central point of their opposition was the proposal that the king should be head of the church. There is some evidence to suggest that the laity, even when accepting him as such, did not intend to exclude the authority of the pope: indeed, Patrick Barnewall declared in parliament, admittedly in a matter when his pocket was an issue, 'that he would not grant that the king as head of the church has so large power as the Bishop of Rome'.[45] Men had spoken that way two centuries earlier, when king and pope disputed their respective competences within what each accepted was one indivisible world. It would take some time before it came to be really accepted that that world could be and had been divided.

In law at any rate the pope was now gone, and the clerical order subject to secular authority. Though Henry was to toy with the possibilities of further innovations in the remaining decade of his reign, in religious matters he was fundamentally conservative, and in fact no real change occurred. Of his three principal ministers in Ireland, the Lord Deputy, the Archbishop of Dublin and the Bishop of Meath, the last-named, together with two successive Lord Deputies, Lord Leonard Grey and Sir Anthony St Leger, did not wish to stir up trouble by pushing change too quickly, while Archbishop Browne of Dublin, while personally inclined to more far-reaching changes in doctrine, was above all determined to be the king's good servant and nothing more.

Even Browne had to admit that he had had no success in getting the clergy to accept that the king was head of the church to the exclusion of the pope:[46] he had to send his own servants, he wrote, to carry out the order to have the name of the Bishop of Rome expunged from the canon of the Mass.[47] Further down the country, Bishop Staples of Meath reported, there was more active opposition: 'the common voice in the Irishry' was simply that the king had forced this false doctrine on parliament.[48] Even in Dublin there was some active opposition, especially from the Franciscan

Observants, who soon emerged as leaders. By this date almost all the friaries of the towns and the Pale had accepted the Observant reform; perhaps even more to the point, most of them had accepted it within the preceding twenty years or so.

What of the laity? As already noted, the penalties for supporting the pope against the king were severe, but for most laymen in Ireland the possibility of being faced with a stark choice was remote. If it did come to a stark choice, the evidence indicates that the royal headship was accepted, but that in practice this made little difference, as indeed it seems to have made little difference to those bishops who took the same road. After all, it is only a small minority of men who are theologians, and — possibly even more relevant here — an even smaller minority who are the stuff of martyrs.

Whatever may have been the new ideas stirring in the towns and the Pale, they had not replaced, or perhaps even greatly disturbed, a general conservative pattern. The fact that the Mass remained must have eased considerably any sense of change or challenge. The Lord Deputy, Lord Leonard Grey, could be seen kneeling, 'very devoutly', before the shrine of Our Lady of Trim, long enough to hear three or four Masses, and the king himself had essentially the same mind.[49] Our Lady of Trim did not escape the reforming zeal of Browne; neither did the famous image of Christ crucified, 'the Holy Cross of Ballyboggan, burnt by the Saxons', as the Annals of Ulster note in 1538; nor even the storied Staff of Jesus, Patrick's crosier, in Christ Church. Evidence of popular reaction is sparse but definite. The case of monastic dissolution may be a little more complex than it has yet got credit for. We have swung from a picture of the good monks turned out by the cruel Protestants to the view that the suppression of the monasteries did little more than give legal sanction to what had for some time been a fact, namely that the monastic spirit was dead and the monastic revenues in the control of laymen. True, much of contemporary monasticism would have scandalised the founding fathers: one shrinks from the thought of St Bernard castigating Irish sixteenth-century Cistercians. Nevertheless, the greater abbeys continued to fulfil a social function not altogether divorced from Christianity. This surfaces in the recommendation by the Lord Deputy and council that six monastic institutions be allowed to remain because they performed irreplaceable social and educational functions.[50] The recommendation was not accepted. The one convent of nuns on the list had an interesting future. It was Grace-Dieu, just north of Dublin. Here under the Augustinian canon-esses 'young children, both gentlemen children and other... of women kind' had been 'brought up in virtue, learning, and in the English tongue and behaviour'. The house and most of the lands passed to Patrick Barnewall, the lawyer who had denied in parliament that the king had as much authority as the pope over the fortunes of monasteries. In 1565 his son Christopher built a great house at Turvey nearby, using the stones of the convent.[51] This Christopher, as described by his son-in-law Richard Stanihurst, seems to present the very lineaments of a Puritan:

> a deep and wise gentleman, spare of speech, and therewithal pithy, wholly addicted to gravity, being in any pleasant conceit rather given to simper than smile: very upright in dealing, measuring all his affairs with the safety of conscience, as true as steel, close and secret, fast to his friend, stout in a good quarrel...[52]

Nevertheless, two years after his death in 1575 it came to the attention of the administration that a group of nuns under a prioress still lived in community at nearby Portrane, in property which had belonged to Grace-Dieu before the dissolution; that they had a chaplain; and that they celebrated their office in the parish church — all this within twelve miles of Dublin Castle.[53] The Barnewall fortunes had been founded on legal practice and confiscated monastic estates. These legal families are a group that all too little is known about. From a very early date they emerge as leading opponents of the Reformation: in his letter of 5 April 1538 Thomas Agard couples with the Observant friars as leaders of the opposition 'they that rule all, that be the temporal lawyers which have the king's fee'.[54] The complaint is to recur; and as the administration of the law at local level was in these men's hands, their opposition must have been very effective.

The doctrinal and liturgical changes held at bay during the old king's lifetime broke through during the reign of his son, the boy king, Edward VI (1547-53). The Second Prayer Book of 1552 appeared in Ireland only in circumstances to be outlined below, but opposition was roused by the First Prayer Book of 1549, which, whatever it was in itself, certainly changed the Mass in a way plain even to the non-theological mind, and even by the Order of Communion (1548), where the changes were less obvious. The irenic Bishop Staples of Meath was clearly frightened by the opposition to his attempts to introduce the Order of Communion into his diocese,[55] while Archbishop Dowdall of Armagh went into exile when it became clear to him that the First Prayer Book was to be imposed, declaring 'he would never be bishop where the holy Mass was abolished'. Lesser men put up lesser resistance when they found themselves in a situation where they had to use the new Prayer Book.[56] They kept on as many of the old ceremonies as they dared — 'holy water, Candlemas candles and such like'. They introduced the new service without any explanation, in effect giving up preaching altogether (in some cases this may have been no great sacrifice); and they made it look as much like the Mass as they could or as they dared — as the wrathful reformer John Bale reported even from loyal Waterford: 'The communion or supper of the Lord was there altogether used like a popish mass, with the old popish toys of Antichrist, in bowings and beckings, kneelings and knockings.'

The author of this irate comment, John Bale, was an Englishman and an advanced reformer who was appointed Bishop of Ossory on 22 October 1552 and consecrated in Dublin according to the rite in the Second Prayer Book on 2 February 1553. After a stormy six months in Kilkenny he left in a hurry when the news arrived of the proclamation of Mary as queen on 16 July. We have only his account of events, but the confrontation seems to have been head-on. Local Butler dominance had ensured a certain measure of at least outward conformity in Kilkenny. Bale described the mayor, Robert Shee, as 'a man sober, wise and godly', adding, however, that these were rare qualities in Kilkenny. The programme he put before his clergy evoked no co-operation. The Mass he denounced as idolatry. Instead they were to conduct service from the Second Prayer Book. To this the reply was that there was no legal warrant for such a service; that it was not being used in Dublin; and that in any case there were no service-books (the First Prayer Book had been printed in Dublin in 1551). He also wished his clergy to give up prayers for the dead and all the 'chanting, piping and singing' at which they wasted so much time to the detriment of preaching the word of God. Finally, he wanted them all to get married and put away their concubines. He seems to have assumed that every priest had a concubine, which was probably not altogether fair to them (in any case, there were no marriages).

In Bale's succinct phrase, 'then followed angers, slanders, conspiracies, and in the end slaughter of men'. With some of the young men he may have had some success. At any rate, on 20 August 1553, the day the news of Mary's proclamation reached Kilkenny, the young men were enacting two of Bale's very antipapal mystery plays. However, across the way on the cathedral hill a procession was taking shape, where, to quote Bale again, they 'blasphemously resumed again the whole papism', copes, candles, holy-water stocks, crosses and censers, Latin litanies, everything. At least some of them appear to have been at least slightly drunk. Bale left Kilkenny.

Queen Mary had no great problems with heresy in Ireland. In the matter of royal supremacy there had been a fair amount of outward conformity wherever the king's writ ran. There had certainly been no heroic resistance. However, the evidence is that many who accepted the supremacy did not believe it and that many more accepted it in fourteenth-century terms rather than in those of the sixteenth century. The destruction of pilgrimage shrines and the dissolution of monasteries may have stirred deeper resentments than their strictly religious values would warrant. There was real resistance to the replacement of the Mass by the Prayer Book service; and when the change was pushed through by a reformer as ham-fisted as Bale the resistance was violent. The return of 'the whole papism' under the Catholic queen was almost universally welcome. No doubt there were some who had reservations, like the Lord Chancellor, Sir Thomas Cusack of Lismullen, Co. Meath. He had committed himself deeply to reform, even to the extent of sanctioning the use of the Second Prayer Book at Bale's consecration in Dublin. But he and others like him kept their reservations to themselves, and their administrative skills were too useful to tempt the authorities to pry into their consciences.

How many people had committed themselves to the state religion in the reigns of Henry VIII and Edward VI? It must be evident that the only answer possible is that we do not know. Of those who accepted the royal supremacy, several, as has been seen, did not accept it to the exclusion of papal authority. Others, especially among the Gaelic Irish, accepted it as part of the process of coming to terms with the king's government in the 1540s known to historians as 'surrender and regrant', but they simply did not believe it was true, and there must have been little if any change once they were safely home from Dublin. There were people who could accept the royal supremacy but who rejected the new church service — the leading example being Archbishop Dowdall. It is indeed not surprising that converts should have been few, for there was almost no one to tell them what the changes were about, and this disastrous lack of effective preachers continued through Elizabeth's reign. The only real reasons put before the laity to abandon the traditional ways were self-interest and fear, closely related motives indeed, and powerful motives, though, curiously, they were in the event not enough.

In 1560 Elizabeth's first parliament had passed the Acts of Supremacy and Uniformity. Fifty years later committed Counter-Reformation Catholics would claim that they were put through parliament by some kind of a trick, but how they passed we simply do not know. One thing does seem reasonably certain: there was no enthusiasm in Dublin or the Pale for the religion now by law established. Two bishops — Meath and Kildare — definitely refused the Oath of Supremacy. It would appear that most of the others who may have attended parliament had prudently made a hasty return to their sees. Even when they submitted to the queen, admitted they held their temporalities of her, and even agreed to be inducted by her representative 'into their ecclesiastical prelacy', they still stuck at a straightforward admission that she was the source of their spiritual authority.[57] Such men were unlikely to be active missionaries for the new ways. In 1562 Lord Deputy Sussex reported to Cecil that there had been scant progress indeed. Only a few showed any enthusiasm; the people, 'utterly void of religion, come to divine service as to a May game'[58] (a Catholic chronicler of about 1600, Peter Lombard, spoke of the people going to church in the early years of Elizabeth's reign with crucifixes, rosaries, litanies and pictures).[59] The clergy were held in contempt, and not without reason. Even in the Dublin cathedrals it was easier to give orders to paint over murals and other remains of popery than to root out popery among the canons. On 18 May 1563 a commission was set up to tender the Oath of Supremacy to all ecclesiastics and state servants, but in so far as this made any progress it was admitted that it rested on compulsion — hopes had to be based on the fact that 'this people fear to offend'. The government realised it had to go slowly, beginning with 'one or two boasting Mass-men in every shire';[60] but though the judges and lawyers had promised co-operation, in a society where judge, lawyer and jury were normally linked in close friendship or even kinship with the accused it was in many cases simply not possible for the crown to get the verdict it sought.[61] It has been noted that from an early date civil lawyers emerged as opponents of the religious reformation; by 1570 it appears that most of them had set themselves against it.[62] That same year the papacy declared war on Elizabeth in the bull *Regnans in excelsis*, issued on 25 February. It declared the queen not merely excommunicated but deposed, and her subjects released from their allegiance. It may have been an outmoded diplomatic weapon, but it made it clear that it was no longer possible to serve both queen and pope, though the Anglo-Irish were to keep trying for a long time to come. Writing to the Lord Deputy on 12 May 1577, Bishop Brady declared:

> I find great boldness generally, as well by word as action, against the received religion. Masses be rife, little less than openly said, friars show themselves openly, two of them being here at the Navan of late were apprehended by some of my men, but quickly rescued, and my men put in hazard of their lives; this act was done by the portreeve of the town and some other of his brethren.[63]

At the end of the decade the Pale had reached, quite literally, its crisis, its judgment.[64] Its people were anxious to be loyal to the queen, but were not willing to give up allegiance to the pope. Before trying to analyse this crisis, it may be worth while to attempt an assessment of what spiritual strengths kept them on a course which by now could demand very real courage. Their first strength was that very few disturbed their belief in the old ways by explaining to them how much better the new ones were. On the other hand, preachers of the Catholic Counter-Reformation can hardly have been very effective until the mid-1570s. The papal envoy, David Wolfe, S.J., did not venture into the Pale, though he had his contacts there (one would like to know very much more about his representative in Dublin, Thady Newman). The positive strengths were the traditional ones: the friars, as Bishop Brady found in Navan; the Mass, clearly regarded in a quite different light from the service of the established church, though few may have been in a position to give anything that might be described as theological reasons for their preference. Then there was the fact of a close-knit society, where the tone was set by quite a small number of magnates and gentry; the whole of Meath, for example, as Wolfe wrote in 1574, was 'united and bound together as if it were a city or republic well governed in love and charity'.[65] Only one magnate, Lord Gormanston, had accepted the new religion, Wolfe claimed. And Meath was the diocese of Hugh Brady, the most religiously effective of its bishops.

In this same report Wolfe claims that in the towns only a handful went willingly to the services of the established church, though he says that in some places — he names Dublin, Drogheda and Cork — they went unwillingly. Three things in particular must have stiffened their resolve. The first was that the town merchants, like the country gentry, formed a small and tightly-knit society. The second arose from a combination of two factors: the large measure of self-government enjoyed by the towns, and the fact that, by and large, members of the municipal corporations were not pressed to take the Oath of Supremacy in the reign of Elizabeth. The third was the religious aspect of the cohesiveness provided by the guilds.[66]

In this matter our information is to all intents and purposes confined to Dublin, but for Dublin we are relatively well informed. Town life was organised around the guilds. The great guild merchant and the various trade guilds all had their religious aspects — the brothers and sisters of the guild regarded themselves as a community not merely for secular purposes but for religious interests as well. In addition to these there were the guilds — we know of six in Dublin — organised for purely religious ends. In the case of one of them, the Guild of St Anne, enough documentation has survived to allow its history to be followed in some detail for a century after the Reformation.

In contrast with England, there had been no law in Ireland vesting the property of chantries and religious guilds in the crown. As much of the guild's funds were devoted to maintaining chantry priests, the fact that they remained in Catholic hands meant that the guild had an important role in providing Catholic worship. The funds of the Guild of St Anne were under Catholic control until 1641. Late in the sixteenth century the guild was still maintaining six 'singing men', whose functions quite certainly included singing Mass, first in the guild's chapel in St Audoen's, and later, when things got tighter, in private houses, when the 'singing men' no longer had a corporate existence, but were in fact Catholic priests supported by the funds of the guild. By the standards of the Counter-Reformation Jesuits, the brethren of the guild may have been 'men of the old faith, poorly instructed in current controversies', but their guilds provided them not just with priests to say Mass, but with a whole system of organised piety.

The Pale, as already noted, reached its 'crisis' about 1580. The old 'nationalist' explanation saw it as a crisis of 'faith and fatherland'. Some modern writing would almost seem to suggest that the crisis was about taxation. In fact it was no simple crisis, but a complex one. Not quite so starkly as Gaelic Ireland, but very nearly so, here was a conservative society under pressure to change its ways. It was expected to adopt the queen's religion. It was expected to give up private armed retainers and instead pay taxes — the hated 'cess' — to support the queen's army to keep the peace. It was expected to assist in administering the queen's justice impartially, even if the accused were a kinsman or a magnate whom lesser men would not have lightly offended in the past. There were many threads in the new social web to be woven.

The chief enemy of the old society was not the Lord Deputy. While he may not have liked its ways, he was usually a man of independent means and did not covet its wealth. He planned to go back to England when his term of office was up. The government officials had no such plan. They had come to Ireland to make their fortune. The wealth of the recalcitrant gentry presented them with an obvious opportunity. They received no salaries, and a man did not grow rich on fees. It was quite natural that they should be enthusiasts for the new government and the new religion, in its most Protestant form. From this it follows that the queen herself was not the leading threat to the lords and gentry of the Pale. Time and again she intervened to say that over-strict insistence on religious conformity must not drive men to political disloyalty.

The crisis of the Pale centres on the revolt of James Eustace, Viscount Baltinglass, in July 1580. That his main motive was religion does seem beyond question. In many ways his development parallels that of James FitzMaurice, who had proclaimed his crusade in Munster twelve months before: like FitzMaurice, he had visited Rome.[67] The central figure, however, was Gerald, Earl of Kildare, greatest of the gentry of the Pale. He was now fifty-five years of age. He had been taken away to Europe in 1540 and was brought up mainly in Italy, where he had been educated by his relative, Cardinal Pole. Returning in the reign of Edward VI, he had been restored to his estates. In successive reigns he had outwardly conformed to the then established religion, but his sympathies were Catholic, though his courage did not quite match them. His wife was much more decidedly Catholic, and their house at Rathangan was full of the comings and goings of priests, including Robert Rochford, who had joined the Jesuits in Rome in 1564 and was to be the close companion of Baltinglass. Kildare had been expected to join the revolt, but he drew back. In consequence, Baltinglass got little support from the Pale. When the Deputy, Arthur, Lord Grey, overran the papal force at Smerwick, Co. Kerry, in November 1580 Baltinglass had to seek shelter with the O'Byrnes of Wicklow.

Sometime that winter he tried to flee abroad. He turned to the port of Wexford, the native town of his Jesuit companion, Robert Rochford. Moreover, Wexford merchants had for some years been acting as couriers between Ireland and James FitzMaurice on the continent,[68] and the Anglo-

Irish gentry there had been active in the troubled year of 1580, their motives being undoubtedly secular as well as religious (the centralising policies of the crown had been especially resented in this small but very tightly-knit enclave, for long an island of Englishry, well used to looking after itself and keeping at bay its Gaelic neighbours, the Kavanaghs).

When Baltinglass arrived in Wexford, however, his cause was so clearly lost that no one wanted to have anything to do with him, except a few poor men, a group of sailors who tried unsuccessfully to get him a passage, and a baker, Matthew Lambert, who gave shelter to him and Robert Rochford. The Wexford gentry had calculated rightly. In the spring of 1581 the Kavanaghs rose in rebellion. That summer the Deputy moved against them, executing the leaders by martial law as he moved down the country. He arrived in Wexford to find many suspects in jail. These were to have the benefit of trial by the processes of common law. Among them was the greatest of the Wexford gentry, Sir Nicholas Devereux of Ballymagir. His guilt seemed proved by his own confession, but the local jury acquitted him,[69] reasoning, no doubt, that while the presence of the Lord Deputy was for the moment terrible he would soon be gone, but there would always be a Devereux in Ballymagir. The family were locally powerful in both secular and religious affairs. Nicholas's uncle, Alexander Devereux, the last Cistercian Abbot of Dunbrody, had become the king's Bishop of Ferns in 1539. He had held the see until his death in 1566, escaping deprivation under Mary because he had not married, and conforming again under Elizabeth. With him the established Devereux practice of introducing relatives into good benefices was extended to alienating see lands to his bastards.[70] He was succeeded by his nephew, John Devereux (1566-78), apparently regarded by the government as the best candidate in the circumstances, believed to be loyal and with an English university education, though, on the testimony of Archbishop Loftus — not always reliable — 'an unfitter man cannot be: he is now of late deprived of his deanery for confessed whoredom'.[71] Nevertheless, he was almost certainly one of the two Leinster bishops who, David Wolfe claimed, 'would much rather be Catholics but that they would lose their sees'.[72]

While we might speculate on the quality of the Catholicism of Bishop John Devereux, there is no doubt in the case of the poor men of Wexford who tried to help Baltinglass. Testimony in this matter has been preserved by another Wexford Jesuit, John Howlin, testimony so vivid that it is hard not to accept that it is that of an eye-witness. Matthew Lambert and the sailors were also in jail. An example had to be made in Wexford, and so 'the men of no property' were hanged. In court they proclaimed themselves Catholics. Matthew Lambert was asked how he reconciled his loyalty to the pope with his professed loyalty to the queen. He replied that he was an unlettered man, unable to discuss such matters: all he could say was that he was a Catholic and held the faith of his holy mother the Catholic church.

Howlin notes another Catholic of humble estate who died in Dublin refusing to accept the queen's supremacy and declaring that he was a Catholic. His name, as given by Howlin, was Walter 'Lakinnus', and he was servant to Maurice Eustace, one of several gentry also executed in Dublin in 1581 and 1582.[73] For these, Howlin's information can be supplemented by material in the state papers. The picture that emerges is of committed Catholics, many of whom have been to Catholic Europe, some of whom had considered becoming priests, several of them coming from homes where a priest was regularly maintained. One of them, Robert Scurlock, was tried by his conforming father, Barnaby. Nor should the women be forgotten. The most indomitable and best remembered was Margaret Bermingham, daughter of one of the gentry of the Pale, married to Bartholomew Ball, a leading Dublin merchant.[74] Her house was a school of Christian doctrine for her menservants and maids. From her they went to other houses, often at their owners' request, and here they instructed the servants, sometimes even the masters. There was always a priest in her household. In contrast to Robert Scurlock, sentenced to death by his father, Margaret was persecuted by her conforming son Walter, Mayor of Dublin in the crisis year of 1581. Not once but several times the house was raided during Mass, and the indomitable lady was led off to jail accompanied by the priest in his vestments. She died in jail in Dublin in 1584. She was then about seventy years of age.

Dublin and Wexford were the centres of crisis for the Catholics in 1581, but the growth of recusancy can be traced in some detail in other towns as well. We are best informed about Waterford, with its links with Kilkenny and Clonmel, towns in the territory of 'Black Tom' Butler, the Earl of Ormond, who certainly served the crown. Waterford was still second only to Dublin among Irish cities, its people 'given to business rather than warfare', according to David Wolfe, who added that they were all Catholics except four or five young men. Wolfe was writing in 1574, to some extent from memory, as he had been imprisoned in 1567, but three separate reports[75] from the opposite interest between 1577 and 1585 show that Waterford was becoming more rather than less Catholic. The inhabitants were 'cankered in popery', with Masses being said everywhere, even in the churches, by the many priests and friars, while a great number of young men of the city were students in Louvain. Only a few went to the official service, and these were not sincere. They behaved disrespectfully, 'and these not small fools but the chief of the city'. The mayor, Patrick Walshe, was the ringleader. No woman went to the official service. They flaunted the rosary beads and other tokens of popery. They had holy images everywhere, even in the churches, for the ministers feared to remove them. Ministers and schoolmasters of the established church went in fear. Only a handful accepted their ministrations. Children were baptised at home, with a priest if possible. Marriages too took place at home, before either a priest or lay witnesses. The cemeteries were controlled by the established church, but there was no religious service at funerals.

Personalities abound, even if it is not always easy to sort out the various Whites and Walshes. First place must go to Peter White, who comes to us so strikingly in the pages of Anthony Wood and his pupil Richard Stanihurst.[76] Native of Clonmel, fellow of Oriel, he returned to become 'the happy schoolmaster' in Kilkenny, continuing to influence a whole generation of young men of the Pale. In 1566 he became Dean of Waterford, when the bishop, Patrick Walshe, had accepted the Protestant reformation, but some time later Peter was deprived for popery and returned to schoolmastering. His brother John, a Catholic priest, preached popery openly, and was 'worshipped like a god' between Kilkenny, Waterford and Clonmel. His nephew Thomas became a Jesuit. A Victor White noted in Clonmel in 1585 is almost certainly a relative in some degree. Maurice MacKenraghty, chaplain to the Earl of Desmond, had been in jail in Clonmel since 1583, and at Easter 1585 Victor bribed the jailer to release him to say Mass in his house. The jailer betrayed both to Sir John Norris, President of Munster. Both were imprisoned, and the priest was executed a few weeks later.[77]

The Sir Nicholas White who filled so many government offices in his lifetime was not of the same family. He had estates in Co. Kilkenny, but was probably born in Waterford city. His patron was the Earl of Ormond, which helped him, no doubt, but made Ormond's enemies his enemies as well. In the critical situation brought about in the parliament of 1585-6 when the gentry of the Pale, having been tendered the Oath of Supremacy, refused to take it and were thereupon threatened with the Court of Castle Chamber, we find Nicholas White pleading for religious toleration. The Speaker of this parliament, Sir Nicholas Walsh, was Ormond's man to an even greater degree. Yet when he came to die in April 1615 he asked to be reconciled to the Catholic church (the testimony is from David Rothe of Kilkenny, who wrote it in the year Nicholas Walsh died). Six months before there had been an even more illustrious convert, 'Black Tom' himself. He died on 23 November 1614 at the ripe age of eighty-three. He too had sent for a Catholic priest.[78]

Anglo-Ireland steadily became more and more committed to Counter-Reformation Catholicism. The 1590s are full of complaints from government servants and clergy of the established church. To turn to Waterford again — they once went, it was claimed, very orderly to church. Then the women stayed away. When they were unpunished the men followed suit. When they in turn were unpunished the city fathers stayed at home. It became the same everywhere — every town and gentleman's house full of 'superstitions and seducing priests',[79] and 'the good town of Waterford' had led the way. When Elizabeth died in 1603 Catholics took over the churches and restored the Mass, first in Waterford, then in Cork, Kilkenny, Wexford and Clonmel. The government soon reasserted its authority, but at least in Waterford and Clonmel, where the Franciscan friaries were still roofed, people gathered every Sunday and holyday to pray, and occasionally risked having Mass on a temporary altar.[80]

Well before the end of the sixteenth century the Catholic Counter-Reformation mission had become more effective than that of the established church. Before going on to consider this development, however, it might be worth while taking a brief look at the literary mind of Anglo-Ireland in the sixteenth century. The look will of necessity be a brief one, for very little remains. Next to nothing of it was printed, and there was no scribal tradition like that of Gaelic Ireland, though there can be little doubt that manuscripts circulated at the time. The most evocative source is a few pages written by Richard Stanihurst for Holinshed's *Chronicles*[81] on 'the learned men and authors of Ireland'. Stanihurst himself was a poet, though his verse can hardly be said to rise much above that of the 'divers scavengers of drafty poetry' he castigates in his dedicatory epistle to Lord Dunsany, a relative and himself a poet. Many of those mentioned in his brief list must probably remain no more than names. For some he gives the interesting information that (in contrast to their Gaelic Irish counterparts) they were experimenting with contemporary verse-forms — writers like Dormer of New Ross, Oxford scholar, who 'wrote in ballad royal The Decay of Ross', or William Nugent, 'a proper gentleman and of a singular good wit: he wrote in the English tongue divers sonnets'. He was of the gifted Westmeath family of Delvin; a relative, Richard Nugent, published in London in 1604 *Cynthia, containing Direful Sonnets, Madrigalls and Passionate Intercourses describing his Repudiate Affections, expressed in Love's Own Language.*[82] There were clergy like Richard Smith, so called because his father was a smith at Rathmacknee, Co. Wexford, who went to Oxford at the age of fourteen, became professor of divinity, and was 'taken in those days for the peerless pearl of all the divines of Oxford, as well in scholastical as in political divinity. Upon the death of Queen Mary he went to Louvain', or 'Poomrell a bachelor of divinity, sometime chaplain New College, Oxford. After returning to his country beneficed in Drogheda, from thence flitted to Louvain', where he died in 1573.

The shift from Oxford to Louvain has several times been noted, but there is still little known of it. The scale of the English recusant exodus to the Spanish Netherlands was considerable, and there are reasons to believe that there was also a considerable exodus from Ireland. John Howlin several times states that considerable numbers of people, women as well as men, fled to Catholic countries in order to practise their religion. There are at least preliminary indications that certain parish registers in the Netherlands might provide rich documentation. Most unfortunately the Louvain matriculation register between the years 1569 and 1616 disappeared during the French Revolution, but Stanihurst, writing in 1577, already notes two young men from Waterford who had made Louvain their first choice, Peter Lombard and Nicholas Cumerford, both scholars of Peter White, who had distinguished careers in the university, Lombard being 'primus universitatis', the leading scholar of his year. Spain too drew the Irish: petitions of impecunious students to the senate of the University of Salamanca are extant from 1574.[83] Stanihurst also notes Robert Rochford, 'born in the county of Wexford, a proper divine, an exact philosopher, and a very good antiquary'. We have met Robert Rochford already. He had been the companion of Baltinglass in 1580 and had gone into exile with him in 1581. He had become a Jesuit in Rome in 1564. He was one of the twenty-three Jesuits who sailed with the Armada in 1588, and one of the three who did not return.[84] With these names we are firmly and clearly dealing with the Counter-Reformation.

It has already been noted that when parliament closed in 1560 it would appear that most of the bishops in Dublin left the city rather quickly. Two — Walsh of Meath and Leverous of Kildare — definitely refused the Oath of Supremacy and were deprived of their sees. Of the others, it may be said with reasonable certainty that seven in all took the oath, though some who are known to have taken it — the outstanding example being Bodkin of Tuam — are probably best described as keeping their own counsel while determined to keep their sees. It was not easy to find effective new bishops for the established church. Hugh Brady of Meath (1563-84), already mentioned, was an outstanding exception. To his name might be added those of Patrick Walsh of Waterford (1551-78) and Nicholas Walsh of Ossory (1578-85), the latter being particularly active in trying to develop preaching in the Irish language. He had been closely associated with John Kearney, whose catechism in Irish had been printed in Dublin in 1571. But as the years went by New English names begin to appear among the bishops of the established church, reflecting the fact that the church itself was becoming New English in character.

The Council of Trent ended in 1563. It had pinned its hopes for a Catholic reform on the provision of good bishops. These in turn would see to it that there should be good priests in the parishes, trained for their task by the mental and moral discipline of the seminaries. To bring this about a reform of the Roman curia was necessary. This Trent had perforce to leave to the papacy, but the post-Tridentine popes took up the task. At the centre of their reorganisation was the idea of distributing the cardinals among congregations or departments of state, each of them charged with specific functions. Offices which had been at the centre of fiscal corruption, such as the chancery and the datary, henceforth functioned only as despatching offices for the decisions reached by the congregations. A congregation for the nomination of bishops was set up in 1572 and was stabilised in the great reforms introduced by Pope Sixtus V in 1588.

So, gradually but not too slowly, the way was made harder for the 'Rome-runners', men like the Dean of Raphoe who went to Rome to seek a bishopric, described by David Wolfe in 1561 as 'a rude, coarse man, fitter to be a soldier than a churchman'. Naturally the provision of an effective Catholic episcopate in Ireland faced increasing difficulties as the government extended its grip on the country. Roman nominations were necessarily sporadic. A number were made in the early 1560s on the recommendation of David Wolfe. Three of them, Donal MacGongail of Raphoe, Eugene O'Harte of Achonry, and Thomas O'Herlihy of Ross, consecrated in Rome in the winter of 1561-2, attended the final sessions of the Council of Trent. Intermittent nominations followed, as the curia freed itself from the idea that possession of the temporalities was important, to sees clearly vacant either by death or because the incumbent was considered to have conformed.[85] In nearly all cases these bishops were given faculties extending over one and sometimes two ecclesiastical provinces. A cluster of provisions around 1580 reflected the hopes raised by James FitzMaurice, but the timing proved unfortunate as these hopes quickly vanished. The most distinguished nominee, Dermot O'Hurley, provided to Cashel in September 1581, was hanged in Dublin in June 1584.

Pope Clement VIII (1592-1605) decided that military action against the regime of Elizabeth was useless. As part of a cautious move towards negotiation he decided to nominate to the Irish sees not bishops but priests not in bishop's orders as vicars apostolic. This device of putting a priest temporarily in charge of a diocese because of difficulties with the civil authorities was well established, and the pope clearly judged it suited to the circumstances in Ireland.

These men, whether bishops or vicars, faced great problems in establishing the Tridentine pattern of good priests in charge of parishes. There is reference to a synod in Ulster held in 1587 to promulgate the decrees of the Council of Trent. It was attended by six Ulster bishops and one from Connacht, together with a great number of clergy, but its effectiveness in establishing a Tridentine pattern was eroded by the advance of government control. More could be done by the individual missionary returning from Europe trained as a priest in the Counter-Reformation pattern. These became available quite early — already in 1564 the government was perturbed by the numbers of young men going abroad, even from the Pale, where the movement was organised by Thady Newman, Wolfe's representative in Leinster, with the support of some parish clergy.[86] Here especially the lack of a systematic examination of Roman administrative archives is a great handicap to tracing development in detail, but some published documents dated about 1580[87] show that in Rome the human resources available for the mission to Ireland were being carefully assessed, both men pursuing ecclesiastical studies on the continent and prominent priests in Ireland known to have been deprived of their livings because they had refused to conform.

The year 1592 saw two events of great significance. On 3 March Trinity College, Dublin, received its charter, establishing the long-thwarted university, its primary purpose being to provide ministers for the established church. That summer the College of St Patrick was set up in Salamanca, with approval and aid from Philip II of Spain, to fulfil the same function for the Catholics. Two years later a College of St Patrick opened its doors at Douai in the Spanish Netherlands. Its founder, Christopher Cusack, is surrounded by a certain mystery, but he was from the Pale, a priest and clearly a person of some substance, and it is probable that he was a son of Robert Cusack, son and heir of Thomas Cusack, representatives of one of the very few legal families to have given active support to the established church.[88]

The Irish Jesuit mission is relatively well documented. Their first appearance in Ireland in 1542 had had little effect, but that of David Wolfe in the early 1560s proved more permanent. From that date there was a steady trickle of young Irish recruits to the Society,[89] mostly from the towns. By no means all returned to Ireland. Some had distinguished missionary careers in central Europe and as far away as South America. Some played a role in the general Jesuit mission of education: they were to be prominent in the foundation of Irish colleges in Europe. In 1603 there were only five Jesuits in Ireland: two in Leinster, two in Munster, and one in jail. But even a handful of these 'shock troops of the Counter-Reformation' could be very effective.

Most of what is known of religious observance among Anglo-Irish Catholics at the end of the century comes from their reports. The Jesuits would have been even more disapproving than earlier humanists like Richard Stanihurst, and they set out to apply their remedies. Their first problem was the ignorance of most people of even the basic truths of their faith. Thomas Field, S.J., writing in 1603,[90] noted that when Catholics refused to take part in the services of the established church they could give no better reason for their refusal than that it was forbidden by their loyalty to their ancestors and by the Catholic church. So the Jesuits preached 'in season and out of season', and they began to organise the laity in the Sodality of the Blessed Virgin Mary.

Another important group, who must probably remain little more than names to us, are the Catholic schoolmasters. When a student was admitted to Salamanca, he had, among other things, to give details of his previous studies. Statements by a hundred students over the years 1595 to 1619 have survived, and in many cases they name the schoolmasters who taught them.[91] As might be expected, they are concentrated in the towns, normally several in each town, but they also exist all over the country (of these hundred students, two-thirds are Anglo-Irish, but a full third are Gaelic Irish). These men were in the humanist tradition, lesser images of Peter White at Kilkenny. There are indications that the profession may have passed from father to son. Stanihurst, writing in 1577, includes among 'the learned men and authors of Ireland' 'Devrox: there are two brethren of the name, learned: the elder was sometime schoolmaster in Wexford', while the Salamanca documents note a student admitted in 1601 taught by James Devereux in Wexford, and another admitted in 1614 taught by William Devereux in the same town. These men must have made a vital contribution, not just to the provision of priests, but to the general level of Catholic education.

After instruction came sacramental practice. Detail becomes plentiful only in the next century, when the Counter-Reformation mission really got under way. The pattern, however, is discernible from the very beginning. The sacraments are to be seen as rites of personal regeneration, not celebrations by the kin-group. Hitherto this had often been the more obvious aspect of baptism, while penance had sometimes been seen as primarily the healing of feuding factions rather than of the individual soul. As for marriage, there was much to be changed before the sacrament reflected the Christian ideal, recently restated by Trent.

In the 1590s a community took shape, consciously Catholic, however ill-instructed by the standards of the Counter-Reformation. While the choice confronting its members had not been as harsh as what the English Catholics had faced, they had had their martyrs. Before he died in Lisbon in 1599 John Howlin had chronicled them, bishops, priests and laity.[92] The fact is clear that in the late 1580s and the 1590s there were mass defections among people who had been attending the services of the established church before this. The explicit testimony comes from those who were dismayed by the development.[93] They were agreed as to why it happened. Nobody wanted the queen's service, and in the circumstances of Ireland it was not possible to enforce the recusancy laws. While the 'sword' was ineffective in the hands of the state, so too was the 'word' in the hands of its established church. By now the 'word' was effective in the hands of the Counter-Reformation mission. Spenser's verdict is well known:

> Wherein it is great wonder to see the odds which are between the zeal of popish priests and the ministers of the gospel. For they spare not to come out of Spain, from Rome and from Rheims, by long toil and dangerous travelling hither, where they know peril of death awaiteth them and no reward or riches to be found, only to draw the people into the Church of Rome: whereas some of our idle ministers, having a way for credit and estimation thereby opened unto them, and having the livings of the country offered unto them without pains and without

peril, will neither for the same, nor any love of God, nor zeal of religion, nor for all the good they may do by winning souls to God, be drawn forth from their warm nests to look out into God's harvest, which is even ready for the sickle and all the fields yellow long ago.[94]

Others were saying the same thing at the same time in less memorable language. Bishop Lyon of Cork lamented that his ministers were leaving their benefices to become seminary priests. In Dublin the Jesuit Henry FitzSimon was engaging successfully in public debate with the Protestants, to the great edification of most of the people, though few of them may have been able to follow the argument in detail.[95] In Cork and Dublin young men carried arms to Mass in private houses to defend the priest and congregation[96] (twenty years earlier David Wolfe had noted that the few genuine conformists in the towns were usually young men).

In a word, in the 1590s the dam burst. It was a quite natural reaction that the Catholics in the southern towns should have taken over the churches on hearing of the death of Elizabeth. Their occupation was short-lived, but all this meant was that henceforth they would seek the ministrations of religion outside the churches. The situation was summed up in a brief from Pope Paul V (1605-21).[97] It exhorted the Irish Catholics to be faithful to their ancestral religion, and ended with a grant of a plenary indulgence to the members of the new sodalities and to those who visited the ancient shrines on their traditional holydays — St Fechin of Fore, Iniscaltra, Skellig, the churches in the Aran Islands, Croagh Patrick, the church of Ciarán of Clonmacnois at Modreeny, the church of St Mary Magdalen at Clane, the cathedral of Armagh, the Franciscan church in Clonmel, and Lady's Island, Co. Wexford. The old and the new had now to blend in fields ready for the sickle and yellow long ago.

Not a
Mission, but a Church

The last resistance to English power came to an end when Hugh O'Neill surrendered to Mountjoy on 30 March 1603. Though he did not know it, Elizabeth I had died six days before, and it fell to the new Stuart king, James I, to exploit the situation in which the royal authority was unopposed over the whole island.

His Irish subjects were, however, far from being a homogeneous community. Historians divide them into three broad groups, and, allowing for some slight shading at the edges, this division is very adequate. The 'New English' were those who had arrived in Ireland since 1530s, when the policy of reducing all Ireland to obedience to the crown had begun. They had come as administrators and soldiers, but as well as serving the crown they planned to build their own fortunes, and in this they were succeeding. As was to be expected, they were overwhelmingly Protestant — indeed, in important respects they virtually constituted the Church of Ireland — but there were Catholics among them, some of whom quite certainly had come because they had rejected the Anglican settlement and judged it easier to be a Catholic in Ireland.

The 'Old Irish' were at the opposite pole. They had borne the brunt of the Tudor wars of conquest, they had suffered most in the plantations, and were soon to suffer even more severely. It was natural that there should be a few Protestants in their ranks — though they were few indeed — who had adopted the new religion as part of their coming to terms with the new political system.

In the middle stood the group who now called themselves the 'Old English'. This group was now much larger than the 'Anglo-Irish' of the Pale and the towns a century before, and included all those of Anglo-Norman origins (it has already been noted that these had kept their distinctive culture even when the English colony was at its weakest in the later middle ages). Again, there were a few Protestants among them, but by and large they had opted for Counter-Reformation Catholicism. They were a wealthy group, having suffered very little in the plantations, and still controlling the economic life of the towns. The difficult political task now facing them was to reconcile their loyalty to the crown with the profession of a religion which was not that of the crown, made all the more difficult because pressure to conform could be stepped up now that the military conquest was completed.

As already noted, the Catholics in the southern towns had taken over the churches when news came of the death of Elizabeth, in the hope that the son of Mary Queen of Scots would be more favourable to Catholicism than the daughter of Anne Boleyn. This hope was disappointed, and it was soon made clear that popery would not be countenanced.

The government's problem was that the anti-popery laws in Ireland were insufficient: there had been no further legislation since the first Elizabethan parliament had passed the Acts of Supremacy and Uniformity. When parliament met in England after the Gunpowder Plot of November 1605 it had adopted a new Oath of Allegiance to be taken by Catholics. It looked less demanding than the Oath of Supremacy, and it did succeed in dividing the Catholic community. Attempts to extend it to Ireland by prerogative were thwarted by the Old English Catholic lawyers, who claimed, successfully, that it could not be legally tendered in Ireland because it had not been passed in parliament there. The administration was forced to what it regarded as the unsatisfactory expedients of issuing personal mandates to prominent recusants to attend the services of the established church, backing these with the threat of being summoned before the prerogative Court of Castle Chamber, a fearsome instrument in that it was not bound by the procedures of common law or the penalties of statute law. The penalties normally imposed by this court were a crippling fine or imprisonment during pleasure, or both; but as the government wished to produce conformity rather than martyrdom, an oath modelled on the English Oath of Allegiance was highly desirable, and this involved summoning parliament.

This in turn involved the problem of inducing the anticipated Old English majority to pass new penal legislation, and the Lord Deputy, Sir Arthur Chichester, decided that the best tactic was to cow them in advance. On 20 August 1611 he got permission from London to mete out exemplary punishment to 'a few titulary bishops', provided it was made clear that the punishment was for civil and not religious offences. At this time there were only two Catholic bishops in the country, David Kearney of Cashel, appointed in 1603, and Conor O'Devany of Down and Connor, appointed in 1582 and now almost eighty years old. Kearney was at liberty, but O'Devany had been captured earlier that summer and was a prisoner in Dublin Castle. On 28 January 1612 he stood trial for treason together with a priest, Patrick O'Loughran, who had been picked out from a number of priests in prison at that time because he had been chaplain to Hugh O'Neill.

This chaplaincy might be said to have been inherited. The O'Loughrans were the erenagh family in the parish of Donaghmore, which comprised the O'Neill mensal lands, the *lucht tighe Uí Néill*. The aged bishop also had deep roots in the Gaelic world, but he had very strikingly made the transition to the new age of the Counter-Reformation. The O'Devanys were hereditary erenaghs of Raphoe, Co. Donegal. Some time about 1550 he had become a Franciscan Observant in the Donegal friary. In 1582 he was consecrated Bishop of Down and Connor in the church of Santa Maria dell'Anima in Rome, and returned to Ireland to bring the ideas of the Counter-Reformation to north-east Ulster. He had been picked up in the sweep of the country that went on in the 'Armada summer' of 1588 and imprisoned in the Castle, but had used the infighting in the council which had gone on after the recall of Sir John Perrot to secure his release. There are indications that he had help from Catholic lawyers in Dublin in preparing his case to be set at liberty. He had refused to play any political role in the Nine Years' War, but this was the indictment against him, duly found by a grand jury, on which he now stood trial.

It had never been government practice to be too nice in handling the evidence once it had been decided to stage a trial for treason, and a verdict of guilty was quickly reached and sentence of death pronounced. The execution was fixed for 1 February.

About two o'clock on that dark and gloomy afternoon in Dublin a procession left the Castle for the place of execution (now George's Hill). At its centre, guarded by soldiers, were the two men to be executed, bound face upwards on carts. The numbers in the procession grew rapidly. Estimates by involved contemporaries are notoriously suspect, but there can be no doubt that it ran into several thousands by the time the scaffold was reached about four o'clock. Both men endured bravely the grisly horrors of an execution for treason, proclaiming from the scaffold that the real reason for their death was their Catholic faith. Soon there was talk of signs and miracles. A memory etched on the mind of everyone present was the fact that the setting sun broke through the clouds as the bishop climbed the scaffold, lighting him up for a brief moment, only to disappear again as he was thrown down.

'As Aidan Clarke has perceptively remarked, 'O'Devany's death was an event of unexpected importance in the development of the Counter-Reformation in Ireland.'[1] Within a few days Chichester was glumly writing to Cecil that 'a titular bishop and priest being lately executed for treason are thought martyrs, and adored for saints'.[2] This large-scale public profession of the Catholic faith in the very capital itself irrevocably committed the Old English community to Counter-Reformation Catholicism. By the time parliament assembled on 18 May 1613 they had been reduced to a parliamentary minority by very questionable methods, including the widespread rigging of elections and the creation of new boroughs which were sometimes no more than points on a map; nevertheless, they fought every inch of the way, and in the end no new penal legislation was passed. The government was left with the intractable political problem that the great majority of its citizens, including men of wealth and property who proclaimed themselves otherwise totally loyal, had determined not to follow the religion of their civil ruler.

The problem was intractable because by the conventions of the time men of wealth and property were regarded as having an active part in the political processes, and as such were expected to be loyal in religion as in all other things. Though an English statesman like Francis Bacon could consider the possibility that some form of toleration of Catholicism, even if only temporary, was necessary in the Irish situation, the acceptance of religious pluriformity was regarded as a political weakness, and any concessions that had to be made would be withdrawn as quickly as possible, as the experience of the French Huguenots was to show. No legal toleration was extended to the Irish Catholics. In particular, the Court of Castle Chamber was now deliberately used as an instrument of harassment; but this court, despite the severe penalties it could inflict, was not able to keep up steady pressure at a local level. An increasingly rigorous insistence on the Oath of Supremacy effectively excluded Catholics from the central administration; but at local level the Old English Catholics remained politically powerful because of their wealth. The established church was too weak over most of the country to act as an instrument of either repression or evangelisation, though, especially at the times when crown courts were held locally, many Catholics certainly lived in fear of being presented as recusants. But the crown officials came and went, and authority rested essentially with the local magnates. They remained a substantial minority in the few parliaments called by the early Stuarts, but their thoughts turned more and more to trying to secure religious toleration by royal prerogative. At times during the reign of Charles I (1625-49) they seemed close to achieving this, but the great confiscations of the 1650s completely changed the terms of their problem.

The central figure in the great public demonstration of Catholic faith in Dublin on 1 February 1612 had been a bishop from Gaelic Ulster. This affords some indication that a new community might be forged in Ireland on the basis of Counter-Reformation Catholicism, but its forging was to be a long and painful process. The Old Irish would have found it difficult to adapt to the new political system even in the most favourable circumstances, but they had been conquered in a particularly ruthless war, and the confiscation of their property begun in the reign of Elizabeth had been greatly extended under James I, not only by the great plantation of Ulster but by substantial plantations in the Gaelic parts of Leinster and Munster. It was only natural that they should pin their hopes for a reversal of the plantations and the restoration of the Catholic religion on armed resistance backed by help from Spain.

The Irish situation was unique in Europe in that the religious recusants

were the great majority of the population. It was doubly unique because of
the way their church came to be organised. By the early seventeenth
century it was coming to be recognised that the religious division of the
Reformation was permanent. Europe was settling into a pattern of confessional states, each with its official religion but also with a religious
minority, beginning to enjoy a grudging factual toleration as it came to be
recognised that they too were to be permanent. In countries with a
Catholic minority the papacy provided for their organisation and pastoral
care by the appointment of vicars apostolic, that is, men in bishop's orders
but directly dependent on the papacy and not appointed to the historic
episcopal sees. It was politically realistic, but it was also fragile, depending
on the goodwill not merely of the government but of the local Catholics.
During the seventeenth century it worked in the United Netherlands, but
it failed in England.

The unique Irish situation did not quite follow this pattern. As already
noted, Pope Clement VIII (1592-1605), as part of his attempts to open up
political negotiations with the government of Elizabeth I, had appointed
in Ireland vicars apostolic who were not in episcopal orders but were
named to the historic sees. Though bishops were occasionally appointed,
the appointment of vicars apostolic not in bishop's orders became almost
papal policy in the early seventeenth century. It is still unclear when and
why this policy changed to one of appointing bishops. Archbishop Peter
Lombard of Armagh certainly influenced it. A native of Waterford, he had
been Hugh O' Neill's agent in Rome, and had been named archbishop in
1601 at O'Neill's request. When O'Neill was defeated this Old English
ecclesiastic had begun to urge the papacy that it could safely appoint
diocesan bishops in Ireland provided they were free from any taint of
association with O'Neill (in 1600 he had dismissed Conor O'Devany as a
person from whom no great help could be expected, because he would not
support the war, while in a long memorandum of 1612 he hinted that he
was precisely the kind of person who should not be appointed bishop in
Ireland).[3] When a separate Congregation of Propaganda was set up in
1622 to oversee the affairs of the 'mission' countries, which included
those in Europe where Catholicism was not the established religion, it too
favoured the appointment of bishops in Ireland. By about 1630 there was
a Catholic bishop in every Irish see. Quite uniquely in Europe, Catholic
Ireland had not a mission, but a church.

David Rothe of Ossory is rightly regarded as the 'founding father' of
this new episcopate. Like Lombard, he was of merchant stock, in his case
from Kilkenny. He had been prominent in the early days of the Irish
College in Douai, and his quest for funds for that struggling institution
had taken him first to Spain and then to Rome. Here he became Lombard's
confidant, and when he returned to Ireland in 1609 it was as
'vice-primate' in Lombard's name as well as vicar apostolic of his native

diocese of Ossory. In 1614 he presided over synods at Drogheda and Kilkenny to draw up regulations for the new Counter-Reformation mission. In 1618 he was appointed Bishop of Ossory. The fellow-bishops who soon surrounded him were the first generation from the continental seminaries. As a group, they were highly capable men, who enjoyed sufficient freedom of action to try to build up the Tridentine pattern of pastoral care which they had been trained to understand and to put into practice. The Council of Trent had built its hopes for Christian renewal on the good bishop in his diocese and the good priest in his parish. The parish church stood at the centre, providing Sunday Mass, sacramental life and catechetical instruction.

In Ireland, what war and neglect had left of the church buildings and what spoliation had left of parish revenues were in the hands of the established church. They would probably have been as much of a hindrance as a help even to a church which commanded the allegiance of a much greater proportion of the population. The Catholics were not altogether without resources. In particular, because there had been no suppression of chantries in Ireland, the substantial funds of the guilds had not been confiscated, and the now Catholic town merchants who administered them devoted them to some extent to the support of priests. In particular, the Catholics were free to ignore the old and often unsuitable parochial divisions: indeed, they were forced to do so because there were not enough priests. Priests were appointed to localities as they became available and as pastoral needs demanded. This gave the flexibility of a mission within the framework of a church. The new parish system which took shape often bore little relationship to the medieval parishes, but as it developed it was probably much more effective, especially in Gaelic Ireland, where the earlier parish system appears to have been at best untidy and in places defective.

The established church suffered from a shortage of ministers even more severely than did the Catholics. In this crucial generation the output of Trinity College could not match that of the Catholic continental seminaries. This forced a reliance on 'reading ministers', licensed only to read prepared homilies. Their religious outlook was uncertain, even, one sometimes suspects, to themselves. They were the end of a tradition, not the beginning of one. While they lasted, the 'reformed' church looked much more like the old 'unreformed' one than did its Catholic counterpart. When they went, the reformed church was even more strikingly the church of the New English.

The supply of Catholic priests from the seminaries kept growing, but these institutions were small and poor and in constant difficulties. It is not easy to arrive at even an intelligent estimate of the numbers of Catholic priests working in the country in the early seventeenth century. A report of 1623 put it at about 800 diocesan priests, about 200 Franciscans, and about 200 members of other religious orders. It is even more difficult to estimate how many of these priests had had a full Tridentine training. The approximately forty Jesuits had certainly had it. So must the approximately forty Dominicans, for that order had been greatly reduced in Ireland in the sixteenth century and had re-established itself from continental centres, chiefly in Spain. For the diocesan priests and the Franciscans, a figure of about 30 per cent with Tridentine training may not be altogether wide of the mark, perhaps a little more in the case of the Franciscans. So the Catholic church had its equivalent of 'reading ministers'. Their distribution may reasonably be presumed to have been uneven. The Old English, especially the town merchants, had had the leading role in establishing the seminaries. It followed naturally that the towns were best supplied with the 'new' priests. The friars concentrated their forces in them, and by the mid-1620s were able to lead a reasonably satisfactory community life behind the unrevealing façade of a large town house. At the other end of the scale, Gaelic Ireland was worst supplied, though the example of Conor O'Devany and the evidence of the Salamanca admission lists clearly indicate that the Counter-Reformation was beginning to have a notable impact here too.

These, then, were the men appointed to the new parishes, first by the vicars apostolic and then by the bishops, in order to build up the Tridentine pattern of pastoral care. As already mentioned, the flexibility of the new system had marked advantages. It also had its disadvantages, notably in that an important consideration in appointing a priest to a locality was whether he could maintain himself there. Particularly among the Old English the priest was frequently maintained by his still wealthy family or relations. This could sometimes mean that he was not amenable to episcopal control. Everywhere the clergy were dependent for their support on the laity, for neither bishops nor priests had any funds under their independent control.

Dependence on the laity and relative independence of the bishop produced an element of competition between the diocesan and religious clergy that led to highly disedifying public quarrels. Ireland was far from unique in this: in England such quarrels had in 1631 led to the collapse of an attempt to establish a vicar apostolic there.

The troubles in Ireland arose out of conflicts between the bishops on the one hand and the Cistercians and the friars, especially the Franciscans, on the other. The Irish Cistercians were comparatively few in number. They had been swept away by the dissolution of the monasteries, though it is possible that one group maintained continuity in the vicinity of Holy Cross, Co. Tipperary. Now they were experiencing a modest revival, springing from a reform that began in Clairvaux in 1615. Their troubles with the bishops arose when they claimed the right to appoint priests in the many parishes which had been impropriated to Cistercian monasteries before the Reformation.

The pressing of this claim led to some highly discreditable confrontations, at times even physical violence, but it was too far-fetched to be really sustained. The problems with the friars were more serious. In the second half of the sixteenth century, when Catholic bishops could be appointed only intermittently and the parish system was in tatters, the Franciscans in particular had manned the Catholic mission when there were few others to man it. To aid their ministrations to the people the Holy See had granted them very extensive missionary faculties, quite incompatible with the role envisaged by Trent for the diocesan bishop. The bishop was indeed the linch-pin of the whole Tridentine system. All pastoral care of the laity was to derive from his authority, even when exercised by exempt religious in their own churches. Their only exemption was in ordering their own lives within what the canon law recognised as 'exempt places', that is, their own religious houses.

The problem was intractable because there were real fears on both sides. The friars, now taken up into the Counter-Reformation movement at least as much as the diocesan clergy, feared that in the conditions they necessarily lived in in Ireland it might be difficult to establish a house that canon law would regard as an 'exempt place', so that if the law were strictly applied they might be completely subject to the bishop and scarcely distinguishable from the diocesan clergy; in addition, there was a natural human reluctance to abandon activities which were long established, with the permission of the Holy See, and which had brought much real credit to their orders. The bishops, for their part, feared that if the friars continued to minister with the same freedom as before, they themselves would lose control over activities it was not merely their right but their duty to supervise.

So friars and diocesans competed to serve the people. Inevitably, there were unseemly incidents, and the worst of them tended to occur at the emotive moment of funerals. All cemeteries were legally the property of the established church, but Catholics continued to be buried in them with Catholic rites. The Irish had traditionally preferred to be buried in monastic cemeteries, so that when the last trump sounded they might be well placed to claim clientship with the holy dead. While Trent had not made burial in the parish cemetery obligatory, it had laid down that the parish priest was entitled to a fee if a parishioner was buried elsewhere. The Irish bishops had further ruled that the cemeteries of the suppressed and deserted monasteries could not be regarded as 'exempt places', and that in consequence the parish priest had the right to conduct funerals in them. The religious naturally resented this, all the more so because the custom had grown up of making an offering for the restoration of the monastery at funerals in monastic cemeteries. Here were all the ingredients for particularly disedifying and public clerical quarrels, and they occurred.

Both sides naturally kept putting their case to Rome and seeking a solution there, hopefully in their favour. The Roman decision was long delayed, and in the end not altogether decisive. In fairness to the Roman authorities, it must be remembered that they were working within the framework of a canon law which envisaged the Catholic church as not merely tolerated but established, and which in consequence could not provide a ready-made solution for the quite exceptional conditions in Ireland. Ireland was exceptional even to the newly formed Congregation of Propaganda, being technically a 'mission' but nevertheless very substantially a 'church'. The question was carefully examined there, and Propaganda tended to favour the bishops' case, though it was hindered by longer-established institutions, notably the Holy Office, the source of independent faculties, and the datary, still claiming to be a source of independent appointments. A decision substantially in favour of the bishops was issued in 1626, and ten years later Propaganda, after a long and careful examination of all the circumstances, issued a kind of charter for the mission of the Catholic church in Ireland.

This document is a testimony to the competence and diligence of the Roman authorities, and while it may not have ended all conflicts, it certainly brought them under control. By this time, the mid-1630s, there is no doubt that substantial progress had been made in establishing a Catholic parish system. This is clear from a number of surviving *relationes status*, or reports on the state of their dioceses Catholic bishops were obliged to make to Rome at regular intervals, and is also confirmed by the detailed report on the diocese of Dublin drawn up by the Church of Ireland archbishop, Lancelot Bulkeley, in 1630. This report makes it clear that the established church had lost the battle for religious allegiance even in Dublin, apart from a few parishes in the immediate vicinity of the Castle. Elsewhere, if there is a Sunday service, the only people to attend may be the families of the minister and churchwarden. In some places there is no service, either because the church is not in sufficient repair or because there is no minister. Funds to rectify this situation are often in the hands of the local gentry, now Catholics, whose forefathers had cheerfully pocketed them during the great spoliation nearly a hundred years before.

The supply of priests for the Catholic mission was growing, and by now approaching adequacy, though as yet not all had a seminary training, and they were badly distributed, with the country parishes tending to be under-supplied, and with the less educated clergy. The bishops had some problems in exercising control, because the diocesan clergy were in one way or another dependent on the laity they served, and the regular clergy were reluctant to accept what the bishop insisted was his lawful authority. But there was a system, and it was working. The bishop carried out visitation of his parochial centres each year. His diocese was divided into deaneries, each committed to a rural dean or vicar forane. The priests of each deanery met regularly in conferences. In some cases it had been possible to arrange an annual retreat for all the clergy. This might have been more widely possible were it not for the tensions between diocesans and regulars. Only the Jesuits appear to have kept up relations sufficiently good to make them acceptable as retreat masters.

What these priests were trying to achieve was a religious practice based on the Tridentine reform. In some respects it had a revolutionary impact. It centred on regular sacramental practice based on sufficient catechetical instruction within the framework of the parish under the direction of the parish priest. It was he who had to sow and nurture the idea that the morally good and the religiously holy were aspects of one and the same ideal at the heart of the Christian life. To do this he had to have adequate theological instruction, for catechesis was central to the whole programme. In this, the seminary priest and the Protestant minister had more in common than might have occurred to them at the time. Both preached a 'religion of the book'. For the Protestant it was the Bible; for the Catholic it was books of dogmatic theology or 'controversies', if only because to be a Catholic now was to know why one was not a Protestant, and books of moral theology or 'cases of conscience', indispensable as a guide to turning the sacrament of penance into an instrument of personal regeneration. The priest's irreducible minimum of equipment was the *Catechism of the Council of Trent*, ordered by the council to be drawn up as a basic manual of instruction for priests, and published by Pope Pius V in 1566. It was a comprehensive survey of Catholic faith and morals: in practice, catechesis centred, as it did everywhere in the Catholic world, on loyalty to the church, appreciation of the Mass, and devotion to Mary.

The success in implementing this programme was uneven. Our most detailed information concerns the towns and their immediate surroundings. The general pattern which emerges is, as might be expected, that the programme was most successful in these towns, and in them among the more educated classes. Success tended to be more modest as one moved down the social scale and out into the countryside. Quite simply, it was easier for those literate in English to acquire the catechetical instruction now demanded. Catechesis of the illiterate, whether they spoke English or Irish, was necessarily more rudimentary. The first Catholic catechism in Irish, O'Hussey's *Teagasg Críosdaidhe*, published in Antwerp in 1611, was aimed primarily at Irish soldiers serving in the Low Countries. When Theobald Stapleton, an Old English diocesan priest from Kilkenny, published his catechism in Latin and Irish (*Catechismus seu Doctrina Catholica Latino-Hibernica*, Brussels 1639) he remarked that the catechesis of many illiterate Irish-speakers consisted only in teaching them the common prayers and the rudiments of their faith in Latin, which they memorised without understanding.

Bearing in mind, then, that the level of achievement gets lower as one moves out from the towns and down the social ladder, some reasonably firm generalisations are possible concerning what was actually achieved. Attendance at Mass gets great emphasis. Allowing for the fact that the evidence comes from clerical sources, which will naturally stress Mass attendance if only as a striking proof of the failure of the Act of Uniformity, there does emerge a real sense of communities being formed around the Sunday Mass. Mass was held in many places. Where Catholics were still propertied it was often in the houses of landlords and town merchants. Where they had lost their property it might be in the open air. But from an early date buildings for Catholic worship were tolerated. They might be called 'chapels' (the word 'church' being reserved for places of worship of the established religion) or, more disparagingly, 'Mass-houses'. Especially in the towns, however, they might have some pretensions to dignity, at least interiorly. The English traveller William Brereton, who visited Dublin in 1635, has left a description of the Jesuit Mass-house in Back Lane, in terms that suggest at the same time certain features of contemporary Jesuit baroque architecture on the continent and look forward to the Catholic chapels in Ireland during the next two centuries, an occasional example of which still survives:

> The pulpit in this church was richly adorned with pictures, and so was the high altar, which was advanced with steps, and railed out like cathedrals; upon either side thereof was there erected places for confession; no fastened seats were in the middle or body hereof, nor was there any chancel; but that it might be more capacious, there was a gallery erected on both sides and at the lower end.

In the mind of the Tridentine reformers, the parish church was also to be the place for the 'parish sacraments', especially baptism and marriage, and for the burial of the dead. These 'rites of passage', as the anthropologists call them, are clearly of great social significance to the kin-group. The task of the church was to relate them to the spiritual life of the individual Christian.

In civil law they fell within the competence of the established church, but by the 1630s a working compromise had been arrived at: Catholics first paid their fees to the Protestant minister (in the matter of marriage, for example, the fee was technically for a dispensation from the publication of the banns), and they were then free to seek the services of their own clergy. For a number of reasons, these services came to be normally provided in the home even in places where there was a chapel or Mass-house.

In regard to baptism and marriage, the Catholic church authorities express no concern that these sacraments are not received. In both cases, however, they do express concern that the occasion shall be seen as one of personal regeneration rather than as a strengthening of the kin-group. They try to insist, as the Council of Trent had insisted, that the number of godparents at baptism be limited to one or at most two, and that these godparents understand the spiritual obligations they are undertaking in regard to the newly baptised — this in place of the numerous godparents, sometimes little older than the child being baptised, that tradition had demanded to symbolise the bringing of the child into the extended kin-group.

Trent's legislation on marriage had to be modified in Irish conditions. The decree *Tametsi* of 1563 had laid it down that marriage between Christians was henceforth invalid unless celebrated before the bishop or parish priest, or a priest duly authorised by either, and at least two witnesses. Because this decree affected all Christian laity, it was further laid down that it was not binding in any parish until it had been promulgated there. Although a Catholic parish system was being built in Ireland, it had to function in quite unusual circumstances. The compromise reached in regard to *Tametsi* was that Catholics must marry before a priest, with at least two witnesses. This proved acceptable and workable.

The church authorities also expressed concern at the lavish feasting which took place at baptisms and funerals. One reason for the concern was religious: such feasting tended to emphasise the social character of the occasion — its significance to the kin-group — rather than its religious character. There was another reason too, not directly religious, but nevertheless affecting the well-being of the Catholic community. Many of the Old Irish in particular were not accommodating themselves well to the new world where being *flaithiúlach* in the traditional manner resulted in a bill to pay, and some of them were being forced to mortgage or even sell what land the plantations had left to them.

The greatest concern was expressed over the most emotive of the rites of passage, the burial of the dead. The concern attached not so much to the funeral, though attempts were made to suppress the traditional 'keening'. An accommodation had been reached with the established church about the cemeteries, and the quarrels between the diocesan and regular clergy proved controllable, however disedifying. Concern centred rather on the waking of the corpse, where the feasting and drinking and the licentious 'wake-games' were strongly marked with a pre-Christian and indeed un-Christian paganism, signifying the assertion of life by the kin-group in the very presence of death. The church had been trying to emphasise the religious character of the Christian's passing for long centuries, and even the Counter-Reformation church still had some centuries of work ahead of it here.

Penance too had to be transformed, by changing the previous emphasis on satisfaction as a regulation of external offences among feuding kin-groups into an emphasis on sorrow for personal sin in a sacrament of individual reconciliation with God. Catechesis was regarded as very important in relation to penance, for the sacrament could be received fruitfully only by a penitent acquainted with the truths of his faith and the. moral obligations of his Christian life. General catechesis was given by the priest at Sunday Mass, and in remoter areas it could be fairly elementary. There are passing references to Catholic schoolmasters, but their work does not come into clear focus. At this time the parish mission was being developed, particularly in France by St Vincent de Paul, but such missions seem to have been very rare in Ireland. The conditions under which parish life existed there were not conducive to them. Neither were the rivalries of the diocesan and regular clergy. As already noted, many of the guild confraternities had survived in the towns, and here too new clerically con-trolled confraternities were set up, especially by the religious orders.

Long-established social practices now manifest themselves because the Counter-Reformation clergy denounce them as abuses — the licentiousness of the wake-games, for example, the professional keening at funerals, the feasting and drinking associated with the 'rites of passage'. Some of the superstition revealed is indeed gross enough, the sheela-na-gigs, for example, those crude fertility images that had made their way into the church buildings. Superstition had also strongly marked the traditional 'patterns' on saints' patronal days or the 'patterns' associated with holy wells and holy trees. The brief of Pope Paul V in 1607 had indulgenced a number of these traditional pilgrimages, and the new Counter-Reformation episcopate in Ireland did try to incorporate them into the round of Christian life as they saw it. In this they were not successful.

Overall, however, they did have a real if necessarily limited success in imposing a new pattern of Christian living, based not on the kin-group, but on the parish, with a sense of the Christian life as resting on instruction and regular sacramental practice. Catholics lived pre-cariously, but their very numbers provided a powerful support. This became evident when the government closed chapels and ordered priests to leave the country in 1629, fearing, not without reason, that the Catholic church was well on the way to becoming the church of Ireland in fact if not in law. The disturbance was severe while it lasted, but it did not last for very long, for the government simply did not have the means to sustain the pressure.

The Catholic achievement was necessarily uneven. It was most successful among the propertied classes in the towns. The Old English in general developed a new sense of identity with Catholic Europe, especially with France. They spoke of 'a new plantation in religion', a 'new civility', much as their forefathers had had their hopes of a 'new civility' in the very different circumstances of the 1540s. Tridentine Catholicism had been implanted in Ireland, even if it did have to adapt somewhat to circumstances there. When Archbishop Rinuccini arrived as papal nuncio in 1645 he found much to displease him when he compared the situation in Ireland with what he knew in the papal states. The Irish, he said, were content with 'a Mass in their cabins', but he was not without hope that they might be reformed. As John Bossy has perceptively remarked, 'It was just as well for Irish Catholicism that he did not succeed.'[4] The Tridentine plan to concentrate all religious observance in the parish church turned out to have its weaknesses, while the strong emphasis on the home forced by circumstances on Irish Catholicism proved to have saving strengths.

There were even indications that their shared religion might be fusing the Old English and the Old Irish into a single nation, but the cultural and political divide was still great. How great was shown up by the stresses of the 1640s.

When the Old Irish rose in arms in Ulster on 23 October 1641 and expelled the planters from much of the province the first response of the Old English was to offer help to suppress them. Only when this was contemptuously rejected by the government did they consider joining them. By June 1642 they had formed a confederacy to defend their threatened interests. In March the English parliament had passed an act offering allotments of forfeited Catholic land in Ireland in return for contributions of money to suppress the rebels there. This act implied that all Irish Catholics were guilty of rebellion, and guilty too of the atrocities which had inevitably accompanied its outbreak in the planted lands, and which soon developed into the propaganda myth that all Catholics were equally guilty of Protestant blood.

At this time sectional interests were forming confederacies in all three kingdoms of Charles I. None regarded themselves as rebels against the crown. The Irish Catholic Confederates certainly did not so regard themselves. Their aims were summed up in the motto they adopted: 'For God, for king and country'. But it was already clear that there were great problems in serving the king while at the same time serving God the way they wanted to, and the crises of the 1640s were to prove that these problems were insoluble. As for country, what the Old English wanted was a guarantee of the property they still held, though it had come increasingly under threat, finally in the act passed by the English parliament in 1642. The Old Irish could ask for no less than the undoing of the plantations, and here the Old English were not prepared to back them.

From their capital at Kilkenny the Confederate Catholics controlled most of Ireland during the 1640s. In the areas they controlled they took over the churches and restored Catholic worship. But much of the energy of the bishops was absorbed in politics, for the Confederates immediately set out to reach agreement with the king, and it soon became apparent that the question of religion was the sticking-point. Even before the

Reformation the church had never been free of relations with the state, and a certain measure of control by the state. This relationship survived Reformation and Counter-Reformation. There were no guidelines or precedents to suggest how a Catholic church might work out a legal relationship with a Protestant king. Even the simpler problem of the French Huguenots was now facing difficulties. They had been granted a large measure of independence which went beyond mere toleration because of political necessity. Their problem was simpler because they did not owe religious allegiance to any authority outside the state, but they did 'divide the state with the king', and by now it was clear that this was unacceptable in the political thought of the time.

The negotiations with the king revealed the differences between the Old English and the Old Irish. It became apparent that the Old English would be satisfied with a toleration of Catholicism by royal prerogative if the rest of the settlement was satisfactory. They did not conceive it to involve a reversal of the plantations. This could not satisfy the Old Irish, and they were all the more inclined to press for a complete restoration of the Catholic religion as well because they had only a limited appreciation of the delicate checks and balances by which the Catholic church had so far managed to exist, and which had been the achievement of the political skills of the Old English. The Old English clergy were really caught in the middle. Their continental training had given them a keen appreciation of the position and prerogatives of the papacy, but they could not but be influenced by the concerns of the Old English laity, many of whom were close relatives.

Tensions heightened with the arrival of Rinuccini as papal nuncio to the Confederate Catholics in 1645. He was Archbishop of Fermo in the papal states, and to him it was unthinkable that the Catholic church in Ireland should be anything other than an established church. The predictable split came in May 1648, and Rinuccini sailed from Galway on 23 February 1649, leaving half the Irish Catholics excommunicated.

By this date the Old English had reached an agreement with the Lord Lieutenant, the Marquis of Ormond. It represented a hard-fought compromise. Ormond had finally agreed that the Catholics should not only retain the churches and church livings they actually held, but should continue to exercise *jurisdiction* in them. This was a key word, for it implied more than toleration by prerogative. It was added, however, that this arrangement was to last only until a final decision was reached by the king in parliament. This was unexceptionable in itself, for the anti-Catholic laws had been passed by 'the king in parliament' and could be repealed only in the same way. But it must remain more than doubtful whether Charles I would ever have agreed to such an arrangement even if he could emerge victor in his struggle with parliament. Throughout the long negotiations he had never regarded the Irish Catholics as more than

pawns in his English conflict, and here his final negotiations with
parliament had broken on his stubborn refusal to compromise on the
position of the established church.

The Irish agreement had been made possible at all only because it was
realised that the collapse of negotiations in England had put the king in
peril of his life. Agreement had been reached in Kilkenny on 19 January
1649, and on 30 January the king was executed in London. What backing
he might give to the agreement reached by his Lord Lieutenant was never
put to the test.

On 15 August 1649 Oliver Cromwell landed at Ringsend as commander
of the army of parliament for the conquest of Ireland. He found his
divided opposition easy prey. The massacres at Drogheda on 11
September and at Wexford on 11 October did not quell resistance as
Cromwell had hoped, but by the time he was forced to return to England
on 26 May 1650 he had bitten deep into the country. His son-in-law,
Henry Ireton, succeeded him as commander. He was more plodding than
Cromwell, but Galway, the last fortified city, surrendered on 12 April
1652. Sporadic resistance continued into 1653, but the war ended
without any formal terms of surrender. The English Commonwealth was
free to do what it wished with Ireland.

In fact the Commonwealth had no option but to confiscate Irish
Catholic property. This was necessary in order to meet the claims of the
'adventurers' who had subscribed money under the act of 1642, and also
to discharge the arrears of army pay. Under both heads it was necessary to
revive the propaganda about the 'massacre of 1641'. It was necessary in
the first instance to motivate the rank and file of the army to fight in
Ireland. There had been mutterings among English religious radicals that
the Irish too were only fighting for the right to worship God as they chose.
The mutterings were muted, for they were dangerous in the view of the
gentry and merchants who had been the real victors in the English civil
war. They too represented the adventurers. The debts to these and to the
army were so great that only a total confiscation of Catholic land could
discharge them. It was in consequence necessary to represent all Irish
Catholics as not only rebels but collectively guilty of Protestant blood.
Cromwell's massacre at Drogheda had taken place in a town which had
never been in the hands of the Confederate Catholics.

The plan which emerged was to confiscate all Catholic property in three
provinces — and part of Connacht — and in all the towns. The dispossessed were to get land grants in Clare, Galway, Roscommon and most
of Mayo. This confiscation proved substantially successful. A small
minority of Catholic proprietors got their estates back after 1660. Others,
with many merchants from the towns, made their way to exile in Catholic
Europe. Not all who received allotments in Connacht settled there: some
remained as tenants on lands they had formerly owned. The adventurers

and the army officers settled down as a new landlord class. Only a minority of the soldiers of the army turned their small grants into land and settled as farmers: the rest sold their rights to their officers. In all this great social upheaval there is still much detail to be worked out, even from what sources remain.

As for religion, it was to the new rulers of Ireland unthinkable that the Irish should continue to be Catholics. Cromwell had proclaimed the principle of liberty of conscience, and there can be no reasonable doubt that he believed in it, but it is a difficult principle to apply in practice. 'Popery' and the 'prelacy' of the established church were to be excluded, since they were contrary to Scripture. While the Act of Uniformity was repealed, and men were not compelled to attend services repugnant to their conscience, the state did keep a close watch over the practice of religion.

But if the Irish were not to be papists, it was by no means clear what they were to be. The state's programme to turn them into something else was even less effective than the mission the established church had hitherto mounted. Abhorrence of popery tended to become an abhorrence of papists, and a reluctance to see them made Protestants. There were not enough ministers to preach to them, and very few able to preach in Irish. The official *Directory* for public worship, adopted by the English parliament in 1645, was not translated into Irish. Commonwealth sources indicate that some Irish in some sense abandoned Catholicism, but reports of 'conversions' from Catholic sources in the 1660s indicate that the change was a very temporary one, taken under pressure. That pressure had begun to ease even before 1660.

Catholic priests were pursued relentlessly. While the war lasted many were executed, and a proclamation of 6 January 1653 extended to Ireland the English statute of 1585, making a priest guilty of treason by the very fact of his presence in the country. Some priests were executed under its terms, but as things settled down the government preferred to deport them. Very many left the country. How many it is impossible to say, but the figure of a thousand may not be altogether wide of the mark. More may have remained that might be suspected: a recently published document lists seventy-four Dominicans in Ireland in 1657, perhaps a fifth of their numbers in the 1640s.[5] It is impossible to count the priests who remained, because they necessarily led a very furtive existence. The parish system had broken down, and the wealthy Catholics who had given them so much protection in the past were now uprooted. They could not ask any of the laity for any protection. Most hid in the bogs, forests and mountains, and there are instances of some carrying on a daring ministry in disguise in the towns. There is evidence that priests were drifting back from the continent in the late 1650s. Archbishop Edmund O'Reilly of Armagh was in Ireland from October 1659 to April 1661. He listed the clergy in the ecclesiastical provinces of Armagh and Dublin. Their numbers were thin everywhere, with the curious but substantiated exception of the diocese of Meath. They were very thin in the province of Dublin, which to a great extent coincided with the area bounded by the Barrow and the Boyne from which it had been proposed to expel all Catholics.

By the end of the Commonwealth period it was possible to convoke provincial synods to take stock of the catastrophe, though not in the province of Dublin. In some respects the picture was gloomy indeed. The parish system of pastoral care had gone. The modest gains in Christianising the 'rites of passage' had been eroded. So had the modest aims of the catechetical programme. In a decade of great strain there had inevitably been a growth in superstition. But the ecclesiastics gathered at these synods set themselves to rebuild as before. A king was coming into his own again — Charles II was proclaimed in Dublin on 14 May 1660 — and they felt that he could not be unmindful of the fact that the last to defend his father's cause had been the Irish Catholics, or unmindful of what they had suffered at the hands of those who had executed him.

The restored king was personally well disposed. His mother was a Catholic, and he himself became a Catholic on his death-bed. Numbers of Irish Catholic gentry had helped to keep up his impoverished 'court' during his exile. But the undoing of the plantation was a political impossibility. Some Catholics did get their lands back. In the rich lands of the old Pale, much of them conveniently held by regicides, men of unimpeachable loyalty found themselves restored. So did some Butlers in Kilkenny and Tipperary. James Butler, Marquis of Ormond, the king's good servant in the 1640s, was created a duke on 30 March 1661 and appointed Lord Lieutenant of Ireland on 21 February 1662. He had no love for popery, but he was prepared to make an exception for papist Butlers.

Elsewhere, however, it was only by the most unusual good fortune that a Catholic could hope to be restored to his estates. Already under the Commonwealth a political alliance had been forged between the 'old Protestants' and the new Cromwellian landlords. They were now in a powerful position to defend what was already being called 'the Protestant interest'. The new landlords ended up easily enough in the established church. The days of religious radicalism were over. The former adventurers had never been very radical, and neither had some of the former army officers. In Ireland as in England these army officers became much less radical in the 1650s. They had inclined to some form of Presbyterianism rather than episcopacy because Presbyterianism placed religion as social control in the hands of the propertied classes, whereas episcopacy concentrated it in the monarchy. Social control now rested with the establishment. These men did not want to come under the terms of the proclamation of August 1660 banning all meetings of 'Papists,

Presbyterians, Independents, Anabaptists, Quakers and other fanatical persons'.

Poor Protestants were few in number outside certain areas planted earlier, notably in Ulster. The Cromwellian soldiery seem to have made remarkably little impact as a population group. It has been noted already that only a minority of them settled as farmers. Quite a number of these seem to have quickly melted into the Catholic population. It was not just their small numbers which caused this, nor the fact that perforce many of them married Irish Catholic wives. These men were the genuine religious radicals of England, and in Ireland they may well have found Catholicism more to their taste than the religion of the established church. There can be strange turns in religious thinking. Thomas Goodwin, Oliver Cromwell's chaplain, a bitter opponent of popery, had published a book of quite subtle theology on devotion to the Sacred Heart in 1652,[6] well before that devotion took shape in Catholic France later in the century.

It would be wrong to view the Irish Catholics as reduced to a common misery. As has been seen, a minority were restored to their estates. Much land was in Catholic hands in the four western counties, over 50 per cent in Galway. A great number of former proprietors ended up as tenants of large farms on advantageous terms, sometimes on lands they had previously owned. Mixed with these people going down in the world were people coming up in the world. They got these farms on good terms because when things settled down in the mid-1650s the new proprietors were only too happy to set land to anyone who could work it. These Catholic 'middlemen' were a feature of Irish life until the end of the eighteenth century, and the descendants of the former proprietors among them continued to enjoy great social respect. Propertied Catholics survived in the towns too, despite the exodus to the continent. Exceptionally, Dublin was a Protestant city — 75 per cent of its population in 1660 being of that religion. In Galway, on the other hand, Protestants were so few that they were barely able to discharge the civil offices, from which Catholics were rigorously excluded in all the towns. But in all of them, except probably Dublin, there were Catholic merchants. They were to build up their wealth and penetrate Dublin itself as the years went by.

Catholics were also rigorously excluded from parliament. The one Catholic elected in 1661 never took his seat. Apart from the 'patriot parliament' of 1689, the next Catholic to be elected to parliament was Daniel O'Connell. Society was polarised between a wealthy privileged 'Protestant interest' at one end and the Catholics at the other. Over most of the island that framework of squire, parish and parson which had provided the stability of pre-industrial England did not exist. The Irish Catholic did not relate to the parson but to his priest. Neither did he relate to his landlord, because he was alien to him in almost every way. Instead he related to the descendants of the old aristocracy, whether, exceptionally, they had kept their lands, or defied the confiscation and gone 'on their keeping' as tories, or accepted it and settled down as 'middlemen' in a diminished but still respected state. The Irish legal parish remained with all its medieval anomalies. In most areas Protestants were too few in number for it to have much religious significance. It never developed as a unit of local government because, among other things, Ireland never had the equivalent of the English Poor Law, which distributed relief through a parish system.

This great transfer of property from Catholics to Protestants influenced Protestant attitudes towards the conversion of Catholics. There might be something to be said for admitting those of them who were still propertied to the ranks of the privileged. There was everything to be said against the conversion of former proprietors. There was, it seems, a growing indifference as to what religion the poor professed. Little more will be heard of the Act of Uniformity, though in so far as it affected Catholics it was not to be repealed until 1793. In Protestant Armagh in 1670 the Earl of Charlemont at the request of Archbishop Oliver Plunkett curbed the zeal of the city magistrates who tried to enforce it. In Catholic Waterford — loyal Waterford — Catholics were allowed their Mass, provided it was not at the same time as the Protestant service, and provided no Catholic appeared in the streets during this time. A person could be a papist if he kept a papist's place.

So when the Catholic clergy set out to fill their ranks and rebuild their mission they had to do it in a radically changed society. Two crucial decisions were taken in Rome in the early 1660s. Both were unfortunate. The first was not to appoint bishops for the time being for fear of provoking the government. The second was to ordain priests as quickly as possible without adequate preparation. In consequence, the vicars apostolic and the few bishops in the country found it hard to organise a difficult clergy. Nor was a seminary background necessarily a guarantee against reversion. Terence O'Kelly had been one of the first students of the Irish College, Rome. Though he was expelled from the college, he succeeded in having himself appointed vicar apostolic of his native diocese of Derry shortly after he returned home. The diocese never came into the power of the Confederate Catholics: it was the only diocese not to have a bishop in the 1640s. Terence O'Kelly survived everything, living in public concubinage, not afraid to appeal to the civil authorities if danger seemed to threaten, until, to use his own word, he was finally 'unhorsed' by Archbishop Oliver Plunkett.

The attempts to reconstruct the Catholic mission in the 1660s were patchy and uncertain, and little information on them has survived. One document may stand as an example of the difficulties. It is a letter from a seminary priest to Propaganda seeking guidance. His tone is matter-of-fact, and he admits that his problem concerns those places where things are at their worst. Here, however, they are shockingly bad, at least to a serious-minded priest with a seminary formation. When people approached him seeking absolution he catechised them on their knowledge of their faith. Their answers appalled him. They told him there were three Gods, even four — the Father, the Son, the Holy Ghost and the Blessed Virgin: the Father became man, the three divine persons became man. Faithful to his training, he refused to absolve such people, though some priests did; in any case, priests visited the districts where they lived only occasionally, so that opportunities for confession were rare. He admitted that he had no convincing answer for a man who when refused absolution because of defective instruction said these were deep matters and quite beyond him: all he wanted was forgiveness for his sins.

Ormond had shown himself hostile to Catholics during the 1660s, but he was replaced as Lord Lieutenant in 1669, and at the same time Rome began to nominate new bishops. Soon most sees were filled, and reconstruction could really get under way. Like the first generation of Counter-Reformation bishops at the beginning of the century, these were highly capable men. Archbishop Oliver Plunkett of Armagh is the best remembered: his heroic and saintly death outshone his sometimes contentious life. The government regarded John O'Molony of Killaloe as the most capable of them all. Others stand out clearly for their broad humanity as well as for their religious dedication, notably Luke Wadding of Ferns and John Brenan of Waterford and Lismore, later Archbishop of Cashel.

There was nothing new or dramatic about their programme. They sought to build up an adequate clergy to staff the parishes and to provide adequate catechesis, Sunday Mass and the sacraments. The thatched Mass-house now became the rule in the rural south. There were times when the landlord gave help to build it, but there were times too when he would not even give a site, so that people had to gather in the open air at the Mass-rock. This was very common in the planted areas of Ulster. In the towns the Mass-house sometimes had more pretension to dignity, but even here the public practice of religion had to be carried out with a certain furtiveness. In Waterford, it will be remembered, Catholics had to remain in their houses during the hour of Protestant service.

Much of the Old English area is sufficiently well documented to allow a fairly detailed picture. The will of Bishop James O'Phelan of Ossory (1669-95) indicates that many Catholics in his diocese were in reasonably comfortable circumstances — not just those who had got back their lands because of the patronage of the Duke of Ormond, but also a number of town merchants, some of whom had fled from Kilkenny when it fell to Cromwell in 1650. There were a number of Catholic schools, concentrated in the city, which is further evidence of a substantial middle class there. Two sets of diocesan regulations (1672, 1676) and a *relatio status* (1678) fill in the detail. In 1678 Bishop O'Phelan had 56 priests, 28 diocesans and 28 regulars, but they were badly distributed, too many in Kilkenny and not enough in the country districts. Though most of them had been educated abroad, the bishop did not pitch his hopes too high. All priests were to have the catechism (presumably the *Catechism of the Council of Trent*) and a book of moral theology or 'cases of conscience'; there is no mention of any further equipment for dogmatic theology or 'controversies'. Clearly not all country priests were able to preach, for those who were not and could only give basic catechesis at Sunday Mass were ordered to get the services of a preacher at least every three months. The basic prayers were also to be recited publicly at Mass on Sunday, and after Mass the priest was ordered to recite the psalm *De profundis* for the dead. Bishop Brenan of Waterford made the same regulation. This appears to be the first reference to what became the practice in Ireland. It has traditionally been explained as a substitute for the Masses for the dead suppressed at the Reformation.

A distinct rigorism appears in Bishop O'Phelan's attitude to the dispositions needed to receive the Eucharist. It certainly suggests the influence of Jansenism. He had been exiled to France as a young priest in the early 1650s, when the Jansenist debate was raging there, precisely on this issue. The synods convened about 1660 had felt it necessary to issue warnings about Jansenism, despite their fairly desperate immediate preoccupations. But, as will be seen, not all bishops who spent the 1650s in France were rigorists, and there were rigorists who had not come under French influence. Nor did the fact that an Irish bishop was a rigorist in the matter of the Eucharist necessarily stamp him as a Jansenist. Bishop O'Phelan still had to order the burning of sheela-na-gigs. So had his neighbour John Brenan in Waterford. Something older than Trent, even older than Christianity, was still rooted in the Irish countryside.

Diocesan regulations for 1672 and 1676 and an extensive correspondence bring Bishop John Brenan and his diocese of Waterford and Lismore into focus. Some Catholic landowners had been restored in the Ormond part of the diocese in Co. Tipperary. There were also prosperous Catholic middlemen. Some Protestant landlords were helpful, but others were hostile. The bishop had good relations with the Protestant bishop and clergy, who were content if they got their fees for the parish sacraments and the Catholics kept a low profile. But no Catholic schools were allowed in the diocese, unlike neighbouring Ossory. The bishop had thirty diocesan priests and twenty regulars, but again the distribution was bad. Waterford city had sixteen of the fifty priests, three diocesans, three Jesuits, five Franciscans and five Dominicans, to serve a Catholic population probably not much greater than 3,000. And, as in Ossory, the country priests were sometimes unable to preach, and had to ensure the services of a preacher at least every three months. There were problems still clinging to wakes and funerals, and the observances at patterns were now less Christian and more secular and superstitious. Yet the bishop was reasonably optimistic:

> The people, generally speaking, are very religious, leading a Christian life without great faults or many scandals. They are most devoted to the Catholic faith and have great reverence for the apostolic see, and I hope, through the divine mercy, that in future they may be able to receive more instruction so as to make more progress in Christian virtue.

The heartland of the old Pale, the counties of Meath and Louth, emerge from the correspondence of Oliver Plunkett (Louth is in the diocese of Armagh) and a set of diocesan statutes drawn up by Bishop Cusack of Meath in 1686. Here a number of Catholics had been restored to their lands, and this made for easier relations between them and the Protestants. The diocese of Meath, as has been seen, was well supplied with clergy even in 1660. In the comparatively relaxed years of the early 1670s Archbishop Plunkett was able to open a school in Drogheda. It was run by the Jesuits, and its primary purpose was to train young men for the priesthood, but Protestants attended it. Bishop Cusack's statutes show that he had a low opinion of his clergy, especially the regulars, and his overall rigoristic approach might suggest Jansenist influence, were it not for the fact that he had been a fellow-student with Oliver Plunkett in Rome. Yet his rigorism is undeniable; indeed, his diocesan regulations achieved a wider notoriety when they were cited by the canonist pope of the middle of the eighteenth century, Benedict XIV, himself no laxist, as an example of how *not* to run a diocese.

The area where the social conditions and religious life of Catholics emerges most clearly is Old English Wexford. Bishop Luke Wadding of Ferns, who died in 1691, kept a notebook which has survived in the detritus of the centuries. In it he recorded many details of his life and work. At about the same time William Molyneux was collecting information for an 'Atlas' planned by the English publisher Moses Pitt. He assembled three accounts of Co. Wexford. One was written by a Cromwellian army officer turned planter, Solomon Richards, and contains information on the practice of 'popery' he saw all around him. The author of the second account, Robert Leigh, is a very interesting person. He was a Catholic of the Old English stock who had performed many services for Charles II during his exile. After 1660 his eldest brother was restored to the family estates at Rathangan, Co. Kildare, while Robert was rewarded with an estate at Rosegarland, Co. Wexford. There were good reasons why he should have little to say about popery, but he does provide valuable information on the Old English. The third author, whose information is confined to the heartland of the Old English, the barony of Forth, is even more interesting. Though he does not name himself, it is clear that he was a Catholic, and he was probably a priest. His special interest in the Sinnott family strongly suggests that it was his own.

The Old English of Wexford had not been restored to their property. Yet the commerce of New Ross was in their hands, and there were Catholic merchants in Wexford. The old proprietors were still there in the barony of Forth, but now as tenants on the lands they had formerly owned. Bishop Wadding was himself of Forth stock, of a family which had held lands at Ballycogley. His father, a younger son, had settled in Wexford town as a merchant. In his notebook the bishop refers to a 'Cousin John Wadding' still at Ballycogley, but now as a tenant. What the great upheaval meant to a society of small gentry substantially undisturbed since the Norman conquest appears vividly in a single phrase. The bishop was listing some family heirlooms that had survived the catastrophe. Among them was 'a small glass bottle of blood which hath been at the castle of Ballycogley since my predecessors first came, what blood it is I know no more than that it was esteemed to be a drop of our Saviour's blood, brought by one Gilbert Wadding who was at the taking of Jerusalem by Godfrey duke of Lorraine'. It does not have quite the soaring arrogance of the Gael — like Aodhagán Ó Rathaille, dying in poverty but consoling himself that his bones will rest with the MacCarthys, 'na flatha fá raibh mo shean roimh éag do Chríost' — but it does reveal a depth of pride in the Norman centuries.

The same sense of nostalgia amid the ruin appears powerfully in the anonymous writer we may call Father Sinnott. Forth is his loved native place — 'the whole barony, at a distance viewed in time of harvest, represents a well-cultivated garden'. There are now ruins in the garden, the eighteen churches and thirty-three chapels destroyed during the Commonwealth, and the

> very many crosses[7] in public roads, and crucifixes, in private houses and chapels in the said barony kept, builded of stone, timber or metal, representing the dolorous passion of our Saviour Jesus Christ, which, wherever found, were totally defaced, broken or burned by Cromwellian soldiers.

But the people were still Catholic, hard-working and sober people keeping feast and fast and waking and burying their dead devoutly and soberly. They had their own special devotions, such as the great pilgrimage to Our Lady's Island, one of those indulgenced by Pope Paul V in 1607, the first detailed description of which comes from Solomon Richards. They sang their own distinctive carols during the 'twelve days of Christmas', as they still do in one parish. Bishop Luke Wadding had two 'old script carol books', an indication that the practice went back to medieval times.

The bishop, whatever his pride in the Norman centuries, was very much a man of his own times. His extensive library (over seven hundred works) shows that he was steeped in the theological learning of the Counter-Reformation and had some interest in the humanities, in English and even to some extent in French. He seems to have been attracted to the English Metaphysical poets, Crashaw in particular. Like Bishop O'Phelan of Ossory, he had spent the 1650s in exile in France, but here he had attached himself not to the Jansenists, but to the more humanist traditions of the Jesuit and especially the Salesian schools. He was a good pastoral bishop. He bought manuals and catechisms by the dozen for distribution among his people, and beads and medals by the gross, some in France, but some in Wexford and New Ross. He built up the Catholic community in Wexford town — the baptism and marriage registers he began in 1671 have continued unbroken since — while keeping a friendly relationship with Protestants that stood him in good stead when he was arrested during the Popish Plot crisis in 1678.

There is much less information on what has been well called the 'permanent substratum of society', largely Gaelic except in the towns and in exceptional areas like Forth and Fingal. Much of what information there is comes from outside and unsympathetic observers, for the literary class of Gaelic Ireland is preoccupied with the past, lamenting the fall of its nobility and castigating the 'upstarts', whether they be the new landlords or the rising middlemen. Some information on the problems of Gaelic Ulster emerges from the correspondence of Archbishop Oliver Plunkett, supplemented by his provincial synods and a synod of the diocese of Kilmore in 1687. In Ulster only two or three Catholics were still landed, and the only great landowner, the Marquis of Antrim, was deeply in debt. A number of former landowners were now reasonably prosperous tenant farmers. They still enjoyed social deference. So did the 'tories', those who kept up the fight against the confiscations, and who were more numerous in Ulster than anywhere else.

The archbishop, with his Roman background, was inevitably concerned by serious problems among the clergy: problems of celibacy, problems of drunkenness, problems of lack of theological and seminary formation, problems arising simply from the continuing strength of the old ways. Some were unable to give even elementary catechesis. In consequence, the old ways were still strong among the laity. In so far as the laity do emerge, they appear as a deeply traditional society, with its quarrelsomeness and superstitions tending to surface in its most deeply rooted religious observances, patterns, pilgrimages, wakes and funerals. There may have been some success in bringing marriage closer to the Christian norms, if only because the aristocratic lifestyle which supported the traditional laxities had vanished. But outside observers do appear to have been shocked by what they saw at wakes and funerals. An English visitor, John Dunton, who was certainly not squeamish, seems genuinely shaken by what went on at wakes, while Sir Henry Piers, who compiled the information on Westmeath for the Molyneux survey, speaks of what happened at wakes and funerals: the lewd obscene dancing, excessive drinking, broken heads and drunken quarrels, the keening — or, as he puts it, 'howling' — mourners accompanying the funeral, pausing regularly at the ritual heaps of stones on the way to say a prayer and 'raise the howl' again.

Great material ruin had come on the Irish Catholics since the beginning of the century, but they still had a recognisable middle class, even a landed class. The ruin had come upon them in great measure because of their adherence to the Catholic religion, and in some respects that religion was drawing them together, though Gaelic Ireland remained a place apart, nursing its traditions and its secrets. In other respects the middle-class Old English Catholics seemed to be reaching some social accommodation with Protestants: as Sir William Petty, that pioneer of social observation, put it, condescendingly but not inaccurately:

> There is much superstition among them, but formerly much more than is now; for as much as by the conversation of Protestants, they became ashamed of their ridiculous practices, which are not *de fide*. As for the richer and better educated sort of them, they are such Catholics as are in other places. The poor, in adhering to their religion, which is rather a custom than a dogma amongst them, they seem rather to obey their grandees, old landlords, and the heads of their septs and clans, than God.

This emerging accommodation was disrupted by the 'Popish Plot', concocted in 1678 to exclude the Catholic Duke of York from succession to the throne. There were proclamations for the banishment of all priests. Peter Talbot, Archbishop of Dublin, was arrested and was to die in prison. In 1680 Edmund Borlase published his *History of the Execrable Irish Rebellion*, renewing all the fears of papist bloodthirstiness. On 1 July 1681 Archbishop Oliver Plunkett was executed at Tyburn, one of the last victims of the plot, a victim of political intrigue and condemned by a travesty of justice, because a popish plot could have no credibility without an Irish dimension, and an Irish dimension to a popish plot could have no credibility unless a popish bishop was involved in it. His death at the end of the century may be balanced against that of Conor O'Devany at its beginning. The Palesman died as bravely, and as innocently, at Tyburn as the man from Gaelic Ulster had died on George's Hill seventy years before. They both died for the same reasons.

The scare died down as suddenly as it had begun: the fact that there never was a plot made it hard to sustain the hysteria. When Charles II died in 1685 the Duke of York succeeded as James II. He might well have sustained his position had he shown more political wisdom, or if he had not had the political misfortune to have fathered, quite unexpectedly, a Catholic heir to the throne. When William of Orange was called in the

Irish Catholics rallied to James II. In 1689 he called an Irish parliament. It was dominated by the Old English Catholics. They demanded toleration of two churches in Ireland. They also demanded a reversal of the plantations that had taken place since 1640, that is, those plantations that had affected themselves, not those that had affected the Old Irish. It is doubtful whether James II could have done anything to give effect to these demands, doubtful indeed whether he wanted to give effect to them. Like his father, Charles I, he had scant interest in the concerns of the Irish Catholics, seeing them only as useful support for his cause. In any case, again like his father, his resolution was not put to the test, for he lost the war.

The Treaty of Limerick, signed on 3 October 1691, promised the Irish Catholics the religious privileges which they had enjoyed in the reign of Charles II, or as were consistent with the laws of the realm, and held out the hope of further concessions. It also guaranteed the property rights of those who had not already surrendered. The religious clauses were less favourable than those wrung from Ormond in the extraordinary circumstances of January 1649, in that the most they promised was toleration of the Catholic church, not recognition of it. They were also riddled with uncertainties and ambiguities as to precisely what toleration the Catholics had enjoyed under Charles II — it had varied greatly at different times — and what toleration, if any, might be consistent with the laws of the realm. Soon these knotty questions ceased to matter, for the treaty was not honoured.

The

Secret People

It was optimistic to expect that the Treaty of Limerick would be honoured. The loose and bad drafting of the articles concerning religion made it easier to break, but the opportunity to break it was provided by the international situation. The war in Ireland had been part of a wider struggle, which was resolved in favour of William of Orange and against Louis XIV of France by the Treaty of Ryswick in 1697. This consolidated William's position as king in England, Scotland and Ireland.

William was not personally in favour of religious persecution. He himself was a Calvinist and had been formed in the relatively tolerant Netherlands, where, however, he had already shown that he would not allow personal conviction to override reasons of state. Already by 1695 his second Irish parliament had passed anti-Catholic laws, and after Ryswick the fears of the 'Protestant interest' ensured the rapid passing of a substantial body of legislation that has come to be known as the 'penal code'. It was effectively complete by the end of the reign of Anne (1702-14).

Though the penal code contained numerous provisions which if put into effect would have extinguished the Catholic church in Ireland, its basic concern was not with religion but with property, above all with landed property, for ownership of land was the key to political power. The proportion of land in Catholic hands fell from 59 per cent in 1641 to 22 per cent after the Cromwellian confiscation and to 14 per cent after the Williamite attainders. It was to fall to about 5 per cent during the eighteenth century under the provisions of the penal code. This prescribed that Catholic land was to be inherited by 'gavelkind', that is, divided among all the sons in the family. If one of them became a Protestant, he was to be the sole heir. This provided a very material incentive to landed Catholics to conform to the established church. Legislation of 1709 ensured that Catholics could not acquire freehold land — all the law allowed them was a lease for thirty-one years on onerous terms. The law of 1709 introduced the 'discoverer', who, if he could show that a Catholic had acquired land illegally, could claim the land as his own.

Catholics had been in practice excluded from parliament since 1660. Now they were legally excluded, by the introduction of an oath for members which no Catholic could take. Since 1661 Catholics had been effectively excluded from town corporations, closed bodies perpetuating themselves by co-option. This should logically have excluded them from the economic life of the towns. In practice, they were rigorously excluded from manufacture but not from trade, in particular the important provisions trade, where many of them prospered. All the professions except medicine were closed to them.

Legislation concerning marriage continued until 1745, longer than in any other matter. Once again, however, the concern was with property, not religion. The established churches of Ireland and England had no legislation comparable to the Tridentine decree *Tametsi* for Catholics. Marriage continued to be governed by the medieval consensus of the canon and civil law, which had accepted marriage as valid solely by the mutual consent of the parties, and as lawful or 'regular' if celebrated before a validly ordained clergyman, however irregular that clergyman might be. This manifestly unsatisfactory situation was remedied in England by the 'Hardwicke Act' of 1754, in itself unsatisfactory in that it laid down that all marriages, except those of Jews, Quakers and the royal family, were invalid unless duly celebrated in the parish church. In Ireland, on the other hand, there never was, and indeed never has been, any civil legislation regulating the marriage of Catholic and Catholic. From early in the eighteenth century, however, there was a series of enactments imposing increasingly severe penalties on Catholic priests officiating at marriages where one or both of the parties was a Protestant; this was because such marriages were valid in civil law, which recognised the priest as validly ordained. The offence was made a felony in 1725, and a few priests were sentenced to death under this provision, which remained law until 1833. In 1745 such marriages were declared null and void in law, a provision which lasted until 1870.

So the basic concern of the penal code was to preserve property and power in Protestant hands. As regards the practice of the Catholic religion, there were two logical choices, either to mount a serious campaign to convert the Catholics to Protestantism, or to allow them freedom of religious practice under strict control. What actually happened was the prohibition of Catholic religious practice by a series of laws which soon proved ineffective.

The established church lacked the means to mount a serious campaign of evangelisation. In any case, like most establishments at the time, ecclesiastical as well as political, it showed only intermittent concern at the religious state of the mass of the population. In the early eighteenth century in Great Britain, and even more in Ireland, 'popery' was essentially a political question. 'Popery in the gross', as it was sometimes referred to, was seen as a political threat to the settlement consolidated in the revolution of 1688, and a real threat as long as life remained in the

Jacobite cause. The only papists whose conversion could bring political advantage were the few surviving Catholic landowners. Archbishop William King of Dublin (1703-29) was one of those who seriously considered mass evangelisation — he had encouraged the teaching of Irish in Trinity College in order to supply suitable clergy. But he too grew disillusioned: as he remarked in a letter of 21 July 1724:

> It is plain to me by the methods which have been taken since the Reformation, and which are yet pursued by both the civil and ecclesiastical powers, that there never was or is any design that all should be Protestants.[1]

So fear of 'popery in the gross' led to the introduction of far-reaching laws against Catholic religious practice, and failure of political will led to their not being rigorously enforced. The Banishment Act of 1697 ordered all regular clergy and all clergy exercising jurisdiction to leave Ireland by 1 May 1698. The great majority went, and the few who remained found some shelter in the provisions of the Registration Act of 1704. This ordered all diocesan clergy to register with the civil authorities, to indicate the parish or parishes where they ministered, and to provide two sureties of £50 each for their continuing good behaviour. The names of a few bishops and a number of religious may be detected among the 1,089 who registerd as parish priests. The long list of laymen who went surety is even more interesting, but it has not yet got the attention it deserves.

What the act proposed was the gradual extinction of the Catholic priesthood in Ireland, because it made no provision for successors to those who registered. The plan broke down completely in 1709. In March 1708 there had been an unsuccessful Jacobite attempt to land in Scotland. In the ensuing scare an oath of abjuration of the Jacobite cause was tendered to the Catholic clergy. It was couched in terms so uncompromising that some Protestants might have difficulty in taking it, if only because Anne was the last Stuart Protestant in the direct line of succession and it was quite uncertain what might happen when she died. In fact only a handful of Catholic priests took the oath, and, faced with this mass refusal, the government was left wondering what to do. It found that its powers to do anything effective were limited.

Priests who had not taken the oath — that is, all except perhaps about forty — lost their status under the Registration Act. They had to endure a sharp harassment for some years. Lay Catholics might be summoned on oath to testify where they had last heard Mass and who had been the celebrant. There emerged a new type of 'popish discoverer', who was rewarded for turning in priests. It was not a highly regarded occupation. There was some sympathy even among Protestants for priests who had refused to take the oath. Soon these 'discoverers' were being referred to by what was accepted as the derogatory term of 'priest-catchers'. John Garzia, one of the most noted, embarrassed the government by capturing Edmund Byrne, Archbishop of Dublin, in 1718. When the archbishop finally appeared in court over a year later Garzia was not there to charge him. It seems certain that his absence had been deliberately arranged by a government unwilling to face international criticism.

Even humbler victims could cause a certain embarrassment, and the priest-catcher's trade was risky, because even in Dublin he could be set on by the Catholic mob. Further down the country the police powers of the government could be very limited and in the remoter areas almost non-existent. In so far as they could be exercised, their principal effect seems to have been to turn the Catholic priest into a kind of folk hero to replace the diminishing group of tories. By the time the second Hanoverian had succeeded to the throne, say about 1730, the persecution had tapered off. The Protestant succession now seemed reasonably secure, but so was the Catholic church. Almost every diocese now had its bishop, and a parish system was well on the way to being re-established. There were weaknesses in what had been achieved, but by any measure it was remarkable, and by now it was accepted by the government. On 1 August 1739 the *Dublin Daily Post* reported the death of Bishop Peter Mulligan of Ardagh, 'late titular bishop of that see...a religious man of the order of the Hermits of St Augustine...one of the most profound humility and unfeigned piety'. This respectful obituary takes no notice of the fact that he was triply in breach of the law, in not having taken the oath of abjuration, in being a regular, and in being a bishop.

Acceptance of popery did not mean an end to fears of popery. It was in fact these fears which generated the report presented to the House of Lords in 1731 and which is the chief source for information on the details of the Catholic reorganisation. This report also shows up clearly that hitherto elusive figure, the Catholic schoolmaster. The prohibition on Catholics teaching school had come as early as 1695, and schoolmasters as well as priests had been harassed during the bad years. The 1731 report showed that this harassment had been completely ineffective, and the main government response to the fears it generated was to set up the Charter Schools in 1733, with the avowed purpose of making Protestants of the children of the poor.

Though this proposal met with little more success than other government tentatives, it did arouse Catholic fears and led the clergy to assess their mission for possible weaknesses. Fears were expressed that there were in fact too many priests in the country, friars and diocesans, and that too many of them had been ordained with quite insufficient preparation. It is true that a small number of bishops ordained priests too easily, and that the friars were rapidly increasing in numbers (the priesthood was one of the very few careers open to Catholics). From the inquiries made there emerged what can be regarded as in some sense statistical information, certainly firm enough to allow some conclusions to be drawn. Many of the parishes were too large and needed either division or the appointment of an assistant priest or curate (this had been forbidden by the 1704 Registration Act, and though that act was now largely past history, the appointment of an assistant was still illegal). The overall number of the clergy was not excessive, but they were badly distributed and some were poorly equipped for their mission. Finally, there were so many friars in proportion to the diocesan clergy that their numbers did pose a problem if pastoral care were to be on the Tridentine model of a parish system.

The decisions were made by the papacy. The pope at the time was Benedict XIV (1740-58), a distinguished figure at a time when distinguished popes were few. He was a skilled canonist and also deeply influenced by the Catholic Enlightenment. In consequence, it is not surprising that his decision, announced in 1751, was heavily weighted against the friars in Ireland. They were to be at the bishop's disposition to a greater extent than elsewhere, though Benedict was taking somewhat similar decisions for the universal church. All novices now had to be sent abroad for training. Within a short time there was a marked decline in the friars' numbers, which was not really reversed for more than a century, by which time they had to share their mission as regular clergy with more recently introduced orders and congregations.

Diocesan priests were obliged to go to the continental seminaries for a course in theology after ordination. This decision to allow them to be ordained first was based on a consideration that they could support themselves at least to some extent by their ministry while pursuing their studies, for the seminaries, increasingly concentrated in France, were not over-endowed. Unfortunately many of them found the ministry in *ancien régime* France congenial and did not return. By the end of the eighteenth century there may be indications that there were not enough Catholic priests in Ireland to minister to a growing population.

Overall, however, the mission of the clergy became more effective as the century advanced because their quality improved. Ireland was at peace after many wars, and this third reorganisation of the Catholic diocesan and parish system was to prove permanent. Before an attempt is made to assess what they achieved some account must be taken of the marked regionalisms within the country, regionalisms which had been clear since the first reorganisation at the beginning of the seventeenth century, and which had indeed been present before the Reformation.

Dublin, which had been largely Protestant in 1660, now appears as a city where the Catholics had become a majority, and where Catholic life is relatively well documented. The basic reason for the change was the great growth in its population, approximately 45,000 in 1685, 92,000 in 1725, and 140,000 in 1760. The Catholic poor were concentrated in the older and increasingly unfashionable quarter of the Liberties, but here too lived those who had prospered in trade, for especially in Dublin, the seat of government and parliament, Catholics kept a prudently low profile. But even here the Mass-houses were closed only intermittently even in the worst years immediately after 1709, and by 1730 Dublin had its parish system and parish chapels, with several chapels of friars. These chapels are shown graphically on Rocque's map of 1756, built in back yards, where they expanded irregularly to fill the space available; the entry was through a discreet alleyway and not directly from the street. Yet even by this date there are indications that interiorly they offered some of the dignity of worship, both in their furnishing and decoration and in the services provided. Even before this there is evidence that Catholic and Protestant were learning to live together. In his will Archbishop Luke Fagan (1729-33) left £15 'for the use of the charitable infirmary'. This, the first voluntary hospital in Great Britain or Ireland, had been founded in Cook Street in 1718 by six surgeons, Catholics and Protestants. It still — at least at the time of writing — keeps its independent existence in Jervis Street, where it moved in 1786.

The Catholic organisation was even more solidly based in the smaller towns, further removed from the central government and with a Catholic merchant community more firmly established: some at least of these merchant families seem to have maintained continuity through all the upheavals of the seventeenth century. But here too Catholics had to keep their place. In Wexford the chapel built inside the walls by Bishop Luke Wadding at the end of the seventeenth century had fallen into disrepair and had to remain so. The parish clergy and the Franciscans shared the friars' chapel, tolerated because it was outside the walls. Here the Catholics worshipped, undisturbed but discreetly: in 1751 Bishop Sweetman felt it necessary to assure the government that no bell summoned them to Mass, for that was the legal prerogative of the established church. In distant Galway the few Protestants were barely able to staff the municipal offices. The special attention given to the town in the 1731 inquiry indicates how insecure they felt themselves to be. But even here, at the opposite pole from Dublin, the pattern was the same — practical toleration of a discreet round of Catholic observance. In 1731 the sheriffs duly searched the three friaries and three nunneries, and duly reported that they could find nobody. The surviving account books of the Augustinians and Dominicans record the spending of money on 'claret to treat the sheriffs in their search', one bottle at the Augustinian friary, two bottles at the Dominicans, which suggests a reasonably civilised co-existence between two groups who had real reason to fear one another.

Connacht began the century with a fairly numerous Catholic gentry. Inevitably, numbers conformed under the pressures of the penal code, in particular the Gavel Act. Here as elsewhere the numbers conforming rose sharply after about 1760. The explanation must probably be sought in the spread of ideas of the Enlightenment, raising the question of whether the difference between being a Protestant and a Catholic was sufficient to justify putting one's estate in jeopardy. The Gavel Act was repealed in 1778, and it is surely no coincidence that shortly afterwards the numbers of conformists declined steeply. In any case, the evidence seems to indicate that those Catholic landowners who conformed were still held in the same social respect. So were former landowners now reduced to the status of farmers, like Hugh O'Donnell of Larkfield, Co. Leitrim, commonly referred to simply as 'the earl' because he was considered to be the legitimate heir to the title conferred on Rory O'Donnell in 1603.

Connacht, then, the least disturbed of the Irish provinces, shows all the appearances of a traditional society, where Catholics and Protestants had learned to live together, though there are indications that landed Catholics were very conscious of how precariously they lived. Though there are instances of Catholics having to meet for Mass in the open air because the landlord would not give a site for a chapel, the reason why there was a Mass-rock instead of a Mass-house was more commonly because the community was too poor to build one.

Ulster, by contrast, was where the old patterns had been most disturbed, especially in that a sizeable Protestant population had been settled there, especially in the east, and there was scarcely a Catholic landowner, apart from the Earl of Antrim. There was a great deal of poor land in the west of the province, and the Catholics were concentrated on it. The returns for Ulster in the 1731 inquiry are less full than those for the other provinces, but they do indicate that here more than elsewhere it was difficult to establish a parish structure. The number of priests appears reasonably adequate, but in Ulster more than anywhere else it was hard for a priest to get a continental education: the 1704 registration shows only nine of the 189 priests in the nine counties of Ulster as having been ordained abroad. Mass-rocks were far more numerous than Mass-houses. The old ways lingered most of all among the Ulster Catholics precisely because of the degree of misfortune they had suffered.

Leinster and Munster had much in common. Though there were poor areas of bogland and mountain, the two provinces contained most of the good land of Ireland and enjoyed the kinder half of its climate. The Catholics had suffered severely in the seventeenth-century confiscations, but it was only in exceptional areas that there were Protestants in any numbers. Resentment at their losses continued to fester among the Catholics, dramatically expressed in the execution of James Cotter in 1720 or the murder of Art O'Leary in 1773. One can sense the same resentment in the many references in the papers of the Earls of Kenmare — Catholics, though in origin 'New English' — to the dispossessed O'Donoghues and MacCarthys, 'idle and proud', who are slow to pay rent not so much because of poverty as of pride, and who still believe in the aristocratic tradition of raiding for cattle. Here too the pressures of the Gavel Act operated. The Butlers of Ormond had showed consistent political prudence since the Reformation and had been rewarded with a dukedom in 1661. James, the second duke, had imprudently supported the unsuccessful Jacobite rising of 1715 and had been attainted in consequence. The next in line was his Catholic cousin, John Butler of Kilcash. When he died childless in 1766 the claim passed to his cousin, Walter Butler of Garryricken; but though he had conformed in 1764, the title — an earldom now, not a dukedom — was revived only after his death in favour of his son John.

These provinces contained many Catholic middlemen, graziers in the midlands, subletting to dairymen in Munster and to tillage farmers in the south-east. Many of them were descendants of dispossessed proprietors, and they kept a lively memory of the lands they had lost. Arthur Young noted in 1776 that 'a gentleman's labourer will regularly leave to his son, by will, his master's estate'. He had got this information from a landlord in Cork, and it certainly expressed real fears on the part of the landlord. Miles Byrne in his *Memoirs* recalls that when he was a child in Monaseed, Co. Wexford, he had had pointed out to him the lands the family had once owned.

Despite these real tensions, the Catholic church was able to organise its diocesan and parish system. The 1731 report shows the Mass-house the rule, more particularly in Leinster and Munster, but there are Mass-rocks, and a detailed investigation — still to be carried out — will almost certainly show that in most cases the lack of a Mass-house is because of landlord hostility. In these provinces too there was always a higher proportion of priests with a full seminary education. Surviving episcopal visitations from the 1750s — detailed and extensive for Cashel, short but informative for Ferns — show that in these dioceses at any rate the Mass-rock had gone by this date. The bishop was in control of a working parish system. The Cashel visitations — and their information can be confirmed from other sources — show what must be regarded as a system of parish schools. The schoolmasters have an important role in the catechesis of children, and some of them are young men preparing for ordination before going abroad for their theological studies.

Bearing in mind these marked regionalisms, and bearing in mind too that there was a steady improvement in the quality of the clergy and in the general quality of religious practice, especially after mid-century, it is possible to attempt some estimate of the Catholic religious culture shaped in Ireland under the penal code. If the Tridentine pattern is to be taken as the norm — and it was the norm for the clergy — the broad pattern is as it had been from early in the seventeenth century: things are best in the towns, best there among the better-off, and become less satisfactory as one moves out from the towns and down the social ladder.

Religious life was rooted in the catechesis of the Counter-Reformation. As already noted, this stressed obedience to church authority, regular sacramental practice, centred on the Sunday Mass, and a regular round of prayers and devotions, especially to the Blessed Virgin. There were notable additions to the catechetical literature in the eighteenth century, including two catechisms in Irish, those of Archbishop O'Reilly of Armagh and of Andrew Donlevy. They consisted of questions and answers to be learned by rote, but they did also contain prayers and devotions, also to be learned by rote, until Butler's catechism asserted a dominance at the end of the eighteenth century.

Those who were literate in English, in particular the urban middle classes, supplemented this basic fare to a considerable extent. From quite early in the eighteenth century Catholic booksellers flourished, and Catholic publishers as well. They naturally congregated in Dublin, though Cork and Waterford had their publishers, and there were few towns without a shop that sold Catholic books. What they sold, even if published in Ireland, was for the most part not written in Ireland. If the booksellers' lists are a trustworthy guide, the most popular author was Richard Challoner (1691-1781), who was vicar apostolic in the London district from 1741. Challoner, and indeed all the other popular authors, were quite firmly in the Jesuit and Salesian tradition of spirituality. This indicates that one must be very cautious in applying the term 'Jansenistic' to the severe and anxious strain which undoubtedly developed in Irish middle-class Catholic spirituality in the eighteenth century. It is true that a severe and anxious spirituality was now the dominant characteristic of French Jansenism, and it is likewise true that by far the greater number of the Irish clergy now received their theological formation in France, but the Irish institutions there had a record of opposition to Jansenism, and while the clergy undoubtedly returned with some Gallican leanings, the Jansenist strain must have been slight. The anxious severity that developed in Irish Catholicism must rather be traced to the devotional reading available in English. Challoner himself does retain much of the serenity and humanism of his master, St Francis de Sales, but a sadder note runs through his writings, beyond doubt the fruit of his experiences as a bishop in penal-day London. Catholic life in penal-day Dublin was also a saddening experience, and it is not surprising that Irish Catholics found Challoner congenial, for they lived under the same conditions as he did.

Little devotional material was available in print in Irish. Bishop James Gallagher's *Sixteen Irish Sermons in an Easy and Familiar Stile* (1736) was the only addition to the catechisms. Indeed, the Irish scribal tradition appears to have put up a positive opposition to the printing-press — it seems strange to find eighteenth-century scribes making manuscript copies of texts which had been printed by the Franciscans at Louvain at the beginning of the seventeenth century. These texts too were translations, of continental origin, not English, and it is hard to see very much in them to nourish a really native spirituality. It is likewise hard to be in any way sure how widely they were disseminated. Nevertheless, the very number of these surviving 'manuscripts of the poor', the great number of religious texts they contain, and the physical evidence of use that they show so clearly, indicate that here is a wide and almost untapped field for research into the religious mind of Gaelic Ireland in the eighteenth and early nineteenth centuries. Even a simple count to indicate what religious texts were most frequently copied could be very informative. But despite the strength of the manuscript tradition, the Gaelic Irish culture was becoming an oral one. Here the popular prayers in Irish must have played an important role, though again it is difficult to quantify. They are often quite striking in their terse theological richness. It is not easy to suggest dates when dealing with a purely oral tradition, but at least those which also occur in Scots Gaelic must be pre-Reformation, and in general they lack that baroque wordiness that characterised some of the prayers of the Counter-Reformation. They are a reminder that there was more to the Christianity of the pre-Reformation centuries than superstitions, and they must undoubtedly have helped to nourish a personal spirituality largely outside the ambit of the Counter-Reformation clergy. They were part of the hidden life of Gaelic Ireland, and, regrettably, as it died, they died.

Sunday Mass was the principal occasion for instruction by the priest. Here regional variations are to be expected, both in the numbers attending Mass and in the quality of the instruction they received there. It was easier to go to Mass on Sunday in a town than in Gaelic Ulster with its scattered Mass-rocks. Yet even here, and at the very worst period of the penal code, there is the testimony of Bishop MacMahon of Clogher in 1714 which indicates a great devotion to the Mass. He gives graphic accounts of Mass at night, Mass with the priest's face veiled, or Mass said by the priest alone in a room with the congregation outside, so that if interrogated they could truthfully say they did not know who the priest was. He speaks too of people kneeling to pray at a time when they knew Mass was beginning somewhere else.

Later in the century there is evidence, particularly from Connacht, that Mass attendance on Sundays was not regarded as a pastoral problem. There was constant pressure on the Irish bishops to reduce the great number of holydays, but the authorities in Rome agreed to this only reluctantly. Between 1755 and 1778 there were a number of holydays on which people were allowed to work but were under obligation to attend Mass. The western bishops in particular pointed out that this was unworkable — if people went to work, as they normally had to do, they were

simply not free to attend Mass, and most of them did not. By implication — and sometimes the implication is close to an assertion — the
bishops found no such problems on Sunday. Other evidence indicates that
at the end of the eighteenth century the Irish Catholics presented the image
of a Mass-going people. In Lismore, Co. Waterford, in 1797 the French
traveller de Latocnaye attended Mass, where, he said, he 'could hardly find
room to stand, both church and cemetery round it being full of people'.

Mass attendance was 'passive', in the sense that people said their
prayers and allowed the priest at the altar to get on with what was seen as
his business — necessarily so when, as at Lismore and so many other
places, most of the congregation could not get into the chapel. Bishop
Plunkett of Meath noted on visitation in a country district in 1780 a 'lack
of respect due to the house of God; for they spoke and were otherwise very
dissipated during Mass'. He also noted disapprovingly 'the custom that
prevails among the women of shouting and groaning at every word the
priest says with emphasis'. In Kerry in 1797 de Latocnaye noted what
appears to have been a widespread custom, that the women were
separated from the men in the chapel: 'I suppose', he commented, 'this to
be to avoid distraction.'

It was in those areas where it was hardest to get to Mass that the quality
of the priest's instruction was likely to be lowest. At worst, the priest
could give an exposition of the catechism, or he could read for the people
summaries of the faith and set prayers. In Munster especially the use of
prepared sermons, modelled on or translated from the French *prônes*,
seems to have been fairly widespread. Everywhere the number of priests
able to preach their own sermons increased as the quality of clerical
education improved. The towns had always been relatively well equipped
with priests able to preach; here, indeed, especially in Dublin, the problem
was rather to find time for the sermon because so many Masses had to be
provided.

The other Counter-Reformation devotions were also better developed
in the towns — confraternities, the stations of the Cross, benediction,
vespers, even sung vespers, in the afternoon. In Wexford at mid-century
one catches a glimpse of the laity following Sunday vespers from their
manuals of prayer.

Devotion to the Blessed Virgin had an important role in Counter-
Reformation spirituality, and strikingly marked off Catholic from
Protestant. When Piaras Mac Gearailt was forced to conform early in the
century he found the absence of devotion to Mary the hardest thing to
accept in 'the Saxon Lutheran religion'. The principal Marian devotion
was the rosary. Already in the 1680s Bishop Luke Wadding in Wexford
had been distributing rosary beads by the gross, and in his visitations in
the 1750s Archbishop Butler of Cashel regularly noted that 'The beads is
duly observed by most of the people.'

While the clergy did not express concern over attendance at Sunday Mass, they were concerned at the problems of getting people to receive the sacrament of penance, even of fulfilling the minimum obligation of confession and communion at Easter. The young priest James Lyons, while working in Dublin, found people who had not been to confession for as long as twenty years, and an Irish Franciscan working in London reported the same problem among Irish migrant labourers there, 'for want', he said, 'of an Irish confessor'. Lyons himself admitted 'a deficiency in my native language, which for the greater part I forgot' while in the Collegio Urbano in Rome between 1755 and 1763. The problem was tackled in the rural areas by the institution of 'stations of confession'. Twice a year, in preparation for Christmas and Easter, the priest went to a number of designated houses in his extensive parish to hear confessions and say Mass. The origins of this distinctive practice are obscure, but it was solidly established in Munster by the 1780s. Though it was rigorously opposed in the nineteenth century by Paul Cullen, it survived in a number of places to become respectable again after the Second Vatican Council.

The 'parish sacraments' became the norm of life. Baptism tended to move from the home, first to the priest's house, as the priest got a house, and then to the chapels, as these came to be equipped with fonts. Marriage, however, remained in the home. The evidence indicates that the full Christian demands in the matter of sexuality had come to be very widely accepted among Catholics of all classes — pre-marital continence and marriage as a lifelong commitment. Inevitably, there were exceptions, notably among the 'squireens', and these occupy a disproportionate place in the records. Merriman's *Midnight Court* is not a sociological survey: it is probably more accurately envisaged as inspired 'pub talk'. There is one character — just one — in the Cashel visitations who would have warmed the heart of Merriman, but he was so harassed by the clergy that he must have paid dearly for his pleasure.

Marriage, however, kept a strongly 'domestic' character even when there was not much of a 'home' to celebrate it in. John Dolan, the historian of Fermanagh, writing about 1730, describes a marriage of the poor:

> When they marry their sons and daughters, suppose their portion does not exceed £20, they think nothing of spending £4 or £5 in a common bottle in the field, the marriage day; for most commonly their simple sort is married in a field, where, after the ceremony, and articles of marriage are concluded, they sit down upon the green, placing their chiefest and clergy at one end and the rest of them in two rows.

It is very much out of the old world, but the marriage is before a priest, and at the wedding feast he sits at what passes for the top table.

The system worked, even though there were opportunities for the

irregular clergyman or 'couple-beggar' well into the nineteenth century,
because the civil law made no regulations for Catholic marriage and the
church authorities were reluctant to introduce the Tridentine *Tametsi*
regulation, feeling it was better to live with the couple-beggar than face
the possibility of civil legislation, which, if it followed the lines of the
'Hardwicke Act' in England, would have obliged Catholics to marry in the
Protestant parish church. It was only in 1827 that *Tametsi* was introduced in the diocese of Meath, the wardenship of Galway, and the ecclesiastical province of Dublin.

It was not only in the ceremonies of marriage that the old world
lingered. Superstition always haunts the human consciousness, the
basically pagan notion of a divinity waiting to strike if the rites are not
duly observed. Martin Marlay in *The Good Confessor* (1743) gave a long
list of superstitions, 'the remains of heathenism', on which he felt
penitents might reasonably examine their consciences. Bishop Madgett of
Kerry in 1760 felt that no preaching by the priests could root out these
ancestral fears and usages, nor was he himself prepared to rule out
altogether the existence of sorcery, because of instances his priests had
given him. Nor were the priests themselves altogether immune. In a
denunciation of superstition in his diocesan regulations for 1771 Bishop
Sweetman of Ferns found it necessary to include priests who 'act the fairy
doctor'.

Usages from the past proved most intractable in the third of the 'rites of
passage', the waking and burial of the dead. Here the efforts of the clergy
to change habits had little effect on the 'unchristian diversions of lewd
songs, brutal tricks called fronsy-fronsy' at wakes, that Bishop Gallagher
of Kildare and Leighlin complained of in 1748, or the professional women
'keeners' at funerals. These practices were so deeply embedded in the
rituals of the kin-group that they yielded only very slowly to Tridentine
Christianity.

The reformers at the beginning of the seventeenth century had tried to
bring the traditional patterns and pilgrimages into this framework. By
and large they failed, and at these gatherings the religious significance
diminished and they tended to become rowdy social occasions. There were
exceptions. The pilgrimage to Lough Derg kept its traditional austerity.
Bishop Hugh MacMahon described it in detail in 1714. It had been
mentioned by name in civil legislation of 1703, forbidding all pilgrimages,
not so much because the government regarded them as superstitious but
because it wished to prevent Catholics gathering in numbers. Yet the
Lough Derg pilgrimage was never interfered with and continued to attract
pilgrims from all over Ireland between the beginning of June and the
middle of August. They spent nine days there, making the 'stations' three
times a day. Masses were said from dawn to midday, with two or three
sermons daily. On the ninth day the pilgrim made a general confession and

received communion at dawn. In important respects there were only marginal concessions to Tridentine Catholicism, but the experience ran deep, the repentance was real, and it expressed itself in the reception of the sacraments. Yet by the closing decades of the century the Catholic bishops had set themselves against patterns and pilgrimages, 'meetings of pretended devotion, or rather of real dissipation and dissoluteness', where 'they profane the name of God and everything that is sacred by the most execrable oaths, and finish the day by the perpetration of the grossest impurities, by shedding their neighbour's blood, by murder, and the transgression of every law'. No doubt such things happened, but it may well be that individual priests did try to keep religious observances alive at the pilgrimages denounced by their bishops. De Latocnaye came on a holy well in Kerry, very famous for its power of curing, resorted to even by Protestants when everything else had failed. The pilgrim rounds were superstitious, and some came without any religious motive. One pilgrim said he came 'to do what the others do and to see the women', and indeed the pattern seems to have been one of the principal local occasions for matchmaking. The priest had tried to forbid the people to come to the well, but in vain: 'The only thing left to the priest is to see that order is observed in these gatherings, and by his exhortations to warn his people against any impropriety or indecency, and in this the priest of this parish has perfectly succeeded.'

This sums up fairly well the position and role of the Catholic priest in late eighteenth-century rural Ireland. He had become a kind of symbol, as is shown in the bitter poetry written about priests who conformed, in contrast with the wry shrug of the shoulders that was the reaction to the layman who had conformed to save his property. In many ways the priest was still 'the man of power'. Before the Reformation he had shared that power with the *file* and the *breitheamh*. Now, almost two hundred years after the political downfall of the Gaelic order, it is not too much to see him as inheriting some of the powers of the *taoiseach*. In peasant Ireland the priest was a father-figure, not to be lightly crossed.

After the middle of the century an increasing number of these priests had a seminary theological formation. Though the ideas of the Enlightenment were beginning to have some impact on seminary training, the French Revolution came too quickly to allow them any lasting effect. The seminary-trained priest still moved in the world of the Counter-Reformation. In Ireland these priests had presided over the introduction of some of the ways of Counter-Reformation spirituality. They had a real but limited success in catechesis and what they saw as the closely related matter of the sacrament of penance. They had more success with Sunday Mass, with the sacraments of baptism and marriage, and in developing certain habits of prayer. It would be wrong to see the situation as a 'Tridentine' priesthood trying to drag a laity out of its old superstitions.

Their continental training may have left the clergy less sensitive to some of what was good in the old ways, but if it is true to say that 'as the priest is, so are the people', the adage retains a good deal of truth when reversed — 'as the people, so the priest'.

Ireland at mid-century was a complex society with many latent tensions. It was not exceptional that this society should be based on privilege, and specifically on the privilege arising from the ownership of land. What made it exceptional was the fact that the privileged land-owners were Protestant, and had to be Protestant as a condition of being privileged, while the bulk of the population was Catholic, with a lively memory of past wrongs. It is significant that in three provinces the idiomatic Irish word for 'Protestant' is 'Sasanach'. In Ulster it is 'Albanach'. The Protestants were the colonists, the people who had taken the land.

The 'Protestant interest' was left with what seemed the insoluble problem of being a small colonial minority. The Earl of Chesterfield, who was Lord Lieutenant in the anxious year of 1745, proposed milder 'popery laws' but a stricter enforcement of them. This was unacceptable, if only because it would have led to a great increase in the numbers conforming. The Irish establishment passed an anxious time during the 'forty-five', even though there was scarcely a stir in Ireland. The pastoral charges issued by the prelates of the established church reflect a deep anxiety and uncertainty of purpose. Josiah Hort, Archbishop of Tuam, could only think of suggesting reasons why no 'modest and reasonable papist' should feel aggrieved, while standing firmly by the 'popery laws' which were the basis of grievance.

Shortly after 1745 the terms of the question began to shift. The Jacobite threat was over. The impact of the Enlightenment was leading to some reassessment of the threat of 'popery in the gross'. In 1756 the forty years' peace between England and France was ended by the outbreak of a new war. A threat to impose the penal code more firmly led Archbishop Michael O'Reilly of Armagh with six other bishops and the support of important Catholic gentry to address a letter to the Catholic clergy in 1759 asking them to pray for the king and royal family at every public Mass, and on the first Sunday of every quarter to read a declaration denying the pope's deposing power and certain other 'odious tenets' imputed to Catholics. Early in 1760 a group of Catholics met in Dublin and took the first steps towards forming a 'Catholic Committee'. George III succeeded later in the year. The war with France ended in 1763, and at the Peace of Paris French Canada was ceded to Britain. The Protestant monarch now had Catholic subjects who had for a long time lived under their own very different laws. Their right to be different under the crown was embodied in the Quebec Act of 1774. This set up a separate government for French Canada. The province was to be ruled by French civil law; Catholics might hold civil office by taking an oath specially devised for them; and the Catholic church was established by being given the power to collect tithes.

The possibility of the Protestant monarch having Catholic subjects nearer home was enhanced by the fact that when the Old Pretender, James III, died in Rome in 1766 the papacy did not continue to recognise the claims of his son. In Ireland the Catholic middle classes had in fact taken the first step on the road towards political accommodation with the Hanoverian monarchy. In June 1774, the same month as the Quebec Act, parliament approved a new oath by which Catholics might testify their allegiance. Unfortunately a few phrases at least implicitly disrespectful to the pope were added as it passed through parliament, and the Catholics were divided. A group of them forced the issue by marching in a body to the Court of King's Bench to take the oath, and this action proved decisive, all the more so as an act of 1778 extended benefits only to such Catholics as had sworn allegiance. These benefits were substantial in the matter of landholding. The Gavel Act was repealed, and Catholics might acquire land on a lease of 999 years. This was in practice equivalent to a freehold, but that emotive and legally and politically dangerous term was avoided.

Despite the popery laws, social relations were easing between Catholics and Protestants. Not everyone would agree with the eccentric Frederick Augustus Hervey, Earl-Bishop of Derry, that popery was 'a mild and harmless superstition', but it did seem to be changing its spots. The Volunteers were set up in 1778 for the defence of the realm while the regular army was absent in the American wars, and soon began to play a political role, championing a reform that included Catholic relief, strikingly embodied in the Dungannon declaration of 15 February 1782. When the first Catholic church was dedicated in Belfast in 1784 the local company of Volunteers 'paraded in full dress and marched to Mass, where a sermon was preached by the Rev. Mr O'Connell, and a handsome collection was made in defraying the expense of the new Mass-house'. This report in the *Hibernian Journal* of 7 June adds that 'great numbers of the other Protestant inhabitants also attended'.

These signs of interconfessional peace proved a false dawn, even though much more far-reaching Catholic relief was granted in parliament in 1782. A number of laws against the clergy which had long fallen into disuse were repealed, but laws marking off papists as inferior were not merely unrepealed but reaffirmed. Catholics might now open schools, but only with the permission of the Protestant bishop. They might acquire land freehold, except in parliamentary boroughs, where freehold tenure might have political consequences. Henry Grattan had put the issue bluntly during the debates: it was a choice between remaining a Protestant settlement or becoming an Irish nation. The legislation as passed showed that 'the Protestant interest' was not yet ready to face this issue, and time was beginning to run out.

Tensions had already surfaced twenty years earlier, in the Kilkenny/Tipperary area. This was a sensitive spot because of the relatively large number of Catholic landowners who had been restored to their estates under the patronage of the first Duke of Ormond in the 1660s. The trouble had arisen here, however, because of the grievances of the poor, and it was neither sectarian nor political, but economic. It was far from being the poorest part of the country, but even here there is evidence that with an increasing population there was a growing cottier class, dependent on a potato-patch for economic and even physical survival. It was one of the areas where a tithe was exacted on potatoes. The problem of survival became critical when, because of a combination of war conditions and an outbreak of cattle disease, Irish beef, pork and butter were allowed into England in 1758, and Irish cattle in 1759. The cottier was not affected by the fact that prices rose, for these items did not figure largely in his diet. What did affect him was the increased demand for land for grazing. This put up the rent of the potato-patch and led to the enclosure of what had been traditionally regarded as common land, though it frequently was not so in law.

Apart from the 'Houghers' in Connacht in the second decade of the century, Ireland had been free of agrarian violence. It could, however, be described as in a real sense a violent society. The Catholic ecclesiastical authorities regularly but ineffectively inveighed against the tendency of every gathering of people to end in violence, indeed against the fact that people assembled simply in order to get drunk and fight. But the 'Whiteboy' disturbances that broke out at the end of 1761 represented organised violence in support of agrarian demands.

Their grievances were economic, directed against enclosures and tithe. At first they were called 'Levellers', because they threw down fences enclosing common land. They came to be called 'Whiteboys' when they took to wearing white shirts so as to recognise one another more easily as they moved around by night. Their organisation was certainly effective: the amount of actual physical violence was limited, as intimidation was often enough.

This intimidation was directed against the Catholic and Protestant establishment equally, and was equally resisted by both. It was resisted too by the Catholic bishops. They had a long-standing tradition of suspicion of combinations and secret societies, and they also saw the disturbances as possibly prejudicing the cautious moves now being made for some recognition of Catholics. Episcopal opposition could sometimes reach a level of insensitivity, as when Bishop Burke of Ossory in 1764 ordered his clergy to read on three successive Sundays and to explain in Irish an instruction which among other things counselled the Whiteboys:

'If they think themselves grieved in any respect, they might be redressed by lawful ways and means. They ought to be amenable to the laws of the nation, and not provoke the government, which is mild beyond expression.'

English-born high officials in the administration, the Lord Lieutenant, the Earl of Halifax, for example, or Sir Arthur Aston, Chief Justice of the Common Pleas, had no doubt that the disturbances were neither political nor sectarian, but caused solely by economic distress. The latter was well placed to know, for he had headed a special commission set up in 1762 to try Whiteboy offences. He judged leniently. When he left Clonmel the road was lined with people kneeling to pray God to bless him. He drew up a report on the problem, which concluded that there was not 'the least reason to impute these disturbances to disaffection to His Majesty, his government, or the laws in general'. The Lord Lieutenant concurred.

The Whiteboys were trying to say the same thing in their own way. A figure called 'Sive Oultagh' frequently appears in what documentation they have left. She is the 'queen', the 'mother', the 'poor old woman'. Sive or Sadb is one of these figures of saga, half queen, half goddess, the 'mother' who has had and discarded many kings in her time. Moreover, she is associated with the Osraighe people and the Fionn saga, which had its roots precisely in the area now disturbed by the Whiteboys. The followers of Sive Oultagh say that all they wish to do is to relieve the poor; indeed, if, as reported, a popular rallying-cry with them was 'Long live King George III and Queen Sive', it can only mean that the old *striapach*, the 'harlot-queen', was now being offered to George III as a bride. In a very different political language, they were saying the same thing as their bishops and betters, though one may doubt if these would have understood what they were trying to say.

The frightened local Protestant establishment would not agree. There was a war with France; a French expedition had actually landed and captured Carrickfergus in February 1760; and any disturbance must be part of 'a popish and Jacobite plot'. Whatever plausibility this version of things might have had in the last war with France over forty years before, it did not have much plausibility now that Catholics were seeking out ways of expressing their loyalty to the throne, but it was based on fear, not on reason. They were dismayed at Aston's leniency, and their pressure in parliament led to the 'Whiteboy Act' of 1765, which set up a number of new capital offences. Their principal victim was Nicholas Sheehy, parish priest of Clogheen.

He *may* have been active in the Whiteboys, but it is more likely that he drew the anger of the gentry on himself because of the way he concerned himself with the needs of the poor. He was first arrested in 1762, but no charge could be made to stick. Harassment drove him into hiding, but he surrendered himself to face trial on any charge, provided he was not tried in Clonmel. He was put on trial in Dublin on a charge of incitement to riot and rebellion. The Dublin jury flatly disbelieved the evidence of the three witnesses against him, and he was acquitted, but immediately rearrested and brought to trial in Clonmel in March 1766 on a charge of having instigated a Whiteboy murder. The chief witnesses against him were the three already discredited in Dublin. A witness who swore that Sheehy was in his home the night the murder was committed was immediately arrested on a charge of being a Whiteboy by the chief magistrate, a Protestant clergyman. The verdict of the court was, predictably, guilty, and Nicholas Sheehy was hanged in Clonmel on 15 March 1766.

As Lecky put it rather mildly, the case 'appears indeed to have been exceedingly flagrant'.[2] The parish priest of Clogheen became a martyr in the eyes of the Catholic poor. It was said that the alleged victim had never been killed, but had gone to Newfoundland, where he was later seen alive. It is quite possible, though it cannot be certain. What is certain is that four years later a man was being hanged at Philipstown in King's County. The scaffold was surrounded by an ominously silent mob. When the execution was over they stoned the hangman to death, and his body lay for two or three days under the gallows, no one daring to remove it. He was the man who had hanged Nicholas Sheehy.

By the time Sheehy was hanged the Whiteboy movement had petered out, not so much because it was repressed as because of the great drought of 1765 which ruined the harvest and threatened real famine. It broke out again in 1769, however, and this time it had a much broader social base.[3] In 1758 parliament had granted a bounty on grain and flour brought overland to Dublin. This had led to a great expansion in corn-growing. Pasture land had been exempt from tithe since 1736, but once it was tilled for corn it became liable. In consequence, this second outbreak of agrarian violence included farmers as well as cottiers. The Catholic church authorities came under pressure to denounce it, and some of them did, under threats that their chapels would be closed and the penal laws enforced. Threats may not have been altogether necessary in some cases. At Ballyragget, Co. Kilkenny, in February 1775 a group of Catholics, led by the parish priest and organised by Archbishop Butler of Cashel, defended against a Whiteboy attack the house of the local landlord, Robert Butler, the archbishop's brother. In March 1776 there was an attack on the house of Eugene Geoghegan, Coadjutor Bishop of Meath, who had forcefully denounced the Whiteboys. He had fired down the stairs at his assailants and killed a known Whiteboy.

The Catholic bishops were in real fear of such movements at a time when the Catholic community was being afforded the first tentative legal recognition. Archbishop Carpenter of Dublin, who had given his approval to the text of the proposed oath of allegiance before it was submitted to parliament in 1774, was at the same time issuing strong condemnations of what might be called the beginnings of trade unionism in Dublin city, which had led to outbreaks of violence, especially where there was a question of 'scab labour'. The position of the bishops was unenviable in that sections of the Protestant interest were still anxious to explain the unrest as a popish rebellion led by the priests. In November 1775 Ambrose Power was murdered in Tipperary. A landlord and magistrate, he had been prominent in the events leading to the execution of Nicholas Sheehy. Two men were executed for the murder in January 1776 at Clonmel, cut down and ritually quartered, while the gentry of the county looked on, heavily armed and guarded by troops. A new and more far-reaching 'Whiteboy Act' became law on 4 April 1776. When Volunteer corps were formed in Tipperary a few years later their principal activity seems to have been the control of Whiteboys. In this they succeeded, but they must have appeared to much of the Catholic population as a kind of 'B Specials'.

It was probably for this reason that the next outbreak in 1785 began on the borders of Cork and Kerry. The original agitators called themselves the 'Rightboys', though contemporaries tended to use the older term 'Whiteboy'. This time the agitation was even more widespread, and the social base was even broader. Foster's Corn Law of June 1784 had made tillage farming even more attractive, so, once again, the central point at issue was the tithe on corn, and indeed the tithe generally. By the spring of 1786 the movement had gained such confidence that marches of great numbers of people were taking place during the daytime. The Rightboys were using the assembly for Sunday Mass to swear in large numbers of men. At the same time they were extending their attack on the tithe to opposition to the exaction of exorbitant dues by some of the Catholic clergy. By now many of these were comfortably off, and some of them certainly did exact excessive dues harshly, though the Rightboy demands recognised that even the best-off among them did not enjoy incomes comparable to those of the clergy of the established church. However, the Catholic bishops, while they denounced the Rightboys for the same reasons as they had denounced the Whiteboys, did accept that the exactions of some priests had given grounds for real grievance.

The level of physical violence was low, because it was not necessary. Intimidation was sufficient for this widespread and confident organisation. The government response was embodied in two acts of parliament in 1787. They contained new initiatives in a proposal for stipendiary magistrates and a plan to establish a barony constabulary, who, though appointed by the local gentry through the grand juries, would be under the control of peace officers nominated by the crown. These proposals were a sensible recognition of the fact that the problem of keeping the peace in Ireland was not the same as it was in England. In the nature of things they would take time to be effective, and the fact that the serious Rightboy disturbances died down quite quickly was not so much because of the new measures taken by parliament as because of a widespread belief that the tithe system would soon be substantially reformed.

Attack on the tithe was now being mounted on a very broad front. It involved not only the cottiers of a generation before, for whom the tithe on potatoes had been the last unbearable burden, but prosperous farmers, even gentry, for whom the tithe on corn was a central grievance. In the north the Presbyterians had long opposed the tithe; the 'small dues' or fees payable to the minister of the established church at christenings, weddings and funerals were a particular grievance in the first disturbances in Ulster in the 1760s. Among the Presbyterians especially the grievance over tithe had broadened into raising the question whether Ireland should have a church establishment at all. A certain whiff of social revolution was detectable from different sources: the possibility began to emerge of Catholic and Presbyterian having common grievances that might develop into common interests. In three successive years, 1787, 1788 and 1789, Henry Grattan had introduced bills to reform the tithe system. All three were defeated. The bishops of the established church were implacably opposed. They pointed out, and rightly, that the right to tithe was an integral part of the church establishment, and the church establishment was an integral part of the 'Protestant interest', or, a more ominous term now coming into use, the 'Protestant ascendancy'. What they did not face was the fact that Grattan was not proposing the abolition of the tithe, nor even a diminution in the returns from tithe, but to make it a less arbitrary charge, easier to assess and in consequence easier to collect.

The meeting of the French estates general in May 1789, the year Grattan's third tithe-reform bill was lost, marked the beginning of the end of the old world. Its disintegration had begun earlier in Ireland, and in a distinctively Irish way, in an area where there was economic rivalry between Catholic and Protestant poor. This was the 'weaving triangle' which covered much of Armagh and parts of east Tyrone. In much of east Ulster there was a dense population, living by cottage industry, able to subsist on tiny farms — poorly farmed, Arthur Young thought — because farming was only a subsidiary occupation. In Antrim and Down this population was solidly Presbyterian. In the 'weaving triangle', however, poor Catholic and poor Protestant competed for survival; more for one meant less for the other. The possibility of Catholic and Presbyterian finding common interests was a middle-class concern.

The Oakboy disturbances in 1763 were easily dealt with. The Steelboys of 1769 were more formidable.[4] The sectarian nature of their agitation emerges from a Steelboy petition to the Lord Lieutenant in 1772:

We are all Protestants and Protestant Dissenters, and bear unfeigned loyalty to his present majesty and the Hanoverian succession. . . . Some

of us by refusing to pay the extravagant rent demanded by our land
lords have been turned out, and our lands given to papists, who will pay
any rent.[5]

This is a claim to be part of the 'Protestant interest' by the very fact that
one is a Protestant. It was rejected. The establishment in the north dealt
with the Steelboys as it had dealt with the Whiteboys in the south. There
was a massive increase in the number of Presbyterian emigrants to
America.

After 1782 the Volunteer corps began to disband. Those which
continued tended to be the more radical, and they admitted Catholics into
their ranks, though Catholics could not legally carry arms. The response
of alarmed Protestant Ulster was the organisation of the 'Peep o' Day
Boys', so called because they raided Catholic houses for arms in the early
morning. The Catholic response was to organise themselves as
'Defenders'. Both groups were organised after an affray at Markethill, Co.
Armagh, on 4 July 1784. The level of violence rose, and it was now clearly
sectarian, with the burning of Catholic chapels and a concerted attempt to
drive Catholics out of Co. Armagh.

So religious sectarianism in a new and popular guise had emerged in
Ulster before the revolutionary decade of the 1790s. So many things
happened so quickly in these ten years that it is hard to keep a sure footing.
There are many things that as yet we do not understand, some things that
may never be understood. The initial stages of the French Revolution
seemed full of promise for the heirs of the 'Glorious Revolution' of 1688.
It was indeed 'bliss to be alive' as the French gave themselves a liberal constitution with a limited monarchy. But the constitution of 1791 did not
work, as there were too many people interested in seeing that it did not.
They included the king, and, to an even greater degree, the queen. The con-
stitution-makers picked what in retrospect was a clearly unnecessary
quarrel with the church. But the greatest wreckers were the Girondin
party in the Legislative Assembly, which met in October 1791 to frame
laws to give effect to the constitution. Lovers of the lofty sentiment and
the sounding phrase, welcoming the thought of bloodshed but shrinking
from the fact, their policy of exporting revolution which did more than
anything else to initiate the great wars that lasted from 1792 to 1815.
War had already begun when the National Convention met in
September 1792. French unpreparedness for war was already inclining
the country towards the dictatorship of the Reign of Terror. The king was
executed on 21 January 1793. A few days later, on 1 February,
revolutionary France declared war on Great Britain.

In September 1791 the French had proclaimed their constitution with
showy ceremony. On 14 October the Society of United Irishmen was
founded in Belfast, to press for reform in 'the common name of Irishman'.

It was suppressed in 1794, and reorganised as a secret society in 1795. One may suspect that some of its founding fathers were unhappy in their new role. It was one thing to issue a call of 'citizen-soldiers, to arms' in December 1792 before war had broken out, but the prospect of real warfare was different. It may well be that historians have concentrated too much on the United Irishmen. In some respects they were the Girondins of the Irish revolution. The really radical forces were elsewhere.

One place where they surfaced was the Catholic Committee. On 27 December 1791 a conservative group led by Lord Kenmare had seceded, and leadership passed to a more radical element led by the Dublin merchant John Keogh. In July 1792 Theobald Wolfe Tone, a founding member of the Dublin Society of United Irishmen, was appointed agent and secretary. In the preceding April a limited Catholic Relief Bill had been passed in parliament. Parliament had refused to admit Catholics to the parliamentary processes or to the holding of office under the crown. A mildly worded petition from the Catholic Committee in February, suggesting that Catholics might now be safely trusted with the limited share in political power which was all they could hope for, was rejected by the house of Commons by 208 votes to 25, a 'patriot' member describing it as emanating from 'the rabble of the town'.

Keogh and Tone decided to organise a national Catholic Convention. The name was ominous. In September 1792 the National Convention met in Paris. In April revolutionary France had challenged Europe to war. The first act of the National Convention was the deposition of the king. At the beginning of December the Catholic Convention met in the Tailors' Hall in Back Lane in Dublin. It decided to ignore the parliament in College Green and go to London to petition the king directly. The delegates, led by Keogh and Tone, travelled by way of Belfast, where sympathisers drew their coach through the streets.

William Pitt, the British Prime Minister, knew that war with France was imminent. When it came, he did not want a combination of dis-affected Catholics and Presbyterians in Ireland at his back door. Under pressure from him the Irish parliament passed a Relief Act on 9 April 1793. It admitted Catholics to the parliamentary franchise on the same terms as Protestants — effectively as 'forty-shilling freeholders' in the county constituencies only, because the closed corporations kept the Protestant monopoly in the boroughs. It also admitted them, with exceptions, to civil and military office under the crown, but they could not yet take a seat in parliament because of the oath required.

This did not completely satisfy the rising expectations of the Catholics. Their hopes rose with the appointment of Earl Fitzwilliam as viceroy. He was a known supporter of further Catholic relief, but his instructions were not to introduce it as a government measure and if possible to defer it until the war was over. When he arrived in Dublin on 4 January 1795 one of his first acts was to dismiss John Beresford, Chief Commissioner of Revenue and centre of a lucrative and expanding network of family patronage that gave him great power. Beresford was adamantly opposed to further Catholic relief. Fitzwilliam's instructions on the question of 'patronage' had been inexact and undefined, but there was a general understanding that he would leave things alone. The question was important, for one consequence of the independence of the Irish parliament in 1782 had been that the landed magnates who controlled parliament now got greater influence in the administration. Fitzwilliam's dismissal of Beresford did not make his task any easier when, faced with the revival of the Catholic Committee and a stream of Catholic petitions, he decided that the Catholic relief question was urgent. In this he was not supported by the British government, which had a great deal more on its hands, and he was dismissed on 23 February. Beresford was back in office shortly afterwards.

'Law and order' now became the watchword of an ascendancy that saw itself increasingly under siege because of the disturbed state of the country and French successes on the continent. There had been rioting to an unprecedented extent in connection with the Militia Act of 1793, which, as it worked out, meant in practice the conscription of the poor. More important, however, was the steady growth of the Defenders. Here especially there is much that we probably will never know, for the Defenders kept their secrets well. The government never succeeded in planting an effective informer among them, whereas it had no difficulty with the United Irishmen. Camden, the new Lord Lieutenant, disturbed by the lack of information, ordered a digest of what was available in July 1795. Trials of Defenders later in the year showed that they had spread as far south as Kildare. Camden's inquiry and the trials provide the bulk of our information, such as it is.

It has already been seen that the Defenders began as a sectarian secret society to defend the Catholics in Co. Armagh. They became highly politicised at an early date and established some contact with revolutionary France. The French seem to have regarded them as more useful than the United Irishmen, as they seemed to promise real hopes of a peasant *chouannerie* that the French knew only too well could be effective. In 1796 the United Irishmen, now a secret society, established some contact with the Defenders. It appears they hoped to use them to spread their organisation, but what happened was rather that the ideas of the Defenders took over. They had begun as anti-Protestant; in Irish conditions this easily shaded into being anti-English. Old millenarian hopes of deliverance blended with a popular Irish version of 'French ideas'. When the French landed at Killala in August 1798 they were met by people on their knees praying for delivery from the 'Sasanaigh'. Eighteenth-century poetry in Irish had looked for a deliverer from beyond the sea. It was to some extent accidental that he had been personified in the Stuart pretenders. The French now represented the deliverer come at last, and they seem to have had some difficulty in understanding their role.

Another fateful development took place in the early autumn of 1795, the foundation of the Orange Order after a clash between Defenders and Peep o' Day Boys at the 'Battle of the Diamond' near Loughgall in Co. Armagh on 21 September. There had always been an Orange tradition in Ireland, cherishing the memory of William the Protestant deliverer, but it had been organised among the better-off, and under the influence of the Enlightenment and freemasonry it had swung towards support of Catholic Emancipation. The new Orange Order was an organisation of the Protestant poor. Their claim to be part of the establishment because they were Protestant had been rejected in 1772. Now in the panic years after 1795 this claim was accepted. The Protestant gentry began to form Orange lodges. Religious polarisation was complete.

The militia formed in 1793 had been mainly Catholic in its rank and file. These were infiltrated by the Defenders, but they won over no officers and only a few non-commissioned officers, and in fact supposedly disaffected regiments stood firm when it came to actual fighting in 1798.[6] But the administration was naturally frightened, and a new corps was formed in 1796, the Yeomanry, and a determined effort was made to keep them exclusively Protestant. This was in November. In December a French fleet sailed into Bantry Bay, and although bad weather prevented a landing, the level of panic was high. It had been high before the French appeared. The Insurrection Act of March 1796 had given sweeping powers to magistrates. These were almost all Protestant — they had been exclusively so until 1793 — and some of them were of comparatively humble social position. Now a small quorum of magistrates could proclaim a whole county and subject it to martial law.

Habeas corpus was suspended in October 1796, and in March 1797 the army under General Lake began the 'pacification' of Ulster. When Sir Ralph Abercromby was appointed commander-in-chief in November he judged that over wide areas of the country the gentry and magistracy had panicked, that the army was 'in a state of licentiousness which must render it formidable to everyone but the enemy', and that the situation was dangerously close to being out of control.

On 12 March 1798 all but two of the supreme executive of the United Irishmen were arrested on Camden's orders. He had been pressed to take this step by John Beresford, John Foster, and John Fitzgibbon, Earl of Clare, three elderly representatives of the 'Protestant ascendancy', who had reluctantly agreed to the concessions of 1793. These arrests meant that if a rising came it would not be anything like what the United Irishmen had planned. In the Catholic south it would approach much more closely the aims of the Defenders. This in turn would have an impact on the northern Presbyterians. Here it seems the rank and file may have been reluctant to follow into battle leaders who had committed themselves too deeply to hold back.

On 23 May there were risings in north Leinster. They were effectively over in little more than a week. On 27 May the conflict began in Wexford. This was a much more serious affair, lasting almost a month, during which most of the county fell into the hands of the insurgents, though attempts to spread the conflict further were repulsed at New Ross (5 June) and Arklow (9 June). On 6 June rebellion broke out in Ulster, but here too it was over in a week. Belfast, where the United Irishmen had been founded, remained quiet: its middle-class Presbyterians were now afraid of popery and afraid for their property.

By far and away the most serious outbreak was in Wexford. In some respects it might seem an unlikely spot, but recent studies by Professor L. M. Cullen in particular have begun the work of clarification.[7] He has pointed out that north Wexford and south Wicklow was an area where there were considerable tensions between Catholic and Protestant. In Munster such tensions had been at gentry level, and in Armagh at the level of the poor. Here they were rather at the middle levels of society. The overall Protestant population was high for the south of Ireland, ranging from 15 to 20 per cent. There were some small Catholic gentry who had held on to their lands, and a number of Catholic middlemen. At all levels of society, but particularly at this level, there was economic rivalry between Protestant and Catholic. Catholics from this area had been prominent among the radicals of the Catholic Committee and at the Catholic Convention.

The county as a whole was politicised to an unusual degree. This had become apparent in the election of 1790. The greater landowners inclined to the liberal side, but the smaller Protestant gentry and Protestant middlemen were hardliners. The election of 1797 showed even greater polarisation (the Catholics had got the vote in 1793), with the Catholic 'middle sort' emerging as the target of their Protestant opposite numbers. Many of these Catholics were members of the United Irishmen. The 'middle sort' of Protestants panicked — landowners, middlemen and magistrates. The northern part of the county was proclaimed in November 1797, and the county as a whole at the end of April 1798.

All this, however, does not explain why the county as a whole was engulfed so quickly in a widespread *chouannerie*. It may be that the historian can get no further than to postulate a Wexford equivalent of the French 'great fear' of 1789. It does seem certain that in the late spring of 1798 every Catholic there was convinced that every Protestant was an Orangeman, and every Protestant convinced that every Catholic was a Defender. Indeed, the actual fighting bore many of the hallmarks of Defenderism, in its ferocity and in its sectarian character. Yet what evidence there is — and, as always with the Defenders, it is inference rather than evidence — suggests that there may have been little if any Defenderism in Wexford. There had been popular disturbances there in 1793, but they were occasioned by a protest against tithes, possibly aggravated by fears arising from the Militia Act. What moved the peaceful — some would say phlegmatic — inhabitants of the 'English baronies' of Forth and Bargy, when the army retreating from Wexford burnt its way through them, to turn to their liberal gentry and demand that they lead them into battle? Who was Richard Monaghan, or 'Dick Monk', the 'Mayor of John Street', a poorer-class suburb of Wexford town, who organised the 'John Street corps' and clearly enjoyed real authority? On what pattern of social respect was that authority based? Who wrote that extraordinary ballad, 'The Croppy Boy', with its spare and nervous language:

> It was early, early in the Spring,
> When small birds tune and thrushes sing,
> Changing their notes from tree to tree,
> And the song they sang was old Ireland free;

with its capacity in a few words to evoke a sense of place and occasion:

> As I was going through Wexford street
> My own first cousin I there did meet,
> My own first cousin did me betray
> And for one guinea swore my life away;

and its mysterious (and in part irrecoverable) allusions to symbols and loyalties:

> I chose the black and I chose the blue,
> I forsook the pink and the orange too,
> But I did them forsake and I did them deny
> And I'll wear the green, like a Croppy Boy.

The mystery deepens if one considers that when the fighting was over, despite fairly savage repression, the county returned to its peaceful ways. Wexford keeps its secrets, like the Defenders and like Gaelic Ireland.

A parliamentary union between Great Britain and Ireland had been mooted for some time, and the rising of 1798 made it the only real option. It was passed in the British parliament on 2 July 1800 and in the Irish one on 1 August, and came into effect on 1 January 1801. By and large, it was welcomed by the Catholic hierarchy and the better-off Catholics, for it was understood that Catholic Emancipation would shortly follow. When people now spoke of 'Catholic Emancipation' what they had in mind was admission to the higher offices of state and the right to sit in parliament. The denial of these during the decade of the 1790s had been a political misjudgment, for had they been conceded, the Catholic establishment might have been expected to align itself positively with the establishment as a whole. The fact that they were not finally granted until 1829 compounded the blunder. There was substantial opposition to the Union from the Protestant ascendancy. There were some who doggedly defended the record of the Irish parliament, even if there were others who had to be bribed because they were glad they had a country to sell. But Protestants learned not only to live with the Union but to support it actively as the Catholic majority in Ireland inevitably made a growing impact on public and political life. In the eighteenth century Irish patriotism had been very much a Protestant preserve. After the crucial decade of the 1790s it was well on the way to becoming a Catholic one.[8]

The
Waning of 'Old Ireland'

In its general social structures the Irish Catholic population at the beginning of the nineteenth century still looked backwards to the past. In many respects its social stratification was still determined by the experience of the great confiscations of the seventeenth century. The families held in highest social esteem were the surviving Catholic landowners. Though their holdings had been reduced to approximately 5 per cent of Irish land, this figure does not give the full picture, for it is clear that many of the old families who had been forced into conformity by the pressures of the penal code did not suffer any loss of social respect because of this. Next in the social order came those regarded as descendants of former proprietors, many of them wealthy 'middlemen', holding large farms on advantageous terms. In the towns there was a great deal of 'new wealth' in the hands of the Catholic merchants who had prospered during the eighteenth century.

About twenty years ago the hypothesis was advanced that the Irish economy in the early years of the nineteenth century might be divided into two sections: a 'money economy' or 'maritime economy' along the east and south coasts, from Belfast to Cork, together with the ports of Limerick and Galway, and a 'subsistence economy' in the rest of the country.[1] The 'money economy', it was claimed, was closely linked with the economy of Britain, indeed part of it. As is the way with all historical hypotheses, this one has been nibbled at steadily since it was first advanced. It has been pointed out, for example, that all over the country, there was a 'monetary stratum' overlying a 'subsistence stratum', though their comparative strength did vary considerably in the two broad regions.

The overall distinction into two areas has survived criticism, and certainly must be borne in mind as a counterbalance to the model of an industrialised Lagan valley set in sharp contrast to all the rest of Ireland. It has been estimated that about three and a half million people came through the Famine on their own resources, most of them in the east and north. These must have been living at something above subsistence level.

The first great catalyst in Irish society was the long war waged by Britain against revolutionary France. War conditions were unfavourable to the old landed wealth. The landlords suffered severely from the sharp rise in prices, for much of their land was let on long leases at fixed rents, and although they took corrective action as these leases fell in, it was too late for some of them. On the other hand, wartime conditions were favourable for the city and town merchants. They increased their wealth and in some cases made great fortunes.

Catholics were well placed to take advantage of changing economic circumstances because of the cumulative effect of the Relief Acts. The last of these had been enacted at the beginning of the war, in 1793. Almost all strictly religious disabilities were removed. Catholics could be admitted to the professions, fairly widely to the public service, and in a still guarded way to the political processes. They had been able to purchase land in fee simple since 1782.

Many Catholics now had the wealth to purchase land, and many Protestant landowners were so financially embarrassed as to have to sell. Catholic wealth was in the hands of both the commercial classes in the towns and the rural middlemen. They began by taking mortgages on the lands of Protestants, and the next step was frequently the outright sale of the land to the creditor. In most cases the amounts of land involved were comparatively small, up to about three hundred acres, and the transfer did little to benefit tenants, for the new merchant proprietors were almost necessarily absentees. The wealthier purchasers, however, did establish themselves as resident landlords, like the Wexford banking family of Redmond, who acquired a large estate, previously Protestant, in 1799.

In some respects these new proprietors still looked backwards. Many of the rural middlemen would have regarded themselves as the descendants of former landowners, and the new merchant landlords often took pains to provide themselves with a pedigree to substantiate a similar claim. It took some time before the old Catholic landowners accepted the newcomers as social equals, but as more and more of them bought their way into landed property the distinction of its origin tended to become a little blurred. In parts of the country at least, substantial Catholic leaseholders remained, even though the new policies forced on the landlords by wartime economic difficulties brought pressure on the middlemen. Wakefield notes that most of the land in north Tipperary was still held by middlemen in 1812, most of them Catholics, like the Scullys, the Ryans and the Maras.

Catholic wealth grew in the towns also. What must be noted, however, is that this wealth was still preponderantly the traditional *merchant* wealth. In the areas more recently opened up by the law — manufacture, the professions, the public service — Catholic penetration was slow in the first half of the nineteenth century, because Catholic penetration was resisted. Discrimination against them was particularly heavy in the growing world of banking. In consequence, while the wealth of middle-class Catholics grew, the social base of that wealth broadened only slowly. In the more deprived areas, much of Ulster for instance, the 'middle class' might consist of a few sizeable farmers, a gombeen-man or two, the Catholic teachers in the National Schools, and the occasional Catholic doctor.

In the towns, however, middle-class Catholic merchants did hold great wealth. A point to be noted here — its religious implications will be discussed in more detail later — is the number of them who spent a great deal of that wealth on religious and philanthropic purposes. In Wexford town, for example, Richard Devereux provided almost all the physical fabric for religious and social life from his great personal fortune. Many other merchants in other towns were active supporters of temperance movements, educational ventures, libraries and schemes of general self-improvement, mostly with a marked religious bent. No doubt there were strong elements of economic self-interest in their actions, but there were also strong elements of real religious philanthropy that resulted in many of the urban poor becoming genuinely literate and in consequence different material for catechesis — whether by priests or later by Fenians.

Uncertainties multiply as we move to the rural poor — the *brúscar an bhaile*, to take the phrase so often on the lips of the diarist Humphrey O'Sullivan. One thing is beyond question — the number of those whose economic condition held out no hope was increasing, not just in absolute numbers, but at least in the more deprived areas as a percentage of the total population. In these areas — and this surely indicates a social order in deep trouble — it appears that it was the better-off who were emigrating, since only they had the means to do so. An increasingly desperate poor remained. These people were coming under no influence of 'modernisation': in so far as they saw structures in their lives, these structures derived from the past. They are a silent people, taught by hardship to keep their own counsel.

Their memories of 'the old stock' were less and less of a defence against the hardships of life. The 'small people' of Catholic Ireland were defenceless and frightened. As Edward Wakefield reported as early as 1812:

> They live in continual apprehension and have no confidence in their own situation; haunted with the terror of persecution, they feel they are without protectors; they are alive to the least alarm; and this must be the case, until they see the aristocracy of their own faith participating equally with the Protestants in the political power of the country.[2]

Lord Cloncurry wrote in even starker terms in 1823, when the wartime boom was over:

> Depravity and a determined spirit of vengeance seem to have taken root in the heart of the despairing multitude. Our rulers think of no other

remedy than the sword and the halter.... In Connacht the military were giving out small portions of potatoes to the starving multitude, at the same time with the bayonet ready to prevent a rush.[3]

From the 1760s the poor had sought to exert some leverage through secret combinations backed by violence or the threat of violence. The Defenders had given a political turn to what had been in origin an economic protest. As more and more people faced the possibility of actual starvation the violence increased. Ireland in the first thirty years of the nineteenth century was a violent country indeed.

The tendency to refer to all secret societies as 'Ribbonmen' has confused the situation further. The real Ribbonmen appear to have been the heirs of the Defenders and active only in the north of the country. They were sectarian in that they fought for Catholic interests against Protestant interests. In the south organised violence was the heir of Whiteboyism, and its objects were economic, land above all as the pressure grew on this only resource in Ireland, but also opposition to the payment of tithes, county cess, vestry cess, and the dues of the Catholic clergy. These societies were the Threshers, the Whitefeet, the Terry Alts, and many more. They seem to have been less organised than the eighteenth-century Whiteboys, in that their organisation appears to have been more local and less permanent, inclined to form and dissolve as local issues presented themselves. In Connacht especially they tended to be more influenced by Ribbonism, while in Munster they merged with the mindless traditional faction-fighting so prevalent in that province. And everywhere the general atmosphere of violence gave an opening to the person essentially the gangster, who loved terrorism for its own sake. Many may have turned to the secret societies for protection because they had no other protectors; but while there was widespread public sympathy, those willing to take an active part may have been outnumbered by those caught up in a web of mindless violence they would have preferred did not exist. Nevertheless, in a society where there was so much intolerable misery, with each group exploiting the group immediately below it, and almost no institutional provision for the really destitute, it was hard for the poor to rule out the weapons of violence and intimidation. The better-off were frequently afraid to do anything. The Catholic clergy consistently opposed the secret societies, often with real courage, and with some measure of success, especially when Daniel O'Connell developed his political organisation. Improved policing, culminating in the setting up of the Irish Constabulary in 1836, also made its contribution, as did the Poor Law of 1838, in that it offered some alternative to starvation or begging, even if at the cost of what was effectively imprisonment in the workhouse.

Sir William Wilde recalled 'the old days' vividly (he was born in 1815). With so little work in the country districts, especially in the winter months, men slept all day and 'went out with the boys' at night. The magistrates were so afraid that they tried to stop all meetings, even 'merrymaking and amusements of the people'. 'Really, the only available or permitted amusements were wakes and funerals — on which account some of the latter were mock.' When there had to be a gathering,

> The only available force were the old barony constables — generally superannuated pensioners from the yeomanry or militia; always Protestants, and most of them foresters, *cleevins*, old servants or hangers-on of the magistrate — who dressed in long blue surtout coats, with scarlet collars, buckskin breeches, and rusty top-boots. Each of these old men was mounted, and carried a heavy cavalry sword, his only weapon, for he was seldom fit to be entrusted with any other. Two or three of these *fogies* might be seen at fairs, patterns, and markets, riding up and down to keep the peace, which, as soon as the superintending magistrate had gone to dinner, they generally broke by getting gloriously drunk. This the people usually bore, however, with good humour, seldom injuring the constable, but affording themselves much amusement by *welting* with their blackthorns their crusty nags, which, knowing perfectly what was about taking place, immediately commenced *lashing*, as if aware that the time was come for the farce, although during the previous portion of the day they remained as sober as their masters.[4]

Had anything serious developed at this stage, the forces available to preserve the peace would have been seriously inadequate.

It would nevertheless be unjust to see the Irish Catholic poor simply as people made desperate by deprivation. All who observed them were agreed that they had many good qualities, such as the chastity of their women and the practical charity of their lives. In a society always gazing into the pit of starvation, with no institutional provision for the destitute, the poor helped out the poor as a matter of daily routine, conscious no doubt that any day it might be their own turn.

It was nevertheless a society where one would expect politics to settle down on class lines, not sectarian ones. In fact sectarianism found it hard enough to take root in what might seem well-prepared soil. Even the shocks of the 1790s did not of themselves ensure a sectarian bias in society. The so-called 'Second Reformation' that began in the 1820s did drive the sectarian wedge further home. Of itself, however, it might not have made politics sectarian. The aim to make the Church of Ireland the church of the nation in fact as well as in law had largely lain dormant since the great confiscations of the seventeenth century. It was now revived because of Evangelical fervour. The first leaders were laymen, some of them English. The Church of Ireland clergy were divided, and many of them had serious reservations. What the campaign certainly achieved was to stir the long memories: the priest-hunter, the Mass-rocks, the lost lands. However, these memories were stirred primarily among the poor, to whom the mission was directed, and among the priests, whose position was directly challenged. It may well be asked what would have been the reaction of the Catholic middle classes had there not been another ingredient in the mix.

That ingredient was the delay of Catholic Emancipation. What the law still withheld from Catholics was the right to sit in parliament and fuller access to the public service. These matters were of advantage only to the better-off. It had been promised that they would be conceded immediately after the Union. All dispassionate observers agreed that they were very reasonable demands. Nevertheless, they were not conceded until the Catholics, led by Daniel O'Connell, had mounted a formidable agitation. The broader political consequences of that agitation concern us very indirectly, but they were quite remarkable. Middle-class Catholics seeking seats in parliament displaced the Ribbonmen as the popular leaders. The movement had been built up by Catholics seeking what were widely believed to be just Catholic demands. The organisation and structures of the Catholic church were pressed into service, if only because over much of the country no other organisation and structures existed. Religious polarisation was ensured when many Protestants resisted these Catholic demands, and when far more Protestants refused to work the system and withdrew into a defensive ghetto once they had been granted. One need not share all the Marxist assumptions of Emile Strauss to perceive the accuracy of his comment:

> The unimaginative stubbornness of the High Church Tories and Dublin Castle had produced the junction between the hesitating middle classes and the masses of the Irish people, which England's cleverest politicians had tried to prevent because of their knowledge that it would make Ireland completely ungovernable.[5]

Politics, no doubt, is always about conflicting interests, but at this stage in Irish history politics settled into a pattern of religious sectarianism rather than of class conflict. The fact that it was the Catholics who had to assert their place in the political nation may afford some of the explanation of the fact that their movements, whatever their faults, were seen as directed to advance Catholicism rather than to oppose Protestantism. The Protestants, on the other hand, formed themselves into defensive alliances to push back Catholicism, as in, for example, the Protestant Tenantry Society, an association of Protestant landlords formed in 1841 for the purpose of putting Protestant tenants in the place of evicted Catholics. Over much of the country causes like this simply could not be won.

In 1824 Bishop James Doyle of Kildare and Leighlin came up with quite startling proposals for a union of churches. It was worth trying, he said, for the political advantages it would bring. Theologically, he felt it was not difficult,

> for in the discussions and correspondence which occurred on this subject early in the last century, as well as that in which Archbishop Wake was engaged, and others which were considered between Bossuet and Leibnitz, it appeared that the points of agreement between the churches were numerous, those on which the parties hesitated few, and apparently not the most important.[6]

There was much in his vision of political advantages to commend itself to the Catholic middle-class laity in the 1820s, but while he may well have picked up his theology when he attended the schools of Coimbra, it was dated everywhere in the early nineteenth century, and particularly dated in Ireland. Yet a number of bishops were very anxious for good relations — the always irenic Archbishop Murray of Dublin, for instance — while even in the years when Orangeism mustered its forces against Catholic Emancipation the consecration of two successive Catholic bishops in Belfast — Crolly (1825) and Denvir (1835) — seem to have been quite ecumenical occasions.

The 'Second Reformation' and in particular the policies of Archbishop Magee of Dublin were hostile. The churches drifted further apart when he precipitated a dispute over Catholic burials. All cemeteries were in the hands of the established church. The law was that Catholics might be buried in them for a fee, though no Catholic service was allowed. In practice, however, the Catholic priest was allowed to bury the Catholic dead. In 1822 Magee forbade a Catholic service in a Dublin city cemetery, and he continued this policy. In St John's in Limerick in 1824 a fracas sufficiently serious to call for intervention by the military developed when the sexton interrupted the priest during a funeral service. A bill to enable the Protestant incumbent to give the priest permission to conduct a service if asked in writing satisfied nobody. Two considerations led to Catholics buying land for cemeteries. One was the fact that new cemeteries were needed, especially in the towns and cities. The second was that there was money available as the Catholic Association was wound up after 1829. Cemeteries were purchased in Dublin at Goldenbridge and Glasnevin. While Protestants were free to use these cemeteries, they were slow to do so. Separation extended to the grave.

At about the same time it became the norm for each Catholic parish to have its own register of baptisms and marriages. Particularly in the towns and cities, a number of registers do go back well into the eighteenth century, but most begin about the year 1829, except in Ulster and the more deprived areas elsewhere. In the nature of things, this further deepened the Catholic sense of common identity.

The Irish Catholics were indeed developing a sense of community at many levels. The fact that the bishops began to hold regular annual meetings inevitably developed their sense of being a corporate body. Provincial meetings had been held in the Tuam province since 1752, in Cashel since 1775, and in Armagh since 1779. The four metropolitans began to hold regular meetings in 1788. After 1795 there were a number of issues that helped to bring about regular meetings of all the bishops, in particular the establishment of Maynooth College and the question of possible state control over the church usually referred to as the 'Veto question'. From 1820 onwards the bishops met once a year to discuss ecclesiastical affairs.[7]

Another development helped to promote harmony between the bishops and their priests.[8] Since 1766 the name of the Stuart pretender had no longer figured in the nomination of Irish bishops. There was now no fixed procedure for the selection of bishops. The Holy See relied for its information on episcopal candidates on such reports as might be sent in by various interested parties, a procedure, or rather lack of procedure, that had obvious drawbacks. Rome sanctioned a new system in 1829. When a vacancy occurred, the parish priests of the diocese, together with the canons of the cathedral chapter, if such existed, met to ballot for three names. These names were sent to Rome and, placed in order of preference, to the bishops of the province. When these in turn met, they could delete a name or names — but not add any — and change the clergy's order of preference. They then sent their recommendations to Rome. During the episcopate of Cardinal Cullen (1849-78) his personal influence frequently led to the nomination of a person not on the list, but otherwise the Holy See normally appointed one of the persons proposed.

The system worked well until it was replaced in 1925. It had some drawbacks. There was no formal obligation to keep the results of the vote secret until 1911, and in fact there was no secrecy. In consequence, there was something of the atmosphere of a parliamentary election, and this increased the possibility of a disappointed faction when the new bishop was named. All in all, however, the system gave the parish priests of the diocese some reason to feel they had a real voice in the nomination of their bishop, and this did help to promote good relations.

The assistant priest or 'curate' was a creature with few rights and heavy responsibilities. The parish system had been restructured in the eighteenth century. Most of the parishes were too large for one priest, especially as the population grew. Assistants were appointed when available, but they were completely dependent on the parish priest, given their keep, usually the keep of their horse, and little more. The bishops' meeting of 1829 set up a subcommittee to report on ecclesiastical discipline. This led to provincial synods in the early 1830s. They produced legislation that included what might be called a 'curates' charter'. There is evidence that it was strongly resisted by the parish priests in Gaelic Ireland, but henceforth the bishop had the right to name a curate to a parish, and the curate had a legal right to a defined share of the parish revenue.

Parish priests or curates, there were not enough of them. Their numbers did grow, but more slowly than the population. In 1800 there was one priest for 2,100 Catholics, in 1840 one for 3,000. The numbers of priests increased rapidly in the 1840s, as Maynooth grew, but it was only when famine drastically reduced the population that the ratio improved on what it had been in 1800. In 1850 there was one priest for 2,000 Catholics.[9] More detailed figures are available for 1834; the following examples may be cited:[10]

Ecclesiastical province of Armagh	1:2,805
Civil province of Ulster	1:2,845
Ecclesiastical province of Dublin	1:2,451
Ecclesiastical province of Cashel	1,3,175
Ecclesiastical province of Tuam	1:3,678
Diocese of Derry (best in Ulster)	1:2,485
Diocese of Raphoe (worst in Ulster)	1:3,381
Diocese of Tuam (worst in province)	1:4,199
Diocese of Ferns (best overall)	1:1,941

The towns had traditionally been better provided for than the country districts. Belfast was an exception. Here the number of priests was far too small for the rapidly growing Catholic population. Elsewhere, however, the contrast between town and country could be striking. In the diocese of Armagh in 1834 (apart from Drogheda) there was one Sunday Mass for every 1,700 people bound by the precept of attendance, while in Drogheda there was one Mass for every 550.[11]

It has been said that the clergy might have provided more Masses.[12] The matter is not quite so simple. The Counter-Reformation church had set its face against the multiplication of Masses, because of the great abuses that had arisen. There was also a tradition as old as the church itself that emphasised the one Sunday Mass as the gathering of the whole community. A priest might get permission to 'binate' or say two Masses on Sunday because of pastoral needs, but this was to be regarded as exceptional. As happens so often, the letter of the law came to count for more than the pastoral needs. In the early nineteenth century, in Ireland as elsewhere, there was a real sense of inhibition against a priest saying two Masses in the same church even on Sundays. Cashel statutes for 1810, for example, allowed him to 'binate' only if he had two chapels in his parish and did not have a curate. Regulations in Tuam and Armagh were even more restrictive.

The problems were increased when, as was often the case, the chapels simply could not accommodate the numbers. It is true that in the towns especially there were new buildings with some pretensions to architectural dignity. This was especially true of the cathedrals: Waterford (1793), Cork (1799), Dublin (1815) and Carlow (1828). Even some very poor dioceses began building impressive cathedrals, such as Killala and Tuam, both in 1827. For the most part, however, the chapels were plain and functional. As described by Mr and Mrs Hall in 1841, they were 'exceedingly ungraceful structures, resembling, in their exterior, rather huge and ungainly barns than edifices for divine worship'. They go on to speak of the bare and whitewashed interior walls, the altar with its 'shabby tinsel ornaments' and 'miserable coloured prints'. There were a few pews or chairs for the better-off, while the poor stood or knelt on the clay or stone floor.[13]

Of the clergy it can fairly be said that they were on the whole worthy men. As a body, they could be described as 'middle-class', in their origins and in their standard of living. Nowhere did their social equals among the laity regard them with any subservience: indeed, as will be seen, the laity had a quite active role in church affairs. As for the poor, they ministered to them faithfully. There was often only the priest to turn to when the charity of neighbours failed. They could be domineering. In 1812 Wakefield noted a priest in Castlepollard who beat his people into respect for the clergy when they displeased him. At the mission in Dingle in 1846 the parish priest kept the queue for confession in order by riding up and down with a whip. The 'silent people' were used to being so treated, and the priest had at least inherited some of the authority of the *taoiseach*. There may not be too much caricature in Carleton's portrait of 'Father Finnerty', at least for the northern countryside that was Carleton's country:

> ...one of those priests who constitute a numerous species in Ireland. Regular, but loose and careless, in the observances of his church, he could not be taxed with any positive neglect of pastoral duty. He held his stations at stated times and places with great exactness; but when the severer duties annexed to them were performed, he relaxed into the boon companion, sang his song, told his story, laughed his laugh, and occasionally danced his dance, the very beau-ideal of a shrewd, humorous divine.... The priests can, the moment such scenes are ended, pass with greatest aptitude of habit into the hard, gloomy character of men who are replete with profound knowledge, exalted piety, and extraordinary power.

Socially, such a group might be expected to be conservative, and such on the whole they were. The bishops in particular were only reluctantly involved by the middle-class laity in the political struggle, even for Catholic Emancipation, and there were even more hesitations when it came to Repeal. They may have felt more comfortable on such an occasion as the proclamation of William IV in Limerick on 5 July 1830, when the Catholic clergy walked in the procession, resplendent in soutane, surplice, stole and biretta, 'a scene not witnessed in Limerick since James II',[14] and, of course, highly illegal under the recently passed Emancipation Act of 1829. For most of them 'the principles of 1793' were still a living memory. They feared revolution, and they had reason to fear it.

Maynooth College was undoubtedly the biggest single factor differentiating the new age from the old. It had been founded in 1795 when revolutionary developments in Europe had closed the continental seminaries. Their closure had created a major crisis for the Catholic church in Ireland. True, there were now some centres at home for the education of priests, notably Carlow. They were, however, totally inadequate as replacement for the losses abroad, and the Catholic bishops simply did not have the means to expand them. Britain was now at war with revolutionary France, and in consequence had an interest in helping the bishops. The help offered took the form of legislation allowing the endowment of a Catholic college and a modest annual grant towards its support. In return the bishops had to accept a governing body — the trustees — not exclusively ecclesiastical and a board of visitors not exclusively Catholic.

It was to be some time before Maynooth came anywhere near replacing the lost continental colleges. Before the Revolution these had provided nearly 500 places in all. When Europe settled down after the revolutionary wars only about 140 of these were restored. The magnitude of the task, the poverty of the institution and the complexity of its structures did not make for painless development at Maynooth. The fact that there were six presidents in the first eighteen years of its history tells its own story. The college had very serious disciplinary problems during these years. Some bishops might feel that the situation could be controlled only by drastic measures, but these could not be taken — or at least they were not taken — because of the structures of college government, and also, probably, because of serious differences and antagonisms among its administrative staff. Contact between the trustees and staff was seriously deficient: for a number of years the trustees met in Dublin, and the college never saw them.[15] The theology course was unsatisfactory, both in its structure and because there were no textbooks. It was a three-year course only, and many students did not complete it, because their bishops, desperate for priests, ordained them sometimes even before they had finished the second year of the course in theology.

The situation was brought under control by Bartholomew Crotty, President from 1813 to 1833. In the early years of his presidency a number of capable men were appointed to the staff: Cornelius Denvir, James Browne, Charles MacNally and John MacHale. The college buildings were extended bit by bit as money was scraped together bit by bit (the fall in the price of provisions after 1815 must have helped). In 1826 Crotty was able to report to a government commission of inquiry that there were 392 students in the college, and that these, together with those on the continent and elsewhere in Ireland, were sufficient to provide replacements for priests who had died. Replacements, however, were not enough, as the population climbed inexorably. The number of priests grew, but not as fast as the numbers of the people. Despite genuinely heroic efforts, the overall situation was worse when the Famine came than it had been in 1800. Thereafter the numbers of priests continued to increase and the population fell. The numbers of Maynooth priests grew especially rapidly after the great increase in the government grant in 1845. Laurence Renehan, President in 1853, was able to tell a government commission in that year that half the priests of Ireland had been educated in Maynooth, and that the college's 516 students represented two-thirds of all Irish seminarians.

The 'Maynooth priest' had arrived. He met a great deal of criticism. He was contrasted unfavourably with the old 'gentlemanly' product of the continental seminaries. He was, it was alleged, a demagogue, coming for the most part from the lower ranks of society, more interested in political leadership than in spiritual ministration, his native bigotry reinforced by his education, which, in the words of one critic, produced 'the habits of a secluded student engrafted on the rudeness of a clown'.[16] This picture is certainly overdrawn to the point of caricature. To begin with, most of it comes from extremely hostile witnesses, suspicious of popery in any form, and especially suspicious of popery in the concrete circumstances of early nineteenth-century Ireland. There is no reason to think that the social class from which the priests were drawn changed any more markedly than the general shifts in the social order. They still for the most part came from among the better-off, though the composition of the 'better-off' class was changing. The priests were certainly more involved in politics, but this was not because they came from Maynooth but because the Irish political scene was changing, and, all in all, the priests were not the leaders in this change. One does come across a charge, how well founded it is not easy to say, that the Maynooth priest was a rigorist because of the character of his theological training, dominated, it was alleged, by the Jansenistic strain imported by his professors, either Frenchmen themselves or Irishmen who had been formed in France, and that this theological rigorism was reinforced by the type of spiritual formation given in the college. All we can say is that there may be something to this charge. It should be noted, however, that in so far as it may have been true it represents something like arrested development rather than a new departure. The staff alleged to be forming Jansenists in Maynooth were precisely the people who would have been forming Jansenists in France if the Revolution had not happened; and if what his critics said of him was true, the seminarian was better placed to resist indoctrination in Maynooth than if he had been in a seminary in France.

The regular clergy were too few in number to make any great contribution.[17] The monastic order had not survived the penal code, but it returned to Ireland when the Cistercians came to Mount Melleray in 1832. The Society of Jesus had been suppressed in the universal church in 1773, but in Ireland as elsewhere its members continued to minister as secular priests. When restoration came in 1814 the Irish province found a new vitality under the leadership of Peter Kenny. Since the Reformation the various orders of friars had been the strength of the regular clergy in Ireland. The decisions of Benedict XIV in 1751, requiring all novices to be trained in the continental colleges, rapidly affected their numbers, and the modification of these decisions in 1774 did not halt the decline. The Dominicans fell from 156 in 1767 to 77 in 1817, and their decline continued. In 1811 the Franciscans had only one priest in most of their houses and had been forced to drop the traditional practice of naming titular superiors to all the pre-Reformation foundations because they had not sufficient friars. In other places they had to abandon a physical presence: the last friar went. In most instances this was in Gaelic areas of their traditional strength. More and more they were concentrated in the towns, and even there resources were stretched. Only the houses in Dublin, Cork, Wexford and Galway had more than three priests, though several Franciscans were acting as parish priests and curates.

Benedict XIV in 1751 had given bishops power to appoint friars to parishes, and they exercised it more freely as their need for priests grew. This had its effects on the friars who remained in their houses, in that their work and lifestyle tended to approximate to that of the diocesan priest, with each individual having control over his own money and any real community life under constant pressure. About 1840, for instance, the friars in Wexford protested against the assignment of a Dublin-born friar to the house, claiming that it was a very old tradition that only Wexford-born friars served in it, and that this had greatly helped in maintaining good relations with the bishop.

From other centres there is evidence of bishops trying to extend their control over the friars. In 1793 Bishop Moylan of Cork demanded that the various religious orders in the city preach in his cathedral. His successor, Bishop Murphy, claimed they had a strict obligation to do so, and when this claim was resisted he closed the novitiate the Franciscans had set up in the city. Other bishops took a similar line. Bishop Abraham of Waterford tried to stop the Franciscans building a new church, and when it was completed in 1834 he tried to stop them using it, as he wished all the friars in the towns of his diocese to work in the parishes.

The closing of the continental novitiates during the revolutionary wars had been a severe blow. The friars tried to set up substitutes in Ireland, the Franciscans, for example, at Cork and Wexford, though, as has been seen, a dispute with the bishop temporarily closed the Cork house. Not long after they regained the houses on the continent a new threat loomed. In the Catholic Emancipation Act of 1829 there were nine separate clauses of what was in effect new penal legislation, aimed at their 'gradual suppression and final extinction' (it was legal opinion that their existence had been tolerated by the Relief Act of 1793). This new penal legislation had been added because there were fears that the act would not pass without such clauses as a sop to Protestant opinion. They were, however, so framed as to ensure they would not be invoked, notably in the stipulation that a prosecution could be brought only by the Attorney General and not by a local magistrate.

In fact they were never invoked, but their very existence was a real deterrent to any expansion in the numbers of the religious orders. Firm figures are hard to come by: the list of those who registered under the provisions of the act does not clearly indicate who were the fully professed priest-members, and the information in the early numbers of the *Catholic Directory* is obviously incomplete. The *Directory* for 1847 does, however, give a total of 215. In all probability this does not represent an increase over the preceding half-century. In 1849 the Franciscans were still complaining of shortages: forty-two friars were trying to staff fourteen friaries. Only Galway and Wexford had sufficient numbers; Cork had three but needed six, and Drogheda and Athlone, each with two, needed three.

The number of schools increased rapidly in early nineteenth-century Ireland, probably even more rapidly than the population. In so far as we can recover the education system of the eighteenth century, it appears as essentially a parish system, with, no doubt, some independent teachers who are harder to bring into the light of history because they have left such little documentation. By the end of the century, however, it is quite clear that the private schools had increased greatly in number, though most parishes still had their schools. Frequently school was held in the chapel — in those parishes rich enough to have built a chapel and not yet rich enough to have built a separate schoolhouse. The private schools were multiplying, however. In his diocesan report of 1790 Bishop Patrick Plunkett of Meath noted 240 of them in his diocese, not far short of what the general survey of 1825 revealed, namely an average of about six schools in each rural parish, with far more in the towns. In the towns too the nuns and Christian Brothers were beginning to make an impact, the nuns at this date (1825) having forty-six schools and the brothers twenty-four.

For most if not all of these schools, the parish priest was a figure of power. The private schoolmaster may not have needed his permission to open, but his disapproval might well close him down. Ecclesiastical regulations for Cashel (1810) and Dublin (1831) envisage two types of school: a parish school where the priest has the most positive obligation to see that it is as large and well equipped as possible, and the other schools, where he has a general duty of supervision, with the right to visit the school, to see that the children know the catechism and that the teachers teach it, and the right to ensure that the teacher is a man of good moral life.

Where did all these teachers come from? It seems beyond question that many of them came from the old learned classes, the scribes and the poets. Some of the poets had been schoolmasters at an earlier date, when the learned classes still had a measure of patronage. As this declined they took to teaching, and many of the growing number of schoolmasters in some sense became recruits to the literary tradition. Schoolmasters were inevitably prominent in diffusing the new revolutionary principles. In consequence, the growing number of private schools in the early nineteenth century were centres for an inflammable fusion of historic resentments and democratic principles.

If the parish priest kept an eye on the teaching of catechism, the state developed a concern for the whole teaching programme. It attempted to provide a counterweight by subsidies to educational societies, notably the Kildare Place Society, founded in 1811. In the circumstances of early nineteenth-century Ireland, it was inevitable that these schools should run foul of the Catholic church authorities on charges of proselytism. The 1820s were filled with a debate on how an acceptable school system might be provided in Ireland. The outcome was the National Schools in 1831.

This system was to be non-sectarian, with respect for the religious faith of each child. All were to receive secular education together, and time was set aside for separate religious education. The Protestant churches found the system unacceptable. For the established church, education was a church matter and no concern of the state. The Presbyterians would accept the new schools only on conditions that would have made them in fact denominational. The Catholics disliked several features of the system, but, quite simply, beggars could not be choosers. Archbishop MacHale of Tuam was hostile from the beginning, but when he decided not to allow the new schools in his diocese the consequences indicated all too clearly that the Catholic church simply did not have the resources to provide an alternative. As the system took root elsewhere there was one particularly interesting development. The key figure was the 'patron', who applied for a school and became its manager. In most cases he was the Catholic priest. Ironically perhaps, the new state system restored to the Catholic church a great deal of the control over the primary school system which it had been in danger of losing over the previous fifty years. As Thackeray put it in 1843:

Look at the National School: throughout the country it is commonly by the chapel-side — it is a Catholic school, directed and fostered by the priest; and as no people are more eager for learning, more apt to receive it, or more grateful for kindness, than the Irish, he gets all the gratitude of the scholars who flock to the school, and all the fuller influence over them, which naturally and justly come to him.[18]

Another point should be noted: the new system began the era of universal literacy. For all the multiplication of schools, the poor were still illiterate before 1831, especially in the rural areas. Pastoral directives and assessments assume that a great number cannot read. Bishop Doyle of Kildare and Leighlin, writing in 1821, is quite explicit. The schools in general were bad, he said, the masters in many instances insufficient, and the buildings so small and cramped that only the most primitive teaching methods were possible. Things were a little better in the towns, but still it was only a very imperfect education that the children of the better-off and most of the farmers' children received. The poor got nothing in the country and little in the towns. And this was where things were at their best, in Leinster and Munster. He had visited Connacht, where 'they are buried in destitution, filth, ignorance and misery'. He had no personal experience of the Ulster Catholics, but he believed things were not much better there.[19]

So in early nineteenth-century Ireland it is impossible to generalise about schools and schoolmasters, any more than about priests and people. In so far as the distinction between 'maritime' and 'subsistence' Ireland is visualised as a line on a map, that line is constantly blurred by economic considerations themselves, the basic distinction between rich and poor, by cultural considerations like the level of literacy and the language spoken, and by the proportion of Catholic to Protestant in any given region (the Catholics of east Ulster must be classed as religiously 'deprived', though they lived in an economically prosperous area). But the most fundamental line of division, as might be expected, was between the better-off and the poor. Everywhere the poor tended to speak Irish and the better-off to speak English. As always, the towns demand separate treatment, and a distinction may now be usefully drawn between other towns and the greater cities (in order of population, Dublin, Cork, Belfast and Limerick). That adds up to four distinct, or at least distinguishable areas. In each of them the experience of 'being a Catholic' was different.

That the level of religious practice did vary between these four areas, at least as tested by the central requirement of Catholic practice, attendance at Sunday Mass, appears quite definitely in the report of a commission set up in 1834 to inquire into religious and other public instruction in Ireland. Its report, published in 1835, gave detailed countrywide figures for Mass attendance. They have been subjected to some analysis by the American historian David Miller.[20] He notes that the figures given are in many cases subject to more than one interpretation and in no sense represent a modern socio-religious study. A further complication arises from the fact that the survey was based on the Church of Ireland parishes, which very often did not coincide with the Catholic ones. On the basis of sampling where the figures seem firmest, he concludes that Mass attendance figures were: the four cities (Dublin, Cork, Belfast, Limerick), 40 per cent to 60 per cent; the other towns, 80 per cent to 100 per cent; the rural English-speaking areas, 30 per cent to 60 per cent; and the rural Irish-speaking areas, 20 per cent to 40 per cent.

Two considerations in particular suggest that these figures may be too low; one is not quantifiable, but the other is. It has been noted above that the survey was 'Protestant' in that it was based on the Church of Ireland parishes. It was also 'Protestant' in that it asked for attendance figures at 'the principal service', which makes sense for a single Holy Communion, but not for possibly a number of Masses. It may be that the figure given sometimes represents the attendance at one Mass only, but if so, there is no way of establishing how many may have attended other Masses — if there were other Masses. This consideration may not affect the percentages greatly in the rural Irish-speaking areas, for, as already noted, it was in these that there were the greatest inhibitions about having more than one Mass in each church.

The second consideration is quantifiable and substantial. Miller makes no allowance for those not under obligation to hear Mass, especially the children under seven. These he should quite certainly have excluded. The annual *Catholic Directory*, beginning in 1836, has in its earlier issues a list of rules for 'conduct in the house of God'. The sixth rule reads: 'Mothers should take care not to disturb the congregation by bringing children under the age required.' Children under seven comprised one-sixth of the population. If we add the aged, the sick, the otherwise impeded — mothers caring for young children, for example — it is a conservative estimate that one-fifth of the population did not come to Mass because the precept of attending did not bind them. Correcting Miller's figures by this factor, we get: the four cities, 50 per cent to 75 per cent; the towns, effectively 100 per cent; the rural English-speaking areas, 37.5 to 75 per cent; and the rural Irish-speaking areas, 25 per cent to 50 per cent. These figures must be regarded as minimum figures rather than as firm figures, because of possible uncertainties in the data. But when all correctives are applied it seems clear that in this matter there has been a deterioration over the previous fifty years; that the deterioration has been most marked in the more deprived areas (though there are indications that in these more Mass centres simply escaped the count because Mass was still said in places other than a chapel and even in the open air); but that nevertheless the general pattern is still the same as has been discernible since the effective beginning of the Counter-Reformation early in the seventeenth century.

Turning now to the cities, it may be noted that the great bulk of the available information concerns Dublin. Just at the time when Dublin had ceased to be a political capital it became an ecclesiastical capital for Catholic Ireland. This was in part because of the development and increasing importance of national episcopal meetings: Dublin was the most convenient place to meet. But it was also because of the calibre of its archbishops, John Thomas Troy (1786-1823) and Daniel Murray (coadjutor 1809, succeeded 1823, died 1852). Troy's Roman connections had been particularly important in the many political questions that arose during his episcopate, while Murray's dedicated saintliness marked an episcopate that deserves more attention than it has hitherto received.[21]

In the cities there was an increasingly self-confident Catholic merchant and middle class. Their Catholic consciousness became more explicit as Catholic progress became more visible in the new churches and with the passage of Catholic Emancipation in 1829. Municipal reform left them poised to take over the corporations, a triumph sealed when Daniel O'Connell became Lord Mayor of Dublin in 1841. But the cities, Dublin especially, contained large numbers of the very poor. Dublin's demotion from being a political capital had hit it particularly severely. The poor were also drawn to the cities because until the new Poor Law of 1838 it was only here they had any prospect of institutional relief, and what little provision there was was largely concentrated in Dublin. The fact that the cities were major ports gave rise to the moral problems associated with major ports everywhere, though Wakefield noted in 1812 that while these problems were serious they were not as bad as in similar circumstances in England.[22] Ten years earlier Archbishop Troy in a report on his diocese had noted a general low level of piety and had singled out drunkenness as a particular problem.[23] Travellers' accounts continue to refer to public drunkenness and multitudes of beggars as common sights in Dublin.

Murray had been consecrated bishop in the old penal-day chapel in Liffey Street on 30 November 1809. The first of the new churches, St Teresa's, Clarendon Street, came the next year. It was followed by St Michan's and SS Michael and John's, reputedly the first Catholic church in Ireland to have an exterior bell. The foundation stone of the Pro-Cathedral (to replace Liffey Street chapel) was laid in 1815, and the church was dedicated in 1825. New churches came more swiftly after Emancipation. Over the years of Daniel Murray's episcopate (1809-52) ninety-seven churches were built in the diocese of Dublin.[24]

The families going to Mass on Sunday morning in the mid-1830s would scarcely have been conscious of the fact that they had entered statistics, but they had. In 1834 they were counted by a government commission. From 1836 onwards the *Catholic Directory* was listing the churches and the clergy. The new churches were beginning to make an impact, and while clerical numbers were still insufficient, they were less so in urban areas than in the rural ones. The fact that the 1834 survey was based on the Church of Ireland parishes is less of a drawback in estimating Mass attendance in the cities, for they can be taken as a whole, and even Dublin was still compact, not yet an urban sprawl. In one respect Dublin, Cork and Limerick conform very closely to a common pattern in that in all three cities two-thirds of those bound by the precept of Sunday Mass attendance did attend. As between the capital and the other two cities, Dublin had rather more people per priest, but the priests provided a better service in that almost every diocesan priest said his maximum of two Sunday Masses. Cork had the most priests per Catholic, but these priests did not provide quite the same level of service as in Dublin. Limerick lay in between; but in all three cities the level of Sunday Mass attendance was the same.

Belfast was different. In some respects it was a disaster area. Its population was growing rapidly, though it was still smaller than Cork. In 1834 it had about 21,000 Catholics, in one parish with two chapels, and, according to the 1837 *Catholic Directory*, three priests. Not surprisingly, only a quarter of those bound by precept to hear Mass did in fact do so. That many more would have gone had facilities been available seems clear from the fact that even greater numbers attended an evening service than attended Mass in the morning, but Belfast was to have its problems until Patrick Dorrian became bishop there in the 1860s.

The Dublin provincial statutes of 1831 laid down that Sunday Mass was to be preceded by the 'Acts of Contrition, Faith, Hope and Charity and a Prayer before Mass', and that at each Mass there was to be a sermon. When, however, one finds Dublin city churches providing up to twelve Masses on Sunday mornings it would seem clear that there simply was not time for a sermon at each Mass, and the early numbers of the *Catholic Directory* indicate that in fact there was a sermon only at some Masses, three being the norm. Everywhere, however, the members of the Confraternity of Christian Doctrine taught catechism for an hour after the last Mass.

Given the great numbers of the very poor in the cities, it is tempting to surmise that they were a disproportionate element in the third of the population that did not go to Mass. There is no evidence to support directly any such surmise. Indeed, a German Lutheran traveller in 1844, J. G. Kohl, noted that at one church in Cork those too poor to pay at the door assisted after their fashion from the steps outside:

> They are satisfied if they but hear the little bell of the assistant of the priest who officiates at the altar: when they have heard that little bell from within, and bowed and crossed themselves, they think they have heard Mass and participated in the worship of God.[25]

However, a consideration of the many sodalities and confraternities that multiplied in the cities, especially in Dublin, in the first half of the nineteenth century, does suggest, as might be expected, a more conscious commitment to religion on the part of the more economically secure. There was the Confraternity of the Blessed Sacrament and Christian Doctrine, which promoted Eucharistic devotion, especially benediction, and quickly organised catechetical instruction in each city church. The Confraternity of the Sacred Heart promoted the devotion of the holy hour and of the first Fridays. The Purgatorian Society visited the dying, tried to put down abuses at wakes and introduce a prayerful atmosphere, and met regularly to recite the office of the dead. Members of the Evening Office Society, initiated by Peter Kenny in the 1790s, met every evening after work to recite vespers and compline or the little office of the Blessed Virgin. The great cholera epidemic of 1832 saw the organisation of burial societies. There was also the Sodality of the Living Rosary. Temperance societies came relatively late, but they antedate Father Mathew's campaign. The Society of St Vincent de Paul was founded in 1845.

One striking feature of these societies of laymen is the extent to which they were run by laymen. Their rules were approved by ecclesiastical authority, and they had their chaplains, but they ran their own affairs under their lay committees. They included all ranks of society down to the level of skilled artisans.[26] That the very poor had no active role in them will be clear from the fact that their activities presuppose literacy. The Evening Office Book published in 1822 ran to 722 pages. It included daily vespers and compline in Latin and English, together with other prayers.

A parish school system had been built up in the eighteenth century. The parish schools in Dublin can be seen in the surviving Catholic *Directory* for 1821.[27] There were very many of them, their main support being an annual charity sermon. This, however, had to be supplemented, and we find laymen very prominent in their organisation. A priest will be 'guardian', but the other officers, president and treasurer for example, will be laymen. What diminished the role of the laity was the rise of the religious congregations of nuns and brothers. The few convents of nuns in eighteenth-century Ireland had conducted schools for girls. The first of the new foundations came in Cork with Nano Nagle. Her Presentation Sisters came to Dublin through Teresa Mullaly, though Teresa herself did not become a nun. The next foundations had their origin in Dublin — the Sisters of Charity, the Loreto Sisters and the Sisters of Mercy. In the cities the most important foundation of brothers was the Irish Christian Brothers, founded by Edmund Rice, who began his work in Waterford in 1802. After very humble beginnings — a disused stableyard in Waterford and a vacant timberyard in Dublin — the names later to become famous began to appear: Mount Sion, Waterford (1803), North Monastery, Cork (1816) and O'Connell School, Dublin (1831).[28]

Catholic general charitable institutions began in Dublin in 1771 with

Teresa Mullaly's illegal orphanage in Mary's Lane. The *Directory* of 1821 lists quite a number of institutions for orphans and widows. Once again the laity were prominent in organising them, but here too they lost ground to the emerging religious congregations. Already by 1821 the orphanage in North William Street was run by the Sisters of Charity. When they opened St Vincent's Hospital in 1835 it was the beginning of a new age.

The people who have so far emerged in the cities are in some sense an elite, literate and ready to form religious organisations to improve themselves and to help others. It is not so easy to document the more general level of religious practice. Those who mention it are agreed that at the beginning of the century there were serious problems — ignorance, drunkenness, violence, unchastity. What seems to have marked a real turning-point was the jubilee of 1826 (the extension from Rome to the universal church of the indulgences of the holy year of 1825). In Dublin at any rate the jubilee might be described as the first parish mission.[29] In every church there was instruction in the early morning, and again at midday and in the evening. Confessions were continuous, and the days of general communion with renewal of baptismal vows turned into a public proclamation of faith. After Emancipation in 1829 there grew up a pride in being an Irish Catholic, pride in an Irish Catholic presence throughout the English-speaking world, and the beginnings of an interest in the foreign missions. A Maynooth mission to India began in 1838.

The Catholic booksellers and publishers had flourished in Dublin even during the eighteenth century. Now they moved out of the net of narrow lanes around Cook Street into the new city, their business broadened by the general improvement in the lot of Catholics and the return of scholars from the continent under the impetus of the French Revolution.[30] The distinction of describing oneself as 'printer and bookseller to the Royal College of Maynooth' was eagerly sought. At 4 Capel Street Hugh Fitzpatrick printed the college's first theological textbooks, and among other things the *Irish Grammar* of its first professor of Irish, Paul O'Brien. Fitzpatrick's successor, Richard Coyne, who died in 1856, was a prominent figure in the Catholic revival. The early meetings of the Catholic Association were held in rooms over his shop: at one of them Maynooth played its part in helping O'Connell to get his way in enrolling the poor as associate members. It was Wednesday 4 February 1824. At twenty-three minutes past three there were seven members present at the meeting, some of them no friends to O'Connell's proposal. The quorum of ten was required by the half-hour. O'Connell dashed downstairs. He met the eighth member going up. In the shop he found two young Maynooth priests buying books. The rules of the association admitted all Catholic clergymen as honorary members, and O'Connell appealed to them to come up solely to make the quorum. They were reluctant, 'there being a good deal of hesitation generally on the part of the clergy to put themselves at all forward in politics, and these young men in particular having all the timidity of their secluded education about them'. Partly by exhortation and partly by physically pushing them, he got them into the meeting with a second or two to spare. The two clerics left the room within minutes, but the meeting had been duly got under way and their job was done.[31]

The booksellers were not confined to scholarly works. An important aspect of the 'Second Reformation' had been the distribution of pamphlets and tracts. At the instigation of Bishop Doyle of Kildare and Leighlin the Catholic hierarchy in 1827 gave approval to what was popularly known as the Catholic Book Society, set up to print and distribute as cheaply as possible Catholic literature, including schoolbooks. It claimed to have printed five million books within ten years. In 1835 the Catholic Society for Ireland was established, to promote parochial libraries, to co-ordinate the work of the sodalities and the Confraternities of Christian Doctrine, and to distribute publications free in cases of real need.

Even with this help, the impact on the more deprived areas was marginal. The Catholic Book Society seems to have done little to promote reading in the Irish language, despite the widespread use of Irish by Protestant Evangelical missionaries; but even had material in Irish been available free, there were many areas where there simply were not enough Catholics of sufficient social standing to make the scheme work. Elsewhere, in the towns particularly and in Dublin most of all, the society was fortunate in having W. J. Battersby as its agent. In some respects he was perhaps over-ready to take risks — his *Catholic Penny Magazine*, launched in 1830, came to an end in 1835 — but in other ways he was a shrewd businessman. His *Catholic Directory* began in 1836, and it lasted. By 1840 he was effectively running the Catholic Book Society, and it was formally handed over to him in 1845. The work of men like Battersby and Coyne undoubtedly did a great deal to strengthen the Irish Catholic sense of community in the first half of the nineteenth century. Their immediate successors are still active — James Duffy, who began as publisher of Young Ireland and became John Henry Newman's publisher in Dublin, and Michael Henry Gill, who opened in Sackville Street in 1856.

The smaller towns presented the same contrasts between Catholic wealth and Catholic poverty, but, especially in the 'old' towns, like Waterford, Wexford, Drogheda or Galway, the smaller numbers resulted in more tightly-knit communities. The number of priests available was more adequate than in either the cities or the countryside; in particular, each town had its friary, some more than one, though the personnel were often fewer than the friars judged to be adequate. The inquiry of 1834 had revealed a Sunday Mass attendance of virtually 100 per cent. There may be some indications that at least with the better-off this represented an improvement in comparison with a generation before: certainly Bishop Plunkett of Meath in his visitations around the turn of the century had noted a 'decay of piety' among some at least of 'the more decent class of people' in the towns of his diocese.

The merchant classes in the towns had benefited considerably from the wartime prosperity. At the same time evidence appears of a deeper religious commitment. It must be stressed, however, that despite some indications of a temporary cooling of religious fervour in the late eighteenth century, the old traditions had come through with real strength. In Waterford, for example, there is an impressive list of Catholic charitable foundations from the end of the 1770s, despite the fact that bequests for Catholic charities continued to be subject to penal legislation. Even the ancient charity of the Holy Ghost Hospital still kept a certain Catholic flavour. It had been founded at the end of the reign of Henry VIII by Patrick Walsh, a merchant of Waterford, on the site of the suppressed Franciscan friary, with the help of the friary's confiscated property. A little over a hundred years later the Walsh family, like many others, was forced into exile because of its commitment to the Catholic religion, but as late as 1735 the founder's rights of Nicholas Walsh were still recognised (he was then living in the Canary Islands), and these rights remained unextinguished even though effective control lay with the Protestant city corporation.[32]

A similar growth in Catholic self-confidence can be sensed in other towns. New churches were going up and old churches being renovated, like the Franciscan friary in Galway, rebuilt in 1781, externally plain but inside a handsome place of worship, though it was noted — with what truth it may be hard to establish — that the friars 'occasionally preach, and daily celebrate the divine mysteries'. Schools were multiplying in Galway too, charity schools with clerical patronage and support but lay management, and also the schools of the new religious communities. The Charter School in Galway had never prospered. It had been converted into an artillery barracks in 1798. In 1814 it became the convent and schools of the Presentation Sisters.[33]

The wealthy merchants were the indispensable element in this Catholic progress. In Waterford it was one of them, Edmund Rice, who decided to devote his life as well as his wealth to founding a teaching order of religious brothers. In Wexford we see the Redmond and Devereux families in particular transforming the whole appearance of the town, with Richard Devereux (1795-1883) providing his church with much of its physical structures. Himself a man of deep personal piety, his piety was marked by rigorism and asceticism, fitting into an overall framework of values that might be described as 'British middle-class', or, perhaps more precisely, as an urge to identify with some of the economic values and attitudes of the Protestant elite (in the earlier years of the century relations between Catholics and Protestants at this social level were still reasonably open). It should be noted further that a man like Devereux tended to diffuse his values. He did this first by providing for formal education: he was a great support in the provision of the Catholic schools of the nuns and brothers. But he and others like him were also prominent in setting up institutions for the 'rational enjoyment and intellectual improvement' of the working classes: the Mechanics' Institute, the Temperance Society, the Catholic Young Men's Society, all of them providing lecturers, libraries and reading rooms. The urban working class seems to have welcomed these developments and made good use of them. The 'intellectual improvement' they picked up had a strong bias towards religious education, and this led to a high level of personal commitment in religious practice. Some detail of the services in the cathedral in Waterford is to be found in the 1840 *Catholic Directory*. On Sunday there were Masses up to noon. On two Sundays a month there was benediction, and benediction with a sermon on the first Friday of each month. The number of communicants averaged 350 each Sunday, with over 600 on the first Sunday of the month. There were devotions each evening in Lent, Advent and May. A few years later W. M. Thackeray, often caustic in his comments on the Irish scene, was impressed by what he saw. The cathedral itself was unfinished and unfurnished, and he did not like what attempt at decoration there was; but, he added, 'A much finer ornament to the church than any of the questionable gewgaws which adorned the ceiling was the piety, stern, simple and unaffected, of the people within. Their whole soul seemed to be in their prayers, as rich and poor knelt indifferently on the flags.'[34] Just about this time the parish missions were reaching the smaller towns as well as the countryside. Athy and Carlow each had a mission in 1843, and in both the results seem to have been striking, with, in particular, an eagerness to receive the sacrament of penance to an extent that seems to suggest that in this respect these people had up to this been neglected.

In defining the rural 'money economy' we are speaking of people rather than of an area, but in geographical terms it may be taken as corresponding to most of Leinster and Munster except Co. Clare and the extreme south-west. In Leinster the English language was dominant, though Irish was strong in much of Munster. Everywhere, however, Irish tended to be the language of the poor, and English that of those in the 'money economy'. Over much of the area the indications are that the rate of population increase had begun to slow down well before the Famine, but the shadow of poverty hung over even relatively favoured places — as Humphrey O'Sullivan remarked in Callan in 1827 as he watched 'a thousand young women and youths dancing', 'Life is pleasant for them unless it ends in beggary' ('Is aoibhinn saol dóibh mura déirc é a dheireadh').[35]

The 'old Catholic stock' were still a power in this community, people like the family known to Patrick Kennedy in his youth, 'a branch of the early Anglo-Norman settlers in Wexford . . . the family lived in a fine old manor house'; or Richard Sutton of Clonmines in the same county, who lived in the tower built by the original twelfth-century grantee, Sir Roger de Sutton.[36] The MacMurrough Kavanaghs of Borris in Co. Carlow had abandoned their ancestral faith only in 1798, but their change of religion made no difference to the immense social esteem in which they were held: the people referred to the head of the family simply as 'the monarch'.[37] Everywhere, however, a new Catholic landowning class was making its appearance. It could not command quite the same respect as the old aristocracy, but it was an important new element in Catholic society.

The number of priests was inadequate, but it was better than elsewhere. The Dublin ecclesiastical province had one priest to 2,451 people; the diocese of Ferns had one to 1,941. The situation was not quite so good in Munster. The ecclesiastical province of Cashel had overall one priest to 3,175 people, but the more prosperous areas had a better ratio. More priests meant in effect more curates, as the number of parishes remained stable. The Dublin provincial statutes of 1831 had established the rights of the curate, without, it appears, very much dissension. The support of the clergy by payment of dues was long established. So also was the right of the bishop to transfer priests, though there are instances of resistance to episcopal appointments. The clergy as a whole had a distinctly 'middle-class' standard of living. Humphrey O'Sullivan always notes the menu when he dined with the priest, and beyond question they dined well.

It may now be taken for granted that the priest has had a seminary education. For more and more of them that education has been provided in Maynooth. Deanery clerical conferences during the summer months were well established, though the experience of Bishop James Doyle of Kildare and Leighlin showed how easily this practice could slip: on his appointment in 1819 he found that no conferences had been held in the diocese since one had been disrupted by yeomanry at Mountrath in the troubled year of 1798.[38] The Dublin provincial statutes of 1831 require the priest to have only a modest library indeed — a textbook in moral theology. These same statutes now make it a precept that priests attend a six days' spiritual retreat every second year.

Over most of this area new chapels — perhaps we may now begin to call them churches — were being built to meet the needs of the growing population, though Bishop Doyle noted that resources for a new building were frequently not available even in his own relatively comfortable diocese.[39] The collection of funds was entrusted to a lay committee; it is frequently noted that the local landlord helped. Even so, it was not unknown for building work to be suspended for years because there was no money. The buildings were plain, their primary purpose being to shelter as many people as possible, though it was coming to be required that they have railed-in sanctuaries around the altar and a separate sacristy for the priest to vest for Mass. The churches were locked during the week, and there was no reservation of the Blessed Sacrament. The priest said Mass in the church only on Sundays and holydays. On weekdays Mass was in his own house or in the house of a parishioner, either a 'station' Mass or a requiem Mass, or sometimes just at the parishioner's request.

Except in the most favoured areas there was still insufficient room in the chapels and not enough priests to provide enough Masses, especially because of the inhibition — in Cashel in 1810 a legal inhibition — against a priest saying Mass twice on Sundays in the same church. The pitfalls in deriving firm figures for Mass attendance from the 1835 report have already been noted, but in this region perhaps something from a low of about 40 per cent to a high of about 80 per cent may not be too far from the truth. There were a variety of reasons for non-attendance, the two most common probably being poverty and distance, often in combination. At the very beginning of the century Bishop Plunkett of Meath noted that Mass was not attended by 'a certain section' of the poor, and a few years later the Archbishop of Cashel spoke of widespread failure in this matter. In relatively prosperous Wexford, well equipped with chapels and priests, it was noted of one parish in 1814 that the poor attended Mass 'in all weathers alike', and of another that most of the inhabitants could turn out on Sundays 'very fashionably dressed'.[40]

From Wexford too there is a detailed account of Sunday morning in a rural church, written by Patrick Kennedy in 1867, recalling his youth nearly fifty years before (he writes in the form of a novel, but his imaginative powers are limited, and much of his account may be accepted as fairly straight recollection).[41] He speaks of the priest hearing confessions before Mass, while groups in the gallery prepared themselves by reading pious books; at Mass the congregation ranged from 'the lazy indifferent *sleveen*', kneeling on one knee at the door, to the devout, either following the service from their manuals or 'wrapt in one act of adoration from beginning to end of the Mass'. The Dublin statutes of 1831 speak of 'the ancient and salutary custom' of the separation of the sexes in church, and this seems to have been very common. In places it might have helped if certain families could have been separated: at least there is a report from east Co. Limerick that some families could never meet without a faction-fight, not even when they met for Mass.[42]

When the church was too small for the congregation, as it frequently was, there were serious problems in giving instruction at Mass. It would appear that the bishops as yet had no very high opinion of their priests' ability to preach. The Cashel statutes of 1810 include lengthy instructions (in Irish and English) which, if diligently read to the people, could have left little time for a personal contribution from the priest; and the Dublin provincial statutes of 1831, while insisting that there be preaching at all Sunday Masses, stress very heavily that it should be solid instruction adapted to the needs of the people, and commend teaching the catechism in terms which suggest that the bishops of the province believe that this is the best way the priest can give instruction, even at Mass. What Patrick Kennedy recalled from the rural Wexford of his youth was 'some practical instructions' after the communion.[43]

If Sunday morning was on the whole a time of devotion, the afternoon and evening was a time of amusement, with, apparently, no inhibitions about doing a job of work if it needed to be done. Though the German Lutheran J. G. Kohl was struck by the absence from the Irish countryside of the external signs of Catholicism, wayside shrines or crosses, as in Bavaria and parts of Austria,[44] other travellers noted that in its general character of relaxation the Irish Sunday afternoon recalled much of Catholic Europe. In the eyes of the clergy, the relaxation was a bit excessive — in particular in the drinking, fighting (especially in the districts where faction-fighting was common) and unsupervised dancing. At 'a dance held unknown to his reverence', Patrick Kennedy noted, 'the only aged people present would be a foul old reprobate or two . . . the very well conducted young men and women would stay away', for it too frequently led to 'a boy taking to drink and a girl losing character'. A favourite stratagem was to hold the dance at the very edge of the parish, where it might be safest from the parish priest. There is, I think, a distinct twinkle in Kennedy's eye as he recalls a long-remembered occasion when a dance at Ballymackessy bridge was scattered when two parish priests converged from opposite directions.[45]

The general level of instruction rose as the confraternities and parish libraries spread out from the towns. Archbishop Butler of Cashel had begun confraternities in his diocese as early as 1778; in 1796 Bishop Plunkett of Meath began the Confraternity of Christian Doctrine, but twenty-five years later he was complaining that it drew poor attendances, while at about the same time Archbishop Everard of Cashel regularly noted on his visitation that instruction was seriously deficient. Lending libraries were also developed, but these helped only the literate. The Dublin provincial synod of 1831 commended highly the Confraternity of the Blessed Eucharist (to encourage the reception of Holy Communion). It also ordered the Confraternity of Christian Doctrine to be set up in every parish where it did not yet exist, and every parish was to have its lending library.

There was a hard-fought battle for the provision of an adequate school system. As already noted, the eighteenth century had seen the effective development of a parish system, but the rising population was straining it. The Cashel statutes of 1810 reflect the eighteenth-century system. In some respects it was being improved: a new schoolhouse, for example, would remove the school from the chapel, and, hopefully, be a building better adapted to teaching. When, however, the Catholic schools refused support from the Kildare Place Society after 1830 the strains grew. The church system was increasingly supplemented by private schoolmasters, and even with this the rural poor were largely illiterate. The Dublin provincial statutes of 1831 ordered the parish priest to ensure that there was a sufficiently large schoolhouse, where the classes could be separated and the new teaching methods introduced. He was to visit the schools regularly to see that the catechism was well taught and well learned. He was reminded that he had the right to see that teachers were of good moral character. One might suspect that the duties laid upon him were getting beyond the resources of many a parish priest until, ironically enough, the National Schools, established in 1831, from unpromising beginnings turned out to be his saviour.

Another basic obligation was confession and communion at Easter. Evidence for the extent of this practice is limited, but one may well accept Bishop Doyle's statement as true of the ecclesiastical province of Dublin, that the country people as a whole had long been in the habit of Christmas and Easter communion.[46] Bishop Plunkett in his visitations of Meath noted that there were defaulters, and that there were parents slow to bring their children to Mass and confession when they were old enough (children were expected to have been several times to confession before being admitted to first communion at about the age of thirteen), but he does leave the impression that such people were a minority in his diocese. Things may have been rather worse in Munster: at any rate Archbishop Everard of Cashel regularly complains of widespread neglect of Easter communion.

What helped most in getting people to the sacraments of penance and the Eucharist was the practice of 'stations of confession', now widespread — indeed, it would seem, universal. Before Christmas and Easter notice was given of the days of the stations and the houses in which they were to be held. All were expected to attend their respective stations; in Cashel those who did not were to be publicly named. The spiritual business of the station — the hearing of confessions, catechism of children by lay members of the confraternity, concluding with Mass and instruction from the priest — was to be over by an early hour. Afterwards business affairs might be dealt with. Inevitably, the business affairs developed into what the church authorities could only see as abuses, feasting and drinking, with the priest expecting his share, though he was supposed to be content with breakfast. The Dublin provincial statutes of 1831 strongly recommended that the 'stations' be held in the church. Over much of Leinster the churches may have been sufficiently adequate to make this change without serious pastoral loss, but even here it did not become obligatory until the 1850s. Elsewhere the stations survived, partly no doubt because of inertia, but also because they still fulfilled a real need.

In the country districts baptism still took place in the home as a general rule. So did marriage, normally in the afternoon. The custom of seeking a dispensation from the publication of the banns was widespread, apparently because it was widely accepted that to have them published indicated disgraceful poverty, an inability to pay the fee for the dispensation. The celebrations that followed the marriage caused the church authorities some concern over clerical conduct, particularly in Munster, where it was the custom to take up a collection for the priest. The Munster clergy had become economically very dependent on the offerings made on the occasion of a marriage,[47] and some apparently made use of the convivial atmosphere to boost the collection. In Munster too the marriage fee itself was high, and the few references to 'Tack-'em' the couple-beggar indicate that he still managed to survive because the fees of the parish clergy were too high. His trade vanished when the Tridentine decree *Tametsi* came unequivocally into force in the whole island in 1827. Henceforth a Catholic marriage was invalid unless celebrated before the parish priest or a priest delegated by him or the bishop.

Men and women married early, though in the more prosperous districts there are indications that well before the Famine economic considerations were beginning to dictate a certain measure of caution. All observers agree that chastity was prized and practised to a remarkable degree. The Halls' praise of Irish women is well known: it is specifically stated to be the sentiments of the English husband, not of his Irish wife. Irish women of all classes, he said, taken in the mass, had the lights without the shadows, the good without the bad. They were the most faithful, the most devoted, the most pure, the best mothers, the best children, the best wives, to a degree unsurpassed elsewhere, and probably nowhere equalled.[48] The illegitimacy rate among Catholics was very low. There was strict social control in that the mother and her illegitimate child faced harsh ostracism. Mostly she was a servant living in conditions that exposed her to temptation from fellow-servants or her employer. The 'kept woman', the 'gentleman's miss', was not uncommon. She was harshly treated by her master, often in effect bought from her mother, and ruthlessly discarded when it suited, with no provision for herself or her children. Yet it was noted that she was scrupulously chaste to young men of her own rank, until necessity might force her to become a prostitute after being cast off. It would indeed appear that most prostitutes were mothers of illegitimate children, driven to it by hard necessity. If such a mother could not marry the father of the child, her necessity was hard indeed. Social ostracism made it almost impossible for her to earn a living. Yet abortion was to all intents and purposes non-existent: probably few girls even knew it existed. Infanticide did occur, but most shrank from this. Many illegitimate children ended up in the harsh care of the foundling hospitals, where most of them simply died.[49]

Despite the publication of *Tametsi* in 1827, by a special dispensation 'mixed' marriages between Catholics and Protestants continued to be valid in canon law in Ireland until 1908 even if not celebrated before the legally designated priest (in civil law mixed marriages celebrated solely before a Catholic priest continued to be invalid until 1870). Protestants held mixed marriages in greater repugnance than Catholics. Where they did take place, the common practice among the upper classes was that the boys followed the father's religion and the girls the mother's. When poorer Protestants married Catholics, however, it was quite common that they themselves became Catholics, while the Catholic seldom if ever became a Protestant. Indeed, over much of the countryside there was some tendency for the poorer Protestants to become Catholics, from sheer social pressure, sometimes reinforced by pastoral neglect.[50] In this as in other matters the battle-lines became more definite with the 'Second Reformation' of the 1820s. 'Protestant' had always been an ambiguous word, denoting the political and economic oppressor as well as the person of different religious faith. Humphrey O'Sullivan, that man of open temperament, dislikes the Protestants intensely. They are the enemy, the tyrants, 'mad to devour the Catholics'. Real venom emerges when he notes that 'Nobody is taking any interest in the fine subtle Irish language, apart from the mean "swaddlers", who try to lure the Irish to join their new cursed religion.'[51] With the peasantry, there was no need of a 'Second Reformation' to nurture a hatred of Protestantism. 'Pastorini's prophecies', forecasting that it would be finally overthrown in 1825, enjoyed a wide popularity; but after 1820, and even more so after 1830, the battle-lines were drawn as the Catholics made their way back to the political nation and the Protestants responded by closing ranks.

Wakes and funerals put up a strong resistance to Tridentine Catholicism. Familiar legislation continued to be directed against familiar abuses. They were slowly eroded, but they died hard. Observers agreed that the Irish Catholics usually died calmly once the priest had administered the last sacraments. The last lingering anxiety was to have a good wake, and the family took care to see to this. Patrick Kennedy describes a Leinster wake in some detail.[52] When people came in they said the psalm for the dead, the *De profundis*. After a while there would be a call for a song. Later, 'to pass the time', they performed 'the wake-house drama', a kind of knockabout farce with a touch of the 'mummers' about it, and later again the 'wake-games', again primarily knockabout and horseplay. Yet he notes also 'young men who became hardened in vice by attending wakes, and young women who lost character thereby.... Girls with any pretence to good conduct never remained in them beyond the early hours of the night, and were always supposed to be there under the guardianship of brother, cousin, or declared lover.' Both Kennedy and Humphrey O'Sullivan approved of the bishops' ruling that young people and unmarried people should not attend night wakes, and Humphrey, a widower of fifty-one, observed the rule personally.[53] The Purgatorian Societies spread from the towns into some rural parishes, where they tried to banish everything from the wake-house except prayer and the office for the dead. The funeral Mass had traditionally been celebrated in the home, but the Dublin diocesan statutes of 1831 ordered that the Mass and requiem office be held in the church; and their admonition to the clergy to conduct the service in a seemly way — one reason given, interestingly, is that on this occasion they are frequently under the eye of Protestants — probably indicates that it had been the practice in some places for some time to have the funeral rites in the church, possibly mainly in the towns, though we find it established at Rathangan in rural Wexford in 1822. The priest did not always go to the graveside, especially for the funerals of the poor. There was some reason for his reluctance, for the church authorities had a very long struggle to ban drink at funerals, and a fight after the funeral was still possible. 'Upper-class' women seldom went to the cemetery either.

The old ways died harder in Munster. The pastoral letter appended to the Cashel statutes of 1810 deals exclusively with abuses at wakes and funerals. The wake-games were rougher; 'fronsy-fronsy' still lived on. The keen, dead in Leinster, was still raised at the wake and funeral. The whiskey flowed more freely, and the chances of a fight after the funeral were higher.

The 'patterns' continued to degenerate. The church authorities had finally set their face against them in the 1780s; the priests ceased to attend, and in many cases the religious element was altogether forgotten. It proved hard to kill completely, however. Humphrey O'Sullivan describes the pattern day at St James's well near Callan in 1829: 'strong and maddening whiskey for those who wanted a row and those who wanted to separate them; open booths full of courting couples; bag-pipers and fiddlers playing music for the young people; and pious people doing the rounds at the well'.[54] Notorious patterns defied all attempts at suppression, like St John's well in Co. Meath, which, because it was so near Dublin, provided a week of 'confusion, drunkenness and debauchery'[55] at the end of June every year, or the Corpus Christi pattern at Doneskeagh in the diocese of Cashel, the scene of 'drunkenness, quarrelling and other abominable vices'.[56] The latter was banned in 1808, by no means for the first time. The advice accompanying the ban, that pattern days should be celebrated by Mass in the chapels and prayer at home, came at the very least a generation too late.

The threat of violence lurked everywhere people gathered, especially when they drank. Humphrey O'Sullivan noted the Whit Monday fair in

Ballingarry, 'the most vicious fair in Munster or Leinster', while Patrick Kennedy describes a gallant as 'well able to clear a fair'.[57] The opposition of the clergy to many popular practices may be palliated to some extent by a consideration of this threat. Many of them, of course, were free of it, like the little girls going from door to door with brídeogs collecting half-pennies on St Brigid's Eve, as described by O'Sullivan, or the boys with the wren in the holly branch on St Stephen's Day.[58] Others were less innocent. On 30 April 1828 he noted:

> I hear the young boys had two golden May balls ('dhá liathróid órga Bhealtaine') in the fields today. They got them from two newly married couples last Shrovetide. They have a Maybush on the top of a stick or long pole with a golden ball in the middle of it, and they dance around it with the young girls.

It sounds idyllic, but he adds:

> There hasn't been a May ball in Callan since 1782, when Seán na Sál killed Butler.

In fact the custom was that the 'young bloods' demanded money as well as the 'May balls', and this money was spent on drink. A row had broken out at Callan in 1782, and Nicholas Butler was killed by a blow of a stone in the forehead. His assailant escaped, but his name was remembered in Callan. One begins to understand why the Dublin priest Henry Young cut down the Finglas maypole, 'the devil's potstick' as he called it.[59] One can see too that the Callan priest who broke up the Easter Sunday hurling match may have been concerned with more than a breach of the Sabbath rest.

It was the age of the Ribbonmen and of the organised and senseless faction-fight. 'Faction country' extended in a broad band across Munster, the worst area being the borders of Limerick and Tipperary. One of Mason's informants in 1814 remarked of the lower classes in Carrick-on-Suir that the best that could be said in their praise was that they were better than the rest of Tipperary. Another remarked of Arklow that the people there had few disputes, even at public meetings: they were, indeed, almost as orderly as their Co. Wexford neighbours.[60] All were agreed that the 'English baronies' of Forth and Bargy were an oasis in troubled Ireland. Even though they were beginning to lose some of their distinctive characteristics, they were 'a reasonable spot', where 'dwell the most orderly people in Ireland', temperate, shy, distant, speaking of 'the dark west' almost as if it was another planet, as indeed in many respects it was. There was no religious dissension, even in the 1840s. The people lived well, on barley bread rather than potatoes, in clean whitewashed cottages surrounded by flower gardens (that incisive improver, 'Martin Doyle' (William Hickey, rector of Bannow) is alone in complaining about the outsides of their houses, but even he admitted that inside most were 'extremely neat and comfortable'). As a matter of course, the poor were supported by their neighbours, and there were no beggars. Every door was left 'on the latch'.[61]

The name of Humphrey O'Sullivan has frequently occurred in the preceding pages. He is indeed an incomparable witness to the social life of 'old Ireland', and there is no substitute for reading his diary. This brief account of the 'maritime economy' might well conclude with a humbler pedagogue's account of how he lived. He was Bartholomew Keegan, schoolmaster at Rathangan in the barony of Bargy, Co. Wexford. On 14 January 1822 he wrote to a fellow-Wexfordman in Rome, Michael Doyle, O.F.M.:

> I am with Mr Barry of Rathangan these three years — a worthy priest he is. The mistress keeps a little shop and between this and the school (tho' not a very good one) we are living pretty well.... I have two fine choirs in the two chapels and music to no end, and we sing the Mass and office of the dead in Rathangan in grand stile on every corpse that comes to the chapel.
>
> I have about £10 a year from the two priests for my care of the two choirs and teaching the poor children of the parish. I have made the science of music my chief study and have made so rappid a progress therein that I am capable of conversing with any band-man in Wexford on theory or practice. I got a lend of a bassoon from Father Ryan of the Glen who is curate at Adamstown, and in one fortnight I could play every Mass we had in the chapel. I also got a lend of a clarionet and practised it for some time and can play all the hymns on it and marches and duets in nice stile. This is the instrument I like, tho' I have not been able to spare one guinea to get one of my own; however I hope to have one before you come home and to play it with singing at your Mass somewhere when you come to old Ireland....
>
> We do have great work here on festivals. On Corpus Christi we have a procession of the Blessed Sacrament, on Palm Sunday a great procession of palm, on 15th of August, our patron day, a grand solemn Mass and procession of candles. Every Sunday in Lent we sing round the Stations, and on other festivals we have a Benediction of the Blessed Sacrament, all which serve very much to excite devotion in the people.

He added, however:

> My school is not the best, as the country abounds with a number of poor people who are not able to pay very much for their children.[62]

The shadows hung over even this peaceful and relatively prosperous land.

To turn to the 'subsistence economy' is to find all the problems that threatened the more prosperous regions in a sharper form, some of them indeed out of control by the 1830s and 1840s. Connacht was a strikingly traditional society. Over the province as a whole the Irish language was dominant. Here too the old gentry continued to exercise great social influence, that did not lessen greatly, if at all, even if they had conformed to the established church under the pressures of the penal code. True, even in Connacht things were changing: in 1838 Thomas Martin of Ross was arrested by the police for leading his tenants into battle with the O'Flahertys in a dispute about land they had fought over for two hundred and fifty years.[63] But the long memories lived on, memories of the old Gaelic system, especially where land was held in rundale. In communities where everyone was struggling to survive it came naturally enough that the poor should help the poor.

There were perhaps three Ulsters. In the industrialising east of the province Catholics may have been economically better off than in many other places, in that many of them had employment of a sort; but theirs were the more menial jobs, they were in a minority, and generally regarded as socially inferior. In the southern parts of the province they were a decided majority, in Cavan about 80 per cent. The land, while it may not have been the best, was workable. In the mountainous north and west, however, their lot appeared pitiable indeed: 'Depressed beyond conception,' Wakefield noted in 1812, 'they bear their degradation without murmur or complaint. . . . They seem neither to know nor to feel the extent of their misery.'[64] No doubt he was right in his account of their economic condition, but he was wrong when he spoke of the total cultural deprivation of this last mountain stronghold of Gaelic Ulster. These were truly 'the silent people', who had learned to keep their own counsel with an inquirer like Wakefield, but were more communicative with people like John O'Donovan or even with William Shaw Mason's informants, who were supplying details on social conditions just when Wakefield was collecting his information. These were the local Protestant clergy, who were living fairly close to the ground. They leave a general impression of a people by no means crushed, cherishing their distinctive inheritance, even though it might place them at an economic disadvantage compared with the Presbyterians. In Inishowen it was noted that the people were 'sober, regular and attentive to business; spirited, warlike and courageous, yet not by any means quarrelsome; they are charitable to the poor, and a kind goodnatured peasantry as ever I saw'.[65] Where rundale persisted it nourished the old ways, as it did in Connacht. And yet over much of Ulster to be a Catholic was to have to accept social deprivation more than anywhere else in Ireland.

As in the other provinces, the Catholic clergy were numerically insufficient. Ulster was not the worst off: its best diocese approached the Leinster average, and overall it was better than Munster. Connacht, however, was approaching disaster: one priest to 3,678 people in 1834, with one to 4,199 in the extensive diocese of Tuam. In Ulster, however, the archaic pattern of clerical recruitment hindered effective clerical deployment. Many still came from the traditional *saorchlanna*, that is, those who regarded themselves as descended from landowners dispossessed by the plantations. They were helped to the priesthood by their people, and in return it was expected that they would have the right to minister among them and that the bishop would have no right to remove them. Such priests could normally count on popular support, and this could and did lead to violent opposition to the bishop's nominee. It was common enough for him to be refused admittance to the chapel, and the scandal was often grave. A priest in the diocese of Clogher was described in 1836 as 'a rude leader of a rude host, surrounded by a strong well-armed bodyguard of determined ruffians, to prevent, forsooth, by force, his desertion of them and any attempt to acquiesce in the commands of the bishop'.[66]

By 1836, however, the days when such incidents could take place were nearly over, but the social pattern was still strong enough to lead to strong resistance to attempts to establish the rights of curates. There were also problems in trying to develop a system of support of the clergy by the payment of dues, because it had no deep roots. The traditional 'familial' system was weaker in Connacht, if only because the province had had a more complex history. It cannot be assumed, however, that it did not exist. Half the townland where Archbishop John MacHale was born had been held in 1640 by five farmers each named 'McKeale'. What did exist on a wider scale in Connacht was a 'familial' system deriving from more contemporary society. Where nearly everyone was very poor, the priest stood out as a rich man, exposed to the hostility of 'Threshers' and 'Carders' where these were active. Yet he was not altogether a free agent in insisting on his dues and fees. His family would have made its contribution to 'make a priest of him', and now that he was ordained he was expected to make an economic return to the family as a whole.

There were problems about the education of the clergy. In the years when the continent was cut off and Maynooth was having its growing pains, some bishops, even in the poorer areas, were forced to set up training centres in their dioceses. Though they referred to them as 'seminaries', they must have been poles apart from, say, Carlow College in Leinster. Even when Maynooth developed, money remained a problem, for until 1845 Maynooth's own resources were slender indeed. Everything was more difficult in Connacht and Ulster — harder to maintain clerical conferences, harder to establish such things as clerical retreats. Of the priests as a body it is impossible to generalise. While progress was slow, the basic stock was not bad. Sometimes, indeed, it may have been too good for its environment. In the diocese of Killala a priest who set out to be a social reformer, John Patrick Lyons, ran into the same kind of opposition as the improving landlord.

The general poverty made it hard to provide adequate chapels, or in some cases any chapel at all. In the diocese of Clogher in 1789 it is clear that there were many Masses in the open air. Thirty chapels were built in the next generation, including a new one in Enniskillen, sited, with some daring, in the town itself — the old one had kept a discreet distance.[67] In the parish of Errigal Kieran in Co. Tyrone the first Mass-house was built at the beginning of the century; it must have been small and poor, for thirty years later it was improved and enlarged. Another Mass site in the parish moved into a barn about 1810, and a Mass-house was built in 1825, but there was a third station where Mass in the open air continued to 1868.[68] Several Mass-rocks appear in west Ulster in the 1834 inquiry.

In Connacht as in Ulster it was a struggle to build a Mass-house. It was not unknown that one could lie unfinished for years, though almost all available parish funds went to building them. In Tuam in 1825 there were 106 chapels, sixteen of them slated; there were many Mass-rocks. Killala in 1832 also reported many Masses in the open air, and in both dioceses where there was a Mass-house it was often far too small, with many of the congregation kneeling outside.[69]

The 1834 statistics do seem to indicate a low level of attendance at Sunday Mass in the area as a whole. However, particularly where there were still Masses in the open air the seemingly detailed statistics may conceal ambiguities that have not been fully adverted to. It must also be noted that in Ulster and probably in Connacht there was a firm inhibition against a priest saying two public Masses on a Sunday. In Leinster there seems to have been no problem about doing this where necessary. In Munster he was allowed to say a second Mass only if he had two chapels in his parish and no assistant. The northern statutes of 1834 are not totally unambiguous, but their general drift is clear. There can be no excuse for omitting the Sunday Mass at its fixed time and place; for example, the need to celebrate a requiem Mass in the house of a parishioner is not a sufficient excuse for omitting the Sunday Mass. And while a priest may say two Masses on a Sunday 'for a public cause', the example given is the need to celebrate a requiem Mass, not the need for a second Mass in his parish.

Turning again to the 1834 statistics, one striking point emerges in the dioceses of Killala, Achonry and Raphoe. In all three the number of Masses noted is less than the number of priests. Making allowance for the odd priest too infirm (or possibly too incorrigible), a real discrepancy remains. The more detailed statistics for Tuam may supply a clue. Here 99 priests provided 108 Masses. Of these, however, thirteen were not in chapels, six being in schoolhouses and seven in private houses (in one case it is noted that Mass is 'in the open air in fine weather'). The only other reference to Mass in the open is in Raphoe, where there are, in addition to the chapels, 'two other places where Mass is performed in temporary shades.' It seems reasonable to conclude that the statistics do not include all the Mass-rocks and therefore not all the Mass-goers.

An interesting cross-check is available for the diocese of Kilmore. It had 67 chapels, and a little over 80 priests in 43 parishes. Ten of the parish priests had no curate. In only five parishes is it noted that there are two Masses on Sunday. Three others have two occasionally, at Christmas and Easter or on the first Sunday of the month. Everywhere else there is one Mass on Sunday. Yet the 1837 *Catholic Directory* reports that there are two Sunday Masses in most chapels. This statistic relates to 1836 at the latest, and must mean that most priests said two Masses. It is true that Kilmore was almost certainly an exception in the north of Ireland. Its bishop was James Browne, appointed in 1827.[70] Born in Forth, Co. Wexford, he was appointed professor of scripture in Maynooth in 1817 and had been sent to Kilmore to combat proselytism. He would have had no inhibitions about a priest saying two Masses on Sundays, and he clearly took advantage of the ambiguities of the provincial statutes in this matter. What is unthinkable, however, is that there should have been two Sunday Masses in only five chapels in his diocese in 1834 and in most of them in 1836. It is another warning to approach the 1834 statistics with great circumspection.

Professor Miller gives an overall figure of 20 to 40 per cent for Mass attendance in the Irish-speaking areas. Corrected by the factor he should have taken into account but did not, namely those for one reason or another not under obligation to attend, we get 25 to 50 per cent. The points made above suggest that this is still too low. By how much it is impossible to say, but when all factors are taken into account the figure is still low. What may be said with a fair measure of certainty, however, is that the generalisation Miller builds on his statistics, namely that the native Irish were never really a Mass-going people, rests on rather shaky foundations. It has been seen already that Sunday Mass attendance was not regarded as a pastoral problem in Connacht in the second half of the eighteenth century. It was in 1834, even by the most optimistic calculation. But the main factors in the 1834 problem had arisen from the growing population and the growing poverty — too few chapels, too few priests, too many people too wretched to come what were often long distances in their rags. In Kilcommon Erris in north-west Mayo there had to be a certain duplication even at stations, to let those who came first go home to give their miserable clothing to a second group.

Poor attendance, but with the congregation frequently unable to find room inside the chapel, did not make for satisfactory instruction at public Mass. There were, of course, the set prayers before Mass, and, at least so the law said, a simple homily or instruction. There was catechesis of children after Mass, and sometimes before it. Attempts were made to provide Sunday catechesis for children who could not get to Mass. There are some indications that the instruction at Mass was often close to catechesis too, but, as has been seen, even in the better-equipped districts this was probably the best way the average priest could spend his time. And what the law said was not always made available: Bishop MacNally of Clogher reported in 1853 that some of his priests occasionally omitted the Sunday sermon, some occasionally gave it, and some never gave it at all.[71] It is only exceptionally that we hear of other Sunday devotions, and then in the towns rather than in the countryside; Loughrea in 1846, for example, had benediction after last Mass on the first Sunday of each month, and the rosary and a sermon on Sunday and holyday evenings. Paul Cullen, fresh from Rome in 1850, introduced novenas and benediction to Armagh. In 1851 he introduced the holy week ceremonies. The people, he said, were delighted; they had never before seen such colour in religious ceremonies; but, he added, 'The singing is horrible, and the other things seem miserable to me when *recordamur tui Sion*.'[72]

Sunday afternoons, as elsewhere, were given to amusement. There would appear to be notably fewer references to it in 'subsistence Ireland' than in the more prosperous areas. One reason for this is that there were fewer observers to record it, but it is possible that there was in fact less of it, especially in the later decades, for there was less and less to be merry about.

We have seen the confraternities and book societies spreading from the towns into the rural areas of the south and east. They impinged on the deprived areas too, but mainly in their more prosperous edges, and even there in the towns. Their effect was necessarily limited because the illiteracy rate was so high. Newry had its confraternity, Sodality of the Sacred Heart and Purgatorian Society in 1834, Belfast its Rosary Society in 1836. More towns joined them in the 1840s. Achonry in 1840 reported Confraternities of the Rosary and of Christian Doctrine in every parish. If true, it was a striking achievement, for two years earlier Tuam had reported one such confraternity, attached to the cathedral. In 1836 the exceptionally thrustful Bishop Browne of Kilmore had confraternities in 'nearly all' his parishes, and even parish libraries in some of them.[73]

The schools provided limited help with catechesis. There were schools, in perhaps surprising numbers, and school was often held in the chapel. But it was seldom the clergy were able to contribute to the financial support of the schoolmaster, and this lessened church influence in the school. Here especially the National Schools were to develop into a strong support for the clerical manager. Archbishop MacHale's decision to have nothing to do with them must be seen in retrospect as a serious misjudgment.

The parish missions came to this countryside only late in this period: the first was at Dingle in 1846. Beyond question they did arouse great religious fervour, with almost uncontrollable multitudes coming to the sermons and to confession. But the spirituality they offered was that of the towns and the more developed English-speaking countryside. It is surely debatable if the net result was loss or gain, even allowing for the fact that much of the area would steadily drift into becoming English-speaking anyway.

Easter confession and communion was inextricably bound up with the 'stations'. There is no doubt that these were universally held, and that in this matter the priests were conscientious and faithful. The Armagh provincial statutes of 1834 made the holding of stations obligatory, but it is doubtful if this directive was needed; with a custom so well established, the imposition of a legal obligation made little difference. Neither did the further legal obligation imposed make much difference — that times should be appointed for confessions on certain days each week. Confession, communion and the stations remained linked. At the station too there was normally a short instruction. After the priest's breakfast he was required to go away. There seems to have been less of a problem with prolonged eating and drinking than in the more comfortable counties. At the stations in the very poorest parishes the priest probably did well if he got breakfast.

Most of the chapels were ill-equipped for christenings, and baptism seems to have been usually administered in the priest's house, though, like Carleton's Father Finnerty, the priest was prepared to go to the parents' home to baptise the children of the better-off. Naturally this raised his fee and provided him with hospitality.

Father Finnerty would also agree to marry the wealthy at home, though Carleton indicates that sometimes even these preferred to go the priest's house. In the really deprived areas 'marriage at home' could have little meaning for many people, because what they had to call 'home' was so wretched. Yet even the poorest seem to have considered it necessary to scrape together the fee for dispensation from the banns. Marriage was often 'runaway' either because the parents refused consent or the priest refused a dispensation, but it was sometimes runaway (at least in parts of Ulster) because marriage without an elopement was considered 'but a lame exploit'.[74] The couple returned after a few days spent in safe tutelage, and everyone came to the wedding, bringing a bottle of whiskey or the price of one.

As in the rest of Ireland, there was a high level of sexual behaviour, though observers noticed that illicit intercourse was more prevalent among poor Catholics in the north, though less prevalent than among their Protestant neighbours. Even where Catholics were a minority, the Protestant partner to a mixed marriage frequently became a Catholic, but the Catholic seldom became a Protestant. In remote areas where Protestants were a small minority they tended to adopt Catholic habits. At Kilrush in Co. Clare many of them raised the keen at funerals, and some had been known to fall into the Catholic (but somewhat un-Protestant) habit of saying 'God be merciful' to the dead. A particularly intriguing piece of information from the largely Presbyterian Island Magee in Co. Antrim in 1838 asserts that 'If a person is suddenly deranged, or a child overseen, the lower orders rarely apply to their own minister for relief, but to some Roman Catholic priest.'[75] It was the priest, not the minister, who 'had the power', even in the eyes of Presbyterians.

As is only to be expected, the traditional usages at wakes, funerals and patterns kept their grip in spite of clerical opposition. A whole neighbour-hood could stop work when a death occurred: indeed, there was often little work to stop. Not to have a wake was unthinkable, and a wake meant smoking, drinking, singing and wake-games. Only exceptionally was the keen not raised at funerals (in Maghera in 1814 it was claimed that it had been discontinued because of Protestant influence).[76] Clerical attempts to forbid whiskey at funerals and wakes seem to have had at best only patchy success. The framers of the Armagh statutes of 1834, while severely attacking the 'wake-games', probably regarded their order that young unmarried people should not attend late-night wakes as more practicable.

Pattern and pilgrimage kept their hold, with the Lough Derg pilgrimage maintaining its honourable exemption from all prohibition: it had the great advantage of getting people to confession. Other pilgrimages and patterns had degenerated, again at least to some degree because the clergy had turned their back on them. They could still attract the devout, though they were also scenes of drunkenness and debauchery, often ending in a fight. 'The humbler classes' had the habit of taking the law into their own hands, with 'a strong propensity to riotous meetings'.[77] And yet it may well be that there was less of this in the really deprived districts. There was no spirit left for it.

The old Gaelic society was weakening, and there were already the first indications of the advance of 'east-coast', English-speaking spirituality. The power of the priest was obviously very great, indeed in some respects increasing as he made his way to political power, at first reluctantly enough, it would appear, but with increasing confidence. The extent to which clerical influence over the poor was weakened by the church's opposition to Ribbonism is a very involved question with no clear answer, while it must always be borne in mind that the influence of any individual priest depended in at least some measure on the individual priest himself. There are some indications of a puritanical strain that must have been irksome, like the parish regulations of Tydavnet, Co. Monaghan, in 1825 that required those who organised card-playing to make public satisfaction on three successive Sundays and those who participated to make similar satisfaction on one Sunday.[78] Yet the priest's position had powerful social support. Life was made miserable for anyone known to have gone against him. Perhaps the last word might be left with the incomparable Humphrey O'Sullivan:

> Father Séamus Henebry was buried today. Young and old, big and small are weeping after him. The little children of the town are crying over his tomb in the chapel, for he was a kind childlike priest among them. He was generous at his own table and he was lively-spirited company, easily satisfied in regard to money, though it is said that he had plenty of it.[79]

There can always be meanings lurking beneath the surface of Humphrey's easy prose, but there can be no mistaking the note of genuine affection here.

Establishment
and Disestablishment

The Great Famine gave a mortal blow to the 'subsistence economy' and marked a permanent change in Irish social structures. Inevitably, it was the poor who had suffered most from death, disease and emigration. After the Famine, even in Connacht and the other poorer areas, the landless labourers were fewer, while the cottier class had practically disappeared. The 'critical nation-forming class', as Emmet Larkin has called them,[1] were now the small to medium farmers, holding thirty acres or upwards. Everywhere they were turning to grazing, first under the impact of the repeal of the Corn Laws in 1846, and then because of the competition from American imports. Despite the growth of Catholic wealth in other areas, such as commerce, the professions and the public service, it was the interests of the tenant farmers that dominated constitutional politics. It was they too who provided the Catholic church with most of its priests, so it was very natural that the political role of the priest should continue.

We can catch satisfying glimpses of the farming family in its home from memoir-type sources, for instance Walter MacDonald's *Reminiscences of a Maynooth Professor*. He had been born in 1854 in Mooncoin, where his father held sixty acres of the good land of south Kilkenny. It was the mother who held the family together, for the father had a serious drink problem. He recalls her as always at work round the house, though 'on Sundays she turned out quite genteel'. Her schooling with the nuns in Mooncoin had been a refining influence, as also had been her friendship with the wife of a Protestant clergyman. She had a brother a priest in America, who died young. Walter MacDonald was by no means uncritical — indeed, in his reminiscences even of these early days there is a certain carping tone — but when he speaks of two things in particular — 'a certain family loyalty, love and pride' and a 'whiteness of soul which ... makes the Irish farmer's son one of the best priests in the world' — one can sense that they are close to the heart of his values.

The family depicted in *The Farm by Lough Gur* moved at a higher social level (the book is the reminiscences of an old lady, born in 1858, four years after Walter MacDonald). They held two hundred acres. The landlord was good, and the head of the house a progressive farmer, something of a patriarch not just in his own family but in the local community. Once again, there was a strong sense of family loyalty and a certain pride of ancestry, a consciousness that on both sides there was a strain of 'gentle blood'. The memory of priest relatives back through the generations was treasured, down to Uncle Richard, the parish priest of Knocklong. The *Freeman's Journal* and the local weekly paper opened up the horizons as far as London; beyond this lay largely unknown lands, with 'a single familiar point', Rome, the centre of a world of faith almost as real as the world about them.

At the other end of the social scale were the labourers, now fewer in number and reduced in social status. They now worked for a daily wage in place of the right to a potato plot which had been common before the Famine. This was regarded as symbolising a reduction in status, even though their meagre rewards had increased in real terms. Violence was still the ultimate defence of the landless, but it was now much more sporadic because of the changed pattern of society. Fenianism made slow progress in the countryside, even among the labourers and marginal farmers, because of its commitment to political independence before agricultural and social reform, but it was only with these classes that it made any real rural impact, and it appears to have met strong resistance from what was left of Ribbonism.

The socially deprived were culturally deprived because of the rapid retreat of the Irish language. Basic literacy in English steadily improved because of the growth of the National School system, but particularly in Munster and Connacht there was a large section of the poor who could not be really literate in English even if they could read and write it, because Irish was the language of their minds. Walter MacDonald noted that though his father and mother were bilingual, their children knew English only. He noted further that some older people of the poorer classes spoke English very badly. No doubt their children spoke it better, and could even read and write it, but a whole world of cultural values decayed with the decay of the Irish language. Religious values were at the heart of this culture, some of them superstitious, but many of them real. In the community at Lough Gur the cultural class distinctions were clearly drawn; for example, it was noted of the maidservants that 'Although they were thankful for holydays and went to Mass, they were really more interested in the old Irish world where fairies, witches and banshees took the place of our angels and saints.' The mother of the family echoed this note of condescension: 'I think only time can cure superstition.' This it did, but it did other things as well.

It was Pius IX (1846-78) who gave the lie to the old legend that no pope would 'see the years of Peter', those twenty-five years that tradition had ascribed to the first pope. His long pontificate saw the Catholic church settle into a mould that has been broken only in recent years, so it may be worth while to give a brief summary of its characteristics.[2] First and dominant was Ultramontanism, a new sense of the centrality of the pope. This was a development with many roots, from the collapse of the protective shell of the *ancien régime* for the Catholics of Europe, to the development of physical communications, the railways that brought people to Rome in unprecedented numbers, or the postal system that made possible much closer Roman supervision of the local churches. And just as Rome exercised a closer supervision of the bishops throughout the world, so too these bishops exercised a closer supervision over their clergy. Everywhere the clergy increased in number. They were a more disciplined body, and also a more professional one, professional in their more single-minded religious vocation and in their preparation for that vocation. Nevertheless, this preparation, though in a real way more intense, was also in a real sense narrower, in that the response to the intellectual and social challenges of the nineteenth century was a defensive closing of the ranks. A genuinely more dedicated clergy was not alive to new intellectual developments, nor did it devise any notable new pastoral methods. By and large, it pinned its faith to the patterns thought up long ago at Trent. True, it was able to develop these patterns more effectively, through the parish clergy and the revivified religious orders and congregations, who had recovered from the near-disaster of the French Revolution. The clergy directed a more personal devotion among the laity, more markedly Italian in general tone, genuinely more human but not without some danger of sentimentality — devotion to the Eucharistic presence, to the Sacred Heart, the Precious Blood and, of course, the Blessed Virgin. There may have been a certain sense of failure when Pius IX died in 1878, a feeling that the church had failed to come to grips with contemporary civilisation, but there could be no doubt that this church had been interiorly strengthened and had a deeper religious life.

These developments in the Catholic church had been so all-pervasive that they would certainly have had a marked influence in Ireland had Paul Cullen never been Archbishop of Armagh (1849), of Dublin (1852), and Ireland's first cardinal (1866). Nevertheless, his long years as bishop in Ireland (1849-78, almost coterminous with the pontificate of Pius IX) ensured that what was new in discipline and devotion in the wider world would be firmly stamped on the Irish Catholic mind.

He was born in 1803, into a family of prosperous farmers, widely related among others of the same class. An uncle had been executed in 1798, and his father had narrowly escaped. In 1820, at the age of seventeen, he went to Rome to study for the priesthood. He was to remain there in a position of increasing power and trust until he was appointed bishop in Ireland. This Roman experience marked him deeply, but it always coexisted with his Irish family heritage. The newspapers of the English establishment assailed him regularly. *The Times* in 1854 caught the two sides of his character: 'a cold bigot ... noted for his unflinching opposition to the policy of England'. To the *Morning Post* in 1861 he was 'a mischievous monk'. His reputation for austerity caused a certain amount of apprehension even to his friends. John Miley, a priest of Dublin, writing to Bernard Smith in Rome on 23 March 1852[3] and assessing Cullen's prospects of nomination to Dublin — which he himself welcomed — noted that many feared him because of his 'monastic severity'.

The *Morning Post* was wrong, however, in describing him as 'rough and rugged as a polar bear'. His health was never good. He never readjusted to the Irish climate, and in consequence suffered from an almost perpetual cold. What was worse, he had a very nervous temperament. This made it hard for him to take decisions, and he faced many difficult and con- tentious decisions in his lifetime. On several occasions he hovered on the brink of breakdown, and at least once, in 1858, he may well have gone over it.

Despite these handicaps, he drove himself relentlessly. That identifi- cation of 'Irish' and 'Catholic' which his much-admired Daniel O'Connell may not have altogether liked, but had in practice learned to live with, was for him axiomatic. Though he could not work for his church without becoming involved in politics, it has been well said that 'he had no political theories, only religious and ecclesiastical ones'.[4] If he had what might be termed a political vision, it was that Irish Catholics would convert the world-empire of Protestant England to the true Catholic faith. It did not seem altogether impossible, given the new mood of confidence he had done so much to develop in Catholic Ireland.

Cullen had come to Ireland with wide powers as apostolic delegate. As such, his first and most important task was to convoke a national or plenary synod of the Irish bishops. It was a long time since there had been such a gathering — arguably not since the great reform synods of the twelfth century. Synods at provincial level were held through the later middle ages. They began again with the Counter-Reformation mission early in the seventeenth century, but they could be held only inter- mittently for the next two hundred years. As has been seen, the Irish hierarchy as a body began to hold annual meetings from the 1820s. However, there was a great deal of informality about these meetings. There was no clear obligation to attend, there were no clear rules of pro- cedure, and no clear agreement on the binding force of any decisions taken. The meeting Cullen convoked at Thurles was, however, to be a full canonical synod. All bishops had to attend or send a procurator; the decisions reached were to be submitted to the Holy See for ratification; and when ratified they were to be binding on all.

The synod opened on 22 August 1850. It is chiefly remembered for the dissensions it revealed among the bishops: a major dissension over the Queen's Colleges, and a relatively minor one over a proposal that no Irish bishop should speak as an individual on any government measure affecting the church until it had first been discussed by the bishops as a body and an agreed stance reached, or, failing this, referred to the Holy See. It seems that Cullen introduced this proposal on the last day of the synod. It was passed by seventeen votes to ten, with one abstention. Five bishops asked to be minuted as opposing the proposal because of lack of time for consideration and debate, and one who voted for it said that on this point he agreed with them.

This was a minor matter, however, compared with the divisions on the Queen's Colleges. The Irish bishops had been seriously divided on this issue since the colleges had been established by act of parliament in 1845 in an attempt to meet the Catholic demand for an acceptable system of higher education. A government endowment was provided, but not for chairs of theology, though chairs of theology could be established by private endowment. This provision gave rise to the taunt of the 'godless colleges', and the abusive term stuck. What was possibly a more serious issue for the bishops was the fact that they had no voice in the staffing of chairs in what were increasingly seen as 'sensitive' subjects, such as history, philosophy or anatomy.

The episcopal divisions had led to missions and counter-missions to Rome, these in turn producing papal decisions dated 9 October 1847 and 11 October 1848, which had condemned the colleges and forbidden the bishops to play any role in them. These papal decisions were accepted unanimously by the synod. The strong papal recommendation that the bishops should set about the establishment of a Catholic university was passed by twenty-four votes to four. The really contentious issues were two: whether priests should be permitted to accept posts in the colleges, and whether the laity should be permitted to send their children to them (priests had in fact accepted such posts, and there were Catholic students enrolled). By the time these matters had arisen Pius IX had been driven from Rome by the revolution of 1848, and all Cullen had to show to back his proposal that the synod forbid priests to accept posts on pain of suspension and that Catholic parents be very strongly exhorted not to enrol their children was a letter from the Cardinal Prefect of Propaganda saying that a negative verdict on these two points was implicit in the previous papal decisions.

There were twenty-eight voters at the synod. Of these, twenty-four were diocesan bishops. There were three procurators of bishops absent because of old age and infirmity. These had been given a vote by a Roman decision. Finally, there was the Cistercian Abbot of Mount Melleray. He had been given a vote by decision of the synod.

Cullen knew the synod was fairly evenly divided. On Friday and Saturday 30 and 31 August he asked each voter to indicate his mind. At the end of the first day the score stood: for Cullen's proposals, six;

against, seven. When all had been polled the bishops were evenly divided, twelve on each side. The abbot and two of the procurators were for Cullen; the third procurator was hesitant, but not prepared to exclude the priests, and while willing to support a synodal decree expressing the general principle that all good Catholics should shun the colleges, was not prepared to agree that an exhortation to them to do so in the strongest possible terms should be included in the joint pastoral to be issued from the synod.

The final vote was taken in an atmosphere of near-revolt, but predictably went in Cullen's favour by a vote of fifteen to thirteen (sixteen to twelve on the point where he had the support of the third procurator). It was clear that the episcopal divisions on the Queen's Colleges had been scarcely papered over.[5]

This issue may have provided the drama at the Synod of Thurles, but it should not be allowed to obscure the fact that the pastoral decisions taken there caused little if any dissension. This was because they contained little if anything totally innovative. Very substantially, they extended to the whole country what was more or less common practice in the eccles-iastical province of Dublin, as set out in the decrees of the provincial synod of 1831. It may be, however, that not all the bishops were fully attuned to the fact that, unlike decisions taken at previous episcopal meetings, the synodal decrees were absolutely binding once they had been approved by Rome. This question came to a head when the Roman author-ities at Cullen's request stiffened the decisions on certain points to bring them more fully into line with the practice of the Catholic continental countries, especially Italy. Their adoption would certainly have posed difficulties in much of Ireland, and they had in fact a long struggle to establish themselves, in the face not only of social patterns but of episcopal opposition.

There were three points of substance. They all concern the transfer of sacraments from the home to the church. Thurles had recommended that baptism should be conferred in the church where this could be done without serious inconvenience. In the decree as finally approved the recommendation was replaced by a mandate. To an exhortation that confessions should be held in the church whenever possible there was added a clause more mandatory than recommendatory, that women's con-fessions should be held in the church and in a confessional except in cases of necessity. In regard to marriage, there were two additions: that it was to be in the church, except in cases of necessity or for a grave reason to be defined by the bishop, and that if celebrated in the home the customary collection was to be either abolished or strictly controlled. As will be seen in more detail later, opposition to these major changes in religious practice was a factor in helping old social habits to maintain themselves.

Legislation is one thing, giving effect to it is another. Cullen's first problem was with the bishops. As already noted, the method of appointing, Irish bishops had been laid down by Propaganda in 1829. It had brought some advantages, but had not solved all problems, notably the question of clerical cliques and dynasties within dioceses. The choice of a coadjutor in Raphoe in 1855, for example, led to serious and public dissension, and the successful candidate, 'Long Dan' MacGettigan, against whom Cullen's help was unsuccessfully solicited, was alleged to have drawn his votes from 'a cabinet of cousins, all curious fellows'.[6] In 1851 Cullen in a communication to Propaganda had named six bishops seriously at fault in their administration. On the death of one of them, Bishop William O'Higgins of Ardagh, in 1853, the Primate, Joseph Dixon, reported that in his diocese there were no teaching brothers or sisters and no secondary schools; that there had been no clerical retreats for eighteen years, and no conferences for four; and that while few priests gave open scandal, there were certain problems of alcoholism and more widespread problems arising from the neglect of preaching.[7] After John McEvilly had gone as bishop to Galway at the end of 1856 he reported that he had visited parts of his diocese that had not seen a bishop for sixteen years.[8]

The greatest thorn in Cullen's side was Archbishop MacHale of Tuam. Their relationship is full of ironies. MacHale had strongly supported Cullen's appointment, but by 1854 they had become open enemies for a variety of reasons, best summed up by saying that Ireland was too small to hold both of them. In one sense the final victory, at least as this world counts victories, was MacHale's, in that he outlived Cullen by three years, though much the older man. In another sense it was Cullen's, for shortly before his own death he succeeded in imposing on MacHale a decidedly unwelcome coadjutor.

A certain charisma undoubtedly emanated from John MacHale. It was true what James Joyce put into the mouth of one of his characters in a short story in *Dubliners*: 'I once saw John MacHale, and I'll never forget it as long as I live.' In some ways he was the very image of the *taoiseach*, but this fact only identified him with an age that was passing away. It may be that his final tragedy was to have lived too long. In his last years even his iron personality lost its grip. His diocese in the late 1870s showed many problems that had almost disappeared elsewhere — clerical dynasties leading to clerical squabbles, with his own relatives holding all the best appointments, with a wide neglect of pastoral duties, preaching and supervision of schools. Admittedly, most of the detailed evidence comes from John McEvilly, the man forced on him as coadjutor, but the general picture seems beyond doubt. His personal battle with Cullen may in some sense have ended in a draw, but he became more and more an anachronism as Irish Catholic society changed, slowly but inexorably.

One reason for the change was the appearance of a new type of bishop, by reason of Cullen's personal influence in Rome. Because of this he was able to put forward successfully the names of candidates not on the diocesan *terna* voted by the parish priests. It became common for a bishop to be appointed who was not a diocesan priest. The promotion of parish priests to the episcopate became less common: the new bishops tended to be successful administrators, college professors, or members of religious congregations. Among the colleges, Cullen did not like Maynooth, and few of its staff were promoted, while the declining proportion of parish priests among the episcopate automatically lessened the proportion of bishops educated at Maynooth.[9]

So, increasingly, the episcopate came to be of Cullen's way of thinking. The completeness of the change must not be exaggerated. Old men lived on, most notably John MacHale. Some of Cullen's appointees may have disappointed him slightly, but to balance things some appointments turned out better than he expected, like that of Thomas Furlong, a professor in the suspect Maynooth, to Ferns in December 1856. Cullen also strengthened his grip over the episcopate by changing the character of the bishops' meetings. After Thurles the annual meeting took the form of a canonical synod, its decisions being referred to Rome for approval, and in consequence becoming unequivocally binding once approved. He did try to centralise power further with a proposal for annual provincial synods to be followed by a meeting of the four archbishops, where he could count on a majority of three to one. He did not succeed in this. The national synod remained, even though at this time the Holy See had a distinct preference for provincial rather than national synods. It remained in Ireland chiefly because the Irish episcopal body insisted on it, so strongly that it was able to get its way.[10]

The diocesan clergy increased both in numbers and quality. In 1850 there was one priest for approximately 2,000 Catholics, in 1870 one for approximately 1,250. There were still local shortages: in 1857 Bishop MacNally of Clogher was being forced to ordain candidates who had completed only half their course in theology.[11] The rapidly growing Catholic community in Belfast had serious problems until Patrick Dorrian was appointed coadjutor in 1860 and succeeded on the resignation of Bishop Denvir in 1865. Overall, however, the ratio of priests to people improved steadily. Here the crucial role was played by Maynooth. A large building grant from the government in 1845 resulted in the college rapidly taking on the appearance that was to remain unchanged until very recently. A greatly increased maintenance grant in the same year allowed it to cater for the extra students without any of the financial anxieties of the earlier years of the century. From now on the great majority of the Irish diocesan clergy were to be educated in Maynooth.

Cullen viewed the institution with a jaundiced eye. It was too independent, being governed by trustees responsible to the state, who included a number of laymen. Its independence was bolstered by its wealth, which did not derive from ecclesiastical sources. Its theological teaching was old-fashioned and suspect. It was also quite simply too large — too many eggs in one basket — but nothing could be done about that. On other matters, however, he made some progress as a result of the investigation of the college by a royal commission in 1853.[12]

Maynooth was a crucial target for the anti-popery agitation after the restoration of the English hierarchy in 1850: the public wanted to know what really went on there. The setting up of a royal commission of inquiry was something of a courtesy, for similar commissions had recently been to Oxford, Cambridge and Trinity. While the inquiry was wide-ranging, it gave particular attention to two topics of interest to Protestants: the nature and extent of papal authority, and confessional practice, especially in sexual matters. On both the commissioners found nothing to disturb Protestant fears; but clearly these were matters where the college staff, in presenting their evidence, had had to show a certain care verging on caution lest they give the wrong impression.

By the connivance of one of the Catholic commissioners, Cullen had the evidence as it was proofed and before it was published. He was further helped by the fact that this became known to the college staff, who protested to the chairman of the commission, Lord Harrowby. This in turn became known. Cullen now had enough information to conduct a visitation of his own. He forced a personal retractation of his alleged 'Gallican' views from one professor, George Crolly, and he made it clear to the staff in general who were the masters. By the time the whole affair was over, control in Maynooth rested substantially with the bishops as a body rather than with the trustees.

Cullen was not fair to the Maynooth staff, even allowing for the fact that he regarded any lack of total commitment on the university question as a form of Gallicanism, or at least as a less than total commitment to Ultramontanism. There is sufficient evidence to show that Maynooth theology was not static but developing. In the field of morals, Edmund O'Reilly, a protégé of Cullen, had introduced the theology of St Alphonsus. O'Reilly, a student of the Irish College, Rome, had been appointed professor of theology in Maynooth in 1838 and had left to become a Jesuit in 1851. It really seems hard that Patrick Murray, professor of dogma, should have been suspected of Gallicanism, for he had substantial writings to prove that theologically speaking he was decidedly Ultramontane. However, he had wavered on the university question, and that was enough.

At this time Maynooth had some hopes of being empowered to grant pontifical university degrees in theology, but Cullen would have none of it. Despite Newman's reservations, he set up a faculty of theology in the Catholic University in Dublin. It was always struggling and never really came to anything. Maynooth had to wait until 1895 for the power to grant theological degrees. Meanwhile it continued to turn out priests more attuned to the new age, partly, but by no means altogether, by reason of Cullen's supervisory eye.

His continuing suspicions of the institution led him to set up a Dublin diocesan seminary at Clonliffe in 1859. He naturally fostered the Irish College in Rome. There had been serious troubles in the Irish College in Paris in the 1850s, but these were satisfactorily solved when the Irish Vincentians were put in charge in 1858. During the period of the French Revolution a number of Irish bishops had tried to provide institutions for the education of priests in their own dioceses. These survived at Carlow, Kilkenny, Wexford, Thurles and Waterford, though many of their ordinands now went abroad to the English-speaking world, where the Irish formed so large a proportion in the Catholic communities. In 1842 the fledgling Irish Vincentian congregation established All Hallows College in Dublin to ordain priests exclusively for work outside Ireland.

The growing numbers of priests were, as everywhere in the Catholic church, more strictly disciplined and with a greater sense of religious commitment. The pattern for the new age had been laid down at Thurles. The priest was to regard himself as a man apart, marked out by his black or dark dress and Roman collar, prayerful, devoted, carefully nourishing his necessary learning, all this supported by regular retreats and clerical conferences. His life was to centre on his church, the focus of sacramental life for his people. This programme for a new age in fact contained little if anything that was really new. It is hard to find anything in Thurles that had not been laid down at Trent. Hitherto the full Tridentine pattern had been difficult to implement in Ireland. Now it was to go the way of Catholic Europe.

On two points in particular the Catholic clergy in Ireland were under tighter episcopal control than elsewhere. As has been seen, assistant priests or curates had been few in the eighteenth century, and still too few for the work to be done in the early nineteenth. As they became available the parish priest claimed the right of appointment (he did in fact have this right under general church law until 1917). The Irish bishops had tried to assert their right to appoint curates, with growing but incomplete success. At Thurles the right was reserved unequivocally to the bishop, and this now became the norm. In proceeding against delinquent clergy the Irish bishop had also unusually wide powers. The normal procedure in general law was by judicial process. Exceptionally the bishop could act administratively, in the technical phrase, *ex informata conscientia*. What was in general law exceptional became the norm in Ireland. There were valid reasons for this. Few Irish dioceses, even Dublin, had qualified personnel to set up ecclesiastical tribunals, and the civil law prohibited the administering of oaths by private persons. This is what the Catholic bishops were in civil law.

The regular clergy played a relatively minor role. For centuries their ranks had been dominated by the friars, and, as has been seen, they found it difficult to define a role for themselves as the Catholic church moved out of penal times. Their demoralisation — the word is scarcely too strong — had been increased by penal provisions against them in the Catholic Emancipation Act of 1829, which had indeed provided for their eventual extinction. Their overall numbers were small, and while a few friars would normally share a house, the religious life in common was practically non-existent. Personal poverty had also disappeared. They lacked the stabilising influence of pastoral responsibility, and some of them appear to have done little if any work.[13]

One of Cullen's mandates as apostolic delegate had been the reform of the religious orders. Inevitably, he saw this in terms of contemporary Italian practice. This increased his problems. In Ireland it was illegal to wear the religious habit in public, illegal for a religious community to own property. Several times he toyed with the idea of giving them parochial responsibility. Among the friars there were divisions. On the whole, the younger men were open to change. The older members were not, being used to a large measure of personal independence, and fearing, not altogether without reason, that a sudden restoration of personal poverty and the common life could result in tyranny and even cruelty. In the face of these complexities, Cullen's temperamental hesitancy led to very awkward situations. In 1855 two Carmelite priests wrote to him saying that the whole Irish province had only seven priests, three of them old. They were divided among themselves. They added: 'For the love of God give us a superior or call on us to elect one and we will never trouble you again.'[14] It was not surprising that reform should have come slowly and painfully, but it did come eventually.

The other major traditional religious order had been the Jesuits. They had always been few in number but high in quality. They had been restored in Ireland in 1814, after the general suppression, by the distinguished Peter Kenny. Their contribution to the general apostolate may be deduced from the fact that they were one of the two congregations mentioned by name at Thurles in connection with parish missions. The second was the Vincentians, or, to give them their official title, the Congregation of the Mission. This group had its origins with six young Maynooth priests, who decided in 1833 to live a common life and in 1841 adopted the Vincentian rule. They became Cullen's most trusted helpers and advisers. The apostolate of the parish mission was strengthened by the introduction of other religious orders from the continent, in most cases by way of England, such as the Passionists (1848), the Oblates of Mary Immaculate (1851) and the Redemptorists (1853). Yet the personnel available for parish missions remained insufficient; because of the continuing shortage Bishop Furlong of Ferns established for this purpose the Missionaries of the Blessed Sacrament, a group of diocesan priests living in community, as late as 1866.

A real explosion in numbers took place with the teaching brothers, most of them Irish Christian Brothers, and with the nuns. There had been about 120 nuns in 1800. In 1850 there were 1,500, in 1870 about 3,700, in 1900 about 8,000. Brothers and nuns were strongest in Munster and Leinster, but they began to make their appearance even in Protestant Ulster. Cullen had introduced them to Armagh during his brief stay there. Foundations could sometimes be thwarted by local hostility, as at Lisburn in 1853, but even in Belfast itself Bishop Patrick Dorrian (1865-85) made nuns, brothers and clerical religious part of the local scene.

It has been necessary to go into some detail in regard to what might be called the 'full-time personnel' of the church, because of the important role they were to play in the years after 1850 in providing a Catholic ethos in the public life of the country, especially, but by no means exclusively, in the schools. The second half of the nineteenth century saw greatly increased provision from public funds for those unable to provide for themselves, especially children. This increased provision had begun with the setting up of workhouses in 1838. The numbers who had to have recourse to them remained remarkably steady after the great pressures of the Famine years had subsided. The workhouses had not a good reputation: they were, in Archbishop Cullen's view, 'an abomination, a sink of vice and misery'. He regularly contrasted them with the more humane provision made for the poor, mainly by the church, in Italy and in particular in the papal states, his grievance being, essentially, that while the Catholic church in Ireland had been stripped of resources it might have used for charity, Catholics were discriminated against in the dispensing of money raised for poor-relief by general taxation. Though the workhouses were supported from public funds, Catholics gained a share in their administration only slowly, even at local level. As late as 1865 there was still not a single Catholic serving as a Poor Law commissioner. The first lady Catholic visitors made their way into the Dublin workhouses only at the beginning of the 1860s. By this date too nuns had begun to make their way into the workhouses as nurses, though not without opposition.

The general atmosphere was such as to nourish ingrained Catholic fears. Children and young people were especially at risk. In 1841 there had been a decision of the Attorney General that foundling children of unknown religion should be brought up in the established church. Though practice varied, this became a bitterly disputed issue in individual cases. At the age of fifteen children were moved in with the adults, often to their moral detriment, it was felt. Poverty was still so widespread that a sizeable number of children fell into the category of 'orphan', either because they were illegitimate or because their parents were dead or unable to provide for them. Much effort had gone into the provision of Catholic orphanages, staffed by nuns and brothers, but funds were very scarce. Two acts of parliament brought about substantial changes.

The first was the Reformatory Schools Act of 1858. Mounting pressure in England for the separate detention of young offenders had led in 1854 to legislation setting up special centres for them. A proposal for similar legislation for Ireland in 1856 was opposed by the Catholic bishops led by Cullen, and the Irish legislation as finally enacted empowered the Chief Secretary to designate certain institutions as suitable for the detention of young offenders; in effect it set up denominational centres with state support. The Industrial Schools Act of 1868 was much more far-reaching in that it extended the system to children 'at risk' because they had no parental care. 'Industrial schools' increased rapidly in number, the Catholic ones being almost exclusively under the care of brothers and nuns.[15] This development in particular greatly reduced, even if it did not altogether remove, Catholic fears of proselytism. How deeply these had been ingrained may perhaps be seen from the fact that national synods continued to advert to the problem until 1927.

These developments led to a great diminution of the number of children in the workhouses, in particular of children without parental care. Religious antagonisms lingered in these workhouses, especially between the chaplains of rival denominations. Cullen had to fight to establish the principle that while the chaplain's salary was paid from public funds, power to appoint and dismiss him rested with the local bishop, but here too he was successful.

Problems of the status of chaplains in the army and navy were more intractable. It was natural that the established church should be in a special position in the armed forces of the crown. It was only in 1853 that it was made a general rule in the navy not to force the Church of England catechism on boys who conscientiously objected, and there were continuing complaints that this rule was by no means always honoured. The appointment of Catholic chaplains came only slowly. The development was set back by the Crimean War (1854-6), which had resulted in chaos in many aspects of military matters, leading to the appearance of self-appointed nurses to care for the wounded as well as self-appointed Catholic chaplains to minister to the Catholic troops. While the war lasted the government was quite in the dark as to what was going on, and when it was over it was determined not to lose control again. In consequence, while it was now prepared to appoint Catholic chaplains, it was insistent that they be fully commissioned officers, like the other chaplains. To Cullen this was highly unsatisfactory, in that the final power to appoint and dismiss them lay with the army authorities, but he had to live with the situation. Paid chaplains were appointed, but their duties were light, especially in that the soldiers went to Mass in the neighbouring parish church because no special Catholic chapel was provided in the barracks. The problem was even more intractable in the navy, for it was not practicable to appoint a Catholic chaplain on each ship, and this led to continuing sectarian squabbles and recriminations in a situation where in practice a sailor was treated as a member of the established church unless he positively opted out, and even then he found problems in fulfilling his religious duties. Similar squabbles and recriminations continued concerning the schools for children of the armed forces, especially because there were now many orphan children in consequence of the Crimean War, and in these schools, as might indeed be expected, there was a strong Protestant ethos that did not yield easily.

The most far-reaching development of a state system which was in practice substantially denominational had come with the National Schools. The issue of proselytism had plumbed the depths of bitterness during the Famine years. Thereafter it was in retreat, though organised groups continued a widespread activity. An important factor in turning back the tide was a series of vigorous parish missions in the 1850s, though these were hampered by lack of personnel and even at their best could be only partially effective. In 1852 a Vincentian mission took place in Oughterard, a parish where there had been large-scale defections. Many returned to Catholic religious practice after the mission, but some of them seem to have expected material recompense for their change of heart, and apparently large numbers ended up attending neither church nor chapel.[16]

More lasting results could come only through a better system of catechesis, and very substantially this was provided through the National Schools, because of the growth in the number of children attending them. While the Christian Brothers withdrew from the system after a brief experiment, almost all the nuns decided they could accommodate their schools within it. Though the system was undenominational in law, the very demographic pattern of the country saw to it that most schools attended by Catholic children were attended by them exclusively or almost exclusively. In 1870 approximately 50 per cent of Catholic children on the rolls were in schools where there was no Protestant. A further 45 per cent were in schools with an average Protestant enrolment of 7 per cent, and only 5 per cent were in what could be regarded as genuinely 'mixed' schools. The system made provision for denominational religious education, and although about 1840 there had been real grounds for fear that this might not be fully honoured, such fears tended to lessen as things tended to improve in practice. The patron of the school was usually the parish priest, and this gave him considerable influence. Its importance could be seen from what happened in the diocese of Tuam.

Archbishop MacHale had withdrawn from the system in 1839. His attempts to plug the gap, mainly with teaching brothers, proved quite insufficient, and he began a grudging return as early as 1852. Even by this date, however, quite a number of National Schools had been set up in his diocese under Protestant patronage, so his scope was limited. An important development emerged from the 'O'Keeffe case' in 1873-4 (other aspects of this crucial lawsuit will be discussed later). Robert O'Keeffe, parish priest of Callan, Co. Kilkenny, had been suspended by his bishop. The bishop informed the National Board of Education, who removed him from his position in the parish schools. The government did not intervene, and in consequence it had become tacitly accepted that a priest's role in the school depended primarily on his nomination to his parish by the bishop, not on his nomination as patron of the school by the board.

The importance of the role of the schools in catechesis is beyond question. 'They saved us from proselytism' — so wrote Bishop Denvir of Down and Connor to Cullen on 21 December 1852.[17] Others were saying the same thing. While what they said was true, much of what had gone right had happened not because of any virtues in the system but because so many of the schools were *de facto* Catholic. In consequence, the bishops continued to press for a fully denominational system, but they had to content themselves with getting piecemeal improvements in the system they had.

The biggest threat to the acceptability of the system arose from the training of teachers. The plan had been to have a Central Training Establishment in Dublin, with preliminary training in thirty-two local Model Schools. The central establishment was set up, but the first Model School came only in 1849. Cullen led the attack on them when one was established in his diocese at Drogheda in 1851, fortified no doubt by the fact that the English Catholics had secured a denominational training college at Hammersmith in 1850, and made more determined when later in the decade it began to appear there might be plans to make the Model Schools the nucleus of an undenominational system of secondary education. In 1862 Catholics were forbidden to attend the Model Schools or the Central Training Establishment, and the bishops pressed for denominational training. It was genuinely difficult to accommodate this within the National system, though in 1864 limited recognition was given to the monitors in 'a few very large and highly efficient schools', in effect giving some large convent schools the same status as the Model Schools. This provided an opening towards denominational teacher-training, and it finally came in 1883.[18]

The National Schools had been a setback to secondary education, at least indirectly, in that as they spread more and more of the 'pay-schools' had to close their doors, and many of these had provided some 'classical' education. Education at secondary level remained in private hands, becoming more and more concentrated in the hands of the clergy and the nuns (the brothers were slower to take on secondary education). Proposals for a national mixed system in 1838 and again in 1858 came to nothing, and Irish secondary education remained handicapped by a lack of aim and lack of means. Walter MacDonald, in a fairly caustic verdict on St Kieran's College, Kilkenny, concluded that 'lack of means — of endowment — was at the root of the whole misery'. In 1871 Catholics, 77 per cent of the population, were only 50 per cent of the pupils at secondary schools. The parents of this school-going population regarded the course as an immediate passport to employment, in, for example, commerce or the civil service. This led to a search for a suitable examining body, such as London University, the Catholic University (in 1856), the Queen's Colleges (in 1860) or the 'South Kensington examinations' in the 1860s. This last was the only one to make grants available to participating schools, but the schools in return had to orient their courses heavily towards scientific subjects. The Intermediate Education Act of 1878 made grants available over a wide range of subjects on the results of public examinations.[19]

University education for Catholics struggled against severe handicaps. The Queen's Colleges lay under ecclesiastical ban. The Catholic University had neither secure endowment nor legal recognition for its degrees (the medical school was a success because its courses won professional recognition). The appointment of John Henry Newman as first Rector had been an imaginative step, but a partially resident Rector and a temperamentally cautious and hesitant Archbishop of Dublin did not allow this first imaginative step to be followed up imaginatively. But the biggest handicap of all was perhaps the fact that the idea that a university education was something they should struggle to afford for their children grew only slowly among the Catholic population. Something of a breakthrough came with the Royal University in 1879. This was a purely examining body, but there were provisions for indirect endowment in the form of fellowships in recognised teaching institutions. The fellowships available to Catholics were concentrated in 'University College' at Newman's old headquarters at 86 St Stephen's Green. From this it was a natural enough transition to the establishment of the National University of Ireland in 1908 — again, a pragmatic solution, which both church and state decided could be accommodated within their principles.[20]

This chapter is turning into a story of institutions, but here it is only reflecting reality. Catholic religious practice was becoming more institutionalised. More pastorally-minded bishops presided over a clergy more numerous, more devout and more disciplined. The mission of the priest centred more and more on his church, with close support from what more and more was his school. The Synod of Thurles had insisted that religious instruction in the National Schools should be denominational. The issue came to a head in 1853, after Richard Whately, the Church of Ireland Archbishop of Dublin, protested to the Board of National Education that his two books, *Lessons on the Truth of Christianity* and *Christian Evidences*, though sanctioned by the board, were not in use even in Model Schools. Cullen reacted strongly, and the outcome was that approval for the books was withdrawn and Whately resigned from the board. Religious instruction of Catholic children in the National Schools was henceforth to be based exclusively on the Catholic catechism. There continued to be a number of catechisms, but most dioceses used the revision of Butler's known as the General Catechism and after later revision as the Maynooth Catechism. But all catechisms in use were in the same mould — exposition by question and answer, to be learned by rote, with the emphasis, continuous since the Jesuit catechisms of the Counter-Reformation, on the Christian life as obedience to concrete rules, with some danger of a dichotomy between Christian knowing and Christian living. Religious instruction in the secondary schools followed the same pattern. Only rarely was a voice raised to suggest that things might be better.[21]

The normal supplement to school catechesis was the Sunday sermon. Fairly rapidly the attendance at Sunday Mass increased. To begin with there were more churches and better churches. The effect must have been particularly marked in the poorer parts, where, with substantial assistance from emigrants' contributions, churches were provided even where there had been nothing before. Bishop Patrick MacGettigan of Raphoe died on 1 May 1861. He was over eighty years of age and had been over forty years a bishop. A few days later Cullen remarked in a letter to Rome, possibly with some exaggeration, but not with much, that the old man had remembered a time when there was not a single church in his diocese, but that he had left it well provided with churches and religious institutions.[22] There were also more Masses. For one thing, there were more priests available. It is true there were still inhibitions about a priest saying two Masses on a Sunday. Thurles had laid down that this was permissible only in cases of necessity and with episcopal approval. However, the new bishops were quicker to recognise necessity and not merely give approval but take the initiative. When John Kilduff went to Ardagh as bishop in 1853 he found many parishes, even town parishes, where there was only one Mass on Sundays. His response was to order a second Mass at an earlier hour.[23]

Naturally improvement came slowly. One test of the quality of the church was its suitability for the reservation of the Blessed Sacrament. Here Thurles had been cautious. When Cullen arrived in Armagh he reported that the churches were usually very poor, many of them thatched.[24] The family in the farm by Lough Gur in Co. Limerick attended

Sunday Mass at St Patrick's Well — 'a poor, plain little chapel...no singing, no incense, no candles, no pictures or stations of the Cross'. A particularly interesting and detailed report was forwarded to Cullen in 1858 by the newly appointed Bishop of Ferns, Thomas Furlong.[25] It was in the form of a letter from Dean Murphy of his diocese. The dean had begun his ministry in 1812. At that time the country chapels were 'miserably insecure', and of necessity the Blessed Sacrament was kept in the priest's house or lodging. His own district was so extensive and calls to the sick so frequent that he could not venture out without taking it with him. But at about the time of Emancipation (1829) the priests, he said, began to build better churches with parochial houses near them, and it became general practice everywhere to reserve the Blessed Sacrament in the church with a lamp burning before it, never to take it out except for a call to the sick, and to return it immediately afterwards.

However, the churches improved, there were more Masses, and more people attended them. In assessing the quality of the Sunday sermon the first criterion is the seminary training of the priest. For most priests this now meant Maynooth. Walter MacDonald has left an account of his theological course in the college, which began in 1873, and even when allowance is made for his caustic approach there would appear to be much truth in what he said.[26] He did not conceal his admiration for the 'great, strong, childlike faith' of his professors, but the implication is strong that this very faith led them to neglect contemporary challenges, and in effect fight the battles of the sixteenth-century Reformation, or at latest the eighteenth-century Enlightenment, against a background of nineteenth-century Ireland (this might not necessarily have made the average priest less effective in his preaching). He had great respect for the Vincentian Father McGowan, who arrived in 1874 to instruct in preaching and teaching Christian doctrine, but he at least implies that he came into a very unsatisfactory situation. Liturgy and sacred music were 'taught execrably or not at all', and the library facilities were poor and dated.

To some extent MacDonald may be falling into a common trap of memoir literature, projecting backwards to his youth things that really became clear to him in later years. Yet the writings of the Maynooth staff tend to confirm his verdict. Up to 1847 there was an extraordinary regulation in the college statutes, forbidding the staff to publish at all. While it was sometimes circumvented, it was only after this date they could consider serious publication. Two names stand out in the field of theology: Patrick Murray in dogma and George Crolly in moral theology. What they did essentially was to give a distinctively Irish bent to contemporary Catholic scholarship. In treating of the church Murray gave special attention to the Anglican position, while in moral questions Crolly gave similar attention to British and Irish law. In so far as contemporary Catholic scholarship was sealed off from the problems of the age, so were they.

After ordination the priest's professional knowledge was maintained by theological conferences, to be held, Thurles had laid down, 'at least four times a year, in accordance with the now universal custom', and to concentrate on practical pastoral matters. This meant that the seminary textbook continued to be important. However, another important influence on the priest's formation was the *Irish Ecclesiastical Record*, a journal still awaiting its historian. It had been founded by Cullen in 1864, with the avowed purpose of forging closer links between Ireland and Rome. In consequence, a regular feature was the publication of Roman documents. Probably in large measure because of the influence of Cullen's nephew and secretary, Patrick F. Moran, it carried many articles on Irish ecclesiastical history, inevitably in the context of religious controversies. From its first number it carried a section headed 'Liturgical Questions'. Shortly afterwards 'Theological Questions' were added, and in due course, with a certain inevitability, questions in canon law. These provided concrete answers to practical, pastoral problems and were widely studied and discussed by the clergy. In 1879 the periodical was transferred to Maynooth. Its Dublin base had simply run out of editors because they kept being promoted to bishoprics, and it had ceased publication in 1876. Its revival in 1879 was due to the efforts of William Walsh, a Dublin priest appointed to the college staff in 1867, President in 1880, and in 1885 Archbishop of Dublin. Thereafter it remained a Maynooth publication.

From this brief sketch of the basic intellectual pabulum of the average Irish priest it may be safely concluded that his Sunday preaching was essentially an extension of the catechism. There was much to be said in its favour. It certainly allowed a structured programme of religious instruction, but like the catechism it may not have avoided the danger of a certain dichotomy between knowing the faith and living it.

The supplement to the Sunday sermon was the parish mission. As already noted, qualified personnel became available only slowly, but while missions were less frequent than they later became, they were in general longer and more intensive. Nevertheless, the missionaries made their way around the whole country, to areas where proselytism was a threat, even into the north, as at Lisburn in 1853, where a mission aroused Protestant hostility. Elsewhere missions might rouse passions that could lead to the intervention of the civil law. At Carlow and Athy in 1858 the people turned on the local 'bad characters' and tried to 'run them out of the town'. This led to the issuing of summonses.[27] The most famous instance was at Kingstown in 1855. Sermons had been preached against immoral books, and quite a number had been turned in. One of the missionaries, Vladimir S. Pecherin, Russian revolutionary turned Redemptorist, proposed that they be publicly burnt. With a nice sense of irony, the bonfire took place on Guy Fawkes Day, 5 November. An extremist Protestant clergyman had incited a young boy to put a few Protestant Bibles into the books to be burnt (it is not altogether impossible that a few others had found their way there by other means). The clergyman then started a propaganda campaign that led to Pecherin's trial for blasphemy in Green Street courthouse on 7 and 8 December 1855. The police had been reluctant to act, as they suspected the evidence. The court took the same view, and Pecherin was acquitted. He was cheered back to Kingstown by triumphant crowds.[28]

The average mission, while less dramatic, seems to have been quite effective in parishes where, at least in the 1850s, the level of instruction was low and religious practice poor. Bishop Kilduff of Ardagh (1853-67) has left a detailed account of the missions he introduced in his diocese.[29] At Athlone in 1853 the mission lasted a month. It was conducted by six Vincentians, the greater part of their total available strength. Every day there were three sermons. With the assistance of the local clergy — three diocesans and three Franciscans — there were confessions from early morning until late evening. The result was described as the total regeneration of the parish. The missionaries left behind them institutions to nourish a more personal spirituality — the Sodalities of the Scapulars, of the Living Rosary and of the Sacred Heart, the Confraternity of Christian Doctrine, and the Society of St Vincent de Paul.

The parish church too became the normal place for conferring the sacraments, but not immediately, and, in the case of penance, never completely.[30] Thurles had ordered that all churches have baptismal fonts and had exhorted priests to baptise in church wherever old customs of baptism in the home could be abolished without inconvenience. At Cullen's instigation the Roman authorities had stiffened this exhortation into a precept. The new practice proved acceptable, and baptism in the church became the norm.

There was much more opposition to the proposal that confessions be held in church, implying as it did the abolition or at least the radical modification of the established practice of the 'stations'. Cullen himself realised that it would be necessary to go slowly here if change were not to result in fewer people going to confession; and although again at his instigation Rome stiffened the original Thurles decree, it remained hortatory, but very hortatory indeed where women's confessions were concerned — these should be in the church and in a confessional. In Cullen's own ecclesiastical province of Dublin there had already been substantial progress towards transferring the 'stations' from private houses to the church. Elsewhere, however, any such proposal was strongly resisted both by priests and bishops, especially in Munster. The Roman authorities found it hard to countenance the hearing of confessions in private houses, especially women's confessions, and on 17 May 1854 issued a decree demanding that there always be a kind of portable confessional screen or *crates* in such cases.[31] Reaction even from Cullen's friends and protégés among the episcopate was swift and sharp. As early as 6 June

Kilduff wrote from Longford that if he communicated the decree to his priests they would think he was mad, while a letter of 22 August from David Moriarty, newly appointed coadjutor bishop in Kerry, indicates that he had communicated the decree to the Kerry clergy, and that while they may not have thought him mad, there had been good Kerry wit at the thought of transporting confessional screens to some of the places where they had to hold stations.[32] The portable *crates*, it might be said, never got off the ground. However, the stations were gradually removed to the churches, where they were gradually replaced by fixed times for confessions. In a few dioceses they survived until the house Mass once again came into liturgical favour after the Second Vatican Council.

Marriage too came into the church ('mixed marriages', between Catholics and Protestants, are discussed below, in the context of relations between the churches). Cullen was opposed to marriages in the home, partly because he wanted to emphasise the sacramental aspect, and partly because he wanted to control the abuse of exorbitant collections by the officiating priest. Again at his instigation, Rome stiffened the original decree of Thurles on these two points, and the new discipline gradually established itself, though priests found it still possible to make marriage lucrative, especially in Munster. Cullen also encouraged the practice of having Mass in church on the occasion of the marriage, a practice hitherto unusual, but which gradually became common.

The church too became the centre of many of the new devotions. Churches where the Blessed Sacrament could be safely reserved increased in number. More parishes were introduced to benediction and the forty hours' adoration; more people were enrolled in Confraternities of the Blessed Sacrament. Devotion to the Sacred Heart had been long established, but now it spread rapidly, developing into the practice of going to confession and communion on the first Fridays of nine consecutive months — 'the nine Fridays', an almost universal practice by the end of the century. Many devotions in honour of the Blessed Virgin made even the traditional family rosary a part of church devotions as well. The tradition of personal devotion, associated particularly with the towns and the middle classes, took on a distinctively Italian colouring in Ireland, as elsewhere in Europe. On 15 January 1856 Cullen wrote to Tobias Kirby, Rector of the Irish College, Rome, saying that next year he proposed to have a Christmas crib in the Pro-Cathedral: 'If you see a few good shepherds or angels going astray in any old shop, send them to us. Such things cannot be found here.'[33]

If the traditions of the urban middle classes were taking on a new colouring, the ancient traditions and usages of the countryside were in full retreat, not just because of ecclesiastical pressures but also because of the changing values of society as a whole. Curiously, the Synod of Thurles had nothing to say about wakes and funerals, but the First Synod of Maynooth

(1875) required parish priests to put an end to unchristian wakes, and the topic recurs in subsequent national synods, as late as 1927 and, somewhat unbelievably, 1956. In these two latest synods, however, there is a distinct impression that the problem was no longer a very serious one. Legislation does tend to continue even after the world that led to it has gone.

What happened was that the traditional wake became socially unacceptable as the general values of society became more 'respectable'. The account of wakes in *The Farm by Lough Gur* is particularly revealing. The mother of the household would not allow her daughters or her maid-servants to go to wakes, and would give no reason. However, Bernie, the curious one among the daughters, made it her business to find out, and this is what she told her sister:

> The next thing that happens at the wake is the arrival of the visitors. The relations bend over the body and say how pretty it looks or how death becomes it, and they cry and lament and say a prayer, but mere friends only kneel and say a short prayer, and then take snuff and tobacco and fill their pipes and glasses and sit down, and some play the first game, which is only clapping hands as people come in. After that the boys and girls play Shuffle the Brogue, which is like Hunt the Slipper, all sitting on the floor. There are other games, the Rope Game and the Horse Fair, and a very wicked one called the Mock Marriage, but really, Sissy, the country people about here aren't like that. Ellie [one of the maids] said a wake on Lough Gur is very gloomy and religious. She said the mistress herself could attend and take no harm. But Bridgie [another maid] told me it is gloomy only so long as the old people are there. When they're gone, the table with the body is pushed on one side and the wake games begin. Even then, every half hour, or oftener, they kneel down and all pray together for the soul of the dead person.[34]

The traditional wake did continue into the twentieth century in some country districts, but what happened was that the elements of paganism and clerical satire disappeared, and the parish clergy did not feel it necessary to offer serious opposition to what was left, usually no more than the general horseplay that Seán Ó Súilleabháin noted at a wake in Mayo he himself attended in 1921.[35] The wake was further attenuated by the growing practice of bringing the corpse to the church for the funeral Mass instead of having Mass in the house. This change was introduced in the ecclesiastical province of Dublin in the 1850s and gradually spread. It became of obligation with the new Code of Canon Law in 1918.

The traditional patterns and pilgrimages were in continuing decline: observers in the 1870s were already speaking of patterns as something that lived only in the memories of older people. Yet the most famous centre of pilgrimage of old Gaelic Ireland, Lough Derg, maintained its ancient pattern of asceticism in the face of changing fashion. Even here, however, one can see a certain tailoring of the observance and greater clerical control. As early as 1780 the traditional Franciscan guardians had been replaced by priors from the diocesan clergy. That same year its most renowned feature, the storied 'cave', was filled in and the first 'basilica' built. Henceforth the vigil would be kept in the church and not in the cave. Apart from this, however, the church authorities preserved the traditional exercises and austerities, and they continued to attract great numbers of pilgrims. After long-drawn-out disputes with the landlords, the Leslie family, the island was legally vested in ecclesiastical authorities in 1917.

There are contrasts and similarities in the case of what had been a great centre of pilgrimage in Norman Ireland, Our Lady's Island in Co. Wexford. Here it would appear that the number of pilgrims had been falling off even before the Famine, and they may have been very few in the 1860s. In July 1867, however, there was a revival, significantly in the form of an ecclesiastical procession around the island, and, again significantly, on the occasion of the closing of a Redemptorist mission. There is no record of this being repeated for the next thirty years. It was only in 1897 that the then parish priest, Father Whitty, organised on 15 August the procession and devotions — high Mass, sermon and benediction — which since then have continued each year. An account in the Wexford *People* commented: 'Catholics of the present day should rejoice that they live in the days of religious toleration, and it is a sign of the times that a couple of Protestants of the locality were interested spectators of Sunday's procession.' One might wonder if they included the ghost of Solomon Richards from two hundred years before.

External observers in Ireland in the 1850s and 1860s noted a Catholic church that seemed full of confidence in its progress, from the English Cardinal Nicholas Wiseman in 1858 to the Irish Presbyterian James Godkin in 1867. The visible signs of that progress were the new churches and ecclesiastical institutions rising everywhere. The increasing misfortunes of the papal states rallied Irish Catholic opinion behind the papacy, in sharp contrast with what happened in England, where the dismemberment and final extinction of the papal states was welcomed because of a feeling that it was part of the general triumph of liberal ideas over an institution traditionally suspect in England, and deeply suspect since the restoration of the English Catholic hierarchy in 1850. The fact was that as the Irish lost one identity they found another, and the new identity was Catholicism. On 14 August 1859, the year after Cardinal Wiseman's triumphant tour, O'Neill Daunt noted in his journal: 'Whatever public spirit exists in Ireland just now is rather religious than political', while in 1872, at a meeting of the council of the International Workers of the World, 'Citizen McDonnell reported that the movement was progressing in Cork and Dublin. He read a letter from a correspondent in Dublin, which expressed a hope that the journals of the Association would avoid any articles expressing atheistical opinions, or condemnation of Catholicism, as anything of the kind would do great damage in Ireland, which opinion Citizen McDonnell endorsed.'[36]

Britain might have a worldwide empire, but there was an Irish world-empire too, with even wider bounds, the empire of the Catholic faith. The Irish had been emigrating in numbers before the Famine, but after it the tide became a flood. It transformed Catholicism in England and Scotland. It built the church round a solid Irish core in the United States of America. The church in the British empire was almost altogether Irish, particularly in Australia. To all these churches Ireland sent a supply of priests, that grew, in Carlow College, for example, from a trickle before the Famine to about a hundred a year at the end of the century. At the First Vatican Council in 1869-70 there were 73 bishops of Irish birth, about 10 per cent of the total, and about 150 of Irish descent, about 20 per cent.

It was not just Paul Cullen who felt that the Irish race could be equated with the Catholic faith, in Ireland and far beyond it. In Ireland the Protestant church establishment was slowly whittled away. Church cess went in 1833; in 1838 the tithe became a rent charge. Final disestablishment came in 1869. The Catholic church was moving in the opposite direction. Under Cullen's leadership it was becoming — it is hard to avoid the phrase — a kind of 'semi-state body'. In using this phrase, however, very large reservations must be made. On the one hand, Cullen would have nothing to do with legal ties between the state and the Catholic church. In connection with church disestablishment, there was widespread support for a 'concurrent endowment' of all churches from the wealth of the established church. Cullen succeeded in persuading Rome that what Ireland should have was 'a free church in a free state', even though the principle of separation of church and state had been formally condemned there a few years before, in the Syllabus of Errors in 1864. For its part, the state, while willing to put increasing public funds effectively at the disposal of the Catholic church, was not disposed to expand this practical help into legal ties. Here two fundamental points were established by the O'Keeffe case in the early 1870s: that the exercise of papal jurisdiction in Ireland was still illegal in virtue of an unrepealed statute of Elizabeth I; and that nevertheless the civil courts would not set aside disciplinary actions within the church, on the grounds that its members had consented to be bound by its rules. The Elizabethan statute was formally repealed only by the Government of Ireland Act (1920).[37]

Cullen saw the whole process as a struggle, usually nerve-racking and exhausting, no doubt, but going in the right direction. 'It is the fight of David against Goliath,' he had written to a correspondent in 1865,[38] but he must have known his Bible well enough to be quite conscious of who had won that particular conflict. It was not a good time for relations between the churches in Ireland. Already before the Famine the Protestant reaction to the entry of Catholics into political affairs had been a defensive closing of the ranks. This became even more marked as the years went by and Catholic progress accelerated. Protestant suspicions were all the greater because of the prominent part played by the Catholic clergy in popular politics at all levels. With Daniel O'Connell this had become part of the very fabric of Irish politics. In this matter Cullen's position had been long and seriously misinterpreted, but what exactly it was is now clear.[39] He did not propose that Irish priests take no part in politics — that is beyond question both from his private correspondence and from the synodal legislation for which he was responsible. The priest in Ireland was necessarily 'political', both because of his general position in society and the general nature of the state. What Cullen wanted was to see that his participation was of a kind compatible with his spiritual ministry, that he did not discuss political topics in church, that he did not in any way become involved in the violence that sometimes marked popular politics, nor indeed involved in politics in any way that might set some of his flock against him as a priest. His involvement in politics should be discreet and not divisive, either between him and his people or between him and his bishop.

Cullen was the giant in this particular contest, and in the event Goliath won. However, some Davids put up a stout resistance. There was, for example, Peter Daly, representative of the old traditions of clerical independence in the wardenship of Galway. He practically ran the town — chairman of the corporation, of the gas company, of the Mechanics' Institute, owner of the Corrib Steam Company, a strong supporter of the local Queen's College. When the Bishop of Galway died in 1855 Cullen trembled at the thought he might be succeeded by Peter Daly: 'He would be a real whip to our backs, for he is violent and hot-tempered.'[40] Even when he finally succeeded in getting an acceptable nomination, John McEvilly, Daly kept up the fight, sustained by support from the metropolitan, John MacHale.

MacHale's support was also important for an even doughtier fighter, Patrick Lavelle, parish priest of Partry in the diocese of Tuam. Lavelle was the only priest openly to defy Cullen on the Fenians. In 1862 he even lectured publicly in Dublin on the moral right of the Irish people to revolt against their rulers. In the end Cullen had to get the Roman authorities to order MacHale to suspend Lavelle from his functions. Even this was ineffective. MacHale sent a swift messenger over the mountains to Partry to warn Lavelle not to be at home when the writ arrived after a slow journey round by road, and Lavelle took good care to be gone before it arrived.[41]

Everywhere the Catholics were advancing, even in Belfast. Well into the nineteenth century Catholics had been a small minority in the city, and relations between the churches had been good. Good relations had been evident even as late as the opening of St Matthew's church in the Catholic enclave of Ballymacarrett in 1831. However, tensions were mounting. The proportion of Catholics in the total population of the rapidly growing city was rising. The census of 1861, the first to distinguish religious denominations, returned them at 34 per cent. Evangelicalism, and with it antipopery, was growing in the Protestant churches, both Church of Ireland and Presbyterian. The first of what might be called sectarian riots began in the 1830s. The first really serious one broke out in 1857, and thereafter they recurred regularly.

William Crolly (1825-35) was the last Catholic bishop to enjoy the old peaceful relations. His successor, Cornelius Denvir (1835-65), kept a low profile. He was, indeed, so slow to build new churches and set up new parishes that the Catholic community in Belfast was seriously neglected. Patrick Dorrian was appointed coadjutor in 1860 and succeeded on Denvir's resignation in 1865. His policy was to meet confrontation with confrontation. New parishes were established and new churches built. Several congregations of nuns were introduced. The Christian Brothers came in 1866, the Passionists in 1868. Belfast's Catholic hospital, the Mater, was opened in 1883.

Relations between the churches deteriorated all over Ireland, for very much the same reasons as in Belfast, even if not quite so dramatically as in that city. Faced with the rising tide of Catholic influence and power, the Protestant community closed ranks. Though Catholic wealth was growing, a disproportionate amount was still in Protestant hands. This was reflected, for instance, in parliamentary representation, as members of parliament still had to be men of independent means. The 1868 general election, though it brought an increase in the number of Irish M.P.s describing themselves as 'liberals', still returned 68 Protestants as against 37 Catholics. The Protestants showed remarkable staying power in the matter of appointments, in certain banks, in the professions, and in government offices, even in the Local Government Board, set up in 1898. One reason for this was that the Protestants as a whole were better educated — in 1871 it was estimated that, though only 23 per cent of the total population, they constituted 50 per cent of those attending secondary schools. But the closing of ranks was a factor sufficiently real to arouse genuine Catholic resentment, especially when it sank to the level of real bigotry, as at times it did, as for example in the regulation of a Dublin hospital in 1858:

> No emissary or official of the Church of Rome shall ever be permitted to cross the threshold ... for the purpose of administering any rite or imparting any instruction or so-called consolation to the patients.[42]

Cullen had no time for Protestants or Protestantism. His fundamental attitude already appears clearly in a letter from Rome to Father Mathew dated 10 October 1841. There were complaints in Rome against Father Mathew, he wrote, because he had been reported in the papers as entertaining 'sentiments too liberal to Protestants in the matter of religion'. Cullen went on:

> We should entertain most expansive sentiments of charity towards Protestants but at the same time we should let them know that there is but one true Church and that they are strayed sheep from the one fold. We should let them know this; otherwise we might lull them into a false security in their errors and by doing so we should really violate charity.[43]

This was a view that might come very naturally to an Irishman in Rome at this date, when it appeared that the Oxford Movement might be mounting a successful challenge to Anglicanism in England itself. Cullen's views hardened when he returned to Ireland as archbishop and was plunged into the fight of David against Goliath. In 1856 he was scandalised when David Moriarty, the Bishop of Kerry, publicly subscribed to a Protestant orphan society, and he was not prepared to accept the excuse that it was done in order to mark off the 'old Protestants' from the proselytising groups. He could not accept the distinction.[44]

It would be unjust to describe this attitude as simple religious bigotry. Its roots were in his theological formation and in the contemporary social scene, but in addition it was strongly reinforced by his character and temperament. This has been very well analysed by John H. Whyte, in attempting to answer the question why Cullen's actions and motives could have been so seriously misjudged for so long.[45] He finds the explanation in the fact that Cullen, despite his many fine qualities, was by nature secretive and suspicious, unable to show any sympathy towards unfamiliar points of view. This was at the heart of his difficulties with Newman over the Catholic University, as Newman was well aware:

> Poor Dr C.! I should not wonder if he is quite dragged down with anxiety. The great fault I find with him is, that he makes no one his friend, because he will confide in nobody, and be considerate to nobody. Everybody feels that he is emphatically *close*, and while this repels friends, it fills enemies with nameless suspicions of horrible conspiracies against bishops and priests and the rights of St Patrick.[46]

Cullen did confide in a limited circle — 'tell the friends' is a phrase that sometimes occurs in his correspondence — but they were all men who shared his views. He did not confide in others, nor did he feel it necessary to explain his actions or his standpoint. Indeed, as Whyte notes, he tended to make a virtue out of being misunderstood. It is doubtful if he could ever have worked with MacHale, for it is doubtful if anyone could, but his secretiveness and suspicions certainly alienated men he might have worked with — other Irish bishops, Newman at the university, Catholic laymen like Duffy and Lucas. His suspicious approach to those who were either Protestant in religion or Conservative in politics or, as quite frequently happened, were both together, was part of the overall pattern of his temperament.

This sharpening of confessional differences showed itself in many ways. Two very different ones might be singled out. The first was historical scholarship. Here we still lack a satisfactory historiography, but it is impossible not to sense a certain drift about mid-century towards clericalism and controversy. The two great Catholic geniuses of the immediately preceding generation were laymen, Eugene O'Curry (1796-1862) and John O'Donovan (1809-61). They left no successors of anything like comparable stature, though O'Curry had been appointed professor of Irish history and archaeology in the Catholic University in 1854. The great Protestant scholar James Henthorn Todd (1805-69) had worked closely with both of them in the common tasks of scholarship. It was perhaps significant that one year, 1864, saw the publication of three books that set historical scholarship on the paths of religious controversy: Todd's *St Patrick, Apostle of Ireland*, and two works, *Essays on the Origins, Doctrine and Discipline of the Early Irish Church* and *History of the Catholic Archbishops of Dublin*, by Cullen's nephew, Patrick F. Moran.

The second question, that of marriage, impinged much more directly on society. In the nineteenth century marriage was the subject of much statutory regulation by civil law.[47] Basically for reasons of history, Irish marriage law tended to come later than the corresponding law in Britain, and to be in some ways different when it did come. The question may conveniently be treated under two heads, Catholic marriages and 'mixed' marriages.

Catholic marriage was regulated by the common law only — it was valid by the consent of the partners, and lawful if contracted before a validly ordained minister of religion. The marriage of two Catholics before a Catholic priest had always been regarded as complying with the requirements of common law, and this was confirmed by two judgments of the House of Lords in 1844 (*R. v. Millis* and *R. v. Carroll*). The civil law naturally took no cognisance of the invalidating regulation set up by Catholic canon law in the Tridentine decree *Tametsi*, so that it regarded a marriage of two Catholics as valid and lawful if contracted before any validly ordained minister of religion, or, after the office had been set up in 1845, before a civil registrar.

The Catholic church authorities were wary of civil legislation for several reasons. They regarded it as state intrusion in church affairs that could have very unwelcome results: in particular, the conflicts in Prussia in the 1830s were always in their minds. On a more practical level, the standard provisions of statute law that a religious marriage should take place in a church and in the morning hours would cut across the established Irish custom of having marriage in the home and in the evening. Even more practically, the clergy, especially in Munster, were heavily dependent on collections made on the occasion of marriage, and there was reason to fear that the faithful might not be so generous if marriage was in church and in the morning. There was a reluctance even to register marriages with the civil registrar. The Irish act of 1845 did not contain the proviso of the corresponding English legislation of 1836, that a civil registrar should be present at all marriages. This problem was resolved only in 1863 (26 & 27 Vict., c. 90), which imposed the obligation of notifying the civil registrar not on the officiating priest but on the husband.

Catholic reluctance to accept civil legislation on marriage was a factor in the long continuation of a penal statute of 1746 (19 Geo. II, c. 13). This had laid down that a marriage where one or both parties was a Protestant was void in law if contracted before a Catholic priest, and that the officiating priest was guilty of felony. The penalty on the priest was abolished in 1833 (3 & 4 Will. IV, c. 102), but the marriage remained void in law, even though legislation of 1844 (7 & 8 Vict., c. 81) allowed Presbyterian ministers to conduct marriages between parties of whom only one was a Presbyterian.

The general Catholic canon law voided mixed marriages not contracted before a Catholic priest wherever the Tridentine decree *Tametsi* was in force. In an earlier chapter it has been seen that this decree came into force in Ireland only by stages, becoming universally applicable only in 1827. However, because of the penal provisions of the civil law, mixed marriages contracted before a Protestant minister had been customarily regarded as valid in Ireland by the Catholic church, and this had been regularised by a papal decision in 1785. This decision continued to apply after *Tametsi* became binding in the whole country in 1827, the papal document being reprinted in the Dublin provincial statutes of 1831 and the Meath diocesan statutes of 1835. *Tametsi* had come into force in these areas only in 1827.

Catholic practice varied in the first half of the nineteenth century. Legally, the church could not countenance a mixed marriage unless certain guarantees were given. The non-Catholic partner had to undertake to respect the faith of the Catholic, and both had to undertake to bring the children up as Catholics. Catholic ecclesiastical legislation on these undertakings had taken shape down the centuries. It had been consolidated by Benedict XIV in 1748 and repeated by Pius IX in 1858. Ireland enjoyed no exemption, though in practice the custom was widespread that the boys should follow the father's religion and the girls the mother's. When the Catholic bishop had granted a dispensation the parties went through the rite of marriage before a Protestant clergyman or, after 1845, the civil registrar. They then presented themselves to a Catholic priest to renew their consent. What form this should take presented certain problems. Some priests used the Catholic marriage service (the question of a Mass at the marriage did not arise, nor did the question of having the marriage in a Catholic church, for Catholic marriages were held in the home and without Mass). Others, fearful of the penalties laid down in the statute of 1746 — a fear that persisted even after these had been abolished in 1833 — used an approved form that was not the Catholic marriage service, but in the nature of things approximated closely to it.

Cullen, as might be expected, did not approve of mixed marriages, and he set out to make them as difficult as possible. At Thurles in 1850 he had insisted that a papal dispensation be sought in each case. For a precedent he appealed to the American fourth national synod of Baltimore (1840), not altogether happily, for the fact was that a proposal to this effect had been successfully resisted there. His position was further weakened when a decision of the English provincial synod of Westminster in 1852, approved in Rome the following year, allowed a priest to grant the dispensation. The outcome in Ireland was that the bishop continued to dispense, in virtue of faculties delegated by Rome.

The situation in civil law was radically changed by the Marriage Causes and Marriage Law (Ireland) Amendment Act of 1870 (33 & 34 Vict., c. 110) and further clarifying legislation in the following year (34 & 35 Vict., c. 49). As from 1 January 1871 a mixed marriage before a Catholic priest became valid and lawful, subject to the normal provisos of civil law. The chief of these were: that due notice be given to the licenser authorised by the bishop or civil registrar, at least seven days before the issue of licence; that this notice be sent forthwith by the licenser or registrar to the clergymen of the habitual places of worship of the contracting parties; that the licence be delivered to the officiating clergyman at the time of the marriage; that the marriage be celebrated in a building set aside for divine worship in the district for which the licence was issued, with open doors, and between the hours of 8 a.m. and 2 p.m. There were some practical problems that were fairly readily resolved. It was accepted that the Catholic parish priest was a licenser as contemplated in the act, in virtue of the authority to conduct marriages attached to his office by ecclesiastical law. From the Catholic point of view, there was a certain problem in that general ecclesiastical law forbade a mixed marriage in a Catholic church. There was, however, a papal dispensation given in 1858, with the situation in Prussia particularly in mind, allowing, for a grave cause, these marriages to be celebrated in the sacristy, or even in the church, according to the locally approved Catholic rite, without, however, the celebration of Mass or the nuptial blessing that was given during Mass. The practice developed in Ireland that mixed marriages took place before the Catholic priest, in the sacristy, not the church, without Mass or the nuptial blessing, now common at Catholic marriages. The practice that the boys followed the father's religion and the girls the mother's tended to linger on, though inevitably this became less common as mixed marriages passed more and more under the control of the Catholic church. The final stage in that control came with the papal decree *Ne temere* that took effect from 19 April 1908. Henceforth Catholics were in all circumstances bound by the Catholic form of marriage, that is, before a duly authorised priest and two witnesses, even when the other partner was not a Catholic.

This chapter has occasionally moved beyond the date of the death of Paul Cardinal Cullen, 24 October 1878. Nevertheless, it should have made clear that by this date the Irish Catholic community had, very substantially, taken on the shape it was to retain until quite recent times. It is also beyond question that in a very real sense Cullen presided over these developments. This raises the intriguing question: what would have been the outcome of events if Paul Cullen had never been born? To this question history, quite rightly, offers no answer. Yet certain points may usefully be borne in mind. There were the basic changes in Irish society, emphasised if not altogether triggered by the Famine. These made its general tone more 'bourgeois', more 'respectable', and went a long way towards ensuring that its dominant spirituality would derive from that of the middle class, particularly in the towns, in pre-Famine and even earlier times. The modifications introduced into this spirituality were part of developments in the Catholic church as a whole, and it is reasonable to suppose that Rome would have found its instrument (or instruments) had there been no Paul Cullen to hand. The changing position of the Catholic church in civil law would also surely have come about as part of the general political developments, though the lack of Cullen's terrier-like insistence might have slowed things down. All in all, it is a reasonable surmise — and it is in the field of surmise we must move — that most of what happened would have happened in any case, perhaps more slowly, but with a certain inevitability. But the last word is far from having been said on that quite remarkable man, Paul Cardinal Cullen.

For a long time Cullen was dismissed by Irish historical legend as being (what he quite certainly was not) 'a Castle hack'. A few recent studies have emphasised the Irish and nationalist element in him.[48] An even more recent work, the first attempt at a formal biography long overdue, denies that there was any such element, and paints him as a narrow bigot, dominated by an exclusive 'Ultramontanism'. He came to a country moving peacefully towards religious pluralism, but reversed all this and put in its place a Catholic 'cultural ascendancy' and 'imperialism'. To put it bluntly, this is an outrageously simplified version of things which is quite unsustainable.[49] Another recent work, after an examination of Cullen that is indeed far from exhaustive, dismisses him as a minor political meddler with little religious significance.[50] It would appear that after a reasonably successful rescue from a role as the *bête noire* of Irish nationalism he is now coming under attack from another quarter. It certainly takes fairly large-sized blinkers to depict the Catholic church in Ireland at this date, and Paul Cullen in particular, as thrusting purposefully towards a sectarian society, brushing aside attempts by the civil authority to keep religious peace by insisting on non-denominational structures. Pending a real study of the man, it would be helpful to find an outside observer who could be regarded as reasonably detached and reasonably competent.

There is in fact such a person, though curiously little is heard of him. Right through the nineteenth century distinguished French scholars visited Ireland and published their impressions and judgments. It can be safely said that Adolphe Perraud, who visited Ireland in 1860, stands high in this group. He published his *Études sur l'Irlande contemporaine* in Paris in 1862. The English translation with a slightly more tendentious title, *Ireland Under English Rule*, appeared in Dublin in 1864.

Perraud was indeed a very distinguished person and a very distinguished scholar, in a distinctively French way. Born in 1828, he had a brilliant course in historical studies in the École Normale. Then in 1852 he joined the Oratorian congregation at Paris and was ordained priest in 1855. This priest who never concealed his 'liberal' political views and strong social conscience became a bishop in 1874, a member of the French Academy in 1883, and a cardinal of the Holy Roman Church in 1893. He was truly a many-sided man of quite remarkable stature.

He speaks with sustained indignation about the lot of the Irish Catholics. He does express his admiration for the fact that the British government, unlike the French, does not dream of restricting the action of the church in managing its own affairs. He notes that there has been considerable economic improvement over the preceding twenty years, but he notes too that while there is less poverty, there is still real poverty, especially in the cities, where, he thinks, there has been only slight emigration among the poor. Certainly Dublin displays rags and bare feet as no other European city does, and parts of Limerick and Cork are as bad. Famine and emigration have thinned the real poor in the country districts, but here too there are areas of desperate poverty. 'A Protestant paper of Londonderry' is his source for the statements that in Co. Donegal about 4,000 people went barefoot in winter, that it was rare to find a man with a calico shirt, and that there were families where five or six grown women had between them only a single dress to go out in. Priests in Donegal confirmed to Perraud that what Beaumont had noted in the 1830s was still true, that frequently when a person came home from Mass he took off his clothes and gave them to another to go to another Mass.

Perraud noted manifold examples of positive discrimination by Protestants against Catholics. Catholics were discriminated against in the civil service, being admitted only to the subordinate posts. Jury-packing was not quite as bad as it had been, but juries were often packed with Protestants and justice denied to Catholics for sectarian reasons. And as well as Protestant discrimination there was Protestant pressure — the Bible societies, the Protestant orphan societies, the Orange Order, which summed up 'the furious hatred which arms Protestants against Catholics in the north of Ireland'. The country seemed to be governed by a succession of coercion acts, even though it was admitted that there had been a marked decline in crime against persons and property.

There had been two particularly horrifying mass evictions while Perraud was in Ireland, one at Derryveagh, Co. Donegal, and the other at Partry, Co. Mayo. When Perraud speaks of these his indignation matches that of Archbishop John MacHale or the parish priest of Partry, Patrick Lavelle. In Partry a whole estate had been evicted because the tenants would not send their children to a Protestant school (it was particularly shocking that the evicting landlord was the Church of Ireland Bishop of Tuam). At Derryveagh the people were evicted because, it was said, they would not disclose the name of a person who had murdered a steward.

These levels of horror were sufficiently untypical to stir up a great deal of controversy. Perraud studied this closely and was obviously moved by what had happened. One striking passage shows his power to select the telling detail: the human reality comes through phrases that started in Irish and ended unmistakably Irish after passing through French and English. A man of eighty and his wife of seventy-four had been evicted in Partry. As they were being turned out she said to her husband: 'Here I am, at seventy-four, without a shelter in the world; I who never wronged anybody, and often opened my door to the poor and unfortunate; what have I done to deserve this?' He replied: 'Peace, my dear, peace; the passion and death of Christ were more than this.'

The ability to catch the authentic voice of 'old Ireland' inspires confidence in Perraud's overall judgment on evictions. It is blunt: evictions were dreaded because they could be capricious; and in so far as they were capricious they were sectarian. Only Catholics were capriciously evicted. It is a verdict worth pondering, in the light of the accepted fact that evictions were relatively few in number but have left an impression on the folk-mind quite disproportionate to the actual numbers.

When Perraud speaks of the Poor Law or the education system his indignation is the indignation of Paul Cullen. Reluctance to give outdoor relief consigns the poor to the workhouse, where 87 per cent of the inmates are Catholics but the officials are disproportionately Protestant. There was a chaplain, but no chapel. Mass was usually said at a temporary altar set up in the dining-room (in Belfast it was in what he called 'a filthy lumber-room', which, characteristically, he insisted on inspecting personally). After Mass the altar was dismantled, and there was no place to pray. In the infirmary of Limerick workhouse there were 430 Catholics and three Protestants. The Board of Guardians appointed three Sisters of Mercy to act as nurses, on condition that they gave a written promise to observe all the rules and be subject to the control of the master. The Poor Law commissioners expressed themselves 'appalled' because 'an element of sectarianism has been thus unnecessarily introduced'. They were even more appalled when the Guardians expressed themselves willing to provide separate nursing for the Protestant sick if they objected to being nursed by the nuns, but they had to sanction their appointment because it broke no rule.

Perraud notes that the British tradition, unlike the French, is for the state to stay out of education. What happened in Ireland was exceptional, but there were good reasons for it. What is not acceptable — he states this quite bluntly — is that the state is not neutral in regard to the education system. Where the National Schools had become acceptable to Catholics it was because in much of Ireland there were few if any Protestants to attend. But there was an inbuilt Protestant bias in the system, and a continuing Protestant pressure to exploit it, that left the schools a real danger to the faith of Catholic children where they were genuinely 'mixed', as was frequently the case in Ulster.

8

Establishments

Historical surveys tend to get longer as they approach more modern times, because communities get more complex and the volume of documentation grows. This may not altogether be true of the present survey. The basic reason is that there was remarkably little change in the central values by which the Irish Catholic community lived between about 1880 and the sudden impact of very great changes some twenty or thirty years ago. On the other hand, there were quite far-reaching changes in the political framework of this community; changes in social, economic and even cultural conditions came much more slowly, but they did come. The problem is to evaluate a community relatively static from the point of view of religious observance but living in a world that in some other respects was changing quite rapidly around it.

There is much to be said for regarding Ireland about 1880 as having two church establishments, one Catholic and the other Protestant, despite the fact that there was no longer a legally established church. The Catholic church was beginning to take on some of the characteristics of an establishment. It was not just that more individual Catholics were entering public life in various ways, or that more of them were becoming richer: as was seen in the last chapter, the church organisation itself was becoming more interlocked with the state, especially in the fields of education and general social concern. In the 1880s too the Catholic church authorities reached an alliance with the nationalist movement which Professor Emmet Larkin has called 'the creation of the modern Irish state',[1] and though the phrase may be a little over-dramatic, it does express a very genuine perception.

Though legally disestablished, the Church of Ireland retained many of the characteristics of an establishment. Its members still had a share in national wealth and political influence out of proportion to their numbers. This unofficial Protestant establishment was greatly strengthened because the Presbyterians had joined it. Here the key role was played by Henry Cooke (1788-1868). He led the Presbyterian church into theological conservatism, but he also led the Presbyterian community as a whole into political conservatism in response to O'Connell's threat of

Catholic democracy. In this decade of the 1880s the existence of two church establishments began to foreshadow the existence of two political communities. When Gladstone's conversion to Home Rule was disclosed at the end of 1885 the English Conservative reaction was 'to play the Orange card'. The Orange Order, languishing for fifty years as a not very respectable and decidedly lower-class institution, was now taken up by wealthy Protestants and was at the centre of implacable opposition to Home Rule. When this long-delayed measure was finally enacted in 1912 the partition of the island began to appear as the most likely outcome, and it was in fact written into the Government of Ireland Act in 1920.

By the 1880s the Catholic church in Ireland was dominated by its clergy to a greater degree than ever before. This was not peculiar to Ireland: a similar development had occurred in the Catholic church generally during the long pontificate of Pope Pius IX (1846-78). The infallible pope was at the centre of this disciplined institution, but while almost all the Irish bishops at the Vatican Council had favoured the definition of papal infallibility, many of them had a strong sense of its limits when applied to political matters. When Leo XIII in 1888 declared the Plan of Campaign unlawful the newly appointed Archbishop of Dublin, William Walsh, wrote some letters of extraordinary bitterness to a correspondent he might have expected to have leaked at least their substance to the pope.[2] Of the two Irish bishops who were altogether inflexible in supporting the pope's decision, the kindest thing that can be said of John Healy, then Bishop of Clonfert, was that he feared for the many people of his diocese who were tenants of Lord Clancarty. The other bishop, Edward Thomas O'Dwyer of Limerick, was later to become famous for his castigation of General Maxwell after the execution of the leaders of the 1916 Rising. This is usually regarded as a remarkable *volte-face*, but it probably was no such thing, for the Bishop of Limerick was always an Irish patriot. His trouble in 1888 was that he believed the papal condemnation of the Plan of Campaign was an infallible decision, because he had been taught an exaggerated view of infallibility when he was a student in Maynooth in the 1860s. Ironically, his teacher would have been Patrick Murray, castigated as a Gallican by Paul Cullen only a decade before.

The Irish bishops remained stubbornly individual: Paul Cullen did not fully succeed in imposing his will on them. He often had to struggle to assert his authority, and its acceptance was never automatic. His office as permanent apostolic delegate did not continue after his death. The bishops met regularly, and the decisions hammered out at these meetings were accepted as binding on all, and about every twenty-five years they met more formally in synod. The first step in the choice of a new bishop continued until 1925 to be an election by the parish priests of the diocese concerned. In that year a new procedure was introduced, which gave much more weight to the views of the bishops of the province. To a great extent thereafter new bishops were appointed by co-option.

The bishops grew more autocratic in their relations with their priests. Once again, this was not a peculiarly Irish development. It occurred all over Europe at this time as the patchwork of exemptions and privileges which had characterised the *ancien régime* churches was eroded by a new and more centralised control. The Irish priesthood had never experienced the privileges of the *ancien régime*, but their conditions of existence under the penal system had given them too a measure of independence of the bishop that was now regarded as intolerable. The case of Robert O'Keeffe, parish priest of Callan, is very instructive.[3] In the early 1870s he clashed with Cullen as apostolic delegate and had very much the worse of the encounter. That he was deprived of his parish can hardly be accounted a real grievance, for he was a cantankerous and wilful man who would probably have been in trouble with any bishop anywhere. It may have been rather more of a grievance that the National Board dismissed him as school manager once he had lost his parish, but this only indicates how closely the Catholic church and the state were interlocked in the matter of education. A much more real grievance was that he had little option but to carry his case to the civil courts, as there were no ecclesiastical courts. Perhaps most ominous of all was that part of Cullen's strategy in dealing with the problem was to have Patrick F. Moran appointed Coadjutor Bishop of Ossory. Moran was his nephew; in this appointment Cullen used him as a kind of *tánaiste*, and this surely shows a potentially fearsome combination of ancestral practices and Roman canon law.

The Irish priest of the nineteenth century has long had a notorious reputation for his role in politics. Once again, however, it is easy to be too insular. 'Political Catholicism' was well known in all the Catholic countries of Europe. Earlier in the century Catholic political parties had been in alliance with religious liberals — the sight of Cullen and Gladstone working together would appear much less remarkable to a European Catholic than to an insular Protestant. By the 1880s, however, there was a change of emphasis. The liberal ethos had become anticlerical and anti-religious, and a new threat had appeared in the form of 'socialism'. While the old 'political Catholicism' lingered on in the deeply religious areas of the countryside, in industrial areas, for example in Belgium and in northern Italy, it was replaced by 'social Catholicism', with an emphasis on the formation of Catholic trade unions and the elaboration of a religious alternative to what the socialists called the 'class war' (this is the background to Leo XIII's encyclical *Rerum novarum* in 1891). Austere and paternalistic Catholic industrialists were prominent in these developments. So were Catholic priests, though sometimes, more particularly in Italy, they might tend to disturb both industrialists and church authorities by displaying a sympathy, if not for the socialist philosophy, at least for socialist political initiatives.

The pattern in Ireland naturally tended to follow that of the European countryside rather than that of the industrial towns. In one obvious way the commitment of the church to politics was less than that in Catholic Europe. There was no Catholic political party, and no Catholic trade unions developed. Ireland also differed from Europe in the extent of the involvement of the Catholic clergy. That they should be involved to an exceptional degree in Ireland was a perfectly natural development. When O'Connell began his organisation of democracy he realised that he simply had to build on the clergy because there was nobody else to build on. They accepted his invitation on the whole reluctantly, but soon many of them came to like their political role. They continued to be indispensable in organisation, in, for example, the selection of candidates and the marshalling of voters on polling day, but such things as the multiplication of polling-booths and Parnell's achievement of a disciplined parliamentary party diminished their organisational role. They had never been in a position to dictate a parliamentary programme, but they were able to push their priorities within a programme on which clergy and laity were agreed. To this extent political issues tended to reflect clerical interests. This essentially pragmatic relationship between the Catholic clergy and the political nation was to prove enduring. The pragmatic nature of this alliance meant that issues which were too divisive could not be pushed. The clergy dared not lead where the laity would not necessarily follow.

The most striking example of this is the education question. While here clergy and laity were in broad agreement, clerical interests tended to give this issue a political priority it might not otherwise have had. The historic alliance made in the 1880s was essentially an acceptance of the Home Rule programme by the hierarchy, in return for which the parliamentary party undertook to press Catholic claims on education.[4] By this date both primary and secondary education had settled into a pattern broadly acceptable to the clergy. The National system of primary education might still have its drawbacks, but they were relatively minor when set against the solid fact of clerical control of the schools. The Intermediate Education Act of 1878 had made some public money available to secondary schools that remained private and denominational. Here it might be remarked that what was distinctive about the Irish system of primary and secondary education was not that denominational schools received so much support from state funds: they received more, for example, in Scotland, to go no further afield. The really distinctive Irish feature was that these denominational schools at primary and secondary level were controlled by the clergy. The question of university education went its intractable way, but this too found a pragmatic solution in 1908.

If the clergy wished to see education get priority, they were quite happy to see second place given to the land question. Most priests came from farming families, many of them from the families of 'strong farmers'. In consequence, priests played a leading role in the land agitation that ended with the replacement of landlordism by a system of peasant proprietors. It was only natural that these farmers' sons should share the attitudes of their social class in regard to the rural labourers, though here they did show a concern for what was often very real deprivation to an extent that sometimes conflicted with their class interests. They seem to have been particularly suspicious of the very rudimentary attempts at the unionisation of rural workers, but more of them displayed concern over the problem of unemployment or under-employment, and even more, it would appear, over the problem of bad housing, especially after the Labourers (Ireland) Act of 1883 allowed the Poor Law Guardians to borrow on the security of the rates to build cottages for labourers, though the protection of sexual morality may have been nearer the centre of the priests' concern than the actual quality of the houses. Some interesting material under this head has appeared recently in a study of Co. Tipperary,[5] but there were still such marked regional differences that there must be many more studies like this before reasonably firm generalisation can replace guesswork.

There was such little industrialisation in Catholic Ireland that it is scarcely surprising that the clergy should have little feel for the real miseries of so many of the town and city labourers. Here again there is much work to be done, for example a study of the social background of the Dublin clergy. There was certainly a very real and not well-informed fear of 'socialism', but this was not confined to the Irish Catholic clergy. As will be seen, the troubled events of 1910 were to show how wide the gap between priest and people could be, though there is much in what is put into the mouth of Father Giffley, the alcoholic priest in *Strumpet City*. Reflecting on his ministry in his slum parish in Dublin, he concluded:

> In the past we have usually managed to say the wrong things, but have contrived quite often to do the right ones — at least the more humble clergy, such as ourselves.[6]

Turning now to the role more proper to the clergy, their part in the religious formation of the laity, it is first necessary to reflect on the nature of the formation they themselves received. Here too a great deal of detailed work is still to be done. It is certain that the discipline of the seminaries was being progressively tightened, with the aim of producing a docile and disciplined priesthood. It is at least arguable that in the end this went too far, and that the regime was better fitted to producing monks than priests who were to be active in parishes. Much also remains to be done in investigating their intellectual formation, but there was something approaching a consensus that it was 'narrow'. This view is pungently and frequently expressed by Walter MacDonald in his *Reminiscences of a Maynooth Professor*, but he was not the only one to express it.

Theology had failed to find a real university setting. While the Queen's Colleges were statutorily non-denominational, religious bodies were free to endow chairs of confessional theology in them. The indefatigable Henry Cooke had actually succeeded in getting a government endowment for four chairs of Presbyterian theology in a college closely associated with Queen's College, Belfast, and while it is not easy to see the Catholic bishops having a similar success in Cork or Galway, it does raise once again the question of the wisdom of their decision to oppose the Queen's Colleges. Cullen's antipathy to Maynooth killed a proposal that the college should be empowered to grant degrees in theology, and the faculty of theology in his Catholic University had little more than a lingering death. Maynooth students began to be presented for degrees of the Royal University after 1879 (but not, of course, in theology). In 1895 the college became a pontifical university, with faculties of theology, philosophy and canon law, and in 1910 it became a recognised college of the newly established National University of Ireland. These developments helped to broaden horizons, but the intellectual development of the seminarian still remained closed and clerical. It is indeed arguable that Irish clerical scholarship achieved more in the field of history than in theology. In the previous chapter something has been said of the two great Maynooth theologians of the mid-nineteenth century, Patrick Murray and George Crolly. Yet even these were worthy labourers rather than original thinkers, and they had no successors to equal them, except perhaps Walter MacDonald, who may have suffered from an excess of originality.

To balance the picture, theologians even more than other academics must be conscious of the fact that it is not their vocation to save the world. The teachers in Maynooth and the other seminaries did not have as their primary aim the production of speculative theologians, but of adequately equipped pastoral priests. The great bulk of their students would have been in agreement. They prepared themselves on the whole con-scientiously to give responsible counsel and direction in the confessional and to preach the diocesan programme of catechetical instruction each Sunday. The preacher's standby was John Hagan's *Compendium of Catechetical Instruction*, published in 1911. Its four volumes treated in turn of the creed, the sacraments, the commandments, and prayer, virtues and vices. This is the pattern of the *Catechism of the Council of Trent*, of which an English translation by Jeremiah Donovan, a member of the staff of Maynooth, had been published in 1829. The Sunday instruction by the priest was backed up by a catechetical instruction in the schools which followed the same pattern, substantially given by the teachers but super-vised by the priest.

This programme had the great advantage of achieving its relatively modest aims. It set out a system of belief, based, as belief must be based, on the creeds of the church. Catholic theology was then in a defensive mood, and at times it may have suggested, and doubtless at times it did suggest, that the answer was clearer than an informed believer had any right to expect; but for the relatively uninformed believer it was clear and it was a system, and despite defects much of the central theological tradition came through. And as well as presenting a system of truths to be believed, the catechetical tradition presented clearly a set of duties to be carried out. The moral theology this rested on was based on casuistry. It has been already noted that casuistic moral theology has very respectable origins, but by now it may have been beginning to show a certain sclerosis of over-refinement. This had been to some extent arrested by the rapid adoption in northern Europe after about 1830 of the moral theology of Alphonsus Liguori (1696-1787), which has been very rightly praised for its practical sense of the need for the individual to make a personal decision of conscience balanced between law and liberty. But in practice moral theology was tempted towards an over-categorisation of offences, in turn tempting the less finely tuned mind to pose the moral question in terms of 'How far can you go?'. There was also a temptation to lose sight of the very basic distinction between the natural philosophy of good action and the theology of good action as revealed in Jesus Christ, but here we may be on heights that most would perhaps be well advised to walk with caution.

That, then, in rough-and-ready form, is the intellectual underpinning of 'traditional Irish Catholicism'. Some few years ago Emmet Larkin spoke of it as a 'devotional revolution' introduced by Paul Cardinal Cullen. More recently Cullen has been dismissed as a tiresome political meddler, and the lion's share of the credit is given to Archbishop Daniel Murray.[7] It must surely be evident that what we are dealing with is a continuous evolution. In the shape in which it became the common heritage of Irish Catholics it has fairly immediate roots in the Council of Trent. In so far as it may be possible to trace these roots further back into history, they may lead us to the preaching of the friars in the later middle ages. One of these stands out vividly, Friar Michael of Kildare. Friar Michael was an English-speaking townsman, and the Tridentine Counter-Reformation had first established itself in the English-speaking towns. What happened in the later nineteenth century was that this line of religious heritage became predominant among Irish Catholics.

'Tridentine' is perhaps too sharp a word: it might be better to blur it into something like 'neo-Tridentine'. In the eighteenth century the Tridentine pattern had been mediated to Ireland through the 'Gallican' atmosphere of northern Europe, especially France. By the end of the nineteenth century even France was coming under influences radiating from Rome. In the optimistic days at the beginning of the century 'romanticism' had encouraged private devotions, to the neglect of the more solid fare of the Bible and the liturgy. As the church closed its ranks defensively later in the century against what it perceived as threats to the faith of believers, even these private devotions began to take on the shape of duties to be discharged.

So the pattern of religious practice, while still basically Tridentine, was by now a web of some complexity. In Ireland the Tridentine pattern had been longest established in the towns. Now it had spread out to become the general pattern of Irish Catholic culture. But at the same time this basic Tridentine pattern was experiencing shifts of emphasis. The same shifts tended to occur in the whole church: the improvement in communications alone ensured that the general pattern of religious observance would become more uniform. At the centre of this uniformity was the papacy and in general the Italian way of doing things.

Life in the Irish countryside was centred in the village, and religious life was increasingly centred in the church, round which many of these villages had in fact grown up.[8] The Catholic parishes as they developed had no necessary relation to the medieval church site. This was often a deserted and decaying ruin, because Protestants were so few in number over much of the country. In other places the 'estate village' with its Protestant church is still frequently easily distinguishable from the 'chapel village' which developed round the Catholic one. The siting of Catholic churches was related most of all to the new roads that were made from the late eighteenth century onwards; even in the richer dioceses poorer outlying regions tended to get their own church only after the Famine. The Catholic chapels were built under the patronage of landlords and substantial farmers and merchants. Around the church there grew the village, providing elementary services, first in trade and commerce, later in government services. This 'chapel village' as the rural political, cultural and social centre began with the agitation for Catholic Emancipation in the 1820s, but its real development came after the Famine, and its full development can be seen about fifty years later, as rural organisations multiplied; one of the most influential in stabilising the parish as a social unit was the Gaelic Athletic Association, founded in 1884. In a phrase made famous by Kickham's novel *Knocknagow*, published in 1879, all effort should be 'for the honour of the little village'.

These social developments strengthened ecclesiastical pressure to make the church the focus of religious life in the parish. Attendance at Sunday Mass improved everywhere, pushing towards the full attendance already the norm in the towns in the 1830s. It would nevertheless be wrong to see the pattern achieved here as 100 per cent attendance everywhere: there were always areas where excusing causes continued to be more readily admitted, such as the need to stay at home to mind young children. Better churches meant that the Eucharist could be reserved in them. The

Confraternities of the Blessed Eucharist and the devotions of benediction and the forty hours' adoration became more widespread. Devotion to the humanity of Jesus under the symbol of the Sacred Heart had first appeared in Ireland at the beginning of the nineteenth century. Medieval in its origins, this devotion had been revived in seventeenth-century France, where after the Revolution it began to take on conservative political tones. Ireland was formally consecrated to the Sacred Heart on Passion Sunday 1873, the year the building of the church of the Sacré Coeur in Paris began. But whereas the builders of the Sacré Coeur had an amalgam of motives in which the Sacred Heart, the prisoner of the Vatican, and France defeated and humiliated by Prussia were often not clearly distinguishable, Irish devotion moved at a more pragmatic level. By the 1890s the devotion of the 'nine first Fridays' in honour of the Sacred Heart had become almost universal, but it may well be asked if the Irish priests who promoted it did so because of the specific graces claimed to follow from the practice or because it ensured that their people would be at confession and communion every month. Marian devotion developed from devotion to the humanity of Jesus. It was nurtured by a series of apparitions from the 1830s onwards, Ireland having its own apparition at Knock, Co. Mayo, in 1879. But Marian devotion in general was personal and emotional; any genuine theological content was mediocre.

The 'rites of passage', traditionally celebrated in the home, made their way to the church. In 1850 the Synod of Thurles laid down that baptism should normally take place there, and I Maynooth (1875) allowed only very few exceptions to this rule. The practice of marriage in church, with Mass and the nuptial blessing, spread more unevenly, but it too became the rule. The traditional funeral Mass in the house also drifted slowly towards the church. In 1917 the new Code of Canon Law laid down that all funeral rites must take place in the church, and this was embodied in the legislation of III Maynooth (1927). This change inevitably lessened the social importance of the traditional wake, and if IV Maynooth (1956) was still legislating against 'profane and unbecoming wakes' it may have been more through force of habit. The practice of 'station Masses' in houses was tolerated only in places remote from a church by I Maynooth (1875), but they were still the subject of regulation at IV Maynooth (1956). They had survived long enough in a few dioceses to link up with the new respectability given the 'house Mass' after the Second Vatican Council.

Old ascetic practices demanding more than the law demanded in the matter of fast and abstinence died out only slowly. In regard to what may be considered as the ascetic practice of avoiding drunkenness, the work of Father Mathew earlier in the century did not endure, but new attempts begun in the 1880s proved more permanent, particularly the Pioneer Total Abstinence Association, founded in Dublin in 1898, and the Father Mathew Union, founded in Cork in 1901.

Here, then, was a society taught a fixed system of beliefs and a definite round of religious practices, which were in fact widely observed. Yet it was not a society altogether at peace with itself. There was much under-development and much real poverty. The land question was resolved in favour of the tenant farmers, but this brought no benefits to the real poor. The Home Rule campaign had lost direction after the Parnell crisis in 1891. The drain of emigration continued, and the population kept falling. While this was a factor helping social stability, especially in that an undue proportion of dissidents or potential dissidents tended to emigrate, enough discontent remained at home. The Catholic clergy had been so prominent in public life that it was with a certain inevitability that anti-clerical writings began to appear. They were indeed so many that it is necessary to be selective and try to concentrate on the most significant.

The novelists can be useful, but here it is necessary to tread with special caution. Patrick MacGill, born in the poverty-stricken district of Glenties in Co. Donegal in 1890, is an example of a dissident who emigrated from economic necessity. His highly autobiographical novel, *Children of the Dead End*, was published in 1914. In its opening chapters there is an acid portrait of the parish priest, who appears simply as an avaricious tyrant. It is not the whole truth about this parish priest, who is well known from other sources. His name was James McFadden, and he was appointed parish priest of Gweedore in 1875. He was authoritarian indeed: despite his lack of inches he came to be known as *An Sagart Mór*. But while he ruled his flock with an iron hand, he used the same tactics in defending them during the Plan of Campaign. Things came to a head with a police inspector who believed in the same methods as the parish priest. An attempt to arrest him after Sunday Mass on 3 February 1889 led to a fracas in which the inspector was killed. The priest and twenty-four others were tried on charges arising out of the murder. He was bound to the peace, but others received prison sentences. A few years later he was appointed parish priest of Glenties, where one of his parishioners was the child Patrick MacGill.[9]

Gerald O'Donovan was a priest who left his ministry during the Modernist crisis. His first novel, *Father Ralph*, was published in 1913. It is clearly autobiographical, and is marked by a typical defect of this kind of novel in that the other characters are introduced to point up the virtues of the hero. The first half is largely an indictment of Maynooth, the second a similar indictment of a town parish in the west of Ireland which he calls 'Bunnahone'. The physical description might indicate Ballina, but in fact O'Donovan had ministered in Loughrea. The central thesis is that the clergy are reduced to sycophants by the system, and that those who rise in it make their careers by willing sycophancy. The outstanding example is the parish administrator, a politician hand in glove with the local gombeen-men. As the 'hillside man' John Byrne is made to say, 'Instead of doing all the bleeding direct, the church lets Hinnissey and his like bleed the people, and then the priests bleed Hinnissey.' Then there is the intellectual of the diocese, Father Magan, who came from Maynooth with a great reputation, though he is in fact an utter blockhead gifted with a prodigious memory; Father Sheldon, a thinking man who temporises, justifying it as 'an old man's weakness'; and the country priest, Father Duff, a farmer among farmers, who has substituted goodness for theology, not ineffectively, rather like Father Giffley in his Dublin slums.

MacGill and O'Donovan were protestors against the establishment, but Canon Sheehan (1852-1913) belonged to it. He had more gifts as a novelist than either of them. In particular, his portraits of the clergy and the rural poor, doubtless drawn from life, are very effective indeed. He too has a rather acid portrait of the Maynooth intellectual Luke Delmege. Luke is intelligent in a way that O'Donovan's Father Magan is not, but his brilliant career at Maynooth has made him hopelessly narrow. In general, his priests fall into two categories: the young priests, who are determined to raise Ireland from its lethargy, and the old ones, who have tried but now know that it cannot be done. 'Daddy Dan' in *My New Curate* is painted as a real father to his people, but in his seventieth year he is resigned to their fecklessness: 'Nothing on earth can cure the inertia of Ireland. It weighs down like the weeping clouds on the damp heavy earth, and there's no lifting it.' Sheehan was only forty-six when this novel was published in 1898, and he may not have completely shared the sentiments of the old. When he died in 1913 at the age of sixty-two he had not quite finished his last novel, *The Graves at Kilmorna*. It was on a Fenian theme, and one can only speculate to what extent he may have sympathised with the view attributed to a character in it: 'The country is sinking into the sleep of death, and nothing can awake it but the crack of the rifle.'

Three substantial works of social comment appeared in the first decade of the twentieth century. The first was Horace Plunkett's *Ireland in the New Century* (1904). Sir Horace Plunkett (1854-1932) was a member of the Protestant branch of a distinguished Old English family, and a highly respected figure. He was appalled by the backwardness of Irish farming and had been prominent in the co-operative movement in the 1890s, where he had worked with such figures as the Jesuit Thomas Finlay. Chapter 4 of the book was entitled 'The Influence of Religious Life in Ireland'. It was an admittedly measured and temperate but nevertheless real indictment of the economic influence of the Catholic religion as interpreted by the Irish clergy. Plunkett may have exposed himself unnecessarily by going on to express the view that there was something inherent in the Catholic religion that made it opposed to economic progress.

Plunkett's thesis on the role of the Catholic religion in Ireland was answered in 1906 by Michael O'Riordan in *Catholicity and Progress in*

Ireland. O'Riordan had studied in Rome, where he had been ordained for the diocese of Limerick. He was later to return to Rome as Rector of the Irish College, where he died in office. In 1906 he was serving in a rural parish in Limerick.

He justified his reply by saying that Plunkett was a respected and influential figure, whose measured criticism demanded a measured answer. Instances from Italy and more especially France and Belgium gave him a satisfactory answer to the charge that the Catholic church was everywhere an obstacle to economic progress. As for Ireland, he pointed out that because of their admitted power and influence many of the Catholic clergy had played a prominent and successful part in the kind of developments Plunkett had at heart. He added that the causes of Irish poverty were deep-rooted and complex, and that it was unfair to attribute a central role to the influence of the Catholic clergy.

The next year saw the publication of a substantial work from an outside observer, the Frenchman Louis Paul-Dubois (*L'Irlande contemporaine*, Paris 1907; English translation, *Contemporary Ireland*, Dublin 1908). He wrote in the tradition of de Tocqueville (1835), de Beaumont (1838), and Perraud (1862). He had impeccable credentials as a social analyst — he was married to the daughter of Hippolyte Taine — and he had visited Ireland several times. On the whole, he came down on the side of O'Riordan as against Plunkett, but he did have some searching observations to make. He did not mince his words in describing Irish problems. He spoke of the 'mental and moral decadence of the nation', the 'general absence of energy and character, of method and discipline' among a people 'distracted by denominational struggles, sectarian fanaticism, and the first phases of anticlericalism'. He noted shrewdly, however, that whereas Protestants were anti-Catholic as well as anti-nationalist, Catholics were anti-English rather than anti-Protestant; among them no one was more popular than a Protestant who was also a nationalist.

The Catholic priest he saw, with some exaggeration, as the only leader in 'an unorganised *plebs* of destitute peasants'. He judged the growth of a middle class slow, even in the towns. The Irish Catholic, he said, 'still bears the mark of servitude', and he recalled de Beaumont's judgment of seventy years before, that he was 'half a slave'. The priest was in truth the father of his people, and no doubt an authoritative enough father. He had immense power, but, Paul-Dubois noted, Plunkett had admitted that it had been 'singularly little abused'. Any charge that the Catholic priest-hood was 'the direct and exclusive cause of all the ills of Ireland' he dismissed as 'a gross and fanatical theory', but he did note areas where its influence was 'apter to restrain evil than to forward good', notably the fact that the Catholic clergy had never ceased to regard their flock as the object of snares set by Protestantism.

Here, then, was a cultural 'nation' in great need of something to hold for pride. The Catholic religion was the clear response to this search for identity and inspiration. One consequence of the drain of emigration was that the Irish Catholics could see themselves as the mother country of many millions in 'Ireland's spiritual empire', especially in the United States and Australia. After the Famine an expanded Maynooth was able to supply the bulk of priests for Ireland, together with the three surviving continental colleges, at Rome, Paris and Salamanca. Those ordained in the other seminaries mostly went to the Irish diaspora: indeed, All Hallows College in Dublin existed exclusively for this purpose. A sense of pride developed from the knowledge that the English-speaking Catholic world was developing so rapidly, and that so many of its numbers, and an even greater proportion of its priests and bishops, were natives of Ireland or of fairly recent Irish extraction.

A new development came towards the end of the nineteenth century in the form of a supply of priests to 'the pagan missions', largely to territories then within the British colonial empire. In missionary work the French Catholics had traditionally made a great contribution. Missionary congregations mainly of French origin began to set up houses in Ireland: the Holy Ghost Fathers (C.S.Sp.) in 1859 and the Society of African Missions (S.M.A.) in 1877. Joseph Shanahan, C.S.Sp. (1871-1943), went to Nigeria in 1902. During an active career of thirty years he showed himself to be a giant among missionaries, pioneering new methods, particularly in the development of mission schools. There were giants too in the missionary congregations of Irish origin, the Maynooth Mission to China (1918) and St Patrick's Society for African Missions (1932), both founded by groups of priests from Maynooth. In them the college took up once again its missionary initiatives of the early nineteenth century. These missionary congregations of priests were complemented by parallel congregations of sisters, and the Medical Missionaries of Mary, founded in 1937 by Mary Martin, was a purely female initiative.

Inevitably, this great missionary movement took on something of the stamp of its times, in that in this heyday of European self-confidence and imperialism it tended to impose its own social and cultural values. The Irish probably brought with them something of their own conviction that Irish Catholicism was in some sense the archetype. The great missionary Columban had said so long ago, and he was the special patron of the Maynooth Mission to China. When the European powers withdrew so swiftly from their colonies after 1945 difficulties could be anticipated. It was perhaps predictable that they should be greatest in the high culture of China, which the European colonisers had never succeeded in over-running.

The search for identity and inspiration developed along other lines as well. The Maynooth Union of Secular Priests originated in a paper read by Walter MacDonald in 1896. The highlight of the 'union day' was a paper, with, from 1906, a second paper in Irish. A list of papers read between 1896 and 1916 was published in 1920. The titles show a wide range of subjects, with a predictable emphasis on ecclesiastical concerns, though more general themes enter too, notably, and topically, labour problems. MacDonald was also closely associated with the launching of the *Irish Theological Quarterly* from Maynooth in 1906. It was not the best of times for such a venture, for the Modernist crisis was just then coming to a head. The journal ceased publication in 1922 and was revived only in 1951.

The Catholic Truth Society of Ireland originated with a paper read to the Maynooth Union in 1899 by Michael O'Riordan. A similar society was already in existence in England. At this time technological advances had made it possible to print more cheaply than ever before, and indeed more cheaply than ever again. The flood of cheap literature was led by the first halfpenny newspaper, Harmsworth's *Daily Mail* in 1896. The Catholic answer was the penny pamphlet. The Catholic Truth Society of Ireland produced over two hundred titles in its first five years. Already a strong 'Irish' slant could be detected. The annual Catholic Truth Conference began in 1903. It was modelled on the German Katholikentag, begun in 1848, and it revolved around about half a dozen papers. Again, the titles of these papers indicate contemporary Irish Catholic interests. At the beginning the panel of lecturers was heavily clerical, but the numbers of the laity grew, in particular the professors of the new National University, founded in 1908.[10]

At the back of all this was the complex phenomenon that we call 'the Irish literary revival'. Whatever truth may be in the assertion that 'the priests killed Irish' — and it is at most a very partial truth — they were certainly among the pioneers of its revival. The Society for the Preservation of the Irish Language, founded in 1876, is not without reason regarded as the forerunner of the Gaelic League. Its leading spirit was a Father Nolan. When the Gaelic League in turn was founded in 1893 the founders were Douglas Hyde, Eoin Mac Néill, and the professor of Irish at Maynooth, Eugene O'Growney. He had been appointed to his chair in 1891, but had to retire because of ill-health in 1894 and died at the age of thirty-six in 1899. The Gaelic League proclaimed itself non-political and non-sectarian: Douglas Hyde resigned in 1915 when it committed itself to a political stand for independence. It campaigned for the teaching of Irish in the schools, where it met opposition from the National Board, the Board of Intermediate Education, and the establishment in Trinity College, but under continuing pressure some concessions were made in 1904. The next campaign was for compulsory Irish as a matriculation subject in the National University. The bitterness engendered by this campaign is at least to some extent explained by the fact that on any rational judgment it was premature to make Irish a compulsory matriculation subject. The most painful incident occurred when O'Growney's successor, Michael O'Hickey, was dismissed from his chair of Irish in Maynooth. The account given by Walter MacDonald in his *Reminiscences of a Maynooth Professor* has become widely known, but it is very partial. The balanced assessment by León Ó Broin is rightly severe on MacDonald not only for his account of the affair but for his part in it: as he sums up, MacDonald fed fuel to O'Hickey's discontent from his own sense of grievance.[11]

The Gaelic League faced dilemmas and contradictions that it never resolved satisfactorily. It has been represented as identifying the Gaelic revival with a glorification of Catholic peasant culture. To whatever extent this may be true, this culture was now only a remnant: the 1901 census had returned just over 620,000 as speaking Irish and English, and just under 21,000 as speaking Irish only, less than 0.5 per cent of the population. These Irish-speakers were divided by dialects, all the more seriously because only a very small number of them could write in Irish: the Gaelic League had come too late to save the scribal tradition. This fact lends some colour to the charge that the League represented only a small elite that increasingly turned to an antiquarian past.

The literary movement in English might seem to have a better hope of escaping this dilemma, but it was even more of an elite; and though its greatest figure, W. B. Yeats, claimed in a book of poems published in 1893 that he

> would accounted be
> True brother of a company
> That sang, to sweeten Ireland's wrong,

that man of European culture, Louis Paul-Dubois, had as early as 1907 put his finger on the essential dilemma of this movement when he said that there was 'something artificial in this literature that is so young in its romanticism, but so advanced in its subtle art and studied symbolism'.[12]

In stark contrast to the art and symbolism of the literary revival were the realities of life in the slums of Dublin. Housing conditions were atrocious, with 36.6 per cent of families occupying a single room. There were some industries, but much casual employment and much unemployment. While there was more work in industrialised Belfast, its mean streets also concealed appalling examples of human deprivation. The relatively skilled craft workers of Dublin had an established tradition of unionisation. Trouble arose when it came to the mass unionisation of the unskilled and casual workers.

The general story of these troubles is fairly well known, though indeed it deserves more attention. In this present context attention might first be focused on the name of Dr Peter Coffey. This priest of Meath farming stock was appointed professor of philosophy in Maynooth in 1902. He soon showed that he had a strong social conscience as well as considerable gifts of intellect. In 1906 he published a Catholic Truth Society pamphlet, *The Church and the Working Classes*. For a priest of farming stock he pulled few punches. The degrading Poor Law and private philanthrophy were not the answers to the fact of poverty. While he condemned 'an un-provoked or unnecessary or unjustifiable strike', he declared that it was as a crime no less terrible than the provocation of a necessary one by a cruel and heartless employer. The employer's 'great and principal duty' was to give his workers a fair wage. The legitimate object of a trade union was to secure by every fair and lawful means that just and equitable treatment that would lead to social peace.

Perhaps it was the fact that he spoke with some approval of 'Christian socialism' that really roused opposition. Certainly thereafter Peter Coffey turned his strong social conscience to the temperance movement. Fears of something called 'socialism' were widespread, coupled with a great uncertainty as to what 'socialism' was, except that it threatened the whole established order, religion included. It should be remembered that at this time such reactions to situations rather like the situation in Ireland were widespread in Europe, and there was perhaps more excuse for them in Ireland because here they were so novel. This will also explain the fact that the clerical response tended to stick to general recommendations, that priests should preach the same moral principles to workers and employers, and to fight shy of positive and concrete suggestions. This is well exemplified in the paper on 'strikes' read to the Maynooth Union in 1912 by Michael J. O'Donnell, recently appointed professor of theology in the college.

James Connolly was undoubtedly the best mind among the labour leaders. The fact that he rejected 'Christian socialism' is less interesting than the reason he gave for doing so. It could not be accepted, he said, because it would give the clergy control over economic affairs, where they had no competence. The reference to the clergy pinpoints Connolly as an Irishman. Catholic Europe had, and still has, its confessional trade unions, and while individual priests participated in them, no one contemplated that they should be run by the clergy. Connolly's advice to working men that they should stand by their rights as citizens while performing their duties as Catholics, and his prediction that socialism would inevitably come and that an adaptable church would adapt to it, also reflect a typically Irish judgment that speaks of 'the church' and really means 'the clergy'.

The clergy saw the labour troubles in Dublin and elsewhere as a syndicalist revolutionary plot, and in their fear did not exactly cover themselves with glory in a display of social concern. It has been well said that the great strike collapsed because the revolutionary leaders tried to lead a working class not really revolutionary, but it may even be asked if the leaders themselves, apart from James Connolly, were really theoretical revolutionaries. As George William Russell ('AE') remarked with some perception, Jim Larkin was not the cause of worker discontent; he was the product of it himself.[13]

To be fair to Walter MacDonald, he did have some probing criticism to offer in *Some Ethical Aspects of the Social Question*, published in 1920.[14] He pointed out that it had been relatively easy for the Irish Catholic priests to support the tenant farmers because most of them were farmers' sons. In this particular struggle they had brought themselves to tolerate measures they could not always justify. They must do no less for the workers. It would be harder, not just because the workers came from a different social class, but because in many parishes the priest drew his material support much more from the employers than from the employees. This was straight talking, even if it was possibly easier to talk this way in 1920 than when Peter Coffey wrote in 1908. Jim Larkin's idea of 'one big union' was now fact: his Irish Transport and General Workers' Union had now about 350 branches and about 100,000 members. Ironically, developments over these years had greatly weakened the labour movement as a political force.

The second decade of the century was traumatic for the nations of Europe, and nowhere more so than in Ireland. At the beginning of the decade most Irish nationalist opinion would rest content with the modest Home Rule Bill now finally put through parliament, but ten years later these same people were locked in a bitter civil war fought about the betrayal of the republic. The key organisation in all this was called Sinn Féin. It had been founded in 1907 and was inspired by Arthur Griffith's view that Home Rule alone was of little value without economic self-sufficiency. It had little mass support, and while it took no part in the 1916 Rising, it proved to be its political beneficiary. In 1917 it added to its programme the aim of an independent Irish republic and elected Eamon de Valera as its president. Six months later, on 16 April 1918, parliament at Westminster passed a measure to extend conscription to Ireland. Sinn Féin, for reasons that were fairly logical in the light of its general programme, had always been opposed to conscription. What certainly helped to make the anti-conscription issue a potent political force was the opposition of the Catholic bishops, declared on 19 April. In the general election held in December the Unionists held their strongholds; the Nationalists were reduced to six, all of them except Captain Redmond in Waterford city being in Ulster. Sinn Féin captured 73 out of the 105 Irish seats. The party had fought the election on the slogan that everything else must wait on the resolution of the question of national independence. Labour decided not to put up any candidates, and this decision weakened it as a political force. While in terms of parliamentary seats Sinn Féin had taken over from the Nationalists, in terms of the social standing of their successful candidates it might be argued that the Nationalists had taken over Sinn Féin. The successful Sinn Féin candidates refused to attend parliament in Westminster and proclaimed themselves the first Dáil of an independent Ireland.

The British government naturally regarded this as an unwarranted claim for 'the rights of small nations'. Violence began when a local unit of the nationalist Volunteer organisation ambushed and killed two policemen at Soloheadbeg, Co. Tipperary, on 21 January 1919. In the bitter guerrilla war which followed, the Catholic church authorities, to borrow Walter MacDonald's phrase about the land struggle, faced the prospect of having to tolerate things they could not always justify. One bishop declared his positive opposition; one or possibly two a positive approbation. The rest could show a kind of general benevolence, because the 1918 election had shown overwhelming democratic support for an independent Ireland, and because the Dáil was in no position to control the guerrilla activities of individuals and groups around the country.

The conflict with Britain ended with twenty-six counties becoming the Irish Free State, with decidedly greater independence than what had been envisaged in the Home Rule Bill, but far short of the aspirations for a thirty-two county republic. The six north-eastern counties got what, ironically, they did not want, Home Rule as envisaged in 1912. This settlement precipitated the civil war. Labour's declaration of neutrality between the parties hastened its political decline, for no one was or could be neutral at the time. The Catholic bishops were not neutral. In a joint pastoral on 10 October 1922 they excommunicated all in arms against the government.

The war ended in April 1923. It left a sorely wounded country, and the bitterness it gave rise to was certainly a factor in the effective ending of any active role by the Catholic clergy in politics. The Irish Free State was overwhelmingly Catholic. Its Protestant population fell from 10.4 per cent to 7.4 per cent between 1911 and 1926, reflecting the fact that many Protestants had left during the troubled years because of a not unfounded fear of physical harm. The British solution rejected by the Dáil, the Government of Ireland Act of 1920, had even provided for Catholic bishops sitting in the upper house of parliament. In fact no Catholic cleric has ever sat in an Irish parliament, and the clause on religion in the 1922 constitution of the Irish Free State was 'about as comprehensive a declaration of neutrality between denominations as any state could make'.[15] It is true that its main lines were dictated by the Anglo-Irish Treaty, but it aroused no criticism and went through the Dáil almost without a debate. It also reflected a long-standing tradition in Irish nationalism of keeping aloof from the clergy in certain matters.

The Irish Free State was fair to its small and understandably fearful Protestant minority. Quite early there emerged a kind of principle to see that they would be assured of a fair share by giving them slightly more, as in representation in the Senate and state aid for their schools. Many would share the wish of Kevin O'Higgins that they should be 'not alien enemies, not planters, but part and parcel of this nation', a small minority equal before the law and in fact slightly privileged.

What remained to be seen was if they could settle into the nation without becoming some kind of 'honorary Catholics'. The population structure alone would see to it that the Irish Free State would take on some kind of Catholic identity despite the religious neutrality of its constitution. And there was more to it than the fact of the great Catholic majority. Nationalist Ireland in 1923 was sore and sensitive. Instead of a free republic there was a partitioned dominion, and the civil war had completed the sense of physical and spiritual destruction. Nationalist Ireland was never in greater need of an identity; it had to be either the Irish language or the Catholic church, and for most people it was in fact the church. Add to this the middle-class nature of the government and the fact that all over Europe there was a conservative reaction to the loosening of traditional values that had happened during the Great War, and it is not surprising that life in the Irish Free State took on a certain conservative Catholic ethos. It should be noted that this did not happen because the clergy brought pressure on the government. The government was as anxious as the clergy to preserve what were regarded as traditional values. Its favoured method was to consult interested parties when these issues arose. The Catholic hierarchy, naturally, was usually among them. The government awaited a consensus and legislated accordingly.

Before 1921 Ireland had no divorce legislation: the only way to get a divorce was by presenting a private bill in parliament. By 1925 it had been decided that no such bills would be accepted in the Irish Dáil. Ireland was especially vulnerable to outside influences because it was English-speaking. The solution was censorship. Films were censored from 1923 and books and periodicals from 1929. While in the circumstances it would not be easy to sustain an argument against censorship in principle, the way individual publications were censored sometimes bordered on the ludicrous. In 1942 a book appeared entitled *The Tailor and Ansty*, an account of the life of an old couple in west Cork. It was sometimes mildly salty, but on the sternest of judgments it was harmless, and on any humanist judgment it was wholesome. Not merely was the book banned, not merely did the priests of the parish force the old man to burn the book on his knees, but in a debate in the Senate some senators averted their ears when passages from the book were read.

There were some things that could not be kept out. Radio broadcasting had begun in Britain in 1919, and the B.B.C. was established in 1922. In 1925 a high-powered long-wave transmitter was set up at Daventry, and its signals could be picked up in the eastern counties of Ireland. Irish broadcasting began in 1926. British radio certainly helped to popularise the new dance music, and a new mobility provided by the motor bus and more slowly by the private car brought young people to the dance halls. 'Company-keeping' assumed a new importance among the mortal sins. Emigration, which had ceased during the war, increased again after it; the population stabilised, or to be more accurate, had a very slight but definite tendency to fall. The proportion of those who never married increased during the 1920s and 1930s.

'Joyless' is too strong a word, but there is a certain temptation to use it. The mood is well caught by Patrick Kavanagh in *The Great Hunger*, published in 1942. Patrick Maguire, the old peasant, sixty-five and single when his mother died aged ninety-one, has lived out his life under her domination:

> Now go to Mass and pray and confess your sins
> And you'll have all the luck, his mother said,

and 'luck' seems to centre in the fact that

> He lives that his little fields may stay fertile when
> his own body
> Is spread in the bottom of a ditch under two coulters
> crossed in Christ's name ...
> Yet sometimes when the sun comes through a gap
> These men knew God the Father in a tree,
> The Holy Spirit in the rising sap,
> And Christ will be the green leaves that will come
> At Easter from the sealed and guarded tomb ...

There is even less joy in Brinsley MacNamara's *The Valley of the Squinting Windows* (1918), which portrays a devout rural community incapable of a single unselfish word or action. Bryan MacMahon's *Children of the Rainbow* (1952) has more, but this may only reflect a difference in temperament between Kerry and points further north. And while he depicts his village of Cloone in the 1920s as still actively alive in its traditional way of life, the novel is shot through with lament for the fact that this is passing: 'What will we be in the heel o' time but a mongrel race draggled at the tail of Christianity?'

Not altogether fairly, all the blame was attributed to 'the church', meaning, as always in Ireland, the clergy. Works by Irish writers joined the list of banned publications in some number. This muting of the critical intellectual voice was, the writers argued, shortsighted, unhealthy and damaging. In *The Irish*, first published in 1947, Seán Ó Faoláin argued that it was in fact fatal. There was no lay periodical which was 'alive'. All clerical periodicals were 'trivial' except the Jesuit quarterly, *Studies*. 'In Ireland today', he wrote, priests and laity rest at ease — with one qualification. Only one group is held at arm's length, the writers or intellectuals.... In Ireland, the church holds her power by the old medieval bond of faith. She does not need political techniques, as the church in other more secularised countries does. ... The priest and the writer ought to be fighting side by side, if for nothing else than the rebuttal of the vulgarity that is pouring daily into the vacuum left in the popular mind by the dying out of the old traditional way of life.[16]

It was not easy for reflections like these to struggle up from the depths of the average subconscious. The year 1829 is fixed in the Irish mind as the date of 'Catholic Emancipation'. In fact the 'emancipation' of Catholics had been substantially achieved by 1793. The achievements of 1829 were relatively minor, and there were still some laws requiring repeal, but in 1929 the Irish Free State publicly celebrated the centenary of 'Catholic Emancipation'. The greatest fusion of Catholic pride and national pride was at the International Eucharistic Congress in 1932. A million knelt at the papal legate's Mass in the Phoenix Park. The voice of John McCormack, Ireland's pride, rang out in the *Panis angelicus*. The new technology brought the voice of Pope Pius XI in blessing, while the faint tinkle of St Patrick's Bell recalled the distant past. It is very arguable that the congress made a powerful contribution to healing the wounds of the civil war.

By the day of that Mass Eamon de Valera headed the Irish government. In the eyes of many, he was still excommunicated for his part in the civil war, but it was his hand that greeted the papal legate. And in his relationships with the Catholic church de Valera continued the policy of his predecessors, not because he was subservient, but because he shared its views over a very wide field. When he did not share those views he went his own way, as O'Connell, Parnell and Redmond had done before him.

There were contradictions in his vision of Ireland that he never resolved: it is hard to see how the country could be an unpartitioned republic, Catholic and Irish-speaking all at the same time. Its people he saw as having modest comfort and as being content with it: as he put it in his often-quoted St Patrick's Day broadcast of 1943, they would be 'a people who valued material wealth only as a basis of right living, a people who were satisfied with frugal comfort and devoted their leisure to the things of the spirit'. This vision was neither new nor peculiar to Eamon de Valera; to give only one example, Michael Collins had said very much the same thing more than twenty years before.[17]

De Valera's vision of Ireland was embodied in his 1937 constitution. It seems certain that it was essentially his own creation, though he did consult a number of people, and among the clergy consulted was John Charles McQuaid, C.S.Sp., soon to be Archbishop of Dublin. The constitution may well be regarded as basically a liberal democratic document with a number of Catholic emphases. Already in the preamble Jesus Christ is invoked as having 'sustained our fathers through centuries of trial' — given the facts of Irish history, clearly the sustainer of the Catholics rather than of the Protestants. Article 44, which dealt with religion, was in sharp contrast to the 1922 constitution, in acknowledging the duty of the state to respect and honour religion, in its formal recognition of the religious bodies existing in Ireland, and in its recognition of 'the special position of the Holy Catholic Apostolic and Roman Church as the guardian of the Faith professed by the great majority of the citizens', while at the same time insisting that the state shall in no way discriminate between one religion and another. Nevertheless, the whole document is shot through with Catholic moral and social teaching; it represents a liberal idea grounded in a Catholic world.

The constitution was enacted by referendum by 685,105 votes to 526,945. Almost 100,000 more voted for the constitution than voted for de Valera's Fianna Fáil party in the general election held on the same day, and it is a very safe assumption that the greater part of the 'no' votes were cast against de Valera rather than against his constitution. The only positive opposition came from a small and loosely organised group of 'intellectuals'. Their father-figure, W. B. Yeats, was now in his seventies and for some years had been drifting into an elitist and authoritarian political creed, ending in a kind of dream world that F. S. L. Lyons has called 'an Anglo-Irish eighteenth century of his own fabrication — a creation which had little to do with history, but a great deal to do with his hungry quest for authority in the modern world'.[18] It was not a vision likely to command a majority vote in a referendum.

The 1937 constitution was permeated not only by Catholic moral viewpoints but also by what had crystallised as 'Catholic social thought' or 'Catholic social teaching'. This had had its origins in Leo XIII's encyclical *Rerum novarum* of 1891, reconsidered and applied to the post-war world by Pius XI's *Quadragesimo anno* in 1931. This latter had in particular stressed the need to supplement parliamentary democracy by the 'vocational' organisation of the different interest groups in the community in order to promote social peace. These organised groups should be encouraged to do things for themselves rather than look to the state for everything. This was called 'the principle of subsidiarity'. Just at this time there is no doubt that the pope was impressed by Mussolini's idea of the 'corporate state' and had been very pleased that the Lateran Treaty of 1929 had ended the long estrangement between the Vatican and Italy. Many Catholics, including Irish Catholics, were thinking along these lines in the 1920s, and *Quadragesimo anno* encouraged their efforts. It had little impact on the organised political parties. Fine Gael, founded in 1933, showed an initial enthusiasm that collapsed before the problem of the Blueshirts, and the only trace of political vocationalism in the 1937 constitution was the method of electing the Senate, which very soon lost any vocational aspect that might have been intended.

On 17 May 1931, by coincidence just two days after the publication of *Quadragesimo anno*, a Tipperary priest, John Hayes, founded Muintir na Tíre, a rural organisation based on the parish. It did a great deal of good in carrying out practical projects and in many intangible ways. It is no discredit to this great-hearted man to suggest that his inspiration came not so much from the Belgian Boerenbond, as he claimed, but from the vision of 'the little village' in Kickham's *Knocknagow*. Much of the strength of his organisation sprang from his insistence that it was not sectional but embraced all the people of the parish. Yet some years later the *Report* of the Commission on Vocational Organisation proposed that it should speak at national level for the farming community. Canon Hayes was a member of the commission, and the proposal must certainly have had his approval; it is highly likely that he himself made it. It was not that he had changed his mind, but rather that he had not rationalised the contradiction.

Another development that showed social concern as well as social thought was the initiative taken by John Charles McQuaid immediately he became Archbishop of Dublin in 1940. This resulted in organisations that not only staved off hunger for many of the poor of Dublin during the bitter years of the war, but transformed the quality of social welfare work, that still had too much degradation of the old Poor Law system attached to it.

In 1939 the government had set up a commission to inquire into the possibilities of vocational organisation in Ireland. Its chairman was Michael Browne, appointed Bishop of Galway in 1937, and commonly regarded as sympathetic to Eamon de Valera and Fianna Fáil. The commission presented its report in 1944. It recommended that the state should move away from a centralised bureaucracy and honour 'the principle of subsidiarity' by acting as far as possible through vocational bodies. There should be a national assembly of such bodies as well as the elected parliament.

Two months after the report was published, but quite unconnected with it, Bishop John Dignan of Clonfert published proposals for a scheme of national health insurance. The proposals were made by the bishop personally, but in this matter he was not altogether a private person, having been appointed in 1936 as chairman of the National Health Insurance Society, charged by the government with the task of tidying up what were admittedly untidy arrangements for health insurance. He was justifiably critical of many aspects of state provision for health and proposed a national insurance scheme which would not be administered by the state.

These recommendations came when in Britain Sir William Beveridge had put forward detailed proposals for the 'welfare state' and the Irish bureaucracy was thinking along the same lines. The collapse of Mussolini's Italy had exposed his 'corporate state' as a hollow sham. De Valera had just won an election with a substantially increased majority and was in no mood to consider sharing power with a national vocational assembly. The report of the Commission on Vocational Organisation was shelved, amid much criticism, some of which was justified, and some acrimony, which was regrettable. With the benefit of hindsight, it might well be argued that it would have been better if it had been taken more seriously; but it is also possible to reflect, a little wryly, on what might have been the reaction of Bishop Michael Browne to a suggestion that he introduce the principle of subsidiarity into his diocese of Galway.

The debate continued. With a certain inevitability it came to centre on the question of state provision for health services, and to manifest itself as a conflict between the government and the church, seen now not as 'the clergy' but as the bishops. The existing system of 'medical assistance' through the dispensary system was a patchwork that had grown out of the old Poor Law. In many respects it was admittedly unsatisfactory, and there were serious and undeniable health problems in regard to tuberculosis and infant mortality.

John Whyte has dispassionately analysed this controversy, and more recently Ronan Fanning has been able to supplement his information on certain points because more documentation has become available,[19] so that it is possible to give a reasonably sure-footed summary of an area where there was much confusion. The government's first attempt to tackle the problems came with the Public Health Bill of 1945. While making more generous provision for need, it retained many of the bad features of the old system. There was very centralised control, no free choice of doctor, and a heavy emphasis on compulsion to avail of the services provided. There was no episcopal response, though John Whyte has found evidence to indicate that the bishops did discuss it.[20] In any case, the proposals collapsed for reasons completely unconnected with their merits.

In 1947 the British health services were introduced into Northern Ireland, and it was immediately clear that, at least in the political situation there, they posed serious problems for voluntary hospitals, and specifically for the Catholic Mater Hospital in Belfast. In the same year the government in Dublin introduced a Health Bill. It lead to a protest from the Catholic hierarchy — as John Whyte notes, 'for the first time since the foundation of the state, so far as is known'.[21] The bill was nevertheless passed, but James Dillon, then sitting as an independent, had an action to test its constitutionality before the courts when the government was defeated in a general election in February 1948. The problem was left to a new coalition government, headed by John A. Costello, with Dr Noel Browne as his Minister for Health.

The details of the 'Mother and Child' controversy of 1950 and 1951 are now so well established that here it will be possible to concentrate on its results. There was nothing new in the provisions for the health care of mothers and children in Dr Browne's proposals, and in some respects they were better than those of 1945 and 1947. The crunch issue was that it was proposed that these services should be free to all without exception. There were strong practical arguments against this, but the British system was a powerful attraction, and 'means test' a very emotive phrase. The bishops' opposition was on the principle that the bringing up of children belonged to the parents and not to the state; that the state had the duty to provide for those who could not provide for themselves, but no right 'to impose a state medical service on the whole community on the pretext of relieving the necessitous 10 per cent from the so-called indignity of the means test'[22] — this last phrase doubly unfortunate in that it was not necessary to the substance of the argument, which was an invocation of 'the principle of subsidiarity' as part of 'Catholic social teaching'.

The stance of the bishops was arguably the most important element, but by no means the only element, in bringing about a general election and the return of Fianna Fáil to power. The controversy figured largely in the election, because — and this was what was quite unprecedented — the issues between the government and the bishops had been made public, largely, but not exclusively, because Dr Browne released to the press his correspondence with the government and the bishops. On one point there was no disagreement — the bishops were entitled to intervene in a matter concerning faith and morals. On the second point, should they have intervened in private, as they did, or publicly, there was disagreement, understandably, because strong arguments could be brought forward on both sides. On the third point, were they justified on the particular point on which they intervened in this particular issue, while there were some who said no, they were few in comparison to the numbers who felt confused and unhappy about the whole issue. The question of health services was resolved by the incoming Fianna Fáil government, though some issues slumbered uneasily in the background.

One of these was a kind of integralist movement operating principally under the name 'Maria Duce', which surfaced in the mid-1940s. In eastern Europe the Catholic church was suffering fierce persecution, while in the west Catholic parties were prominent in national governments, even in France. The Maria Duce movement put forward the claim that the recognition granted to the Catholic church in Ireland by the 1937 constitution was quite insufficient: it should be constitutionally recognised as the one true church. The judgment of the Supreme Court in the Tilson case on 5 August 1950, that pre-nuptial promises regarding the upbringing of children were valid in civil law, raised fears that Catholic canon law might become part of civil law, even though the court stated as the basis of its decision the fact that it judged both parents to have equal constitutional rights in this matter. In any case, this judgment did not set a precedent. Then in 1957 a boycott of local Protestants by local Catholics broke out in the little village of Fethard in Co. Wexford, again arising out of the question of the religious education of the children of a mixed marriage. It was generally represented as a matter of religious bigotry, though in fact it was in the main about an equally emotive issue, land. It was another instance where Eamon de Valera had no hesitations in opposing 'the church'. He condemned the boycott in the Dáil on 4 July, and expressed the hope that 'good sense and decent neighbourly feeling' would prevail. In fact good sense did prevail, and decent neighbourly feeling was never driven as deep underground as was sometimes represented.

The real Irish problem in the 1950s was economic depression. By contrast, the British economy was booming, and the boats were full of young people, not just seeking a job but, as one of them poignantly said, finding it hard to fit into 'the more civilised mode of living' in Britain after 'the more cramped and less free standards prevailing in Ireland'.[23] It was hard to see the boats pulling out without thinking of the phrase then applied to the refugees from East Germany just before the building of the Berlin wall — they were voting with their feet.

Disturbing reports of failure in religious practice drifted back from Britain. Bishop Beck of Brentwood addressed the Maynooth Union on the topic in 1950. His paper was followed by a heated and heavily defensive discussion. Yet the Irish Catholic clergy were sensitive to problems. The Christus Rex Society to encourage social studies among priests had been founded in 1941 and began publication of a journal in 1947. In 1950 that gritty and courageous character, Gerard McGarry, professor of pastoral theology at Maynooth, launched *The Furrow*, and the *Irish Theological Quarterly* was revived in 1951.

At the Maynooth Union meeting in 1955 Bishop William Philbin of Clonfert read a paper suggesting that the union needed new direction and proposing a summer school of theological studies. The 1956 union meeting was devoted to a discussion of this proposal. To prepare for the discussion the officers of the union had canvassed clerical opinion. Almost everyone favoured the proposal. What was very interesting was the response to more detailed questions. To a question on emphasis 21 per cent opted for 'strictly theological topics', but 79 per cent for 'pastoral topics'. Amongst 'theological subjects' 35 per cent opted for moral theology, 22 per cent for dogmatic theology, 22 per cent for liturgy, and 16 per cent for scripture. A number of points emerged with reasonable clarity: there was some sense of crisis and of the need to do something about it; as to what was to be done, there was wide agreement that 'strictly theological topics' had a low priority; and as to who was to do what was to be done, it just does not seem to have entered anyone's mind that it could be other than the clergy. The decrees of the national synod held at Maynooth that same year scarcely convey the sense of crisis felt by the priests. To read them through is to get the impression that little had changed since the previous synod of 1927; indeed, even earlier synods might suggest themselves without demanding any great change in the text of 1956.

The fortunes of the movement known as the Legion of Mary may be instructive here, and a recently published little book lifts a number of veils. Frank Duff, a Dublin layman, had founded the Legion in 1921. It attracted many committed laity, not only in Ireland but throughout the Catholic world. Each branch of the Legion had its chaplain, but it was decidedly a lay movement, reminiscent in this of the sodalities and confraternities of the early nineteenth century. It engaged in charitable activities, but insisted that these be rooted in a personal spirituality in turn rooted in theology. Some would have seen this theology as in some respects unbalanced, but what was not sufficiently realised was that the centre of Frank Duff's vision was theological. He met with deep suspicion from two successive Archbishops of Dublin, Edward Byrne and John Charles McQuaid. In a very revealing few pages his biographer argues his own conviction that at the centre of Archbishop McQuaid's opposition was the fear that, in insisting on this theological core to its activities, the Legion might be 'stepping too far'.[24]

The world outside broke in suddenly on this closed and uneasy society. Its first task was to solve its economic ills: as Bishop Philbin argued in 1957, the Irish had erred in believing that political freedom would solve all ills, and among the many problems neglected the greatest was the failure to provide the young with an acceptable alternative to emigration. In the following year the First Programme for Economic Expansion set out to provide precisely this by attracting foreign capital. For at least a decade it seemed to be working. Not merely did emigration stop, but there was a certain 'ingathering of the exiles'. A newly confident country welcomed in the modern world, and the modern world came to it. In 1953 the B.B.C. began television transmissions from Belfast; Dublin picked them up gratefully. Transmissions from Dublin began on 31 December 1961; of necessity many of the programmes were of foreign origin. In Rome a great council of the Catholic church opened on 11 October 1962, and its conclusions, as they slowly sank in, were certainly challenging, if not downright revolutionary.

When the six counties of the north-east were established as a separate political unit by the Government of Ireland Act in 1920 Catholics, at about one-third of the population, were a very sizeable minority. They felt a sense of betrayal and abandonment: and it is hard not to agree that at least Tyrone and Fermanagh had been lost in sterile debates about sovereignty. More than the rest of nationalist Ireland they felt that partition simply could not last, and they were reluctant to come to any terms with the new state. In consequence, it was born in violence, and the Protestant majority found arguments to justify their reluctance to come to terms with the Catholics. 'Catholic' and 'Protestant' are the most convenient shorthand, especially in the present context, but the issue was not religion but political power. 'Who began it?' is the most sterile of human questions, but the fact is that political power lay with the Protestant majority, and only they could take real steps to try to reconcile the minority. They did not do this, but instead took steps to exclude them positively.

Political power took on a guise that must be described as sectarian. Security took on a sectarian face with the development of the B Special police. Steps were taken to make political power at all levels secure for Protestants, with the abolition of proportional representation (enshrined in the Government of Ireland Act) and manipulation in the redrawing of electoral boundaries that necessarily followed on its abolition. At local level especially, powers to allocate jobs and housing went with political control.

In the thorny question of education, neither Catholic nor Protestant clergy were willing to abandon the control that had come to them under the old National Board. Indeed, some Catholics at first flatly refused to break their links with Dublin, and some teachers' salaries were actually paid from Dublin for a short time. The Minister of Education, Lord Londonderry, set up what was meant to be an interdenominational system of primary education, with provision for private schools on less generous financial terms. This public system was unacceptable to the Catholics. The Protestant clergy, in alliance with the Orange Order, applied relentless political pressure to transform the state system into a denominational Protestant system. In this they had succeeded by 1930, and though Catholic schools got a grant of 50 per cent towards building and running costs, what happened was in fact a state endowment of the Protestant churches in regard to education.[25] All such endowments had been excluded by the Government of Ireland Act.

If all Protestants were equal, some were more equal than others. Inquiries in the 1920s disclosed irregularities and even plain graft in the housing programme of Belfast corporation, and it is reasonable to suspect that monopoly of political power must have been a factor. In 1932 the hungry and humiliated poor rioted in the streets of Belfast, and for a brief time no man asked his neighbour if he were Catholic or Protestant. When the city suffered devastating air-raids in April and May 1941 it was found that among the refugees from the slums there were about 5,000 people who were described in a cabinet paper as 'unbilletable' because they were 'nearly sub-human'.[26] These unfortunates came from both sides of the sectarian divide. Northern Ireland was a poor region of the United Kingdom, and life at the bottom of the heap was horrible for Protestant as well as for Catholic.

After the war the benefits of the British welfare state were extended to Northern Ireland. In the nature of things the Catholics benefited out of proportion to their numbers: there were more poor Catholics. But for all, employment, health care and education improved dramatically in the 1950s, just when the Republic to the south was struggling with economic depression. It is not surprising that the I.R.A. campaign of the late 1950s failed for lack of popular support. But it did build up a strong Protestant reaction, and names like Ian Paisley began to make the headlines.

Revolutionary situations develop when rising expectations are seen as thwarted. Two symbolic events occurred in 1965. In February it was decided that the new university to be opened would be at Coleraine, and in June that the new city to be built would be in the Lagan valley and would be called Craigavon. Both decisions were at the expense of legitimate aspirations of preponderantly Catholic Derry and west Ulster. Growing Catholic impatience met growing Protestant resistance. As David Harkness has put it, 'The question was . . . whether or not a state created to protect Protestant unionism could ever risk full participation by Catholics, even if they did not openly profess nationalist ambitions.'[27] Sadly and literally, it was an explosive situation.

At the beginning of the 1960s, the Irish Catholics existed in two political communities that were showing signs of coming adrift, and in some ways the voice of their church was uncertain. There was no clear answer to the question of what was that central inheritance for which people may be asked to make the sacrifices necessary to sustain an organised state, the question of what past to keep for pride. The Irish had pioneered the struggle against colonialism, which was just now a great 'wind of change' blowing across the world. They had seen themselves as a kind of Celtic 'centre' orbited by more fragmentary survivors, in Brittany, Wales, Man and Scotland. Above all, they had seen themselves in the role of mother country to the English-speaking Catholic world.

It was overall a somewhat fragile inheritance, even the religious inheritance that seemed so strong in so many ways and was beyond question the strongest. What was referred to with such certainty as 'traditional Irish Catholicism' was a fairly recent experience in the heritage of most Irish people. It had its roots in the Tridentine reformation as adopted in the first instance by the English-speaking towns. The Tridentine programme for religious renewal had had its shortcomings, but on the whole it had been a reasonably adequate response to the questions thrown up by Renaissance humanism and by the Reformation.

The fact that this programme could not be fully implemented in Ireland had not been altogether a disadvantage, especially in that the inability to centre religious life in the church building allowed some good features of the old 'household' observance to survive.

Gaelic-speaking Ireland came fully into this pattern only after the Famine. By then it had taken on the shape of what I have called 'neo-Tridentinism'. The shortcomings of this pattern of religious observance became more apparent as the church became more defensive in the later nineteenth century. It would, however, be a mistake to underrate its effectiveness. Acceptance of a clear system of belief and a clear round of duty could and did lead to real religious experience, but because on the whole the system was not open and growing, it was by a kind of law of life in some sense necessarily closing and getting more rigid. In this, Gaelic-speaking Ireland was especially unfortunate in that its rich religious tradition was embodied in a language it was losing. Neither the Gaelic League nor the language policy of the Irish Free State was able to restore what had been lost. In reading the 'Blasket literature', for example, especially its most powerful writer, Tomás Ó Criomhthain, it is apparent that the overriding theme is nostalgia. The old people appear in a kind of archaic pose, and the reader is not sure if that is how they really saw themselves or if it represents what people like Robin Flower told them they were. Interestingly, this note of nostalgia for a lost past comes through even with the young man who left the island, Muiris Ó Súileabháin.

Patrick Kavanagh published *The Great Hunger* in 1942. That same year he wrote what is in every way a bigger poem, *Lough Derg*. He appears to have dashed it off and never returned to it: it was published only in 1978, eleven years after he died. It may be that he preferred to publish the poem on 'Patrick Maguire, the old peasant' because he was surer of this relatively minor theme. Yet it is hard to read *Lough Derg* without being struck by the sureness of his grip on a greater one, the spiritual hunger of Ireland.

The pilgrims gather at Lough Derg, ranging from 'solicitors praying for cushy jobs' to

> a Leitrim man
> With a face as sad as a flooded hayfield.

The devotions are routine and low-key:

> The rosary is said and benediction...
> The same routine and ritual now
> As serves for street-processions or congresses...
> But something that is Ireland's secret leads
> These petty mean people...

Then there comes up a powerful image of 'the Great Hunger', evoked by the heaps of stones of the penitential 'beds':

> The middle of the island looked like the memory
> Of some village evicted by the Famine...
> So much alike is our historical
> And spiritual pattern, a heap
> Of stones anywhere is consecrated
> By love's terrible need...
> And these pilgrims of a western reason
> Were not pursuing French-hot miracles
>   ...were not led there
> By priests of Maynooth or stories of Italy or Spain,
> For this is the penance of the poor...
> Lough Derg, St Patrick's Purgatory in Donegal,
> Christendom's purge. Heretical
> Around the edges: the centre's hard...
> The twentieth century blows across it now,
> But deeply it has kept an ancient vow.
> It knows the secret of pain...

To explore further might be to spoil things, but a few questions might suggest themselves. Are the clergy quite so central as their official image might have suggested? — an image that, in all fairness, was often modified in reality by Father Giffley in the Dublin slums or Father Duff in the rural west. Are the intellectuals, when they assault the shortcomings of 'traditional Irish Catholicism', criticising the clergy for something where the fault is shared by the laity? — again, in all fairness, they show themselves conscious of this: Austin Clarke's portrait of Martha Blake at Mass and communion must be balanced against his 'straying student' reflecting on the problem in

>   this land, where every woman's son
> Must carry his own coffin and believe,
> In dread, all that the clergy teach the young.[28]

Is there not a great deal to Seán Ó Faoláin's contention that

> The priest and the writer ought to be fighting side by side, if for nothing else than the rebuttal of the vulgarity that is pouring daily into the vacuum left in the popular mind by the dying out of the old traditional way of life.

Dónall Mac Amhlaigh was a young man who left Ireland for England in the depressed decade of the 1950s. In 1960 he summed up his experiences in a book called *Dialann Deoraí*. An English translation appeared in 1964; it was entitled, why it is hard to say, *An Irish Navvy*. The book is in striking contrast to the 'Blasket literature': here is a young Irish person who is very much alive in the world of his day. He shows a real resentment of the social and economic conditions that forced him to emigrate, together with a possibly naïve conviction that the government could do something about it. He has a real appreciation of the good qualities of the English, which often contrast favourably with bad qualities shown by some Irish emigrants, but nevertheless the English always remain 'they'. The most important reason why 'they' remain separate from 'us' is that they are not religious:

Good Friday. I always feel very guilty on this day and I'm always glad when it's over. There's a great difference between Good Friday at home and Good Friday here. To the English, it's only the beginning of the holiday, a day on which you eat hot cross buns; and they work on that day so that they can have Easter Tuesday off. Some of the Irish are just as bad and they think nothing of going out drinking and celebrating that night. Well, it wasn't like that for the old people who would have nothing to eat but a bit of dry bread or to drink but a drop of black tea and who would spend most of the time saying the rosary.[29]

The book closes as the boat taking him back from a holiday in Ireland pulls out of Dún Laoire. As the bourgeois shoreline recedes it prompts the thought:

Doesn't Dún Laoire look beautiful with the mountains behind it? The quay is lined with little sailing-boats, and wooden rowing-boats. The wealthy own them, those who can stay behind here.

On the boat he has spotted a little group from Connemara, talking in Irish. Somewhere a man is singing 'The Rose of Tralee'. Then comes the last throwaway sentence, translated as 'We're a great people surely.' Translation is an art that varies from the difficult to the impossible. Here is it very near the impossible, for what Dónall Mac Amhlaigh wrote was 'Is iontach an dream muid cinnte.'

Anyone who can put so many layers of irony into a single word deserves, and demands, a religion which is hard at the centre. One thing the writers would be widely agreed on, and their record here is a proud one, is that it is impossible just to turn away from the old traditions. It may not be possible to recover fully the depths within depths of hard theological religion once available to the popular mind in a single phrase like 'Rí an Domhnaigh'. It may even be hard to hang on to it in its impoverished later forms. G. K. Chesterton attended the Eucharistic Congress in Dublin in 1932. What struck him most was that

In that strange town, the poorer were the streets, the richer were the street decorations....Men who could hardly write had written up inscriptions; and somehow they were dogmas as well as jokes.... Somebody wrote 'God Bless Christ the King'; and I knew I was staring at one of the staggering paradoxes of Christianity.... A priest told me he had heard a very poor threadbare working woman saying in a tram, with a resignation perhaps slightly tinged with tartness: 'Well, if it rains now, He'll have brought it on himself.'[30]

Chesterton did have a sprightly imagination, quite capable of embroidery. But he also had a real gift of what can only be called intuition. He does seem to be hitting the dead centre when he summed up Ireland's Catholicism:

Her religion has always been poetic, popular and, above all, domestic. Nobody who knows anything of her population will think there was ever any special danger that her Deity would be only a definition. He was always so intimate as rather to resemble, in a pagan parallel, a household god or a family ghost. Ireland was filled with the specially human spirit of Christianity, especially in the sense of the pathetic, the sensitive and the great moral emotions that attach to memory.[31]

I have suggested that the Irish national inheritance, those shared values for which people are prepared to make the necessary sacrifices, is a complex thing and may well be a fragile thing. I have also suggested that the strongest element in it may well be the religious inheritance. The Irish have only slender traditions of a philosophical humanism, much less of a secularist humanism. What humanism they are capable of is rather rooted in religion. It is in some ways a daunting thought that the real elements of pluralism in Ireland may well be the confessional churches; but if this is so, there is nothing gained by a refusal to face it.

I have suggested in the introduction to this book that the Irish Catholic inheritance — like all religious inheritances — can be understood only by co-operation between theology and the humanities. It is only this that will give us a real Irish theology, hard at the centre not only with the great central tradition but with the Irish tradition as well. And it is difficult to resist the thought that without this hard centre much effort in other areas may be, perhaps not exactly wasted, but wasteful.

Notes

Chapter 1: Saints, Kings and Vikings (pp 1-29)
James F. Kenney's monumental *The Sources for the Early History of Ireland*, Vol. 1: *Eccesiastical* (New York 1929; reprinted with additions by Ludwig Bieler, 1966) is still indispensable, both as a guide to the sources and for measured and balanced historical judgment. With it may be mentioned Kathleen Hughes, *Early Christian Ireland: Introduction to the Sources* (London 1972), which followed her learned and readable *The Church in Early Irish Society* (London 1966). I myself have written a short survey, *The Christian Mission*, in Corish, *Ir. Catholicism*, i, ch. 3 (Dublin 1971).

The literature on St Patrick is so vast and sometimes so contentious that it is with some trepidation that I single out R. P. C. Hanson, *Saint Patrick: His Origins and Career* (Oxford 1968) for its success in probing Patrick's brief writings in search of a person.

1. Penitential of Vinnian, no. 46, and Old Irish Penitential, no. 8, in Ludwig Bieler (ed.), *The Irish Penitentials* (Dublin 1963), 93, 279.
2. See, e.g., Donncha Ó Corráin, 'The Early Irish Churches: Some Aspects of Organisation' in *Irish Antiquity*, the volume of commemorative essays edited by him (Cork 1981), 327-42. He promises a more extended treatment in the forthcoming *New History of Ireland*, i.
3. T. F. O'Rahilly in *I.H.S.*, viii (1953), 273; James Carney, *The Problem of St Patrick* (Dublin 1961), 46; D. A. Binchy, 'St Patrick and his Biographers: Ancient and Modern' in *Studia Hib.*, ii (1962), 60. This view had been earlier propounded by Eoin Mac Néill (see John Ryan (ed.), *St Patrick* (Dublin 1964), 154-5).
4. *Letter to the Soldiers of Coroticus*, nos 1, 2, 16.
5. I have treated the subject a little more fully in 'The Early Irish Church and the Western Patriarchate' in Próinséas Ní Chatháin and Michael Richter (ed.), *Irland und Europa: Ireland and Europe* (Stuttgart 1984), 9-15.
6. 'Rule of the *Céli Dé*', nos 58, 64, ed. E. J. Gwynn in *Hermathena*, xliv (1927), 81, 85.
7. Hughes, *Early Christian Ireland: Introduction to the Sources* (London 1972), 188-9.
8. Françoise Henry, *Irish Art in the Early Christian Period*, English trans., i (London 1965), 209.
9. G. S. M. Walker (ed.), *Sancti Columbani Opera* (Dublin 1957); Bede, *Hist.*

Ecc., iii, 5 (Aidan); A. O. Anderson and M. O. Anderson (ed.), *Adomnan's Life of Columba* (Edinburgh 1961), 524-6.

10. Plummer, *Vitae SS Hib.*, i, 206; ii, 119; i, 265.
11. Whitley Stokes (ed.), *Félire Oengusso: The Martyrology of Oengus* (London 1905), 211.
12. R. P. C. Hanson, *Saint Patrick* (Oxford 1968) is especially perceptive on these points.
13. Translation from Ludwig Bieler (ed.), *The Works of St Patrick* (London 1953), 71.
14. Letter to Mellitus, in Bede, *Hist. Ecc.*, i, 65.
15. See, e.g., the analysis of the penitential of Burchard of Worms by George Duby in *The Knight, the Lady and the Priest*, English trans. (London 1984), 63-74.
16. Nos 42-46 in Bieler (ed.), *The Irish Penitentials*, 91-2.
17. Cf. 'Second Synod of Patrick', xxvi (Bieler, op. cit., 195); Old Irish Penitential, ii, 36 (ibid., 265).
18. Hughes, *The Church in Early Irish Society*, 153, 177.
19. Quoted in Kathleen Hughes, 'The Church and the World in Early Christian Ireland' in *I.H.S.*, xiii (1962), 109.
20. 'Second Synod of Patrick', xiii (Bieler, op. cit., 188).
21. Hughes, *The Church in Early Irish Society*, 277.
22. Migne, *P.L.*, lxxii, 789, translated in Ludwig Bieler, *Ireland, Harbinger of the Middle Ages* (London 1963), 28.
23. E. J. Gwynn and W. J. Purton (ed.), 'The Monastery of Tallaght' in *R.I.A.' Proc.*, sect. C, xxix (1911-12), 153.
24. 'Canones Hibernenses', i, 26-9; 'Bigotian Penitential', iv, 6; Old Irish Penitential, v, 17, 18 (Bieler (ed.), *The Irish Penitentials*, 162, 230, 273).
25. See Peter Dwyer, *Céli Dé: Spiritual Reform in Ireland, 750-900* (Dublin 1981).
26. Gerard Murphy, *Early Irish Lyrics* (Oxford 1962), 18-23.
27. 'Rule of the *Céli Dé*', no. 64, ed. E. J. Gwynn in *Hermathena*, xliv (1927), 85.
28. See D. A. Binchy, 'The Passing of the Old Order' in Brian Ó Cuív (ed.) *The Impact of the Scandinavian Invasions on the Celtic-Speaking Peoples* (Dublin 1975), 119-32.
29. For an interesting recent contribution see Richard Sharpe, 'Armagh and Rome in the Seventh Century' in Ní Chatháin and Richter (ed.), *Irland und Europa: Ireland and Europe*, 58-72.
30. See Murphy, *Early Irish Lyrics*, 4-5; David Greene and Frank O'Connor, *A Golden Treasury of Irish Poetry* (London 1967), 84-5.
31. Cited in Robin Flower, *The Irish Tradition* (Oxford 1947), 30-1, from Stokes (ed.), *Félire Oengusso*.
32. Murphy, *Early Irish Lyrics*, 67-9.

Chapter 2: Normans, but no King (pp 30-62)
We still have a great deal to learn about the religious life of later medieval Ireland. For the twelfth century in particular Aubrey Gwynn distilled his great knowledge in *The Twelfth-Century Reform* in Corish, *Ir. Catholicism*, ii, ch. 1 (Dublin

1968). He also contributed *Anglo-Irish Church Life: Fourteenth and Fifteenth Centuries* (ii, ch. 4, 1968), while Geoffrey Hand wrote on *The Church in the English Lordship, 1216-1307* (ii, ch. 3, 1968).

The many writings of John Watt are particularly useful, especially *The Church and the Two Nations in Medieval Ireland* (Cambridge 1970) and *The Church in Medieval Ireland* (Dublin 1972).

For Gaelic Ireland the most useful introductions are Canice Mooney, *The Church in Gaelic Ireland: Thirteenth to Fifteenth Centuries* in Corish, *Ir. Catholicism*, ii, ch. 5 (Dublin 1969) and Kenneth Nicholls, *Gaelic and Gaelicised Ireland in the Middle Ages* (Dublin 1972).

1. Gwynn *The Twelfth-Century Reform*, 11.
2. See Aubrey Gwynn and Neville Hadcock, *Medieval Religious Houses: Ireland* (London 1970), 117.
3. T.C.D. MS B 1 1, printed in Gwynn, *The Twelfth-Century Reform*, 59-60. The text breaks off abruptly at the end.
4. D. A. Binchy, 'The Passing of the Old Order' in Brian Ó Cuív (ed.), *The Impact of the Scandinavian Invasions on the Celtic-Speaking Peoples* (Dublin 1975), 119-32.
5. Watt, *The Church and the Two Nations in Medieval Ireland*, 47.
6. They are listed in John J. Webb, *The Guilds of Dublin* (Dublin 1929), 4-8.
7. St John D. Seymour, *Anglo-Irish Literature, 1200-1582* (Cambridge 1929), 81-8.
8. Text in Edmund Curtis and R. B. McDowell, *Irish Historical Documents, 1172-1922* (London 1943), 38-46. The passage quoted is on p. 44.
9. For the details see Gwynn and Hadcock, *Medieval Religious Houses: Ireland*.
10. Watt, *The Church in Medieval Ireland*, 50-2.
11. For a clear and succinct summary see Mooney, *The Church in Gaelic Ireland: Thirteenth to Fifteenth Centuries*, 10-13.
12. Seymour, *Anglo-Irish Literature*, 103-17.
13. Ibid., 52-76.
14. 'The Professional Poets' in Brian Ó Cuív (ed.), *Seven Centuries of Irish Learning, 1000-1700* (Dublin 1961), 52.
15. *S.P. Hen. VIII*, ii, 11.
16. Aubrey Gwynn, 'Provincial and Diocesan Decrees of the Diocese of Dublin during the Anglo-Norman Period' in *Archiv. Hib.*, xi (1944), 31-117; 'Two Sermons of Primate Richard FitzRalph', ibid., xiv (1949), 50-65; Katherine Walsh, *A Fourteenth-Century Scholar and Primate: Richard FitzRalph in Oxford. Avignon and Armagh* (Oxford 1981), 239-348.
17. Gearóid Mac Niocaill, 'Registrum Cantariae S. Salvatoris Waterfordensis' in *Anal. Hib.*, xxiii (1966), 135-222.
18. William Hawkes, 'The Liturgy in Dublin, 1200-1500: Manuscript Sources' in *Reportorium Novum*, ii, 1 (1957-8), 33-67.
19. Seymour, *Anglo-Irish Literature*, 120-1.
20. See M. V. Ronan, 'Religious Customs of Dublin Medieval Guilds' in *I.E.R.*, series 5, xxvi (1925), 225-47, 364-85.
21. Ruth Dudley Edwards, 'Ecclesiastical Appointments in the Province of Tuam, 1399-1477' in *Archiv. Hib.*, xxxiii (1975), 91-100.

22. E.g. J. H. McGuckin, 'The Medieval Priests of Artrea' in *Journal of the South Derry Historical Society*, ii, 1 (1981-2), 116-21.
23. Watt, *The Church in Medieval Ireland*, 201-2.
24. What he wrote in *The Irish Tradition* (Oxford 1947), 107-73, remains very worthwhile reading.
25. Richard Butler (ed.), *The Annals of Ireland by Friar John Clyn and Thady Dowling* ... (Dublin 1849), s.a. 1494.
26. Watt, *The Church in Medieval Ireland*, 210-11.
27. Heather A. King, 'Late Medieval Crosses in County Meath, *c.* 1470-1635' in *R.I.A. Proc.*, sect. C, lxxxiv (1984), 79-115.
28. Catriona MacLeod, 'Medieval Wooden Figure Sculptures in Ireland' in *R.S.A.I. Jn.*, lxxv (1945), 195-204; lxxvi (1946), 155-70.
29. See Nicholls, *Gaelic and Gaelicised Ireland in the Middle Ages*, 3-4.
30. Edmund Curtis, *A History of Medieval Ireland*, (Dublin 1927), 426.

Chapter 3: King or Pope? (pp 63-95)

The fifteen or twenty years just past have seen a probing new examination of sixteenth-century Ireland, with the almost predictable result that while old certainties have disappeared, what has replaced them is more in the way of uncertainties. At the centre of the old certainties was the acceptance of the fact that the conflict in sixteenth-century Ireland was essentially, indeed almost exclusively, about religion. This conflict is now quite rightly seen as a much broader clash of cultures. There may be some danger of concluding that the conflict was not really about religion at all, but about something else, possibly taxation, but this will settle down.

The new ideas are emerging through the periodical literature and are only slowly finding their way into books. In consequence, the annotation to this chapter has to be rather more extensive than that to some others.

1. See the lists in J. T. Gilbert, 'The Manuscripts of His Grace the Duke of Leinster' in *H.M.C. rep. 9*, app., pt ii, 288-9.
2. For an excellent summary see Penry Williams, *The Tudor Regime* (Oxford 1979), 253-92.' See also J. J. Scarisbrick, *The Reformation and the English People* (Oxford 1984).
3. See Richard Mant, *History of the Church of Ireland* (London 1840), i, 271-5.
4. Brendan Bradshaw, 'Sword, Word and Strategy in the Reformation in Ireland' in *Hist. Jn.*, xxi (1978), 475-502; Nicholas Canny, 'Why the Reformation Failed in Ireland: *une question mal posée*' in *Jn. Ecc. Hist.*, xxx (1979), 423-50.
5. Brady to Cecil, 14 Mar. 1564, 10 Jan. 1565, in Shirley, *Ch. in Ire., 1547-67*, 135-8, 160-3.
6. Cited in Edwards, *Church & State*, 139.
7. Craik to Dudley, 30 Apr. 1561, in Shirley, *Ch. in Ire., 1547-67*, 95-7.
8. Sidney to the queen, 28 Apr. 1576, in Brady, *Ir. Ch. Eliz.*, 14-19.
9. Ibid., 93-4.
10. Brady to Cecil, 14 Mar. 1564, in Shirley, *Ch. in Ire., 1547-67*, 135-8.
11. Sidney to the queen, 28 Apr. 1576, in Brady, *Ir. Ch. Eliz.*, 14-19.

12. Lawrence Marron, 'Documents from the State Papers concerning Miler Magrath' in *Archiv. Hib.*, xxi (1958), 75-189.
13. 'A Letter from Sir John Davies concerning the State of Ireland' in Morley, *Ire. under Eliz. & Jas I*, 377-8.
14. Sidney to the queen, 20 Apr. 1567, P.R.O., S.P. 63/20/66, *Cal. S.P. Ire., 1509-73*, 330.
15. Ed. Aubrey Gwynn in *Archiv. Hib.*, xiii (1947), 24-6.
16. See Gwynn, *Med. Province Armagh*, 269.
17. *Cal. Carew MSS, Book of Howth*, 181.
18. Theiner, *Vetera Mon.*, 521.
19. Tanner to Cardinal Moroni, Rome, 26 Oct. 1571, in *Cal. S.P. Rome, 1558-72*, 467-8.
20. Williams, *The Tudor Regime*, 290.
21. Brendan Bradshaw, 'Native Reaction to the Westward Enterprise: A Case-Study in Gaelic Ideology' in K. R. Andrews and others (ed.), *The Westward Enterprise* (Liverpool 1978), 68-80; T. J. Dunne, 'The Gaelic Response to Conquest and Colonisation: The Evidence of the Poetry' in *Studia Hib.*, xx (1980), 31-45; Nicholas Canny, 'The Formation of the Irish Mind: Religion, Politics and Gaelic Irish Literature' in *Past & Present*, 95 (May 1982), 91-116.
22. See his 'Device' addressed to the English council in 1541 in *S.P. Hen. VIII*, iii, 326-30.
23. Wolfe's phrase is from his first report on his mission, finally presented in Rome in 1571: English translation in M. V. Ronan, *The Reformation in Ireland under Elizabeth* (London 1930), 471. The phrase from Andrew Trollope is in a letter he wrote to Walsingham on 12 Sept. 1581: Brady, *Ir. Ch. Eliz.*, 48-55.
24. An English translation of Cuellar's account is available in several editions, e.g. H. D. Sedgwick (trans.), *A Letter ... by Captain Cuellar ...* (London and New York 1896).
25. John Derricke, *The Image of Irelande* (London 1581).
26. Liam Butler and Eileen Power (ed.), *Holinshed's Irish Chronicle* (Dublin 1979), 112.
27. Wallop to Burghley, 10 June 1582, in Brady, *Ir. Ch. Eliz.*, 58-9.
28. Agard to Cromwell, 5 Apr. 1538, in *S.P. Hen. VIII*, ii, 569-70.
29. Brendan Jennings (ed.), 'Brussels MS 3947' in *Anal. Hib.*, vi (1934), 40-55.
30. Edward White, clerk to Clanricard, to Sidney, undated, but enclosed in Sidney to Burghley, 7 Dec. 1572, P.R.O., S.P. 63/38/52, *Cal. S.P. Ire., 1509-73*, 490.
31. See the account by John Howlin, S.J., in Moran, *Spicil. Ossor.*, i, 91-3.
32. John Hagan (ed.), 'Miscellanea Vaticano-Hibernica' in *Archiv. Hib.*, v (1916), 161, 163.
33. Brendan Jennings (ed.), 'Brussels MS 3947' in *Anal. Hib.*, vi (1934), 71; Philip O'Sullivan Beare, *Historiae Catholicae Iberniae Compendium* (repr. Dublin 1850), 134.
34. See, e.g., the record of the examination of Richard Creagh, 24 Feb. 1565, in Shirley, *Ch. in Ire., 1547-67*, 165-7.
35. Brendan Jennings (ed.), 'Irish Students in the University of Louvain' in

Measgra i gCuimhne, Mhichil Ui Chléirigh (Dublin 1944), 74-97.

36. See note 23 above. The account of FitzMaurice is on p. 470.
37. Ciaran Brady, 'Faction and the Origins of the Desmond Rebellion of 1579' in *I.H.S.*, xxii (1981), especially pp 305-7.
38. Nicholas Canny, 'Why the Reformation Failed in Ireland: *une question mal posée*' in *Jn. Ecc. Hist.*, xxx (1979), 447-50.
39. Bishop Lyon to Lord Hunsdon, 6 July 1596, P.R.O., S.P. 63/191/8, *Cal. S.P. Ire., 1596-97*, 13-20.
40. O'Sullivan Beare, *Historiae Catholicae Iberniae Compendium* (repr. Dublin 1950), 134-7.
41. *Pacata Hibernia*, i, 163-4.
42. Edmund Hogan, *Ibernia Ignatiana* (Dublin 1880), 38-40.
43. Cowley to Wolsey, Sept. 1528, *S.P. Hen. VIII*, ii, 141.
44. Ibid., 15.
45. Cowley to Cromwell, 4 Oct. 1536, ibid., 372.
46. Brendan Bradshaw, 'George Browne, First Reformation Archbishop of Dublin' in *Jn. Ecc. Hist.*, xxi (1976), 301-26.
47. Browne to Cromwell, 8 Jan. 1538, *S.P. Hen. VIII*, ii, 539-41.
48. Staples to St Leger, 17 June 1538, *S.P. Hen. VIII*, iii, 29-30.
49. Thomas Alen to Cromwell, 10 Oct. 1538, *L. & P. Hen. VIII*, iii, 103. For Henry's devotion to the Mass see J. J. Scarisbrick, *Henry VIII* (London 1968), 472-8.
50. Lord Deputy and council to Cromwell, 21 May 1539, *S.P. Hen. VIII*, iii, 130-1.
51. John Kingston, 'Catholic Families of the Pale' in *Reportorium Novum*, i, 2 (1956), 336-41.
52. Butler and Power (ed.), *Holinshed's Irish Chronicle*, 93.
53. Mervyn Archdall, *Monasticon Hibernicum* (Dublin 1786), 217-18.
54. *S.P. Hen. VIII*, ii, 569-70.
55. Staples to Bellingham, Dec. 1548, in Shirley, *Ch. in Ire., 1547-67*, 22-5.
56. Browne to Earl of Warwick, 6 Aug. 1551, ibid., 58.
57. So Lord Deputy Sidney in April 1576: *Cal. Carew MSS, 1575-88*, 352.
58. Sussex to Cecil, 22 July 1562, in Shirley, *Ch. in Ire., 1547-67*, 117-18.
59. Peter Lombard, *De Regno Hiberniae Sanctorum Insulae Commentarius*, ed. P. F. Moran (Dublin 1868), 122.
60. Thomas Wroth and Nicholas Arnold to the privy council, 16 Mar. 1564, in Shirley, *Ch. in Ire., 1547-67*, 140.
61. Loftus to the queen, 17 May 1565, ibid., 194-7.
62. Brady to Cecil, 6 Feb. 1570, in Brady, *Ir. Ch. Eliz.*, 8-9.
63. P.R.O., S.P. 63/58/16, *Cal. S.P. Ire., 1574-85*, 114.
64. See especially Ciaran Brady, 'Conservative Subversives: The Community of the Pale and the Dublin Administration, 1556-84' in P. J. Corish (ed.), *Radicals, Rebels and Establishments* (Belfast 1985), 11-32.
65. English translation in Ronan, *The Reformation in Ireland under Elizabeth*, 477.
66. H. F. Berry, 'History of the Religious Gild of St Anne' in *R.I.A. Proc.*, sect. C, xxv (1904-5), 21-106; M. V. Ronan, 'Religious Customs of the Dublin Medieval Guilds' in *I.E.R.*, series 5, xxvi (1925), 225-47, 364-85; Colm

Lennon, 'Civil Life and Religion in Early Seventeenth-Century Dublin in *Archiv. Hib.*, xxxviii (1983), 14-23.

67. Loftus and Wallop to Walsingham, 20 Oct. 1583, in Brady, *Ir. Ch. Eliz.*, 71.
68. See the spy's report enclosed in Drury to Walsingham, 14 Apr. 1577, P.R.O., S.P. 63/58/2, *Cal. S.P. Ire.*, *1574-85*, 112.
69. Lord Deputy to the privy council, 10 July 1581, P.R.O., S.P. 63/84/12, *Cal. S.P. Ire.*, *1574-85*, 310.
70. Sidney to Cecil, 19 Aug. 1566, in Shirley, *Ch. in Ire.*, *1547-67*, 264-6.
71. Loftus to Cecil, 5 Oct. 1566, ibid., 269-71.
72. English translation in Ronan, *The Reformation in Ireland under Elizabeth*, 480.
73. Moran, *Spicil. Ossor.*, i, 95-103.
74. Ibid., 105-6.
75. Drury to Walsingham, 14 Apr. 1577; Bishop Marmaduke Middleton to Walsingham, 29 June 1580; John Shearman to Archbishop Long, 12 July 1585 (Brady, *Ir. Ch. Eliz.*, 22-4, 39-42, 99).
76. Anthony à Wood, *Athenae Oxonienses* (London 1813-20), i, 575; Butler and power (ed), *Holinshed's Irish Chronicle*, 59-60.
77. Moran, *Spicil. Ossor.*, i, 89-90.
78. These claims were made in print a few years later by David Rothe, *Analecta Sacra . . .*, ed. P. F. Moran (Dublin 1884), 43-5.
79. John Dowdall to Burghley, 9 Mar. 1596, P.R.O., S.P. 63/187/19, *Cal. S.P. Ire.*, *1592-96*, 484-8.
80. Brendan Jennings (ed.), 'Brussels MS 3947' in *Anal. Hib.*, vi (1934), 78-80.
81. Butler and Power (ed.), *Holinshed's Irish Chronicle*, 95ff. See also St John D. Seymour, *Anglo-Irish Literature*, *1200-1582* (Cambridge 1929), 93-101, 145-65.
82, Pollard and Redgrave, *Short-Title Catologue . . .*, no. 18745; and see the entry under his name in *D.N.B.*
83. Printed in *Archiv. Hib.*, iv (1915), 96-130.
84. Hogan, *Ibernia Ignatiana*, 15, 30.
85. The briefs of appointment are listed in Moran, *Spicil. Ossor.*, i, 71-2.
86. P.R.O., S.P. 63/11/81, *Cal. S.P. Ire.*, *1509-73*, 245.
87. *Archiv. Hib.*, v (1916), 158-67.
88. John Brady, 'Father Christopher Cusack and the Irish College of Douai' in *Measgra i gCuimhne Mhichíl Uí Chléirigh* (Dublin 1944), 98-107.
89. Hogan, *Ibernia Ignatiana* and *Distinguished Irishmen of the Sixteenth Century* (London 1894).
90. Hogan, *Ibernia Ignatiana*, 108-11.
91. Printed in *Archiv. Hib.*, ii (1913), 1-36.
92. 'Perbreve compendium in quo contintur nonullorum nomina qui in Hybernia regnante impia Regina Elisabetha vincula, martirium et exilium perpessi sunt'. Printed, not always accurately, in Moran, *Spicil. Ossor.*, i, 82-109.
93. See, e.g., Loftus to Burghley, 22 Sept. 1590, P.R.O., S.P. 63/114/37, *Cal. S.P. Ire.*, *1588-92*, 365-6, Brady, *Ir. Ch. Eliz.*, 124-8; John Dowdall to Burghley, 9 Mar. 1596, P.R.O., S.P. 63/187/19, *Cal. S.P. Ire.*, *1592-96*, 464-8; Bishop Lyon of Cork to Lord Hunsdon, 6 July 1596, P.R.O., S.P. 63/191/8, *Cal. S.P. Ire.*, *1596-97*, 13-20.

94. Spenser, *View* in Morley, *Ire. under Eliz. & Jas I*, 203.
95. Hogan, *Ibernia Ignatiana*, 40-4.
96. Ibid. Bishop Lyon (see note 93) confirms this.
97. Printed in *Archiv. Hib.*, iii (1914), 260-4. Undated, but probably 1607.

Chapter 4: Not a Mission, but a Church (pp 96-122)
I have left this and the following chapter almost without annotation, as I have recently treated the subject at greater length and with reasonably full reference to sources and literature *(The Catholic Community in the Seventeenth and Eighteenth Centuries*, Dublin 1981).

1. *New History of Ireland*, iii (Oxford 1976), 209. The impact of Conor O'Devany's death spread rapidly: over a dozen accounts, many of them printed, circulated in Catholic Europe within a few years.
2. On 6 February 1612: P.R.O., S.P. 63/232/8, *Cal. S.P. Ire., 1611-14*, 244.
3. Compare *Archiv. Hib.*, ii (1913), 301 with *Archiv. Hib.*, iii (1914), 297-8.
4. In a truly seminal contribution, 'The Counter-Reformation and the People of Catholic Ireland, 1596-1641' in *Hist. Studies*, viii (1971), 155-70.
5. Hugh Fenning, 'A List of Dominicans in Ireland, 1657' in *Collect. Hib.*, xxv (1983), 24-9.
6. Louis Bouyer, *A History of Christian Spirituality*, English trans., iii (London 1969), 140-2.
7. Twenty-two such crosses, dating from *c.* 1470 to 1635, survive in the Pale in Co. Meath; no others are known. See Heather A. King, 'Late Medieval Crosses in County Meath, *c.* 1470-1635' in *R.I.A. Proc.*, sect. C, lxxxiv (1984), 79-115.

Chapter 5: The Secret People (pp 123-150)
1. Cited in Richard Mant, *A History of the Church of Ireland* (London 1840), ii 230.
2. Lecky, *Ire.*, ii, 41.
3. J. S. Donnelly, 'Irish Agrarian Rebellion: The Whiteboys of 1769-76' in *R.I.A. Proc.*, sect. C, lxxxiii (1983), 293-331.
4. J. S. Donnelly, 'Hearts of Oak, Hearts of Steel' in *Studia Hib.*, xxi (1981), 7-74.
5. Quoted in Froude, *Ire.*, ii, 132-3. The three main religious traditions in Ireland have historically described themselves as 'Catholic', 'Protestant' and 'Presbyterian'.
6. Thomas Bartlett, 'Indiscipline and Disaffection in the Armed Forces in Ireland in the 1790s' in P. J. Corish (ed.), *Radicals, Rebels and Establishments* (Belfast 1985), 115-34.
7. L. M. Cullen, *The Emergence of Modern Ireland, 1600-1900* (London 1981), 210-33; 'The 1798 Rebellion in its Eighteenth-Century Context' in Corish (ed.), op. cit., 91-113.
8. The point is succinctly made by Marianne Elliott, *Partners in Revolution* (Yale 1982), 238-9.

Chapter 6: The Waning of 'Old Ireland' (pp 151-191)
There have been two full-length studies of this period in recent times: S. J. Connolly, *Priests and People in Pre-Famine Ireland, 1780-1845* (Dublin 1982) and Desmond Keenan, *The Catholic Church in Nineteenth-Century Ireland* (Dublin 1983 — the title is misleading, for the study does not go beyond 1860). Their points of contact seem curiously limited until one realises the extent to which they do not take full account of the rich diversity that was the hallmark of this last chapter of 'old Ireland'. Connolly focuses on rural Ulster Catholicism and Keenan on urban 'east-coast' practice.

This rich diversity was to be severely reduced by various pressures after the Great Famine. Diversity had always been characteristic of Ireland, but in the first half of the nineteenth century it is, by Irish standards, well documented. Ecclesiastical sources of a genuinely archival nature are still patchy, but, especially in Dublin and Cashel, they are now much more extensive, while the visitation records of Bishop Patrick Plunkett of Meath (in Anthony Cogan, *Ecclesiastical History of the Diocese of Meath*, iii, Dublin 1870) are very informative. After 1836 the annual *Catholic Directory* provides statistical and other information.

Biographical studies of leading ecclesiastics are disappointingly few, with little to add to W. J. Fitzpatrick, *The Life, Times and Correspondence of the Right Rev. Dr Doyle* (enlarged ed., 2 vols, Dublin 1880, cited as Fitzpatrick, *Doyle*) or even the tendentious work by Bernard O'Reilly, *John MacHale, Archbishop of Tuam* (2 vols, New York 1890, cited as O'Reilly, *MacHale*). A good biography of Archbishop Daniel Murray of Dublin is badly needed.

Synodal legislation provides evidence of a continuing attempt to put the house in order. Diocesan or provincial decrees exist for Cashel (1810), Tuam (1817), Dublin (1831), Armagh (1834).

The forty years between the end of the Napoleonic wars and the coming of the 'tourist' with the railways were the heyday of the 'traveller', who still needed to be fairly wealthy, was, perhaps in consequence, fairly well educated, and, again perhaps in consequence, was determined to write a book about his experiences. These works are quite fascinating, and I can only indicate those where I have found the most useful information:
John Carr, *The Stranger in Ireland* (London 1806, cited as Carr, *Ireland*)
Mr and Mrs S. C. Hall, *Ireland: Its Scenery and Character* (3 vols, London 1841-3, cited as Hall, *Ireland*)
J. G. Kohl, *Travels in Ireland* (English trans., London 1844, cited as Kohl, *Ireland*)
Leitch Ritchie, *Ireland Picturesque and Romantic* (London 1838, cited as Ritchie, *Ireland*)
W. M. Thackeray, *The Irish Sketch-Book* (cited from the collected ed., London 1879).

Then there is a group who might claim to be social or political scientists rather than mere 'travellers', led by the two Frenchmen, Alexis de Tocqueville (1835) and Gustave de Beaumont (1838), to whom may be added Edward Wakefield, *An Account of Ireland Statistical and Political* (2 vols, London 1812, cited as Wakefield, *Ireland*) and W. S. Mason, *A Statistical Account or Parochial Survey of Ireland* (3 vols, Dublin 1814-19, cited as Mason, *Parochial Survey*).

The resources of the government were being increasingly brought to bear in attempts to analyse the problems of Ireland, most of them related in one way or another to the problem of poverty, and the 'blue books' or 'parliamentary papers' begin to pour out their information.

Finally, this society itself is vocal. In the Irish language, I should like to single out the *Diary* of Humphrey O'Sullivan. For the English language, the novelists are important — Kennedy, the Banims, Carleton — all the more important because they are not great novelists: they tend to record rather than create. If I have leant rather heavily on Kennedy, I would like to feel that it is not out of any *pietas* but because his real limitations as a creative writer suggest that he may be quite important as a recorder (or in his case a recaller) of events.

1. Patrick Lynch and John Vaizey, *Guinness's Brewery and the Irish Economy, 1759-1876* (Cambridge 1960). Cf. Joseph Lee, 'The Dual Economy in Ireland, 1800-1850' in *Hist. Studies*, viii (1971), 191-201.
2. Wakefield, *Ireland*, ii, 568.
3. Cited in Fitzpatrick, *Doyle*, i, 259.
4. Sir William Wilde, *Irish Popular Superstitions* (Dublin 1852), 82-3.
5. Emile Strauss, *Irish Nationalism and British Democracy* (London 1951), 93.
6. Fitzpatrick, *Doyle*, i, 330.
7. See Seán Cannon, *Irish Episcopal Meetings, 1788-1882* (Rome 1979).
8. T. P. Cunningham, *Church Reorganisation* in Corish, *Ir. Catholicism*, v, ch. 7 (Dublin 1970), 11-14.
9. Emmet Larkin, 'The Devotional Revolution in Ireland, 1850-75' in *A.H.R.*, lxxvii (1972), 625-7.
10. S. J. Connolly, 'Catholicism in Ulster, 1800-50' in Peter Roebuck (ed.), *Plantation to Partition* (Belfast 1981), 157-71.
11. Louis O'Kane, 'A Statistical Return of Armagh Diocese in 1836' in *Seanchas Ardmhacha*, iii, 1 (1958), 181-9.
12. David W. Miller, 'Irish Catholicism and the Great Famine' in *Journal of Social History*, ix (1975), 81-98.
13. Hall, *Ireland*, ii, 18-19.
14. John Begley, *The Diocese of Limerick from 1691 to the Present Time* (Dublin 1938), 479.
15. Some interesting 'observations' by Louis Delahogue, one of the first professors, are printed in Seosamh Ó Dufaigh, 'James Murphy, Bishop of Clogher, 1801-24' in *Clogher Rec.*, vi, 3 (1968), 482-7.
16. Ritchie, *Ireland*, 201.
17. See in particular the extracts from the general archives of the Franciscans in Rome presented by Patrick Conlan in *Collect. Hib.*, xviiii-xix (1976-7), 132-83; xx (1978), 104-46; Hugh Fenning, 'A List of Dominicans in Ireland, 1817', ibid., ix (1966), 79-82.
18. Thackeray, *The Irish Sketch-Book*, 56-7.
19. Fitzpatrick, *Doyle*, i, 176.
20. David W. Miller, 'Irish Catholicism and the Great Famine' in *Journal of Social History*, ix (1975), 81-98.
21. William Meagher, *Notices of the Life and Character of . . . Most Rev. Daniel Murray* (Dublin 1853); Moira Lysaght, 'Daniel Murray, Archbishop of Dublin, 1823-1852' in *Dublin Hist. Rec.*, xxvii (1974), 101-8; Keenan, *The*

Catholic Church in Nineteenth-Century Ireland.

22. Wakefield, *Ireland*, ii, 767.
23. Report in Moran, *Spicil. Ossor.*, iii, 625-46.
24. See T. P. Kennedy, *Church-Building* in Corish, *Ir. Catholicism*, v, ch. 8 (Dublin 1970).
25. Kohl, *Ireland*, 184-5.
26. For an excellent summary of lay societies see M. V. Ronan, *An Apostle of Catholic Dublin* (Dublin 1944), 123-205.
27. Reprinted in *Reportorium Novum*, ii, 2 (1959-60), 324-63.
28. Desmond Rushe, *Edmund Rice: The Man and his Times* (Dublin 1981), 105.
29. Ronan, *An Apostle of Catholic Dublin*, 206-10; Meagher, *Notices of...Daniel Murray*, 106-7.
30. Thomas Wall, *The Sign of Dr Hay's Head* (Dublin 1958); 'Catholic Periodicals of the Past' in *I.E.R.*, series 5, ci (1964, i), 234-44, 289-303, 375-88; cii (1964, ii), 17-27, 86-100, 129-47, 206-23.
31. The story was told by John O'Connell. See Denis Gwynn, *The Struggle for Catholic Emancipation* (London 1928), 220-1.
32. Patrick Power, *Parochial History of Waterford and Lismore* (Waterford 1912), 263-6.
33. James Hardiman, *History of... Galway* (Dublin 1820), 267, 278.
34. Thackeray, *The Irish Sketch-Book*, 47.
35. Full text edited by Michael McGrath (Irish Texts Society, xxx-xxxiii, 1936-7). Extracts edited by Tomás de Bhaldraithe, *Cín Lae Amhlaoibh* (Dublin 1970), and in English translation, *The Diary of Humphrey O'Sullivan* (Dublin 1979). Extracts from the diary are here identified by citing the precise date: this entry is for 12 July 1827.
36. Patrick Kennedy, *The Banks of the Boro* (Dublin 1867), 172-3; Hall, *Ireland*, ii, 152.
37. Wakefield, *Ireland*, ii, 598.
38. Fitzpatrick, *Doyle*, i, 107.
39. Ibid., 284.
40. Mason, *Parochial Survey*, i, 458, 470-1.
41. Kennedy, *The Banks of the Boro*, 76-8, 199-200.
42. Mason, *Parochial Survey*, ii, 87.
43. Kennedy, *The Banks of the Boro*, 76.
44. Kohl, *Ireland*, 182-3.
45. Kennedy, *The Banks of the Boro*, 130.
46. Fitzpatrick, *Doyle*, i, 147.
47. See the interesting letter from Archbishop Slattery of Cashel to Daniel O'Connell, 8 Apr. 1842, in Maurice R. O'Connell, (ed.), *The Correspondence of Daniel O'Connell*, vii (Dublin n.d.), 148-51.
48. Hall, *Ireland*, ii, 314-15. The testimony of contemporary observers is indeed unanimous.
49. K. H. Connell, *Irish Peasant Society* (Oxford 1968), 51-86.
50. E.g. Mason, *Parochial Survey*, i, 458; Ritchie, *Ireland*, 70, referring to the predominantly Protestant Island Magee, Co. Antrim.
51. O'Sullivan's Diary, 14 May 1827.
52. Kennedy, *The Banks of the Boro*, 56-66.

53. O'Sullivan's Diary, 24 Apr. 1831.
54. Ibid., 26 July 1829.
55. Wakefield, *Ireland*, ii, 605.
56. 'Instructions on patrons' issued to the clergy by the Munster bishops in 1808 (Cashel diocesan archives).
57. O'Sullivan's Diary, 26 May 1828; Kennedy, *The Banks of the Boro*, 231.
58. O'Sullivan's Diary, 31 Jan. 1828.
59. Ronan, *An Apostle of Catholic Dublin*, 256.
60. Mason, *Parochial Survey*, ii, 44.
61. See, e.g., Hall, *Ireland*, ii, 165; Kohl, *Ireland*, 121; Henry Inglis, *A Journey through Ireland in 1834*, reprinted in *Past*, vii (1964), 178-80; N. P. Willis and J. Stirling Coyne, *The Scenery and Antiquities of Ireland* (London n.d.), ii, 97. The comments by 'Martin Doyle' are in his *Hints Originally Intended for the Small Farmers of the County of Wexford* (Dublin 1833), 19-23.
62. Pádraig Ó Súilleabháin, 'Sidelights on the Irish Church, 1811-38' in *Collect. Hib.*, ix (1966), 74-6.
63. T. N. Brown, 'Nationalism and the Irish Peasant, 1800-1846' in *Rev. Pol.*, xv (1953), 411.
64. Wakefield, *Ireland*, ii, 736.
65. Mason, *Parochial Survey*, i, 184.
66. Peter Livingstone, *The Monaghan Story* (Enniskillen 1980), 241-2; Seosamh Ó Dufaigh, 'James Murphy, Bishop of Clogher, 1801-24' in *Clogher Rec.*, vi, 3 (1968), 419-92; Patrick Mulligan, 'The Life and Times of Bishop Edward Kernan', ibid., x, 3 (1981), 322-48; Donal Kerr, 'Charles MacNally, Maynooth Professor and Bishop of Clogher', ibid., x, 3 (1981), 364-91.
67. Livingstone, op. cit., 244-5; Ó Dufaigh, op. cit., 466-70; Mulligan, op. cit., 323.
68. Brendan McEvoy, 'The Parish of Errigal Kieran in the Nineteenth Century' in *Seanchas Ardmhacha*, i, 1 (1954), 118-50.
69. W. P. Burke, *The History of the Catholic Archbishops of Tuam* (Dublin 1882), 232-3; O'Reilly, *MacHale*, i, 328-32.
70. Donal Kerr, 'James Browne, Bishop of Kilmore, 1829-65' in *Breifne*, vi, no. 22 (1983-4), 109-54.
71. Donal Kerr, 'Charles MacNally, Maynooth Professor and Bishop of Clogher' in *Clogher Rec.*, x, 3 (1981), 385.
72. Cullen to Kirby, 16 Apr. 1851, in Peadar Mac Suibhne (ed.), *Paul Cullen and his Contemporaries*, iii (Naas 1965), 81.
73. S. J. Connolly, 'Catholicism in Ulster, 1800-50' in Roebuck (ed.), *Plantation to Partition*, 166; the information on Achonry, Tuam and Kilmore is from the relevant issues of the *Catholic Directory*.
74. George Sampson, *Statistical Survey of the County of Londonderry* (Dublin 1802), 457.
75. Ritchie, *Ireland*, 71.
76. Mason, *Parochial Survey*, i, 596.
77. Wakefield, *Ireland*, ii, 739.
78. Patrick Mulligan, 'The Life and Times of Bishop Edward Kernan' in *Clogher Rec.*, x, 3 (1981), 348.
79. O'Sullivan's Diary, 10 Jan. 1834.

Chapter 7: Establishment and Disestablishment (pp 192-225)
What is needed most for this period is a good biography of Paul Cardinal Cullen. The need has not been met by Desmond Bowen, *Paul Cardinal Cullen and the Shaping of Modern Irish Catholicism* (Dublin 1983). Desmond Keenan, *The Catholic Church in Ireland in the Nineteenth Century* (Dublin 1983), despite its title, stops in 1860. So does Bernard O'Reilly, *John MacHale, Archbishop of Tuam* (2 vols, New York 1890), for reasons that can only be tantalisingly conjectured, because of the disappearance of MacHale's papers. Emmet Larkin, *The Making of the Roman Catholic Church in Ireland, 1850-1860* (University of North Carolina Press 1980) is a skilful, if lengthy, analysis of epsicopal policies in the 1850s. E. R. Norman, *The Catholic Church and Ireland in the Age of Rebellion, 1859-73* (London 1965) is a work of solid scholarship that has worn well, but it is basically about ecclesiastical politics rather than about religion. Regrettably, the pages on the chapter on 'Priests and People' (ch. 3, pp 171-256) in K. Theodore Hoppen, *Elections, Politics, and Society in Ireland, 1832-1885* (Oxford 1984) arrived too late to be worked in.

From the middle of the nineteenth century genuinely archival material multiplies. It was not just that there was a wish to see things better organised; such developments as the new cheap postal service led to the proliferation of paper, much of it still to be turned over by historians. I have explored, but certainly not exhausted, the material in the archives of Propaganda Fide in Rome (cited as A.P.F.), the Dublin diocesan archives (cited as D.D.A.), and the archives of the Irish College, Rome (see my calendar of material in *Archiv. Hib.*, xxx (1972), 29-116; xxxi (1973), 1-94; xxxii (1974), 1-62.

1. Emmet Larkin, 'Church, State and Nation in Modern Ireland' in *A.H.R.*, lxxx (1975), 1245.
2. The best study is still Roger Aubert, *Pie IX* (Paris 1952).
3. A.P.F., Acta 214, ff 284v-285r.
4. Norman, *Cath. Ch. and Ire.*, 10.
5. These details are spelled out in two informative diaries kept by participants in the synod (D.D.A., 46/2), especially that by one of the three secretaries, the very pro-Cullen Peter Cooper.
6. Enclosure in a letter from Hugh McFadden, P.P., Falcarragh, to Cullen, 12 Oct. 1855 (D.D.A., 332/7).
7. Dixon to Propaganda, 21 Mar. 1853 (A.P.F. Congressi, Irlanda 31, ff 410-12.
8. McEvilly to Cullen, 10 July 1857 (D.D.A., 339/5).
9. J. H. Whyte, 'The Appointment of Catholic Bishops in Nineteenth-Century Ireland' in *Catholic Historical Review*, xlviii (1962), 12-32.
10. Seán Cannon, *Irish Episcopal Meetings, 1788-1882* (Rome 1979), 73-86; Larkin, *The Making of the Roman Catholic Church in Ireland, 1850-1860*, 400-2.
11. MacNally to Cullen, 26 Feb. 1867 (D.D.A., 339/5).
12. P. J. Corish, 'Gallicanism at Maynooth: Archbishop Cullen and the Royal Visitation of 1853' in Art Cosgrove and Donal McCartney (ed.), *Studies in Irish History presented to R. Dudley Edwards* (Dublin 1979), 176-89.
13. For Franciscan material see Patrick Conlan in *Collect. Hib.*, xviii-xix (1976-

7), 132-83; xx (1978), 104-46; xxi-xxii (1979-80), 160-204; xxiii (1982), 86-115; xxv (1983), 178-208. There is much material concerning a number of religious orders in D.D.A., especially in the 1850s.

14. Bernard Verdon and Michael Mahon (O.D.C.) to Cullen, Loughrea, 31 Aug. 1855 (D.D.A., 332/7).
15. Joseph Robins, *The Lost Children* (Dublin 1980), 271-309.
16. See the eleven-page report to Cullen by John Kilduff, appointed Bishop of Ardagh in the following year (D.D.A., 325/1).
17. D.D.A., 325/1.
18. D. H. Akenson, *The Irish Education Experiment* (London 1970); Ignatius Murphy, *Primary Education* in Corish, *Ir. Catholicism*, v. ch. 6 (Dublin 1971).
19. S. V. Ó Súilleabháin, *Secondary Education* in Corish, *Ir. Catholicism*, v, ch. 6.
20. Fergal McGrath, *The University Question*, ibid.; *Newman's University: Idea and Reality* (Dublin 1951).
21. Michael Tynan, 'The End of an Era' in *Furrow*, xxv (1974), 660-71; William J. Walsh, 'Our Catechisms: Is There Room for Improvement?' in *I.E.R.*, series 3, xiii (1892), 1-28.
22. Cullen to Barnabò, 3 May 1861 (A.P.F. Congressi, Irlanda 33, f. 85).
23. John Monahan, *Records Relating to the Diocese of Ardagh and Clonmacnoise* (Dublin 1886), 256.
24. Cullen to Barnabò, 20 Sept. 1851 (A.P.F. Congressi, Irlanda 30, f. 705r).
25. Dean Murphy to Bishop Furlong, 22 Feb. 1858 (D.D.A., 319/1).
26. Walter MacDonald, *Reminiscences of a Maynooth Professor* (London 1925), 50-67.
27. For Lisburn see Denvir to Kirby, 12 June 1854, calendared in *Archiv. Hib.*, xxxi (1973), 17, and for Carlow and Athy C. B. Lyons to Cullen, 9 Nov. 1858 (D.D.A., 319/2).
28. Eoin MacWhite, 'Towards a Biography of Father Vladimir Pecherin (1807-1885)' in *R.I.A. Proc.*, sect. C, lxxx (1980), 138-9.
29. Monahan, *Records Relating to the Diocese of Ardagh and Clonmacnoise*, 253-4.
30. T. P. Cunningham, *Church Reorganisation* in Corish, *Ir. Catholicism*, v, ch. 7 (Dublin 1970), 16-25.
31. Propaganda to Cullen, 17 May 1854 (D.D.A., 449/7).
32. Both letters are in D.D.A., 332/1.
33. Calendared in *Archiv. Hib.*, xxxi (1973), 88.
34. Mary Carbery, *The Farm by Lough Gur: The Story of Mary Fogarty* (Cork 1973), 169.
35. Seán Ó Súilleabháin, *Irish Wake Amusements* (Cork 1976), 9-11.
36. Karl Marx and Friedrich Engels, *Ireland and the Irish Question* (Moscow 1971), 527.
37. Cunningham, *Church Reorganisation*, 6.
38. Cullen to E. F. Collins, undated, but late Jan. 1865 (D.D.A., 121/4).
39. See especially J. H. Whyte, *Political Problems, 1850-1860* in Corish, *Ir. Catholicism*, v. ch. 2 (Dublin 1967), 24-38.
40. Cullen to Kirby, 28 July 1855, calendared in *Archiv. Hib.*, xxxi (1973), 55.

41. Cullen described it as 'a comedy' in a letter to Kirby dated 13 May 1864, calendared in *Archiv. Hib.*, xxx (1972), 41. One might suspect that he saw it as black comedy.
42. Peadar Mac Suibhne (ed.), *Paul Cullen and his Contemporaries*, v (Naas 1977), 299.
43. Ibid., ii (Naas 1962), 11.
44. Cullen to Kirby, 21 Aug. 1856, calendared in *Archiv. Hib.*, xxxi (1973), 61.
45. Whyte, *Political Problems, 1850-1860*, 36-8.
46. Newman to Ambrose St John, cited ibid., 37.
47. I have dealt with the topic a little more fully in 'Catholic Marriage under the Penal Code' in Art Cosgrove (ed.), *Sex and Marriage in Ireland* (forthcoming).
48. E. D. Steele, 'Cardinal Cullen and Irish Nationality' in *I.H.S.*, xix (1975), 239-60; Larkin, *The Making of the Roman Catholic Church in Ireland, 1850-1860*.
49. Bowen, *Paul Cardinal Cullen and the Shaping of Modern Irish Catholicism*.
50. Keenan, *The Catholic Church in Nineteenth-Century Ireland*.

Chapter 8: Establishments (pp 226-258)
Archival material is abundant for this period, but it is largely unexplored. The published decrees of the four Maynooth synods of 1875, 1900, 1927 and 1956 are at least useful indications of the mind of the hierarchy, but they have not been studied against the background of contemporary Catholic society.

The published work is, for very understandable reasons, mainly concerned with 'political' issues. Emmet Larkin's three volumes cover the period from 1878 to 1891: *The Roman Catholic Church and the Creation of the Modern Irish State, 1878-1886* (Dublin 1975), *The Roman Catholic Church and the Plan of Campaign, 1886-1888* (Cork 1978) and *The Roman Catholic Church and the Fall of Parnell, 1888-1891* (University of North Carolina Press 1979). These are followed by David W. Miller, *Church, State and Nation in Ireland, 1898-1921* (Dublin 1973) and John H. Whyte's invaluable *Church and State in Modern Ireland, 1923-1979* (2nd ed., Dublin 1980). The one worthwhile biography — Patrick Walsh, *William J. Walsh, Archbishop of Dublin* (Dublin 1928) is also heavily 'political'.

There are useful modern summaries of general history in Joseph Lee, *The Modernisation of Irish Society, 1848-1918* (Dublin 1973), John A. Murphy, *Ireland in the Twentieth Century* (Dublin 1975), Ronan Fanning, *Independent Ireland* (Dublin 1983) and David Harkness, *Northern Ireland since 1920* (Dublin 1983). Terence Brown, *Ireland: A Social and Cultural History, 1922-79* (n.p. 1981) is, as its author says, necessarily 'a provisional and speculative sketch', and in his treatment of Catholicism he adopts uncritically Larkin's now much-criticised thesis on the 'devotional revolution'.

In the present state of our knowledge any treatment must be impressionistic. If the annotation is also impressionistic, I can only plead the state of the question.

1. Larkin, *The Roman Catholic Church and the Creation of the Modern Irish State, 1878-1886*.

2. See especially his long letter to Tobias Kirby, 3 July 1888, calendared in *Archiv. Hib.*, xxxii (1974), 16.
3. For a lucid summary see T. P. Cunningham, *Church Reorganisation* in Corish, *Ir. Catholicism*, v, ch. 7 (Dublin 1970), 2-6.
4. This is explicitly the thesis of Emmet Larkin's book cited in note 1 above.
5. James O'Shea, *Priest, Politics and Society in Post-Famine Ireland: A Study of County Tipperary, 1850-1891* (Dublin 1983), especially pp 119-35.
6. James Plunkett, *Strumpet City* (London 1969), 392.
7. Emmet Larkin, 'The Devotional Revolution in Ireland, 1850-75' in *A.H.R.*, 625-52; Desmond Keenan, *The Catholic Church in Nineteenth-Century Ireland* (Dublin 1983), 252.
8. For a pioneering study see Kevin Whelan, 'The Catholic Parish, the Catholic Chapel and Village Development in Ireland' in *Ir. Geography*, xvi (1983), 1-15.
9. See the details in Seán Ó Síoda, 'The Gweedore Case' in *Scáthlán*, i (1980), 47-51.
10. The papers from 1903 to 1938 are listed in *Catholic Truth Society of Ireland: First Fifty Years* (Dublin 1949), 45-51.
11. León Ó Broin, 'The Gaelic League and the Chair of Irish at Maynooth' in *Studies*, lii (1963), 348-62.
12. Louis Paul-Dubois, *Contemporary Ireland* (Dublin 1908), 425.
13. There are good things in Dermot Keogh, *The Rise of the Irish Working Class* (Belfast 1982). See also Michael Laffan, '"Labour Must Wait": Ireland's Conservative Revolution' in P. J. Corish (ed.), *Radicals, Rebels and Establishments* (Belfast 1985), 203-22.
14. See especially his summing-up, pp 143-4.
15. Whyte, *Church and State in Modern Ireland, 1923-1979*, 14.
16. Seán Ó Faoláin, *The Irish* (West Drayton 1947), 125-7.
17. Michael Collins, *The Path to Freedom* (Dublin 1922), 127-8.
18. F. S. L. Lyons, *Culture and Anarchy in Ireland, 1890-1939* (Oxford 1979), 169.
19. Whyte, *Church and State in Modern Ireland, 1923-1979*, 96-330; Fanning, *Independent Ireland*, especially pp 181-7.
20. Whyte, op. cit., 137-8.
21. Ibid., 143.
22. Ibid., 404-5.
23. Quoted in Fanning, *Independent Ireland*, 191.
24. León Ó Broin, *Frank Duff: A Biography* (Dublin 1982), 61-7.
25. This is the conclusion of D. H. Akenson, *Education and Enmity: Control of Schooling in Northern Ireland* (New York 1973), 86-7.
26. Quoted in Harkness, *Northern Ireland since 1920*, 89.
27. Ibid., 156.
28. Austin Clarke, *Collected Poems*, ed. Liam Miller (Dublin and Oxford 1974), 188-9.
29. Dónall Mac Amhlaigh, *An Irish Navvy*, trans. Valentin Iremonger (London 1964), 175.
30. G. K. Chesterton, *Christendom in Dublin* (London 1932), 13-16, 59.
31. Ibid., 68.

Index